DATE DUE

Chi Town
Norbert Blei

Chi Town

Norbert Blei

Ellis Press
1990

Acknowledgements

Some of these pieces and photographs originally appeared in the following publications: *Chicagoland Magazine, Chicago Magazine, the Chicago Tribune Sunday Magazine, The Chicago Sun-Times Midwest Magazine, StoryQuarterly Magazine, The Door County Advocate*. The author is grateful to these periodicals for permission to reprint these pieces and photographs here.

Jazz drawings by Ross LewAllen, Santa Fe, New Mexico.

Bill Mauldin cartoon copyright (c) 1945 by Bill Mauldin, used by permission.

Painting on the dust jacket and pencil drawings in the text by Charles Peterson, Ephraim, Wisconsin. Used with permission of the artist.

Blues passages from *The Meaning of the Blues* by Paul Oliver, Collier Books, 1963.

Photographs: Don Zimmer and Jerome Holtzman by Charles Cherney, *Chicago Tribune*; Marty Robinson by Sherwood Fohrman; Street Musician, Field's Clock, El Tracks by Cynthia Pochron; Klas Restaurant by Brandy Pesole. The author is grateful for permission to print these photographs.

Published by Ellis Press, David Pichaske, publisher, P.O. Box 6, Granite Falls, Minnesota 56241.
Typesetting by Michelle Payne, Granite Falls, Minnesota.
Design and lay-out by David Pichaske.

ISBN: 0-944024-10-6

FIRST EDITION
1   2   3   4   5   6   7   8   9   0

in memory of my grandparents
  and the little village, 26th and Pulaski

To nejhorší mám za sebou
—říkám si—, jsem už stár.
To nejhorší mám před sebou,
ještě žiji.
Ale kdybyste mermomocí chtěli vědět,
byl jsem šťásten.
Někdy celý den, někdy celé hodiny,
někdy jen pár minut.
To stačí.

— Jaroslav Seifert

(The worst is behind me
—I tell myself—I'm already old.
The worst is yet to come,
I'm still alive.
But if you must know,
I was happy.
Sometimes a whole day, sometimes a whole hour.
sometimes only few minutes.
That's enough.)

Song Of The Soul Of Chicago

On the bridges, on the bridges—sweeping and rising, whirling and
   circling—back to the bridges, always the bridges.

I'll talk forever—I'm damned if I'll sing. Don't you see that mine is not
   a singing people? We're just a lot of muddy things caught up by
   the stream. You can't fool us. Don't we know ourselves?

Here we are, out here in Chicago. You think we're not humble?
   You're a liar. We are like the sewerage of our town, swept up stream
   by a kind of mechanical triumph—that's what we are.

On the bridges, on the bridges—wagons and motors, horses and
   men—not flying, just tearing along and swearing.

By God we'll love each other or die trying. We'll get to understanding
   too. In some grim way our own song shall work through.

We'll stay down in the muddy depths of our stream—we will.
   There can't be any poet come out here and sit on the shaky rail of our
   ugly bridges and sing us into paradise.

We're finding out—that's what I want to say. We'll get
   at our own thing out here or die for it. We're going down,
   numberless thousands of us, into ugly oblivion. We know that.

But say, bards, you keep off our bridges. Keep out of our dreams,
   dreamers. We want to give this democracy thing they talk
   so big about a whirl. We want to see if we are any good
   out here, we Americans from all over hell. That's what we want.

—Sherwood Anderson

Chi Town

March, 1989

Dear Norb,

When you come to Chi Town, come visit. I bought an espresso coffee pot. I can still remember our outings with Dave Brubeck at the piano and running all around downtown in your Volkswagen and parking under Wacker Drive and seeing all the drunks laying down there and you telling me, isn't this picturesque?

Love ya,

Audrey

April 5, 1989
Cicero, Ill. 60650

Dear Norbert:

I went down to the Loop Tuesday, stopped at the old bank, [the Continental Bank] and was really disgusted with its appearance and the stories I've been told.

The trip on the Elevated was also very grim, all the ruined buildings and burned out homes is unbelievable. I'm going to try to stay out of the Loop. It's not worth it to travel there anymore.

Everything's OK. A good ballgame for the Cubs. And Richard M. Daley's our new mayor.

Stay healthy.

Your Dad

Prologue: Chi Town Blues

When you settle into the quiet of the country, far removed from a life lived and loved in the big city, you experience a period of withdrawal, a homesickness, which can last for months or years. Some learn to adjust to the isolation, the slower rhythms of nature, the absence of city sounds, city streets, city talk, city people. Others remain out of sorts, out of place.

It is not an easy juncture. You live, at best, between places, in exile, never forgetting where you came from, never sure why you left. Never certain you will return.

There is an hour just before dawn in the country known as the blue hour. It is an hour of incredible emptiness, beauty, desire and despair . . . an hour of remembering and forgetting. An hour of beginning all over again. It's the hour I often begin to write.

In the wee midnight hours, long 'fore the break of day,
In the wee midnight, long before the break of day,
When the blues creep upon you and carry your mind away. . . .

I miss Chicago most in October, exiled in Wisconsin, the tip of the Door Peninsula, hundreds of miles from home, though only a walk through fields and woods to the edge of the very same lake which touches the city I love and left years ago.

I miss the cold October rain, the stiff wind holding people to a standstill. The city watercolored Cobalt Blue, Payne's Gray. Coats and dresses swept away. Black umbrellas, red umbrellas . . . yellow and white. Heads lowered into the wind, collars turned, hands holding hats, tugging lapels close to the neck. Words caught in the throat, fragmented in passing conversations, swallowed whole.

Taxis, cars, carriages, trains, buses. The smell of exhaust fumes. The movement of people up the street down the street across the street beneath the street. Up elevators, down escalators. Revolving doors, department stores. The city inhaling, exhaling.

Catch its beating heart from the Michigan Avenue Bridge. Take it all in,

1

every direction: north up Michigan from the Tribune Tower to the old Water Tower, the Hancock Building, the Drake; south down Michigan to the Art Institute, Orchestra Hall, the Auditorium. East to the great lake, along the Chicago River—the Wrigley Building, Wacker Drive, the Sun-Times, Marina City. The river below you, moving beneath bridges of beauty, of steel lace. Day river. Pea-soup and St.-Patrick's-Day-green river. Night river of the moon and the stars down there in your eyes.

City you can't shake off, that keeps coming back: the river, the bridge, the lake, the Loop. The movement through and around, back and forth, back and forth . . . the recurring dream.

City of parks: Lincoln, Grant, Burnham, Jackson. City of architectural awe and arrogance. Of Sullivan's Carson Pirie Scott, of Wright's (never built) "Mile High" skyscraper, of Mies van der Rohe's towers of glass, of Helmut Jahn's State of Illinois Building, launching into the next century. City of museums. Of monumental sculpture old and new, from Lorado Taft and Ivan Mestrovic to Calder, Dubbuffet, Oldenberg, Miro, and Chicago's own Picasso.

Of old movie palaces: the Oriental, the Woods, the McVickers, and the grande dame Chicago Theater. City of the Merchandise Mart, Marshall Field's, and Maxwell Street. Uptown, downtown, crosstown, Old Town, New Town, Chinatown, Greektown, Niggertown, Bucktown, Jewtown—ethnic soul enclaves of Scandinavian, Irish, Hispanic, Black, Italian, Yugoslav, Polish, Czechoslovak, Native American, Southern White, Lithuanian, Hungarian, Russian, German, and Jew. North Shore, South Shore, northside, southside, westside, upper Wacker, lower Wacker, Calumet City, Cook County, *Chikagou.*

City of sirens, shouts, whistles, hustlers, horns, newshawks, Salvation Army Santas ringing bells, street music, beach waters, foot traffic, fountains. City of corners: State & Randolph, Clark & Van Buren, Madison & Wabash, Washington & Wells, State & Lake, Jackson & Dearborn, Lake & Michigan, State & Madison. The scene: one young man, alone, unemployed, envisioning himself a writer, on his way through dark canyons of steel, concrete, and glass. The glow from shopwindows and streetlights illuminates the way. He is comfortably hunched inside himself, his own fantasy—hair blowing, pipe burning, hands pocketed, newspapers and books tucked under his arms. Plot: to find a "clean, well-lighted place" of his own—downtown Chicago. Character/conflict: the insecurity and confidence of youth in pursuit of a grand love affair. Theme: to make an impression, to leave his mark . . . as others have before him. How else will this Lady of the Night with the heart of gold and eyes so watery blue ever remember him?

Well it's blues in my house, from the roof to the ground,
Well it's blues in my house, from the roof to the ground,
And it's blues everywhere since my good woman left town.

Blues in my mail-box, 'cause I cain't get no mail,
Blues in my mail-box, 'cause I cain't get no mail,
Says blues in my bread-box, 'cause my bread got stale.

Blues in my meal-barrel and there's blues upon my shelf,
And there's blues in my bed, 'cause I'm sleepin' by myself.

He recalls seeing Sandburg like God himself one summer evening, walking down Chicago Avenue (where else?) in white cap and long white hair, turning the corner on Dearborn, plunking down pennies at the newsstand for a final edition (Red Streak) of the *Chicago Daily News*, pausing to jabber with the people and the newsie awhile. The old poet perfectly at home, perfectly in place, still with a feel for the streets. "I will be the word of the people. Mine will be the bleeding mouth from which the gag is snatched. I will say everything." And seeing him again, months later, on stage in the Civic Opera House, strumming his guitar, letting loose his lingo, his singsong voice: "I know a Jew fish crier down on Maxwell Street with a voice/ like a north wind blowing over corn stubble in January. . . ." A Chicago Sandburgian opera unto himself—the beating heart, the common tongue of an old poet nearing the end of his time, trying to get his last words in. "Good-by now to the traffic policeman and his whistle/ The smash of the iron hoof on the stones/ All the crazy wonderful slamming roar of the street—/ O God, there's noises I'm going to be hungry for."

The young man haunted by all of this, the power of one writer to define an entire city . . . the blind alleys, the dark streets, the contrary hearts, the native tongue. The difficulty for anyone to find the words and the way.

Yet the journey continues, his own rendezvous in the city of steel girders, rivets, El platform billboards of torn posters—the Man from Marlboro, the Woman in Red—flap, flap, flapping in the wind. Bare bulbs burning under white metal lampshades. Red Wrigley Spearmint gum machines. Green benches. A cluster of iridescent pigeons at the waiting passenger's feet. Silver rails and blue-white sparks in the distance. Memory and desire. Child, boy, man. Here comes the El . . . the lifeline of one writer's journey to the heart of Chicago.

I lived on the El as a boy, the 58th Avenue Station, three cents to Downtown, around the Loop, and back. (Hide behind the seat at the end of the line and ride around the Loop on the El all day, especially Saturdays.)

Conductors in blue uniforms with silver watch chains draped across their vests. Grim conductors with round, blue caps low and light upon the forehead. Smiling-Irish conductors (Mr. Kenny who lived across the street) who would let a neighbor kid stand outside on the black-iron gated platform between the cars, for the thrill of riding the Douglas Park El—the ascent between Cicero Avenue and Pulaski (Crawford) . . . because it was summer . . . because the wind in the face felt cool . . . because this was the closest thing to flight a kid in the 1940's

3

would ever experience . . . because some Irish conductors were kids at heart themselves.

The El ascending, aloft, passing people you could almost touch in upper storey apartments . . . windows opened to tableaus of Chicago domestic tranquility: a man in his undershirt at the kitchen table, a quart of cold beer in his hand; a woman across from him blowing cigarette smoke. El stations marked with blue and white enamel signs: Kedzie, California, Western Ave., Hoyne, 18th St. . . . Polk St. . . . the medical center. The dark, red brick building where they locked crazy people up for good . . . the Hospital for the Incurably Ill. (One shuddered to look upon it for fear of being snatched away.)

On the ground, aboveground, underground. Around the bend. Over the river, under the river, beneath the Chicago Post Office. From elevated way to subway. The kid either emerging from the lower depths of the city into the day, up toward the tops of skyscrapers waiting to receive him as they loomed closer with each step . . . or the kid left aloft to drift on his own, to hang over the platform railing of the State & Lake station and stare down State Street . . . the bright moving lights of the Chicago Theater, the traffic, the rush of people, the policemen's whistles, Field's clock, the city at his feet. The vibrations of trains and passengers coming and going, reverberating through his body. Another miracle El ride from way out in Cicero—on the ground, in the air, over the streets, houses, parks, rivers, factories, people—to here in no time at all, around the Loop, into Downtown Chicago! What next? Whether to go down the steps and enter the stream of things or to board the next El home and keep riding to the Loop all day?

Sometimes, on some streets, on sunny days, ladders of light and shadow beneath the El rails . . . Lake, Wabash, Wells . . . another Chicago image to keep and carry always, like Sandburg alive on his own streets. "Come and show me another city with lifted head singing so proud to be alive. . . ."

Sometimes on State Street, old Casey Jones, "chickenman," street entertainer, playing his harmonica as a chicken danced on the sidewalk or perched on his head. Rewarding the dancing bird with a shot of beer.

City of the man who danced with his wife. City of the bet bottom dollar where you'll lose the blues. City of the great State Street and Michigan Avenue's magnificent mile. Streets electric, awash in neon.

City of criminals, character, and characters: Terrible Tommy O'Connor, John Dillinger, Bugs Moran, the St. Valentine's Day Massacre. From Jane Adams and Mother Cabrini to Scarface Al Capone: "I hear the police have been looking for me. What for?" City of powerhouse politics from ward bosses to City Hall. From "Bathhouse John" Coughlin and "Hinky Dink" Kenna; from saloon keeper-alderman Mathias J. "Paddy" "Chicago-ain't-ready-for-reform" Baulder to commoner, King, Richard J. Daley: "You know, people like it when every now and then you make a mistake in grammar and in your way of speaking. They feel you're more like them." Man of his word, matter of fact, manner

5

of speaking at the 1968 Democratic Convention in Chicago: "Shoot to kill arsonists and shoot to maim looters."

> *You poets*
> *and all your Big Words*
> *your River Lethe*
> *your to be or not to be*
> *your lovely, dark, and deep woods*
> *all your promises . . . your social significance.*
> *We don't buy that shit back in Chicago.*
> *We got the greatest Irish ballad on four legs*
> *for a mayor.*
> *We got a police station named Shakespeare.*
> *We got Italian sonneteers who keep our waters*
> *woods fresh with dead bodies—1,004+ gangland*
> *murders unsolved, 645 for the year of the family*
> *kind.*
> *We got a motto that says "I will."*
> *And I do.*
> *We all do in Chicago.*
> *In '68 we pounded a poem*
> *out of flesh and blood,*
> *and the whole world sang . . .*
> *without any help from you Poets*
> *your Big words*
> *and all your bullshit promises to keep.*

City of the first woman mayor, Jane Byrne, and the first black mayor, Harold "Chicago, Chicago, That Toddlin' Town" Washington. City of the succession of Daleys. Said father, King Richard I, to son, King Richard II, one day, "I can put you on the ballroom floor, but you'll have to dance yourself." And dance he does. City that Billy Sunday could not shut down.

> *Did you ever wake up with the blues and didn't have no place to go?*
> *Did you ever wake up with the blues and didn't have no place to go?*
> *An' you couldn't do nothin' but just walk from door to door?*

Just another dark October morning, the writer-who-was-a-young-writer-then on the streets again, now under the El on Wabash, headed down Randolph, across from the Chicago Public Library. Now in his place at the window of the all-day-and-night cafe, looking out. Grilled cheese and black coffee around midnight, a chocolate-covered donut and black coffee in the morning. A pipeful of fresh Troost tobacco (or Three Star Blue) purchased from the gentle old man at Iwan

6

Ries on Wabash near Kroch's, or a pack of imported Turkish cigarettes. Just readin', dreamin', and lookin' out . . . catching his reflection in the cafe window (the cafe long gone). The chair, the table, the window to the city made for the likes of him then —a writer hopelessly in love, carrying the torch, a long love affair with a city wasting his time. Morning, noon, night . . . he could never get enough of her. She was a passion that took the face of every woman passing by. Oh, for the dreaming, the wanting, the love of that October lady in blue . . . windswept, drifting away and out of touch, out of focus, out of sight.

Drifting into the visionary's realm of light returned to the eyes of the beholder, blinding images merged, desire dispossessed. Lost again and forever beyond the window glass.

Lesson #1 for the would-be Chicago writer: to write is to witness.
(Lesson never learned: to want is not to have.)

> *Between midnight and dawn, baby, we may never have to part,*
> *Between midnight and dawn, baby, we may never have to part,*
> *But there's one thing about it, baby: please remember I've always been your*
>   *heart.*

I thought we were meant for each other. Forever.

City of reality. City of illusion. City you sometimes have to imagine to believe.

Here I sit from a great distance, self-exiled, the hour of blue giving way to another cold, wet, gray October day, conjuring images, remembering a Chicago I once knew, considering the words of Ben Hecht: "I once saw a city that seemed to picture the past that lingers in every aging head. . . . I sat on one of its high walls and looked on the ghost of grandeur. . . . So do we all look on our youth. We note windows missing . . . but a poem lies in thes ruins."

Pining away, pondering anew the uncertain directions in any man's life, staring south from the window of this coop in the woods where I work, witness the world, convinced if I look in that direction long enough, hard enough, all the Chicago I loved will reappear, from the early childhood years (late 1930's) on the westside, to boyhood and young manhood (the late 40's, 50's, and 60's) on the far westside. All my visits since then . . . my present impromptu, infrequent rendezvous. . . .

My early Chicago was "Old Chicago," from my birth at St. Anthony's (2875 W. 19th, you could see it from the El, the black and white sign painted on the brick wall) to the age of five, when I lived in the Czechoslovokian enclave around 26th and Pulaski (Crawford)—which came to be known as "the little village."

26th Street was the lifeline of the neighborhood, where people could board a red, wooden streetcar that would eventually take them to downtown Chicago.

26th Street was alive with fruit and vegetable stands, butchershops, bakeries, taverns, dimestores, department stores. The language of the Old World—mostly Czech—could be heard everywhere on the streets: "Jak se máte?" "Já se mám velmi dobře, děkuji." [How are you? I'm fine, thank you.]

There was the Atlantic show (where my father remembers vaudeville acts), Kaplan's Clothing, Mach's Import, Stetina's Bakery, Tabor's Furniture Parlor, Cizek's, Neverkla Men's Clothing, Petrzilka's Funeral Parlor, the Leader Store, Krejci's Ice Cream, Woolworth's, Tancl the Undertaker, Zelezny Building & Loan, Crawford Sausage down the street, Bleier's Fruit & Vegetables.

26th and Troy was the Pilsen Brewery and a place called Pilsen Park, where families picniced, where Czech women on Sundays wore beautiful Old World costumes as they waltzed and danced the polka to the music of buttonbox concertinas. The men drank beer, told stories, and played pinochle in the shade of trees. My mother, as a young girl, danced in Pilsen Park. So did my aunts and uncles. So did Babi, my Grandma Papp.

All the relatives lived nearby . . . aunts, uncles, cousins, grandparents. There was an air of the European village in Chicago neighborhoods then, something we tried to preserve when we moved to the next Czech enclave in Cicero, in the late 1940's . . . something that began to disaappear as the suburbanization of America eroded ethnic cultures after the War, into the 1950's.

There in the little village of 26th Street, my people always referred to themselves as "the tribe." The tribe was all going to Grandma Papp's to eat on Sunday . . . roast pork, *knedliky* and *zeli*. The whole tribe would be there at Svobodas' wedding or Kadlecs' twenty-fifth wedding anniversary behind the corner tavern on Saturday night.

My uncle, Bill Burda (a star on Sparta's soccer team), was a local butcher—Burda's Butchershop, 27th and Springfield, famous for smoked hams. Another uncle sold fruits and vegetables on the street during the Depression. Another wanted to be a drummer. Grandpa Papp worked in an icehouse. Grandpa Blei was a machinest at Liquid Carbonic in 31st and Kedzie.

Uncle Bill the butcher and Aunt Julia lived across the hall from us above Brachtl's Drugstore on 31st and Hamlim—where they still live today. The butchershop disappeared a few years ago. Most of the neighborhood taverns and shops are gone. The Czech language has given way to Spanish. Only the names of the streets and some of the buildings remain.

Both sets of grandparents lived within walking distance of each other, but they never visited. The Bleis (my German side, one quarter) lived in a traditional Chicago bungalow on Avers Avenue, near 31st—just down the alley from where I lived above the drugstore with my parents until the age of five.

The Papps (my Slavic side) lived mostly in the basement of their bungalow on Pulaski, next door to a warehouse smelling of coffee and tea, near the Burlington railroad tracks where I watched and waited for the streamlined Silver Zephyr to pass by.

9

Marty Robinson

Railroads, streetcars, Elevated trains . . . images of chidlhood that marked my earliest Chicago years. Steam engines, train whistles, train stations, railroad crossing guards, red lanterns. The light of a distant engine, the light in passenger cars at night bound for the city of Chicago. The rumbling of freight cars. The man in the red caboose waving. The clanging and whining of streetcars . . . sparks from the overhead wires. Blueflashes and shooting sparks from the iron weight of wheels on the El rolling by.

As a small child of working parents, I was shuttled between both sets of grandparents, both worlds. Everything dutiful, protective, calm, loving and quiet with the Bleis. Everything dark, spontaneous, explosive, mysterious and uncertain with the Papps.

It was like waiting for a streetcar or the El, or playing near the railroad tracks: excitement, the possibility of danger, the certainty that someone would arrive on time to rescue you. It was like walking the rails . . . finding your balance, with arms outstretched.

A pad of paper and a knife-sharpened pencil on a sunny kitchen table, a dog, and a canary in a green cage occupied my time at Grandma and Grandpa Blei's. There were buttons, string, cards, dice, wooden matches, chicken feathers, meatbones, dough rising, a wood stove, boiling pots, floured hands, a foreign tongue (Babi, talking to herself) and the dark abyss of the basement at Grandma and Grandpa Papp's.

My little life was predictable and secure at the Bleis', fraught with fear or sudden love in the basement of the Papps. The back door might suddenly burst open: the violent explosion of my grandfather, Czech or Hungarian spewing from his mouth, an aunt in tears over a bad love affair, a strange woman standing in the doorway holding a jar of dark liquid to cure stomach pain, an uncle stumbling in drunk, playing an instrument. My mother coming to take me home after work.

This was Chicago to me then: our tribe and all its traditions of language, food, celebration, settled around 31st and Pulaski—a small European village of mystery and excitement . . . with intimations of a different life, a greater city out there, accessible by streetcar, motor car, steam engine, and Elevated train.

My Grandma Blei spoke English and knew Czech. My Grandma Papp never learned English and spoke only Czech, which made her a greenhorn to most American-minded cityfolk. Beyond her own neighborhood she was lost, a stranger in a strange land indeed. I don't believe she ever saw downtown Chicago, or even knew where it was.

My Grandma Blei cooked well-balanced meals, ate carefully, and read health books. My Grandma Papp bought live chickens home from the local markets and butchered them in the basement. She didn't cook food for the family, she consecrated it. Cooking was ritualistic, mystical, sanctifying. Cooking was her faith, the kitchen her church, the stove her altar. When the family broke bread, they tore it apart with both hands. Knives were everywhere and ever-sharp.

Sometimes they flew in the air. Grandpa Papp put food in his mouth with the point of a knife. The Bleis kept knives hidden in the backs of dark drawers.

Each grandparent loved me, and I loved each of them. Losing them in death was a most difficult thing for me as I entered my twenties (already separated from them, living in Cicero), as their Chicago world began to fade. The streetcars suddenly disappeared. Corner neighborhood shops became apartments. The language on the streets was stilled. The family scattered to the suburbs. The world became "super," "modern," and finally "instant."

When I discovered I could conjure memories of them (not unlike the way Babi cooked) in that old Chicago neighborhood at that time of horse and wagons, streetcars, fruit peddlers—when I first began to write in the 1960's—it was the spirit of Babi that guided my rite-of-passage: woman of peasant stock, of darkness, strength, light, stubbornness, and blood. Woman of the Old World confronted by the New.

Her language was her hands. Her love was unconditional: earth, children, family, dreams. She was earth-mother, medicine woman, artist. She knew the secret of time—past, present, future—how it all came together at any one moment, how it would all come back to me, her first grandson. My work was to remember. From the window of a second-storey flat above the drugstore on 31st and Hamlin, from the warm window-seat of the silver radiator in my bedroom, I viewed the setting—sky, buildings, streets, the black iron fire escape—a perfect perspective for a child's recreation of a world.

In daylight I watched women going to market with their black leather shopping bags, men carrying home foamy buckets of beer from corner taverns, children chalking the streets and sidewalks in games. I heard milkmen rattling glass bottles of milk (two inches of cream in the neck); I heard the "raggggssaliooon" cry of junkmen on horse-pulled wagons, factory whistles at noon, machines pounding steel, steam engines puffing, pulling, switching boxcars in freightyards, streetcars screeching their way home down the long steel rails . . . streaks of silver curving into the neighborhood, then shooting back out again.

A winter's night view from the window was a dreamscape of drifting snow and pools of yellow streetlight . . . white flakes and the lights in the windows of the houses, the storefronts, the darkened fortress of Gary School across the street. An occasional automobile ("machines," Grandpa Blei called them) and the city skyscrapers, as I imagined them, soaring into layers of darkness, clouds of snow . . . trains, streetcars, and Els gliding on silver rails, burrowing through night and new snow, passengers framed in small squares of windowlight, arriving, departing for downtown Chicago, where my father worked. Where he would disappear each day at first light. Where Grandpa Blei would sometimes take me for an El ride to watch a parade.

Now look here. Mister Blues, I want you to leave my door.
Now look here, Mister Blues, I want you to leave my door.
And when you go this time. I don't want you back no more.

J. Robert Nash

"Time? The storyteller you can't shut up, he goes on", said Sandburg.

Wasn't it only weeks ago? months ago? last year? I rode the El downtown again for old time's sake and stood on the middle of the Michigan Avenue Bridge on a sunny morning listening to Lil' Howlin' Wolf blowing his sax? Didn't I stop to see writer/friend Lowell Komie, to swap plans, recent adventures from my old Bohemian neighborhood in Cicero/Berwyn to Central America, the Southwest, Eastern Europe, and Door County, Wisconsin? Wasn't it another one of my mad dashes through the city, trying to cram a week into a day?

Didn't I stop at the Art Institute for a quick look at Hopper's "Nighthawks"—and everything else in sight—in the few minutes I could spare? (Don't I miss this Chicago place most of all?) Didn't I buy some books at Kroch's on Wabash? (Wasn't I tracking one of my old routes through the city?) Wasn't it just another great day in downtown Chicago, like it used to be ten, twenty, thirty years ago?

Didn't I stop at the Goat for a shot of nostalgia and a beer, recalling the good times, days and nights in the greatest underground neighborhood tavern in downtown Chicago . . . conversation, laughter, stories, dreams (Old Billy Goat Sianis himself still on the scene) basking in the good company of Jay Robert Nash, Mike Royko, Harry Mark Petrakis, Curt Johnson, Brian Boyer, John Fink, Clarus Backes, Dick Takeuchi, Tony Monahan, John Blades, journalists, poets, writers, editors, friends . . . the best people in the best of places, in the best of my Chicago times?

Didn't I lunch at Riccardo's with the golden voice himself, Marty Robinson, TV and radio host (WFMT, WTTW)—classical music connoisseur, opera buff, jazz aficionado, lover of literature, ethnic enthusiast, piano bar man, *bon vivant*, superb storyteller, Mr. Mellifluous? Didn't he once tell me, "I'm really a Chicago street kid, a brawler who got kicked out of Lane Tech for cutting school. Every kid thinks he's going to be a movie star. When I first thought of radio, I was driving a cab in Chicago and dating a girl who danced in the chorus line of the Silver Frolics. She was gorgeous. She didn't have a clue to anything, but she told me I had a nice voice. I began reading the newspapers out loud."

Spoken like a true Chicagoan—something to do with street smarts and *savoir-faire*, making something of it, saying what's on your mind and having the mind to say it. (Beyond candor.) Speaking up and *not* forever holding your peace. A touch of the wise guy. (McMahon in headband labeled ROZELLE.) Being the real McCoy. (Ditka in a press conference: "There are teams named Smith and some named Grabowski; we're Grabowskis.") Compassion unlimited and understated. Humor that hits home. (Studs on the air. Royko on Daley, Royko on Reagan, Royko on anything.) Something to do with Sandburg's idea of poetry: "the synthesis of hyacinths and biscuits." Hemingway's concept of a writer needing a built-in shit detector.

Of course it's the Windy City. Of course it's the Second City. Of course

14

it's the Midwest. Character like this does not weather well in New York or California. Read Royko. Hear Studs. Watch Ditka, Nash, Zimmer, Halas, Holtzman, Hecht, Algren, Sandburg, Petrakis, Sage, Kogan, Petros, Byrne, Szathmary, Scala, Daly (I and II), Veeck, Washington, Wright, Broonzy, Belushi, Bauler, Capone. There it is, unmistakable. The beat goes on—past, present, future. And birthright is not the only guarantee. Strangers too at times have what it takes to be from here. If John Kennedy was a Berliner wasn't Lech Walęsa a Chicagoan in Daley Plaza, November 1989? It was written all over his face: this is *my* kind of town, too, Mr. Sinatra. What is it about Chicago? asks the stranger. Why do I feel at home here?

"The American spirit has discovered its manliest voices, as well as its meanest here," Algren reminds us.

Then didn't I walk all the way down Michigan to Water Tower Place, pausing outside the door to hear a black man blowing blues?

> Make a music squander
> Hurried throats,
> While the harsh notes wander—
> Flurried notes—
> Oh, the scorns and horns and drummings-strain
> Chicago's daffy, laughy pain!

Sang Maxwell Bodenheim in a poem, "Chicago Jazz II" (1930).

Didn't I stop at Rizzoli's to buy books and South American tapes? Didn't I walk on over to Cricket's on Chestnut from there to check on bartender and friend, St. Pat?

Didn't I return to Riccardo's for the Friday-5 o'clock-cocktail hour (looking for waiter extraordinaire Bobby Estrada, man of infinite refinement, culture, kindness—the dean of waiters in Chi Town), still seeking the Ghosts of Great Times Past at Ric's? Nights beginning there with Nash holding court, the crowd around him growing louder, wilder, beyond the booth or three-deep at the bar . . . growing, finally, beyond Riccardo's, north to Nash's favorite watering hole, O'Rourke's in Old Town, where Nash could really be Nash—larger than life, wise guy, storyteller, entertainer, literary authority, film buff, friend of literary luminaries from Hemingway to Dylan Thomas, Jack Conroy, James Farrell, Algren, Bukowski, Brooks, Mailer, not to mention Chicago's Jim McCormick, Offen, Cuscaden, Etter, Ritalin, Peuchner, Schrager, Smith, Clark, Boyer, Jonjack, Balchowsky, Johnson, McCarrell, Blazek, Torgersen, Burleigh, Roger Ebert ("Disestablishmentarianists," he dubbed us) . . . novelist, editor, publisher, crime expert (which he later became, authoring dozens of books and encyclopedias), not to mention all-time-great bar scuffler: "OK, Buster. You're a dead man!" Nash inevitably taking on the biggest, baddest guy at the bar . . . and always a winner—in my eyes. To this day, invincible . . . every Chicago writer's great

15

friend.

Back here in Dairyland, the radio can't quite pick up WGN this morning—as usual. And it'll never bring in Brandmeier on WLUP, Steve and Gary, or Studs on WFMT. Too forlorn a place. Too far gone. Absence and the fond Chicago heart. It comes with the territory of exile. Some, like Algren, never leave home to know the pain: "Well, we're all born equal and anyone in Chicago can now become an expatriate without leaving town."

> *Well, I went to the gypsy an' I laid my money on the line,*
> *Well, I went to the gypsy an' I laid my money on the line,*
> *I said "Bring back my baby, or please take her off my mind."*

If I never intended to leave, I never intended to stay away this long. Still the aspiring writer (too late, too long gone), still looking for Chicago written in his name.

Remembrance of things past—always the writer's calling card. Well, you've got to begin *somewhere*.

16

When I began, I began with the family, the neighborhood, the people, the city. Many stories herein reprinted reflect that time and place: Chicago, the 60's, 70's. Portrait of a young writer in Chicago, aspiring to short stories, novels, and poetry, freelancing his way to survival. Trying to put into practice all he had learned from all he had read. No excuses. No other qualifications. Trying to bring the people, the place, the story alive. First person journalism, new journalism, old fashioned who/what/when/where journalism. It was all news to him. No "journalist" by education, no guts to ever call himself one. "Writer" is the only name of the game he knows.

"If people did not want their stories told," Sherwood Anderson said, "it would be better for them to keep away from me. I would tell if I could get at the heart of it. . . ."

The young man in these small Chicago tales seems obviously enamoured of the place, in love with what he is doing, obviously seeking love in return. In a whirl, beside himself at times. Feeling his oats, happy to be alive, on the streets, among people . . . talking, listening, telling all about it. ("Extra! Extra! Read all about it!" . . . sounds of the city now replaced by coins stuck into metal newsboxes.)

Obviously his is not the whole Chicago story. Obviously some of his Chicago has changed, disappeared. Prices have doubled and redoubled. Chef Louie Szathmary has retired and closed the Bakery; Stop & Shop is no more; both Burr Tillstrom and Fran Allison have passed away, which means the end as well for the whole world of the Kuklapolitans; Royko has turned gray; Dr. Preston Bradley died in 1983; Nick Klein, the rocking horse man who gave joy to so many, found little joy in old age, and one morning walked into the southbound traffic of Lake Shore Drive, dead at 79. But Petros still dances in Greektown, and Studs will live forever. Stories never end. Everything a man writes becomes history—he learned just the other day.

Obviously, regretfully, there is much that he missed, much he witnessed but never got down, much he wishes he could some day return to:

Sieben Brewery and beer garden, Cafe Bellini on Rush Street, Rush Street, Mister Kelly's, Second City, Slim Brundage and the College of Complexes, Bill Smith, Tip Top Tap and the Allerton Hotel, the Italian Village, Henrici's, Ike Sewell and the Pizzeria Uno, the Blue Note, Miles Davis at the Cloister Inn, George Shearing, Erroll Garner at the London House, Josh White at the Gate of Horn, Berghoff's, Bug House Square, Discount Records, Sayat Nova, Kungsholm, George Diamond, Jacques, David Mamet, the women of Michigan Avenue, the Goodman Theatre, the pressmen in their newspaper hats, City of Clout/City of Chicagoese, the Blackhawk, the Gaslight Club, Charley and the Wrigley Building Restaurant, Red Grooms' "City of Chicago" (1967), Oak Street, The Clark Theater, the Chicago Film Festival, Hugh Heffner and *Playboy*, the Morrison Hotel, the Post Office News, Union Station, Chicago North Western Station, Colonel McCormick, Holy Name Cathedral, the Lyric

Opera, Bob Wallace, State Street tatoo parlors, Milwaukee Avenue, Solti's Chicago Symphony, Elmer Gertz, the Blizzard of '67, the Reader, Cellini Pipes on South Wacker, Old Town, Christmas in Chicago, Lincoln Park, readings by Norman Mailer, e e cummings, Robert Frost, Carl Sandburg, Kenneth Rexroth, Ferlinghetti, Ginsberg, Comiskey Park, Herman Kogan, Punchinello's, Figaro's, the Happy Medium, the Quiet Knight, Music Till Dawn with Jay Andres, the Empire Room, the Greyhound Bus Depot, Arthur Shay, River City, Riverview, Richard Hunt, the Red Star Inn, the Earl of Old Town, Cape Cod Room, Bratislava, the Atlantic Hotel, Meyer's Deli, Lutz's Pastery Shop, Cafe Bohemia, the Chez Paree, Christine Newman, Gwendolyn Brooks, Saul Bellow, John Fink, Sauer's, the Stock Yard Inn, Chances R, the Dill Pickle Club, the Old Corona Cafe on Grand, Stephen Deutch, Papa Milano's, Bobby Estrada Zum Deutschen Eck, Lyon & Healy, Rose Records, Hyde Park, John Barleycorn, lower Wacker Drive, Big Table, Minskey's, the Fulton Fish Market, Soldier Field, Kup, Chagall's mosaic, Newberry Library, the Pump Room, North Avenue Beach, Thai restaurants, John Fischetti, Cardinal Cody, the Golden Ox, Horder's, the Palmer House, Checker Cabs, Yellow Cabs, Ivan Albright, The Billy Goat, Sears, Bozo, Smokey Joe's, Jesse Jackson, the Cliff Dwellers, the Oxford Pub, Ivanhoe, rib joints, the Bismarck Hotel, Su Casa, Barney's, Norman Ross, Miomir's, Fritzel's, Harry Caray, Rickett's, Monroe Cigar Shop, Eli's, Butkus, *Poetry* Magazine, McClurg Ct., Ditka, Randolph Street Market, Trader Vic's, Paul Sills, Big Bill Broonzy: "Young people have forgotten to cry the blues. Now they talk and get lawyers and things."

> *I wrote these blues, I'm gonna sing them as I please,*
> *I wrote these blues, I'm gonna sing them as I please,*
> *I'm the only one liking the way I'm singing them, I'll swear to goodness*
> *there's no one else t'please.*

Home may be where someone waits for you, but the Lady of the Lake waits for no one, and this loverboy of long ago feels just a stranger himself in town these days.

Hell, I hardly recognize the old girl anymore.

Still the whore-with-the-heart-of-gold attraction: I'll give you the time of your life, Mister City-Lights-Shining-in-Your-Eyes. But nobody owns me, and you'll never be satisfied. Leave the money under the lamp while I tend to business. What did you say your name was again, Mister?

It's not that I've given up trying to win back her heart, or whatever time she once gave me. I check out the action these days with streetwise St. Pat (a k a Patrick Fagan), Brother Blarney, who lives out of a suitcase, carries his life savings in his pocket, has worked bars and first-class bistros all across the country, and is now day bartender at Cricket's in the Tremont. At P.J. Clarkes, "Yes, now, when I walk in, since I have been here a year and half, from one end of the

bar to the other, I've got to say hello to a hundred ladies. I do! 'Hi, St. Pat.'—
That's what they're calling me now. . . . At Cricket's, I'm getting more of the
Fourth Estate in there, and the most beautiful, wealthy women in the world,
who are actually sitting at the bar, tossing barbs at Chicago's finest writers. On
Wednesday nights, I sit at the Billy Goat, hoping to have a drink with my very
dear friend, Mike Royko! This city is bustling with activity. Excellent restau-
rants. Theaters of all types. . . ."

St. Patrick

People, if you hear me humming on this song both night and day,
People, if you hear me humming on this song both night and day,
I'm just a poor boy in trouble, trying to drive the blues away.

"Sandburg's Chicago, Dreiser's Chicago, Farrell's and Wright's and my own Chicago, that was somebody else's Chicago," said Algren in 1961. In 1975 he left with a broken heart.

She remains what she always was: a good-time lady. Any man's one-night stand. And for any lover who's ever put in the time with her, it always ends in heart and all its variations: broken, rusty, mean, bitter, faint, empty, hard, half, cold, little or no heart at all. To have is not to hold for keeps.

They tell me you are wicked . . . and crooked . . . and brutal. . . .

But, of course. Only the numbers change. Crime wakes each morning, puts on a new face, takes another name, but cruises the same territory— Chicago and Vicinity; Cabrini Green, City Hall, Circuit Court, North Side, South Side, West Side. Black Panthers, Greylords, gangs, muggings, drugs, rape, racism, mayhem, murder on the CTA, where death and danger now ride a writer's once-beloved El train.

Still, you gotta love her for what she is. And was.

City that's there. City that isn't.

Expect no more than what you remember.

Sometimes, in the morning light, giving the lady what she wants is to say thanks. And so long.

Man in the Window

He sits always at the window in Pixley's, attempts to drink hot coffee and read his morning paper. There are distractions, though, always distractions on the outside–and the coffee gets colder. Sometimes it's a beautiful woman—a welcome distraction. Other times it's one tragic sight after another. Some mornings it's all tragedy, and the newspaper is no help at all.

> A 16-year-old Niles West High School student collapsed and died
> Wednesday night while running to a class of religious instruction.

Outside, an old Black woman, paper suitcase bound with newspaper twine, checks the destination of every bus, but is lost, totally lost in conversation with herself. Her bus will never come.

> Writer Gorden Langley Hall, adopted son of Dame Margaret Rutherford,
> has changed his sex through an operation and is planning to marry a
> South Carolina Negro man—with the approval of most of his British family.

The hippies parade in striped trousers, hairy vests, beads, bells, and boots and get all the attention they deserve. Where the hell are they bound, he wonders. How long is a day and a night to them? And what could morning mean? Of all the people passing, only the hippies seem oblivious of any destination. (Even the black woman thinks a bus might be her answer.) How many people live only for a parade?

> Actress Zsa Zsa Gabor checked into a London Hospital Wednesday night
> with her wrists and ankles bandaged, claiming she had been beaten by
> five Spanish Island policemen.

Two heavy, blind men, dressed in gray jackets and orange Day-Glo caps, step slowly and awkwardly to the tune of coins rattling in tin cups. They look so much like brothers. They make their way through the crowd with a minimum of contact. Only the glow of their caps stays in the eyes of the passersby. The coffee gets colder.

> A bullet inside the brain of a holdup victim was repositioned by
> whirling him in a centrifuge normally used in space research by the

21

National Aeronautics and Space Administration.

Here comes a woman crying. There goes that man again, with the overcoat down to his ankles, filling his pockets with butts. A bus driver shuts the door in an old woman's face. An average looking All-American respectable business-man stops dead in his tracks, turns, and stands mystified at how minimal a mini-skirt is on a young girl, blonde hair swinging freely in her time.

> Distressed motorist Mrs. Ula B. Scanlon (left) is bypassed by hitchhiker
> and waited 17 minutes for aid, while miniskirted Temro Jaco had no
> trouble getting immediate offers of assistance near Long Beach, Calif.

Maybe Ann has the answer this morning:

> Dear Ann: I have had some very disturbing dreams lately. I dream of
> being intimate with the butcher, the garage mechanic, the TV repairman
> and even the paperboy. I am a respectable married woman, mid 30s,
> with a fine family. I have no interest in anyone other than my husband.
> My dreams have made me feel unworthy and I am filled with guilt.
> Can you explain this?
>   ASHAMED TO SLEEP
>
> Dear Ashamed: Dreams are uncensored thoughts and desires that get
> loose in the unconscious. Freud said they are the disguised fulfillment
> of repressed wishes. Robert Louis Stevenson once wrote: "We all have
> feelings that would shame hell." Some of those feelings come out in our
> dreams. But it's how we conduct ourselves, not what we dream, that
> counts. The fact that you are ashamed of your dreams indicates that
> you would probably never do, in your waking hours, the things you
> dream about.

Ann has only more questions. The coffee is ice cold. There are no answers in the newspaper this morning, he is sure of that. It's just another one of those mornings where he finds it difficult to sit still and concentrate on who he is and what is going on. One of those mornings where he must do what he can to keep from walking through the plate glass window himself.

22

Chicago's Basements:
The Best Bargains in Town

State Streeting it today, the inveterate bargain hunter, looking for a kill that will do my marked-down, ethnic soul good. Something I can show my Bohemian ancestors with pride and say, "You'll never guess what I paid for these great socks with the clocks on the ankle! 29c a pair! How can a guy go wrong on a bargain like that?"

I carry an old, shocking-pink shopping bag under my arm (a souvenir from the old neighborhood) which blazenly states, WESTERN NATIONAL BANK OF CICERO, 5801 West Cermak Road, FREE PARKING DRIVE-IN BANKING WALK-UP WINDOWS. Old shopping bags never die in the hands of true basement bargaineers. They soften with age and become sacred with each mission.

If there's one thing Bohemians have in their blood, it's basements. And if there's another thing, it's bargains. There's something about hard times and the lower depths that's almost mythical to their culture.

First it was the Depression, then it was the War. Next it was the Recession, and now it's inflation. The Bohemian lives with the threat of economic collapse from the day of his birth until the day of his death. Even then, he's afraid the undertaker, the lawyer, or a relative probably did him out of all his money. ("Did you have to spend $3000 to bury me? Couldn't you find a better bargain than that in the old neighborhood?")

But no matter the name or wave of history, the ethnic shopper (especially the Bohemian) was bred on bargains and honed in the neighborhood handicraft of stretching the dollar. Shopping was a risky sport at best, which sometimes bordered on an art. It was not so much *what* you had shopping-bagged in neighborhood department stores and the bargain basements downtown, as how much you saved by buying that maroon tie with the mallard ducks for only 89 cents. "It's a genuine hand-painted silk tie from Italy worth $2.98 at least," you try to convince yourself.

Ethnic economics aside, all the world loves a bargain, and basements used to be the place to find them. Enter the nostalgic shopper with that far-away look in his eyes. In these reduced days of first floor—even entire stores—of "discount

23

shopping," bargains come almost too easy. What's left for the old battlers of basement bargains? Can one still go down to the basement and emerge with some rare trophy?

Yes, I say, yes . . . descending to the lower depths of Weiboldt's on State Street, down, down, down to the Budget Store. At first I'm transfixed by the sight and sound of the pet shop in the basement, and then I'm suddenly seized by a department store sound I haven't heard since childhood: ding . . . ding . . . ding. All my youthful shopping days are memories of these notes which sounded like someone wopping wooden tones on a xylophone. I never knew what they meant, but I knew that's what department stores sounded like.

Wieboldt's basement is close to classic in bargain basement shopping; to be just down is not enough. The more a bargain shopper is made to feel humbled by the atmosphere, the more significant the bargain.

And you always go through these places sort of lost, forever adrift. Bargain basement shoppers actually have nothing particular in mind. They really don't care to know where they are at or where they're headed: Millinery, Handbags, Dresses, Sportswear, Foundation Garments, Bakery, Cards . . . what have you? What's the bargain?

Take these women's house slippers, 2 pair for $7. Not one, but two pair! Now that's a bargain. Ding . . . ding . . . ding . . . There it goes again. "Look," says one bargain huntress to another, "They got cheap umbrellas here, $3.98. But they have the old wooden handle." Ah, for an old umbrella with a wooden handle.

Behind me I hear Spanish-speaking voices sparking the air as two women throw piles of shoes around. One of them finds a particular treasure, shows it to the other, who subsequently turns up her nose, and they're off again, digging deeper and deeper into the treasure of Sierra Wieboldt's.

Through Infant Wear and into Men's Furnishings, feeling more and more in touch with bargain basements of yore as the very floor gives way, it seems, and now turns wooden, bare and worn, transmitting a certain softness and character formed by thousands of bargain hunters through the years.

Knee Length Pajamas, $2.99 . . . Dress Shirts, $3.49 . . . Ties, 69 cents (some beautiful old battle types) and T-shirts, says the sign, $1.19; IF PERFECT, $1.99. "If Perfect." I like that . . . the conditional, philosophic overtones for a shopper to ponder.

A sales woman on the phone says to some customer calling up on a bargain from God knows where: "It's hard to describe the slacks . . . They're on the table now . . . no, I wouldn't be able to tell you what color or size . . . yes, they're on the table now . . . but let me tell you something, these are not polyester . . . no, truthfully, these are not the modern pants."

No, and truthfully, the Van Heusen and Arrow shirts are labeled IMPERFECTS, but at $4.59, there's nothing in a bargaineer's world as beautiful as an IMPERFECT Arrow shirt.

These great old, open counters, I pause to reflect, battered and so sorely in need of paint. But these are the battlegrounds. The scenes of hand-to-hand combat in piles of twisted ties and shirts and pants.

Even now, holding one leg of a $2.99 pair of pants, while the woman across from me clinches the other, I can feel the bargain in my hand. Remembering, though, that maroon is not for me, I relinquish my grip on the pants only to see the woman hold them up in some kind of victory gesture, then toss them down again in front of me.

Oh, the anguish! But ah, the purely physical play of bargain shopping. More contact. More emotion. They've taken all this away from us in stores today. A real bargain, the true essence of shopping, was always more meaningful if you not only saved money but successfully wrenched the item from another person's hand.

In a far off corner, I see men's suspenders, $2, and smile a little. Who wears suspenders in these denim days of ours? By God, this is dinosaur country down here. But how beautiful to keep the faith, to keep the old bargains alive. Men's garters, $1.

And look at these beat-up, old fashioned straw hats on open shelves going for a mere $1.99! I try them all on though not one seems a perfect fit. They're all bent. The straw is bad. The weave seems highly irregular. Putting one on, I look like a reject pinochle player from some Polish or Bohemian picnic. I love it, but decide State Street's not ready yet for me and my bent straw hat. Ding . . . ding . . . ding.

Onward to Carson Pirie Scott & Co. and their Budget store. A little more class here, a little brighter looking, even a rather mind boggling directory to the lower depths: Ready to Wear for misses, women, juniors; Children's Shoes; Women's Shoes; Key Shop; Snack Bar; Honey Bear Food Shop; Intimate Apparel; Cosmetics; Shoe Repair; Girl's Wear; Children's Wear; Men's Wear; Boy's Wear; Tartan Tray; Infant's Wear.

I strike out in all directions at once, but really find little that suits my bargaining fancy. I down a quick Coke at the empty Snack Bar, then hang around the Key Shop for awhile because I like to watch keys being made. But there's not much doing in the Budget Store this morning. Bargains maybe have bargained out?

Food again gets the best of me as I step into the Honey Bear Food Shop in the corner of the basement, trying to satisfy the always-present hunger in a Bargain Shopper. I find a salesgirl sorting through various hunks of cheese that seem to be getting just a bit over-ripe.

Ah, hah, I figure, back in the old neighborhood this is a sure sign to do some heavy bargaining. . . . "Hey, Mr. Fruit Man, these bananas are brown. How about a nickel a piece?" Or, "Mr. Baker, you got some day-old Bohemian rye for the birds?"

"I'll bet you're going to sell me some of this good cheese at half price, because it's moldy, maybe?" I try the salesgirl for openers.

"No," she smiles and goes right ahead rearranging and repackaging the stuff.

"You mean, no bargain on moldy cheese?"

"No. Just cut the mold off."

Away I go, bargainless, up from Carson's basement, down State Street, ducking briefly into Baskin's, only to learn from the salesman, "There is no budget floor. Everything's up here." And a quick once-around Lytton's where again I am informed there is no bargain basement. "We used to have one years ago. There are no more bargains."

So I ponder that as I enter the Valhalla of bargain shoppers—Goldblatt's. Just in case you're still not sure, there's a sign as you're going down the escalator: GOLDBLATT'S BARGAIN BASEMENT.

Signs of all sorts (especially hand-painted) are a true indication of real bargain basement shopping. EVERYDAY LOW LOW PRICES. People with bargains on their brains need to be reminded of the good deals in their midst. And Goldblatt's goes all the way with sign language . . . authentic-gauche yellow signs popping out of everywhere.

At the bottom of the escalator I'm assaulted by a mixture of hard and soft, sweet and sour smells that can at best be described as "definitely delicatessen." And so it is . . . Goldblatt's Bargain Basement style. Half Price Baby Corn, 69 cents; Polish Type Praski, $1.49 a lb., Hot & Mild Short Polish, $1.39 lb . . . beautifully displayed in four open boxes.

I smell dill pickles, I smell spicy sausage, rye bread, cheese . . . I'm alive again, thanks to Goldblatt's Bargain Basement. This is the way it was. Food, clothing, people, everything mixed together . . . all the senses working . . . the whole scene wonderfully alive like Old World markets and Middle Eastern bazaars. Almost a sense of "carnival" to it . . . Goldblatt's has all this going, in the basement, naturally, without the systematic and artificial effort many stores employ to hype a particular sale with ethnic gusto.

I buy a couple pounds of bargain Short, Hot Polish Sausage, drop them into my shopping bag, and press on with the hunt. Now I'm sorry I didn't buy that straw hat at Wieboldt's. With a shopping bag, Polish sausage and a straw hat (and maybe stripped down to a tank type T-shirt) how could I be anything but the best dressed ethnic on my block?

Moving into the thick of it, I find a three-foot mound of men's underwear, 3 for $2.85, jeans for $2.99, men's dress shoes for $3.88, swim suits for $2.99. "Has inflation forced you into bargain shopping?" I ask one customer. She replies with a pained look, a grunt, and leaves me standing there amidst the underwear.

"Well, in times like these, there's nothing like being able to buy a pair of shoes for less than $4," I comment to an old gent. "These are good shoes," he says, "but they're all the wrong size."

"What's the difference? A bargain's a bargain."

"Yeah, but I got big feet."

Bargain shoppers are not necessarily great talkers. No time. Their eyes, brains, hands, are centered on only one thing: the merchandise at hand. Do I or don't I buy this five-piece shower curtain set with the Polish flowers for $2.99, or pass it up and go home to my bathroom with the storks and live to regret it?

Deep now into men's clothing, I spy a true steal—Leisure Suits. A $110 outfit going for just $20! Both me and a young guy are overwhelmed by the immensity of the bargain.

Retrieving my handy pink shopping bag with the Polish sausage inside, I meander into the world's schlockiest collection of glassware. There's an ugly, orange swan that only a blind bargaineer could love, dusty bowls, obscene vases . . . $2.99 to $6.99 . . . help yourself. There comes a time when some bargains must be passed up just to save a shopper's nickel-and-dime integrity. The only reason I might consider buying that orange swan would be the thrill of dropping it accidentally, immediately.

Glancing at the Wig Department I discover that Capless Wigs, a $12 value, are going for $4.97. BLONDES HAVE MORE FUN, says another original Goldblatt sign, LIGHT COLOR WIGS, $2.97. Afro Wigs, a $10 value, are going for a remarkable $3.97. I pull one on quickly, glimpsing a hazy resemblance of a white Jesse Jackson, and throw it back on the pile before I'm suspected of being a Goldblatt's Bargain Basement detective.

"What's the Five Million Dollar Sale?" I ask a saleswoman, pointing to the sign above. "I don't know," she says, grasping her throat in confusion. "I really don't know." "Then where's the Bargain Basement?" I counter. And her mouth drops, and she kind of side-steps away.

I tune in now to the bargain shoppers themselves. I eavesdrop on a couple of late, middle-aged women sorting through a counter of women's pants. The more fashionably bargain-basement-attired of the two (about 55) says, "First is money, then is sex. So I'm making him happy. I give him what I got. When a man spends $50 on you and takes you out to the best places. . . ." Ah, a bargain romance in Goldblatt's!

On the escalator going up, I attempt a conversation with a well-dressed gentleman, sensing he just may be Goldblatt's personnel and know something of the sale on hand.

"Well, I work here indirectly," he confesses. "The Five Million Dollar Sale? Where's the sign? I'm really not sure, but 5 million dollars is not that much when you're dealing with a 250-million-dollar-a-year business such as Goldblatt's does."

I hop over then to Sears, where I learn, much to my amazement, there is no bargain basement, only a self-service Hillman's Fine Food Store.

Crossing over and working my way back along the west side of State, I try the State Street Store where I'm informed that the bargain department is on the 3rd floor. Taking the elevator up, I step into a scene of hungry sales girls and lean pickin's. Aside from the rock music crowding the room, there are no customers and no bargains as far as I can see.

Bond's basement coming up . . . going down . . . a nice, neat, almost antiseptic store for the bargaineers. "Where are all the shoppers?" I ask. "In the suburbs," I'm advised. "Or maybe at Goldblatt's," I suggest.

Bonds has clothing . . . ties for $1.99, belts for $2.99, walking shorts from $2.99 to $4.99 . . . but who really goes out of his way to bargain basement shop in this place for these items, I wonder? When you can buy a decent belt for a buck at your local drugstore these days?

Montgomery Wards has a legitimate-enough bargain basement (the Budget Store) going, although it's corralled (you must actually pass through turnstiles) in the southeast corner of the basement. There's a solitary bargain shopper as I enter.

But Big Brother Bargaineer then suddenly clicks on over the intercom with some reminders: "Ladies blouses, 40 to 46, $1 each . . . navy blue blazers, $9 . . . ladies shorts now on sale, $1.50 . . . have a good day and thank you for shopping at Wards."

I wait a few minutes for the onslaught of bargain shoppers, but when nobody shows, I quietly tip-toe out and hit the street again with my two pounds of Polish, which is beginning to ripen.

For a final fling, I give Marshall Fields bargain basement a fast whirl. Fields , however, refers to it as "the Budget Floor . . . Moderately Priced Merchandise . . . A Store in Itself." Women's dresses, Toiletries, Linens, Stationery, Men's Store, Lamps, Women's Jewelry. Field's basement is bountiful and beautiful in display, quality of merchandise and the whole operation of sub-shopping.

But as for bargains? Well, there are bangle bracelets for 25 cents each, some budget-priced paintings for under $50. I check some nifty French berets in the Men's Store going for $6, which you'll probably never find in Goldblatt's basement. Truthfully, though, you will not find this a happy hunting ground for the ethnic bargaineer. There's just too damn much taste and quality around.

What the bargain shopper has going here, then, is a sort of reverse psychology. A bargain may be just a bargain in any basement. But a bargain in Fields' basement, where the very word "bargain" is seldom mentioned, or ever seen, is something bordering on "good value."

It's a suave way to shop in your head, but I prefer the primitiveness of Wieboldt's and Goldblatt's basements when I'm shopping for the kill. Besides, I feel out of place here with my shopping bag of Polish sausage.

Outside once again, I'm about to call it the end of another bargain basement day, take my trophy of Polish sausage home, when I think, what the hell, I really need that bent straw hat for $1.99 to match my shopping bag and complete my image for my long ride home on the Douglas Park L. Back to Wieboldt's.

Ding . . . ding . . . ding . . . down the stairs, but this time swinging into the Pet Shop first, which I missed last time. Bargain basement pets?

There are mice, rabbits, snakes, hamsters, turtles, fish and birds to be had. A veritable zoo in the basement of Wieboldt's. It's the parrot, though, that catches my fancy. A big, green, South American jungle beauty that I would love to have, though I hate to see birds caged for life.

But there's no bargain on the parrot. It's going for a cool $425 . . . probably the most expensive item in Wieboldt's basement.

"Why don't you buy the parrot?" says the salesgirl who seems to understand my need for it. "$425, and I'll throw in the cage. Or buy two of everything here, male and female, and start your own pet shop."

Hermit crabs are going for $2.75. And there's a sale on parakeets . . . green, $11.95, blue, $12.95, fancy, $13.95. Reptiles start from $1.59.

I go back to bid good-bye to my parrot. "Polly want a piece of Polish sausage?" The bird just blinks its eye, ooh so slowly.

Winging through the men's department, I see my favorite bent straw hat perched on a shelf, still waiting for me. I plunk down the $1.99 plus tax, shove the hat in my shopping bag, and head for home.

Ding . . . ding . . . ding . . . I hear again as I'm about to leave the store. "What does it all mean?" I ask an old saleslady in umbrellas.

"Oh, it's for the offices and the various departments. We all have our bells."

And I have my bargain basement bent straw hat, I smile, pulling it out of the pink shopping bag (reeking a little from Polish sausage) and setting it on the very top of my head (bad fit) for all the world to see and understand the joy in the eyes of a basement bargaineer going home with a real kill. I wish I had a green parrot for my shoulder.

Chef Louis: Supercook

We may live without poetry, music, and art;
We may live without conscience and live without heart;
We may live without friends; we may live without books,
But civilized man cannot live without cooks.

—Athenaeus

He sits there, tasting pears, in the kitchen of his famous restaurant, the Bakery. Barrel-chested, double chinned, stuffed in a chef's uniform topped with the classic cream puff hat, he looks for all the world like the kind of jovial cook one finds pictured in children's books or happy Hollywood movies. There's a touch of Billy Gilbert about him. There is that certain romance surrounding any cook. Chef Louis Szathmary has all these ingredients. Plus more.

The very photograph of him on the cover of his book, *The Chef's Secret Cook Book*, radiates a sort of ebullience, though the eyes are closed, ovens baking and dough raising elbow deep.

He's Hungarian. He's a bit difficult to understand at times. He gets excited, words gush, and you are left with fantastic images, wild syllogisms, and blank spaces which you must fill in for yourself. That's the difficulty of interpretation. That's the poetry of the man.

I came quite fed up with all the business about The Bakery: how quaint it is, how continental, how superb the food, how incomparable the food anywhere in Chicago. Everyone, it seemed, has had his say about The Bakery.

I did not care to add to their accolades. Furthermore, as a neighborhood gourmet, I'm quite weak on even the nomenclature of continental cuisine, let alone the taste. I can't tell a bloody Beef Wellington from a tough turbot. Move into the heady area of French desserts, and I'm lost without a dish of Jello.

And as for the pondering fat man seated before me—well, he was the owner. He was the cook. He was Chef Louis, pat-a-cake, pat-a-cake, baker man. And about the only lead I had on him was some whispered advice that he was Hungarian, and all Hungarians, of course, were con men. (Which I resented since I am

31

part Hungarian.) And maybe with The Bakery booming so, maybe Louie was on the verge of cooking up a Howard Johnson-land for himself or a Kentucky Coloneldom.

I could write about recipes, but it didn't work out that way. I could write about Louis in action in the kitchen, but I never saw him lift a lid off a pot or poke a fork into anything.

The only thing to begin with then, is Louis. He's all there is. And he's a little teed off at the moment because I am almost two hours late.

A great beginning. Silence. Watching the great chef eat with four or five cohorts lined up at the table (all Hungarian freedom advocates, one a fighter and a poet) plus his wife, Sada, a secretary, and even more of the kitchen entourage hovering about. Louis, no matter where he moves, is the center.

"You teach?" he asks, staring into his pears.

Sometimes.

"You write?"

Most of the time.

"You hungry? I thought you be here for lunch."

I'm sorry. A mix-up.

"That's all right. Not enough time, though. Must fly to Indiana for the book in a little while."

Then a swift command in Hungarian to a woman in white, and in three deep breaths I'm faced with a plate of Hungarian goulash, noodles, bread, and a silver pitcher of beer. I smile and nod my appreciation to Louis. That's what I like about chef's-power.

Now he is talking to the men across from him, they are talking, a secretary is reminding him of an appointment, and I am eating, with my notebook closed beside me. Louis, I say to myself, you really know how to disarm a writer. Put food in his hands.

A photographer suddenly slides into the scene to show Louis a picture of a church in Louis's native Hungary, a church Louis is helping preserve because of it s historical significance. I ask about this, about religion, his country. "You can commit genocide many ways," he says. "You can destroy a culture . . . no one in the United Nations would care," and with this, tears begin to well up in his eyes.

What about the money you send to Hungary for the restoration of the church? How can you be sure it's getting there?

"Anybody who takes money, you can trust," smiles Louie. "Because they always want more."

Chef Louis Szathmary is no mere rolly-polly cook. Since when do cooks talk like philosophers?

He is an eclectic man. He has his hands in the kitchen, in other enterprises, his whole being whirring into history, literature, religion, psychology, philosophy and art.

32

"You see," he smiles and mesmerizes you with those beady, bouncy, black Hungarian eyes, "God blessed me with insomnia . . . so . . . you are lucky, you can play more than other children, read more than other children, do everything more. Spread myself thin?" he laughs. "Me?" He grabs hold of his massive body. "You have to learn to spread. No boundaries. None."

I ask him about his future. Is there another Bakery in the horizon (aside from The Bowl & Roll and The Cave which he also owns in Chicago)? Is there a Bakery East in the future? A Bakery West perhaps?

"I feel I'm an organic part of Chicago. I don't know what Chicago will be like five years from now, but I am part of the city and the city is part of me. This city put its imprint on me, and I put mine on it."

Any regrets about being a chef?

"My mother would like me to be a priest," he laughs.

Louis is listening to me, he is listening to the man across from him bid good-by, he is telling his personal home economist to check out something on the menu for him, he is watching someone on his kitchen staff assemble a tray of Beef Wellington, and he is being approached by a middle-aged Hungarian woman with a grown son who is saying hello to Louie and pushing her son forward to meet the chef.

"Tell Louis what you want to tell him," says the mother poking the son.

Louis winces a little, looks the young man in the eye, gives him about a tenth of his attention and says, "Well, you speak Hungarian? No? Russian? Chinese? What?"

"English," the young man smiles.

"So, what you want to tell me?"

"Well, Louie, ah, you see Louie, ah, I work for this company called Amway, ah. And I've got a lot of products and things you might want to use in your kitchen. . . . " Louis seems to have turned him off entirely and is saying something to his wife while the young man makes his pitch. But then he cuts right into a plea for Amway and says, "Yes, so what? So what?"

"Well, Louie, Amway, ah, has been in business for a long time. And if you'd like to try one of their products, I'm sure you'd be satisfied. And if not, there's a money back guarantee!"

Louis coughs, sizes the young man up, and says in a quiet rage, "I never in my life buy anything with money-back guarantees! If a company gives you money back, they don't trust what they sell and can't be no goddam good!" Which completely destroys the young man, save for Louis's electric smile, a handshake, and a gesture to talk to someone else on his staff.

Both the young man and the mother exit with smiles and a thousand thank you's, as if they'd just received a papal blessing.

And even before they've turned away, he switches instantly to me, taking up a thread of a conversation begun some 20 minutes ago. "So you see, my main thing today is to get my book over as much as possible. Not for money. I don't have to write books for that. This is a cookbook that was needed. A book without learning all the rules and regulations of cooking. You can open up the book, try one recipe and succeed."

This American fascination with food. Cookbooks, it seems, are the all-American best sellers. People don't want stories or poems or even history books. They are interested only in eating.

"The great fascination with cookbooks is world wide," says Louis. "When Gutenberg invented movable type, we asked, 'Who are we?' Then the next question, 'Where are we?' which gave us geography and history. Then we said, 'How does it look? What is it?' . . . travel books. And then we ask, 'What are we feeling, thinking?' And so comes literature. Now, today, the question is, 'What is it?' What we want to know are the components. What is it made from? The ingredient world.

"First they want to know their destiny, their place, their dreams. Now we want to know, 'What are we dreaming?' To me, today, it is the electronic age. To defy gravity means to make things happen. It is not the problem anymore to make an airplane faster . . . it is how to put on the brakes before it starts.

"Where is the easiest to learn, 'What is in it?' Food! More and more people are realizing food is not nourishment alone but a serious thing. The poor dream about food which is nourishing. The rich dream about food which is not nourishing."

Another interruption from another member of his kitchen staff. He leaves the table for a minute, returns, and takes me on a quick tour of the main kitchen, a banquet room, and then upstairs to his office and whatever else cooks behind closed doors. On the way, I ask him about American cooking. I expect him to take a couple of grand swipes at what we sometimes call "good old American food."

"To me, American cooking is the greatest without any doubt. All sauces in France are based on one basic sauce, Espanol . . . all French desserts . . . chocolate and vanilla . . . all of it products of Pre-Columbian American Indian. All the cooking . . . done on a stove which was invented by an American from Connecticut, Thompson."

We are upstairs now in Louis's crowded office. He has eight secretaries, five for The Bakery alone. Moving into a neat, small kitchen, he introduces me to his private home economist, who tests every recipe before serving it in The Bakery.

We enter still another room, a dining room of sorts, where a woman is busy clipping items about Louis and The Bakery. Then into an ornate sitting room, thick furniture, heavily Hungarian in atmosphere.

There is still another room beyond which turns out to be a library in which an old man seated at a desk pours over some books. (I am reminded of Jack Benny going down to his vault.) This is Louis's personal librarian, overlord of some 5,000 books on food, some so rare that they are handwritten and contain but a single recipe.

Behind the library lies still another room, another office of sorts, with two huge desks face to face. Louis sits behind one and picks up a carving knife. He begins to sharpen it and ponders the question about man and food. How does it all work? Where did it all begin? Is there a philosophy to man the eater?

Louis keeps honing the knife, then slowly begins building a conversation, a lecture, a discourse on man and food in his own style of broken English, precise English, long pauses, dramatic gestures, blank spaces, laughter, tears, and perhaps even prayer.

"What I firmly believe . . . since life left liquid and went on land . . . the human being always tries to defeat gravity. The second of birth gives only one surprise: you are heavy—drop. The first touch of gravity. Every human being dreams to have wings. When you fly in your dreams . . . is normal. Babies are always playing dropping things. Gravity is the only real surprise when you are born.

"If you try to think electronically . . . if you want to put any philosophy into a computer . . . a simple system needs less holes to punch in.

"Every living philosophy means this: to live means to devour and not to be devoured. You have to nourish yourself. You destroy what once was to live. So . . . to live, man needs an offensive system to devour, and a defensive system, not to be devoured.

"Primates? Who eats the primates? Saber-toothed tiger.

"OK, look at the human being . . . no difference between the defensive and offensive system. If you are the hunter and the prey, then you must have all that the hunter has to defend you. The only living being that kills its own kind in a fight is the human being. Two elks fight, the winner never kills the loser.

"OK, so you have the Divine Design. Only one God, not other God. And the God designs people, making something like its own image. Man eats God. Man did eat each other only. Why? This was the only way to get to the top. The only way to have a perfectly balanced defensive, offensive system. If you hunt each other and eat each other, we hunt the hunter . . . we are cannibals.

"The one great occasion when we all meet together, the family, the one time when we must be together is the funeral. We want to prove that we are the hunter."

End of lecture. I am confused, excited, shaken, and again left a bit in awe that all this is coming from a cook rather than a college professor. A cook, nonetheless, with a Ph. D. in psychology from Budapest University.

Louis puts down the knife, checks his watch and says, "I must go. You come back again, yes? We will talk some more."

We move to a back office where he studies his calendar. Every day and night seem full of one obligation or another—talk shows, interviews, dinners. Chicago's own celebrity cook. We select a late-night return engagement, a few weeks later.

35

One of the first things I tell him at our next meeting is to stop writing cookbooks, and begin writing the real book about himself, about all the things he's been telling me. But he only smiles and says, "I am not the writer. You do it."

It is late in the evening. The Bakery is still bustling with tables of hearty eaters plus a full waiting room. Louis whisks me through one dining room, two kitchens, and stations me behind a kind of divider in the banquet room where he wants me to stand still, listen, and wait for him. He must give a short speech. Afterward, we will talk some more.

Louis, it turns out, is wining and dining a long tableful of Sears Roebuck & Co. executives. I peek around the divider and discover that the meal is now over, dishes are being removed, and a waiter is pouring brandy. It is time for an after-dinner speech.

And Louis, of course, is the main attraction. Sears has recently made him a household word by putting him in a short commercial for the Kenmore dishwasher.

Louis stands waiting in the wings, then moves toward the head of the table as the master of ceremonies drones on. "Louis has come a long way from his native Hungary. And now he has finally achieved stardom in our TV commercial for the Kenmore dishwasher. There have been a lot of steps along the way for Louis—a professional soldier, an actor, and even a marriage counselor . . . and now the author of *The Chef's Secret Cook Book*, which is also featured in our commercial . . . and now, Chef Louis!"

A great round of applause. Louis, in spotless chef's's uniform, bows briefly, nods, raises his hand, and stands 10 feet tall . . . Supercook!

"Marriage counselor I tried to be for seven years, but it was premature," he says. "They wouldn't let me demonstrate," which brings down the house. With that for an opener, the Great Comic Chef keeps belting them out, line after line of Hungarian dialect, Hungarian humor, that would put the best of our professional comedians to shame. A natural storyteller, in the great tradition of Old World storytellers.

"My life is a series of happenings," Louis goes on. "Every step I make forward takes me 10 steps backward . . . "

His wife, Sada, comes up behind me and whispers, "He's a fantastic speaker, isn't he? Spontaneous . . . "

"Everyone has a dream to be something else. Every chef has a secret dream. My secret dream is to be a dishwasher." Again he brings down The Bakery. But even this is only a warmup for an anecdote, a tremendous, ribald story spun around one of his experiences as a marriage counselor.

He winds up his little speech with praise and appreciation to Sears for all the company has done for him. "My association with Sears is by all means not new. I do many different things for many larger companies. But none of them are as good to me as Sears. You people make me a very happy and very wealthy man in the Sears family."

36

A standing ovation. Louis acknowledges the applause like a veteran actor and begins handing out personally autographed copies of his book to each executive present. And after this, he calls upon Chicago folksinger Win Stracke to sing.

We meet momentarily in the main kitchen. "Are you hungry?" he asks. He reads my mind.

We are standing before a butcher block where one of his cooks is performing surgery on a hunk of meat. Louis, in a fantastic exhibition of Chef's Power, snaps his fingers, rolls out a litany of Hungarian, and within a few magic seconds, the butcher block is draped with a white tablecloth and set for dinner for two.

"You want some wine?" I give him my best European shrug of "why not," to which someone responds with two bottles of red.

I don't know what to call what we ate. A choice piece of steak, I would guess. With fancy trimmings. With an incredible dessert steeped in chocolate. With an after-dinner suggestion of brandy.

And bread. French style. Which I eat, and which Louis breaks into tiny pieces as we talk on into the night, much the same as he had sharpened a carving knife during our last discussion.

We cover many areas once again, including another rather heavy discussion (lecture) on man, morality, and food. I decide to leave this to Louis and his next book, which I hope someday he will write.

We edge once again into the field of his own success. How does it all happen? Why one man and not another? And what is left for Louis to do, granting that he now has his full measure of recognition?

"Go on!" he says with great exuberance. "Live! The happy man jumps up and opens the door when opportunity knocks; but the unhappy man complains about the noise. You choose from the possibilities coming, the ones that suit you best. You achieve power through performance. Sooner or later people will know that I love to be here, I love to be of service.

"Mark T. McKee, who was the founder of Greyhound and is still a director of Pan Am . . . a self-made man. And he told me when we met, 'You know, Louis, only two proverbs are American in origin. Both have something to do with movement. Number one, life must be a two-way street because one-way streets usually lead to a dead end. Number two, when the going gets too easy, you better check your brakes because most likely you are going downhill.'

"And I always felt the only way I should take is if I can give. And the only way I can give is if I can expect to take something. And I really think that basically The Bakery succeeds as a business because of this. I'm giving as much as I expect to take from you."

And The Bakery, his proper milieu, brings him back home in a kind of reverie of place. It would be hard to imagine Chef Louis in different surroundings. This is his stage, his private fantasy which he has somehow made real and shared with others.

Why "The Bakery"? What's in a name?

"The Bakery"—it has pleasant memories for everybody. We are not able to remember tastes, but for sweet, sour, salty. But we can remember over 300 smells. We have to recognize food by its shape, by its smell. When it's in your mouth, it's too late. We have to recognize it before it gets to our taste buds.

"So, I want to have a name which makes people think through their noses. And nobody has ever been offended by the smell of baked goods."

Louis remains hunched over his bread, continually breaking it down into pieces, until mound after mound rises before him.

"One night in the kitchen we had 20 Nobel Prize winners. These people feel that this is more than a restaurant. Show people, young people . . . everyone who is looking for something like this. Segovia sends a telegram before he comes. He eats nothing but soup and loves to study the tables, the people.

"What I give people here is a sense of honesty. A chair is a chair, a table a table, a floor a floor. Nothing fake. No plastic flowers."

He breaks the last piece of bread, leans back, steadies the chef's hat, rests his eyes, and dreams, undoubtedly, that he has wings.

The Museum of Science and Industry

Tourists around the world are known for their absurd adventures. I once met a man, on his way to Rome for the afternoon, who swore he did Paris in ten minutes. And time, being both scientific and industrial (not to mention philosophical) as we all know, waits for no man or woman.

So you've got this cousin in Iowa, you recall, and he's on his way to maybe Indiana, just passing through, and he has the nerve to actually take you up on one of those open invitations, customarily extended to long-lost relatives who tend to appear out of the woodwork at wakes for other long-lost relatives . . . "Well, Woodrow, next time you're in Chicago, give me a call."

Behold, one hung-over morning, there's old Cousin Woodrow on the phone, between buses, planes, or trains. He's on his way to a convention in Indianapolis, and he figures maybe you can show him the high points of Chicago in an hour ('cause that's all he can spare). Things he's always dreamed about—Buckingham Fountain, the Merchandise Mart, Tribune Tower, State Street, the Board of Trade, The Sears Tower, Old Town, the Field Museum, that Picasso thing, the lakefront, and mostly that Museum of Science and Industry he's heard so much about.

So you dash down to the Loop ("Where's that?" Woodrow asks. "You're in it, man!") pick him up, and do some quick flashes with him down State Street, around the Civic Center, down Michigan Ave., doglegging it over to Old Town, then cutting out, onto and down Lake Shore Drive in a suicide mission of traffic. Destination: Museum of Science & Industry.

If you're like most Chicago guides of out-of-town visitors, you've hardly seen most of these places yourself, and would be hard pressed to describe just what Buckingham Fountain really looks like, or just where and what the Board of Trade is.

So you're tooling somewhere beyond Soldier Field.

"That sure is a pretty lakefront," says Woodrow admiringly.

"Woodrow, that's the soul of Chicago," you throw in mechanically as you pull into the huge museum parking lot.

"I got about fifteen minutes," says Woodrow.

Well, you may not believe this, but Woodrow and I did the museum in fifteen minutes flat, and you can, too.

We hit the INFORMATION desk . . . there's no time for information . . . we move (I move) instinctively to the left, past the check room (no time for that either) and for some strange reason, into the HALL OF ELEMENTS and *déjà vu* . . . I've been here before . . . boring, boring chemical exhibits . . . "Here, Woodrow, check this!"

We do a quick right and fade into FOOD FOR LIFE, for a glimpse of the baby chicks hatching. You push and shove through a bunch of mesmerized kids meditating on the mystery of the egg to get a close-up view. Kids will wait for hours just to see a chick poke through the shell.

"There's a hole," says a kid. "One's coming out!"

"Wish him a happy birthday for us, will you?" I tell him as I collar Woodrow. We do a quick take of a commercial aviation exhibit, check the mock-up of a 1st Class cabin section of a Beoing 747, and sashay right in front of Apollo 8.

(It's the real, true, re-entry burned space capsule that Lovell, Anders, and Borman swung around the moon in. Looking inside, Cousin Woodrow says what probably millions of other museum visitors say: "How did they ever get three guys in there?" Which is no problem at all for technocrats. "The question, Woodrow, is why?")

But then . . . music . . . circus music . . . From Apollo 8 to the circus! Why not? More celestial mechanics, not to mention metaphysics. Beautiful, beautiful . . . THE CIRCUS, presented by Sears, Roebuck and Co. What better place to ease a hang-over than the circus? Especially when you've been on the tight rope yourself the night before.

Check my watch. Three minutes already gone. As we enter the midway ramp of the circus exhibit, miniature circus wagons, tents, animals, clowns demand our attention; we are engulfed in a sound system of the circus parade; it takes the circus to reconfirm the child in all of us.

Woodrow, I discover, has his head stuck in the wall. "Woodrow, what the hell are you doing?" He is getting even closer to the spirit of circus; Woodrow is involving his face in an exhibit where, when you stick your head through this opening, lights go on, and your face is miraculously reflected, colored, marked, transformed into that of a clown! Finally, there's my chance; an empty opening for me too!

By the time I finally pop my head out to take a bead on Woodrow, I catch him running up the ramp and disappearing behind the red door of the Circus Cinema.

I find myself sitting in a small theater beside Woodrow, a handful of people scattered about. There are white, high wire acts and a white bicycle above me sort of floating in pitch black infinity, and also a couple of incomplete white spheres. Lights, action, camera, an oldtime black-and-white movie circus wagons and the Big Top going up over Grant Park, and suddenly . . . the screen explodes . . . no, shoots up! (Actually it's a Cinemascope screen viewed from bottom to top, rather than side to side.) And there's the technicolored ringmaster, about 1,000 feet tall, looming over you, making it all happen, right before your eyes . . . sound, color, splash . . . lions, tigers, clowns and a trapeze act so real you can hear the bar whipping through the air . . . you want to reach out and grab that luscious lady aerialist (all 1,000 feet of daring woman) and save her from disaster . . . then those white balls start spinning with images of clown faces projected on them . . . and it's all too much . . . the greatest sound, light, and picture show circus on earth, here in Chicago. And free!

"Come on, boy, we gotta make tracks. We got maybe only five minutes," Woodrow says.

Bam! We double back through the circus, past the pecking chicks (same kids still watching) and over to the model railroad, because I remember this layout with great excitement as a kid. I always wanted one just like it in my basement.

"Here comes the old Santa Fe, Woodrow, near the canyon, around the mountain, over the bridge, through 3,000 square feet of the Southwest. I still wish I had this damn thing in my basement, even though I don't have a basement anymore . . . Look up! Up on the ceiling! See 'em? Old airplanes . . . beautiful, aren't they? Hanging there the way we used to hang all our model airplanes from the ceiling when we were kids."

We race now past a quick glimpse of "Spirit of America," first jet-powered car to top 500 m.p.h., through Motorama (not a second to apply the brakes) and into Main Street . . . ah, wonderful Main Street, where you (I) stop in your tracks because the nostalgia for the way things were is thick.

You want to race through here, but you can't. The atmosphere just won't let go of you. Main Street was made for strolling. There's old Henrici's. (Oh, for the way it once was on Randolph Street.) And look here, a political address tonight by Hon. J.J. Hone: "Shall Women Vote?"

"Hurry, Woodrow, down this way . . . nope . . . here . . . nope . . . Coal Mine . . . Where the hell's the Coal Mine? Here, up this way. Woodrow, you've got to understand. I'm working off an old map in my head that goes back 10, 15, 20 years or more, and let me tell you, I remember the Coal Mine, but not the way. Here it is. . . . "How long does the descent through hell take?" I ask the caged lady.

"Fifteen minutes."

"You can't do it this time, Woodrow, but believe me, it's all there. The trip down the mine shaft, the machinery, the miners in their hats, the coal, the little electric train run. . . ."

We're (you're) on the balcony now, literally running through the South Gallery, Computer in the Park, Electricity . . . Magnetism, The Magic of Motion. "Fascinating, huh, Woodrow, physics?" My own memory's kind of magnetized now by grade school days. First it was the Coal Mine with Charmaine, then checking those babies all preserved. . . .

41

I don't even have the time to explain to Woodrow that if you grew up in my time in Chicago, the museums provided you with the major riddles of life (in the flesh, so to speak) to speculate upon forever and after. You went downstairs at the Field Museum as a kid for a fearful and face-to-face confrontation with the mummies, and that old bugaboo Death. You dreamed about it for weeks and months afterwards, but to this day, mummies at the Field Museum are a far-out memory.

But the Museum of Science & Industry, ah, that place was just the opposite. And there were more buttons to push, more to involve us physically, so we went there more often. The Museum of Science & Industry was Live and Love and even S-E-X!

When we went down into the Coal Mine with our 7th and 8th grade sweethearts, we weren't particularly interested in the mining industry. We learned all that the first time we went down. We went down to hell for only one reason: to neck with our girlfriends on that three-minute, simulated electric train ride in the coaly darkness! (Ah, Charmaine, where are you today? I can't even remember what you looked like except that every guy in seventh grade had a crush on you, but only I got you down into the Coal Mine.)

And as for Life and S-E-X, there were these (and here they are now, as I pull up fast before them) human embryos. From the first one at four weeks, to the last one at 37 weeks. These spooky, white, wrinkly, weird, and truly most amazing and wonderful "things" that became us! Furthermore, that we (and whoever our Charmaine's were to someday be) had the potential to reproduce!

That's what the Museum of Science & Industry has always meant to me (I suddenly discover). I want to tell Woodrow, who stands transfixed before Tam, the transparent anatomical model, who is illuminating the industry of her various internal parts and telling him all about it in a downright sexy, scientific voice . . . "this is my circulatory system. . . ."

You and I both know what kind of illumination Woodrow is waiting for, but his fifteen minutes are up, and so it's once around and through the pounding, 16-foot open human heart, past the Sickle Cell exhibit, down the red staircase, past the Souvenir Shop, and on his way to Indianapolis. The science and industry of chicken machines, Tam, the Circus, and even the mystery of the Coal Mine will forever illuminate his beating heart. I didn't even have time to tell him all that he missed, today's attractions and all the coming attractions, tomorrow, next week, next month, next year, and ever after.

Sydney J. Harris: Strictly Personal

"Every community needs a newspaper that is better than it deserves; if the paper simply reflects the community, it is not doing a good enough job."

"The most truly lonesome people are those who have not been able to make themselves necessary to somebody."

"The creative person knows every man for his brother, in some way. He recognizes that he himself is potentially a hero and a villian and a dupe; and he says, along with Terrence: 'I am a human being, and therefore nothing human is alien to me.' "

—Sydney J. Harris

HARRIS

The editor of the Door County *Advocate*, Chan Harris, once referred to me in an editorial as "Door County's No. 1 writer." Though I appreciated the compliment, I couldn't honestly accept it. Door County's number one writer was a man of national and international acclaim, Sydney J. Harris, who lived in Fish Creek a good part of the year, wrote out of Chicago, was published in the Chicago *Sun-Times* and hundreds of newspapers throughout the country. His last book, *Pieces of Eight* (Houghton Miflin, $12.95), was a bestseller in Chicago.

What was so important about Sydney J. Harris? Everything—to me. He was the last of the great traditional essayists in America. He was our Emerson, our Bacon, our Montaigne. No one else does what he did in a few short paragraphs. No other columnist wrote with such conciseness, clarity, and common sense. Andy Rooney may be the rage these days, but Harris could make him eat his smile in 400 words or less any day. Harris will continue to be read years from now, while Rooney will go the way of all American fads, from hula hoops, to pet rocks, to Arthur Godfrey.

My first introduction to Harris came in the 1950s when I was a student in high school. One evening at the supper table my father handed me the editorial section of the Chicago *Daily News* and said, "Read Sydney J. Harris. He makes a lot of sense." That was the extent of my literary influences from the kitchen table of a family that never read books, but did read newspapers. And I've been forever grateful to my father for that bit of guidance. In fact, I think I began to truly read newspapers at that moment, never realizing that one day I would write for all the Chicago newspapers, be published for the first time in Harris' own Chicago *Daily News*, and eventually even meet Harris himself in Door County outside of Bunda's Department Store in Sister Bay one morning in the 1960s.

To go back to that moment of reading Sydney J. Harris for the first time. I did not drop everything and decide immediately to become a newspaperman. I never wanted to become a newspaperman, though I did flirt with the idea later and actually put in the customary stint of many would-be newspaper writers in Chicago, working for the City News Bureau, probably the best education any young writer could have. I may have had a slight glimmer of wanting to write by the time I was fifteen, but even that seems doubtful, since I hated high school with a passion (especially the first two years) and periodically wanted to quit, find a factory job, and escape the boredom. By my junior and senior years I had straightened things out and begun to grow up. Harris, among others, including a few exceptional teachers, was one of the influences.

A dark, postage stamp size drawing of Harris accompanied those first "Strictly Personal" columns I read. There was something deep, meditative, and eye-catching about that drawing of Harris as he stared into the distance (crewcut, shirt and tie), pondering the old imponderables of truth, beauty, justice, knowledge, love, and freedom. And though at first he was just a newspaper columnist to me, and though I was really first learning who and what and how to read, I think Harris' taut little essays (I didn't even know they were essays then, let alone 'taut') filled me with a kind of heady exhileration, a sense of rebelliousness, if you will.

If there was one thing I was (or thought I was) in high school and college, it was a rebel. (And if there was another thing I was later to realize about a writer's life, it is just about all rebelliousness, or the writer is not worth a damn). I nurtured my outsider-ness every way I could. The Beatniks were beginning to stir. I discovered that bohemians and writers and artists and beats and rebels were all one, and that's what I was or wanted to be.

As for Harris? He was just there (he always is) at the right time. I have before me a very fragile, yellowed column pulled from my files, a column which must have spoken to me then: "Are the Beatniks Meaningless Rebels?" In it he says, among other things, "Of course, many of the Beatniks are fakers and dead-beats. But, then, so are many persons in other strata of life. I know a considerable number of young men in business who wear clean shirts daily, have impeccable family connections, and titles on their office doors—and they, too, are simply paid loafers who happen to have jobs because of affluence or influence."

44

I loved that, knew it to be true, and probably jumped out of my chair over the way he ended the essay: "A civilization must tolerate, must give room and air and liberty, to its cultural dissidents as well as its political dissidents. One of the marks of social health is its permissiveness to be different, for the best as well as the worst grows out of eccentricity. The beatniks may be dirty, but the ultimate influence can be a cleansing one."

Much of the value of Harris as a writer can be found in that passage. It's as true today as it was then, whether or not the Beatniks evolved into the hippies, the hippies into anti-war demonstrators, environmentalists, even the present day nuclear freeze people.

So it was merely a pose, perhaps, that I first picked up from Harris, a way I wanted to be, an attitude. A moral and creative perspective (something writers and teachers so seldom suggest today). And while simple posturing may lack depth, it can lead to questioning everything (which is what education is really all about) and eventually action (those things an individual must do for the good of himself and others.)

Writers, especially young ones, are always in search of role models, and though I had no idea of what Harris really looked like, how he dressed, or wrote, or acted, I could identify with the man's ideas, especially those which championed the individual over the conforming masses. (Later in college I was to recognize these ideas in Emerson and Thoreau. And still later I was to realize, through Harris' own admission, that none of his thinking was original, that all writing is a form of plagarism.)

All this was ripe stuff for a young student, a young writer (who couldn't even call himself a writer), pretty much self-educated in an ethnic neighborhood where the word "intellectual" had no meaning, let alone a translation from the Czech or Serbo-Croat.

I studied to become a teacher before I became a writer, though the writer within me remained restless, expressed itself in teaching techniques, continued scratching to be let out. Twice I came close to becoming a full-time newspaperman, but each time I pulled back for fear I'd never be able to write what I truly wanted to write, even though I was uncertain what that really was or what form it would take.

I kept Harris alive in my years as a high school teacher, often reading his work to students, giving assignments based on Harris's ideas, attempting to make Harris a regular reading habit. (Later on, when I became a writer, and still later when I attempted to teach writing, I always used Harris's essays as models for nonfiction writing.) Former high school students who became teachers still tell me they read and teach Harris to their students.

My first glimpse of the man came unexpectedly. During one of my flirtations with newspaper work, I went to the old Chicago *Daily News* building seeking a job as copy boy. Somehow I got into the city room. Suddenly the face of Sydney J. Harris became real: there he was in red suspenders, standing at his desk. (Why the red suspenders have stayed with me through all these years, I'll never know.) I remember telling my father, "I saw Sydney J. Harris today." I'm not sure he believed me.

I caught a second glimpse of Harris when, years later, he actually visited my neighborhood, Cicero, Illinois, and spoke to a group of teachers at the Warren Park Community Center—my hangout as a kid! I was in the audience (a college student studying to become a teacher), and I remember delighting in his wit as time and time again he attacked colleges of education, and teachers in general— how refreshing (after courses in education and professors with Ph.D.s in education) to finally hear a man speak his own mind. Yet here I was studying to become part of the very institution he was attacking. But, I decided, I would sustain the rebelliousness he seemed to favor, until the time came to undermine false educators and the whole damned bureaucracy.

I don't recall the particulars of his speech that evening, but he could have said something similar to one of his essay on education: "Children, for instance, do not 'naturally' rebel against mathematics; they rebel against the way it has been taught in the past. Much as a teacher may wince at the thought, he is also an entertainer—for unless he can hold his audience, he cannot really instruct or edify them. . . .

"Except for the professional school, teachers should be chosen more for their personal attributes than for their scholarship: For if they cannot make their field seem exciting and challenging to young minds, then they are in the wrong profession, and should devote themselves to research or some other solitary occupation."

As the years passed, I became a teacher, I left teaching, I became a writer, I began publishing short stories, newspaper articles, book reviews, poetry, and books . . . and always there was some image of Harris in the background.

I had further glimpses of him from time to time in downtown Chicago, on the streets, in bookshops, once in an office supply store. I even nodded to him upon occasion, and sometimes he nodded back. I was aware that he was aware that some people recognized him, and something about him said, "Please don't bother me or bore me." I respected that.

Other newspapermen and writers in Chicago, I learned, quietly respected Harris, although nobody really knew him. From all indications he was a loner. He didn't hang out in the bars where most newspapermen hung out. One editor recalled attending a dinner at which Harris was present, how he sat right across from him, but they never spoke. "He's kind of aloof," the editor told me. "I didn't have anything to say to him."

Those stories of Harris's cool arrogance stayed with me. Whenever I unexpectedly discoved myself in his presence, I always respected his privacy. Much of my information on this matter, granted,was based upon Harris hearsay—how one teacher, during a convention, was so insulted by his attack upon teachers that she walked out. How, according to another inside source in Door County,

Mr. Harris, who loves to play bridge, is not necessarily the world's number one bridge player. That sort of thing. (Rumor also had it that one could feel damned intimidated just by the look in Sydney J. Harris's eye.)

It was in Door County, in the mid-1960's, outside of Bunda's Department Store in Sister Bay one summer morning. that I finally got up the courage to approach the man. Knowing how Harris revered words and language, I found myself nervous in his presence, mumbling some stupidities about the weather, never quite expressing my deep admiration of his work or his influence upon me. I couldn't bear to tell him I was a teacher and a writer, for fear he might take me to be the very kind of fumbling teacher or writer he denounced in his columns and speeches. He asked what I did, and I told him I freelanced for the Chicago papers, taught, and spent my summers in Door County. He asked if I could write from Door, and I said yes, I could, and he said he couldn't, and that was it. We shook hands, parted, and I had finally met Sydney J. Harris. What a great guy! I told everyone. When friends visited me, my tour of the county always included a drive past Sydney J. Harris's place in Fish Creek. "That's where Sydney J. Harris lives," I'd tell them, as if he and I were the best of friends.

After that, I often saw him each summer in Door. Sometimes he'd be driving down Highway 42 in a nifty little sports car, sometimes sauntering into Wilson's for an ice cream cone, sometimes eating at Al's, often in the company of rather distinguished looking people. Famous European philosophers, artists and musicians, I surmised. Some of them probably were. He, of course, never recognized me after our first meeting, and I could hardly expect him to. He was in a league by himself. And what the hell, really, did the two of us have in common?

His columns, through all these years, began to fill another need: the need to know what Harris felt about writers and writing. And so any column of his even remotely concerned with writing became gospel, a favorite Harris column of mine to clip and keep . . . a new book to buy when they were eventually gathered between covers. From them I gleaned much sage advice:

"Chesterton needed a grammar book no more than Da Vinci needed a numbered paint set. Men of overwhelming talent make their own rules, guided by some pulse of the heart that beats truer than all the formal textbooks."

"A college senior of my acquaintance, who is majoring in what his school hopefully calls 'Creative Writing,' asked me at dinner last night what I think is the most important single quality that a writer must have . . . the word I think that best describes it is 'empathy' . . . the ability to get inside another person and see the world through his eyes."

"Temperament, not talent, determines how a man works. His technique is derived from his unconscious structure, not from any conscious formula . . . creation comes out of the dark pit of the soul which no textbook can illuminate."

47

All this makes as much sense to me now as a writer as it did then. In all the book reviewing I've done in the past fifteen years, I have never been fortunate enough to be asked to review a new Sydney J. Harris book, and I have never been able to understand why, since I feel I'm such an authority on the man's work. I wanted, sorely, to review Harris' latest book, *Pieces of Eight*, for Chicago, Milwaukee, California, New York, anywhere.

It's another collection of his brilliant essays that keep working on your head and heart, teasing your sensibilities. Whatever the man writes about, he's worth reading. And rereading. Any of Harris' books can last a lifetime. *Pieces of Eight* is no exception. He should be read at random, five minutes a day, by everyone—students and teachers especially. He can raise the quality in a person's life.

Harris has remained constant in my life, since my father first passed him on to me. Oh, the drawing of him changed with the times. He let his crewcut grow out. (So did I.) In the 1960s the drawing was replaced with a photograph, and in the age of "Hair," Harris let his own hang out and even sported a mustache and long sideburns.

Occasionally I'm asked how well I know Sydney J. Harris, how often we might socialize. "I know him a little better than before," I say. And no, we don't get together at all, though once or twice he asked me to stop by. But that was just being polite, I figured.

I still can't imagine what we might say to each other after the first five minutes. Two writers alone are not often the best companions. Invite both to the same social gathering and you will find them in opposite corners of the room, each nursing his own solitariness with the most potent drink on hand. (If only punch is served, both have probably gone home.)

Most writers get along best imagining others they like or dislike in the trade, listening to gossip concerning the other's lifestyle, occasionally exchanging notes, and sometimes reading (admiring or disliking) what the other has written, but feeling a little self-conscious about telling him so.

To be accepted by the general reading audience is one thing for a writer. But to be accepted by one's peers is another dimension entirely.

In the summer of 1978, with the publication of my first book of stories, *The Hour of the Sunshine Now*, Marge and Hal Grutzmacher of Passtimes Books held a small autograph party for me from 1 to 3 p.m. At ten minutes before the hour, when things had quieted down and most of the people had left, Sydney J. Harris walked in. It was like Hemingway standing at your front door. I couldn't have been more excited or surprised. We shook hands. He introduced me to his daughter. Then handed me a copy of my book to sign. "We writers must stick together," he said.

I don't remember much after that, but I'm sure I tried to explain much of what I'm trying to deal with here on paper: how he played a big part in my growing up as a human being, and as a writer.

"You'll never guess who showed up at the autograph session!" I told my wife later that afternoon. (She didn't.)

"You'll never guess who showed up with a book to sign!" I told my father weeks later in Chicago, sitting around the same kitchen table where he once introduced me to the man's writing. (He didn't.)

I don't know whether there were any witnesses or not. But I know I signed a copy of my stories to Sydney J. Harris and felt a confirmation of sorts in the brotherhood of writing.

When my first book about the county, *Door Way*, was nearing publication, my publisher sent Harris a copy of the galleys in the hopes that he might make a comment which would help spur interest in the book. I doubted Harris would have the time or inclination to do such a thing. Part of me longed for just such endorsement, while part of me feared the intrusion on his privacy and the possible silent reaction or curt remarks.

Weeks later the publisher called. "I got it," he said.

"What?"

"A statement from Harris." He proceeded to read a letter from Sydney J. Harris as beautifully crafted and expressive as one of his perfect "Strictly Personal" essays. It was printed on the front cover flap to *Door Way*, where I was sure my father would see it.

Sydney J. Harris died in December of 1986.

I miss him in the newspapers.

I miss him on the streets of Chicago.

I open the top drawer of a file cabinet beside my desk and begin rummaging through some old manila file folders on writers and writing, sources of inspiration for the fledgling author. Things Hemingway, Sherwood Anderson, Sandburg, Steinbeck, Wolfe, Algren, Petrakis, did or said. I have not looked in any of these for years. I pull the file with "Sydney J. Harris" pencilled on the tab.

Inside are nearly a hundred clips of his "Strictly Personal" columns, yellowed with age, many from the 50s and 60s and the old Chicago *Daily News*. Images of him accompanying each essay (drawings and photos) reflect time past as well: from the young man in crewcut to the old sage in beard.

I push the typewriter aside and begin reading each essay.

Everything he said remains true, from "Man: Creature of Destruction" to "The Steinbecks Are Disappearing." The lessons of his art are clear and self-sustaining. I feel vindicated for my less-than-certain life. Renewed.

I am reminded of my own Chicago youth. The dream of becoming a writer. The excitement of reading Harris for confirmation of the writer's art and life in those early days. There was always so much uncertainty.

I smile at the discolored, time-ravished, newspaper image of the man in the crewcut which I hold in my hand. "We writers must stick together," I say.

To Stop & Shop

Hungry in the heart of Chicago. Me, a man with a memory of neighborhood markets gnawing inside—the texture of fresh bread, the scent of sausage in old butcher shops, ah . . . the lure and the lore of it all.

Dogging through downtown, gripped by food shopper's mania. Where, how to satisfy a lust for liverwurst in the Loop? Not some plastic liverwurst, but the best: Braunschweiger, fashioned by the sausage house of Usinger's of Milwaukee—sausage to pique the tired taste buds of any packaged-food aficionado.

A sharp turn on the corner of State, and west down Washington . . . a shopper led almost literally by my nose. There, at 16 West Washington is the sign: STOP & SHOP. Yes, of course. A place to come home to, of sorts. A real find. A rediscovery. A rememberance of things past and perfect.

Through the revolving doors . . . an interior decor reminiscent of Chicago in its heyday. From floor to walls to ceiling—a lingering air of tradition. Picture Berghoff's as a supermarket, or the late great Henrici's on Randolph.

Ladies and gentlemen, food-conscious consumers, I'm talking about class, maybe the last vestige of class, given the location: a neighborhood store serving one of the densest neighborhoods in the country—downtown Chicago.

The produce, the bakery, the food counters beckon . . . but first, a trip upstairs to see who and what is behind this preserved shopping sanity. (Ah, what is that? Do I catch a whiff of cheese? A breath of Brie? A smack of smoked cheddar? A gust of Gruyere?) I turn my back on it and head for the office of John W. Loeb, since 1973 the chairman of the board and chief executive.

He sits in a comfortable room three floors up and explains his 20-year-plus association with the business, and how Stop & Shop is part of Hillman's Inc., but a different animal entirely.

"Stop & Shop was founded in 1872 by Tebbetts and Garland on 18th and Wabash in a 20-foot store," explains Loeb. "In 1890, they moved to 16th and Calumet, where they handled all the trade from the fashionable Prairie Avenue socialites . . . the Pullmans, the Fields. We still use the Tegar lable [in honor of the founders].

51

"At the turn of the century the store moved to 18 North Michigan, and around 1916 or 1917 it was bought by Aaron Younker, who changed the name [from Tebbetts and Garland] to Stop & Shop. In 1925 Herbert Loeb, Henry Stern, and Max Adler bought Stop & Shop from Younker and opened a temporary location on Wabash Avenue between Washington and Madison, until this building was completed. It opened in October, 1928. We celebrated our 50th anniversary this fall. Today, the Loeb and Stern families are principal stockholders."

The traditional symbol of Stop & Shop is a silhouetted horse and carriage (circa 1890) with a long-gowned, high-hatted, bustled woman (package in hand), obviously pleased that she has stopped and shopped where it mattered.

John Loeb explains: "For many years Stop & Shop was an upgraded special-ty food store serving the carriage trade of Chicago. We still offer many services uncommon to most supermarkets: telephone orders, deliveries in metropolitan Chicago, corporate charge accounts, credit cards, a complete-service meat depart-ment, almost unheard of today. While Hillman's is a conventional supermarket, Stop & Shop is a food store that offers the finest quality available in every area.

"Stop & Shop is an operating division of Hillman's Inc. Gaper's, the third division, is the largest social-catering service in the Midwest and perhaps in the country today. Gaper's is also the manufacturing division of many of Stop & Shop's specialty foods—salads, ice cream, bakery products."

Not having seen a horse and carriage on Chicago's streets in some time (not to mention a woman with a bustle), one wonders just whom this fine old store appeals to in these station-wagon days of suburban shopping plazas.

"We've been trying to broaden our market," claims the chairman and chief, "from the carriage-trade appeal, which we continue to encourage, to the primarily younger people who enjoy the fine food. Young professionals, lawyers, many of the City Hall people. At the same time, we have brought Stop & Shop into the North Side neighborhoods with our junior stores [260 East Chestnut Street and 1313 North Ritchie Court], which carry a full line. Essentially, they have everything the big store has with the exception of candy. Also, they do not have a full line of specialty groceries. We don't try to overreach ourselves. We don't think people are going to come downtown from Lake Forest just for Stop & Shop. Our main market: people working in the Loop and the Near North."

So what makes a specialty food store special? What has Stop & Shop got over your average brightly lighted supermarket with wide aisles, rattling shop-ping carts, food boxed or encased in plastic, and computerized cash registers that hum into the night? (Not to mention the absence of blood and butchers.)

John Loeb will tell you there is a difference: "Because of our size, we're able to obtain the relatively small quantities of high-quality perishables that the big-ger chains can't get because there isn't enough to go around. For instance, for Christmas last year we had the only 100 cases of the largest Delicious apples that were grown. There were literally only 100 cases in the U.S., and we had them all!

"Our beef . . . well, we offer more prime beef in the selection of the original level of prime-quality beef, which has become more difficult to get. Every piece of meat has been stamped by our own buyer. This allows us to get the quality level where we want it. The large chains need such tremendous quantities that they're not available. It's all they can do to get twenty loads of USDA choice, let alone select this new wider grade, or the top half of prime.

"We're also much bigger in candy than a supermarket chain. Our candy competes with Marshall Field's, as opposed to a supermarket's. Our delicatessen department? Nobody can touch us in those items that our catering business produces for us. We think we have the city's finest luncheon-meat department. And the biggest variety of top quality cheese to be found anywhere. We serve our neighborhood—which in this area is the Loop. Most of our domestic sausage is Usinger. I'm pretty sure we're their oldest customer in existence today. They are the Cadillac of the sausage business. We buy every product they produce.

"The biggest part of our cheese is the imported cheese. We also carry domestic. We have a sandwich bar down there . . . Italian beef has been very popular. We have ice cream cones. Our bakery department is the finest in the city, we think, all the products baked either by a specially selected supplier or by Gaper's.

"Only the finest-quality fish. Only fresh, when it's available. We always tell customers when it has been previously frozen. We fly in a lot of products, brook trout, a lot of fish, when available, from the East Coast. We fly in stone crabs from Forida, which is becoming a very important area for fish procurement. We're one of the very few retailers of beluga caviar. Our veal, by the way, only Provimi . . . prime milk-fed veal that is produced in very limited quantities."

Grocery items? I ask offhandedly. "What you can't find anywhere else, you can find here," smiles John Loeb. "Imported foods . . . crackers and biscuits from Holland, Ireland, England. French foods . . . truffles. A variety of imported and domestic bottled waters. Imported mustard from Europe. Spices, coffee, exotic foods of all sorts, an extensive gift department, plus wine and liquor. . . ."

Customers? Some particulars, some names. . . .

"Probably the 500 best-known industrialists and professional people use Stop & Shop," he says without flinching. "Our best-known customer at the moment: Heather Bilandic. Marshall Korshak is here buying his lunch once a week. Mrs. Daley shopped here. . . . "

A tall, dapper, distinguished-looking gentleman enters the office and shakes hands, a carriage-trade person of the old days. Class. He's a walking history of Stop & Shop, Gardner H. Stern, Sr., chairman of the finance committee. He measures his words carefully, graciously. "Mayor Daley," he edges into the conversation, "helped celebrate our 100th anniversary. He cut the ribbon." Any memorable conversation, corned beef and cabbage or something? "No," says Gardner. "All he and I ever talked about were the White Sox."

I prepare to investigate the premises, thanking Loeb and Stern for the flavorful history. I want to be surrounded by the main floor's delectables. In seconds, the elevator lands me in the midst of plenty.

In preparation, I step outside for a moment of Chicago's freshly polluted air, clear my head with heavy breathing, and meditate on emptiness—the signal my stomach is sending me. Then, in the style of an old carriage-trade shopper (without authentic carriage or cash), I whirl through the revolving door to feast my senses.

Perishables: grapefruits the size of watermelons . . . mangoes, papayas, eggplant, artichokes, rhubarb, turnips, anise, leeks, dry shallots, okra, dill . . . pecans, walnuts . . . a fantasy of fruit, a small flourish of fresh flowers at $2.99 a bunch, a mixture of color and scent that one associates with the bright craziness of European markets.

Candy! Sweets to gladden the bitter heart of any Chicagoan. Perugina Florentine, Italian nougat, Blum's assorted creams, Russian mints, Bavarian mints, petit fours, Bogdon's Reception Sticks, Astor liqueur. . . .

A sophisticated woman with an English accent stands before the candy-counter clerk and asks, "May I take it off the shelf, do you think?" (Not a touch of bargain-basement shopper in her.)

Candy Counter, Part II—Specialties. Dried apricots, dried pears, dried peaches, red and natural pineapple, lemon, orange, and citron halves, dehydrated pineapple. . . .

The deli counter now, a deli divine of endless shiny stainless-steel-and-glass cases. Beginning with pans filled with ambrosia salad, potato salads, bean salads, egg salad. Or how about fried smelt, Chinese egg rolls, beef Knishes, potato pancakes, Irish meat pies, stuffed peppers and cabbage . . . a veritable U.N. of deli delectables. Greek olives, Sicilian olives, halavah, barbecued ribs and chicken, smoked chub, pepper sable, smoked eel and sturgeon and trout, regular lox, Nova Scotia lox, herring. (God help the hungry man at this counter.)

You say you haven't enjoyed real sausage heartburn in years? How about no-garlic corned beef or garlic corned beef? Domestic boiled ham, imported ham, roast beef, German hard salami, sulze, tongue, mortadella, teawurst, Bohemian-style prasky, and ahhhh . . . there it is: Usinger's Milwaukee liver sausage, Braunschweiger, at $2.29 a pound. Guaranteed to melt in the mouth like whipped cream and go down with a zing.

Another lady with a foreign accent, this time heavily Germanic, blond, dressed to the teeth (big sunglasses, gold earrings, mink jacket, bright silk scarf) and generating a wispy cloud of the right perfume, says to the man behind the case, "Give me from that Usinger a quarter pound." And he moves quickly.

Sausage begins to give way to cheese—but not just yet. On top of the case: trays and row after row of salami. Plus ranks of the Usinger sausage army: bratwurst, knackwurst, bockwurst—the spicy lilt of it all levitating any true sausage shopper at least a link off the floor.

Now let's hear it for cheese. Cases of it. Danish Port du Salut, Holland Edam, Norwegian Jarlsberg, English Caerphilly, Danish Tilsit, French Doux de Montagne, French Mordier.

The Old Chicago Style Deli marks the end of the deli line. Hot and cold sandwiches to go: thuringer, roast beef, veal cutlet, Italian beef and sausage, turkey. A sign directly behind me raises my chili consciousness to new levels of sophistication: HADLER'S HEART WARMING GOURMET CHILI, $1.69.

Bakery is next and an instinctive pull to the center counter, the very heart of the store. A mixed metaphor of sense impressions—from sausage to a delivery cart full of fresh bread, sweet- and warm-smelling rolls, pies, and coffee cakes. French crumb and apple loaves. Danishes, almond crescents, and schnecken. Chocolate flake cake, banana layer, torte, cheesecake, lemon fluff. Plus a panorama of whipped cream and custard items, all with high drifts of topping.

Senses reeling, stomach churning, I surface for air, seeking the relief of human contact. I speak for a moment to Jerry Riordan, store manager, young, yet a 20-year Stop & Shop veteran. "I started with the company as a high school student," he explains. "Let me know if I can help you." He's whisked away by a lady shopper with a problem and passion concerning yogurt, and I am left stranded between shelves of coffee, adjusting my senses once again to the nostalgic aroma. From grind-your-own coffee to cans of Colombian, Salvador La Paz, Mexican Coatepec, Guatemalan Antigua, Brazilian Santos, and more, much more, including a three-pound can of Mocha-Java-blend roasted whole-bean coffee for $14.19.

Teas—English, Irish, Chinese . . . from Lady Londonderry to Irish blend to Chinese green tea. Or See-Touch-Nee and a full line of Celestial Seasoning from Morning Thunder to Pelican Punch.

Onward to the meat department with real, live butchers in residence. There they are, dressed in white aprons and blood just like the good old days. Filet Mignon at $6.49 a pound, super-lean gound beef at $2.29. Oxtails, pork loin, baby rack ribs, and butterfly pork chops . . . all there, behind the glass and ready to be closely inspected, even touched, should the shopper so desire.

What's that sound? Just a butcher going at a hunk of meat with a hand saw! Then the saw's singing is traded for the clunk of a cleaver, and the splat of the flattened flesh.

"Which one of you can help me?" asks a woman customer.

"Right here. Just look into my blue eyes," says the butcher. (Ah, butchers, characters all. An almost-forgotten bunch of neighborhood folk heroes.)

Then fresh fish. Turbot filets, halibut steaks, smoked cod, king-crab legs, blue-point oysters, cherrystone clams, whitefish, walleyed pike . . . even fresh-water catfish.

The variety, the specialness of everything boggles the mind. I could fill three old-fashioned horse-drawn carriages with meat, bakery goods, and sausage alone. And yet there are still canned goods, preserves, and specialties galore.

Delicacies like a chestnut spread from France, preserved kumquats, and a six-ounce can of round morels (wild mushrooms in natural juice), imported from Switzerland, for $7.09.

Jerry Riordan, the manager, suddenly appears near a display of McCann's quick-cooking Irish oatmeal just in time to unboggle my mind and settle my stomach with a few final facts to send me on my way, empty but complete, all my senses reawakened to the old, true possibilities of food.

Only he comes to comfort me with the exotic news about chocolate-covered grasshoppers. "They're just not sending them anymore," he says quite seriously. "Most of this stuff is on the endangered species list . . . fried grasshoppers, yeah." He pulls out a sample from the shelf—$2.49 for 1.5 ounces.

"Certainly ants aren't on the endangered list. But there are several organizations against the guys who pack hippo meat, and they're just laying off the stuff. We used to have a section called Spooky Foods. We used to have a big counter with reindeer meat, rattlesnake, elephant. . . . We had colored quail eggs too, a pretty green and blue. Now we just have white. We also had caterpillars."

Jerry's been on this floor too long, my stomach tells me. I ditch him and his talk about caterpillars, take a quick turn down another aisle (looking for a way out) only to come face to face with a jar of quail eggs (white), imported from Canada, six ounces for $3.59. Next to it, reindeer meatballs—from Norway.

But the store manager has trapped me again, is leading me back to the meat department to confront a butcher named Don. "Don, where's that special-order price list on hippo meat and stuff?" asks Jerry. Both these guys are dead serious. "Game to Order" begins the list: "grouse, wild turkey, peacock," explains the butcher. "On hand every day is squab, partridge, pheasant, mallard duck. . . . "

My eyes, though, are riveted to the list: hippopotamus (rib), lion (legs), zebra (top butts), rattlesnake (whole, skinned). . . . I try to envision what a plate of zebra might look like. My appetite has been appeased.

I drift past the deli on my way out, but my stomach is psychologically unprepared for revival. Even a sandwich of Italian beef to go fails to register. And my lust for liverwurst has subsided.

I linger momentarily over Romanoff caviar but with beluga (large eggs) going for $250 a 14-ounce tin, I realize at last that I am not cut out for shopping of such depth and magnitude.

Then I spot a jar of large dill pickles on my way out, and my mouth suddenly salivates. I opt for a pickle to go for 55 cents. One juicy, crunchy bite triggers memories of neighborhood butcher shops and all the dill ever hung and left to dry in my grandmother's basement.

To stop and shop and rediscover that alone—the wonder of traditional food—is enough, even as the juice of the dill pickle runs down my wrist, eliminating me, do doubt, from the class of carriage-trade folk. Though a taste for real food, alas, is universal.

Europe In Chicago

Within the Chicago setting, cold and inhuman as it rides off to work each day and burning in nervous neon through the night, there are patches of calm where one can loll as if in a foreign country.

Europe humanizes a person. It puts one in close touch with beauty, tradition, nature, and other people. It makes one better than before and more concerned with the way things are.

A sidewalk cafe is the sort of place where one gets this feeling.

My sidewalk cafe in Chicago is not outside, but it is close enough for me to feel the excitement of people passing.

Pixley & Ehlers, across from the Chicago Public Library, is my cafe. There I take a table by the front window early in the morning, and watch the street outside grow rich with color, motion, and people. Green and yellow buses stop [marked "Union Station via Ohio"]. A string of cabs await each new wave of passengers from the Illinois Central terminal. A newsstand blossoms with magazines.

And the people. The business man in starched frenzy, the student in nonchalance, the beggar with time enough to spare, rummaging waste-baskets for the brown paper bags. The women, perhaps the best reason for cafe sitting in Paris, are worth watching here, too. They dress either beautifully or comically, and either style deserves attention.

Pixley's is not quite Paris, but it is sufficient. No one bothers me. I make my own time—it is part of the art of cafe sitting. On a good morning, when the weather and time of year are right, the early sun cuts through the window and angles on my table in an orange warmth that can be compared only to Paris.

Then, too, whatever the time of year, if I sit in the right position by the window, I can see buckets of fresh flowers on Garland court. Roses, carnations, mums. That's Paris. That's Chicago.

The Chicago river is our Seine. It lacks the fishermen, the artists, the bookstalls, the lovers of Paris, and it has no Notre Dame. But there is an American beauty to the river that cannot be denied. Whether I hang over the Michigan

Avenue bridge on the east or west side, there always are the floating, fragmentary images of skyscrapers by daylight, and the underwater fireworks of shattered light by night.

The Halles, the market of Paris, famous for its onion soup, has its counterpart at Chicago's Fulton and Randolph Streets—one of the busiest and most exciting places in the city.

Our market has just as much color, confusion, beauty as the Halles. The knots of angry trucks on Fulton defy any pedestrian. Sides of beef hang in ranks waiting to be packaged for human consumption. Poultry is in crates, fish is packed in ice. There are smells of animal and earth.

Randolph market with its boxes, baskets, bags of produce: lettuce, cabbage, apples, potatoes, peppers, lemons, egg plant. Bananas that hang like tropical sculpture.

The Halles/Fulton market. All the backward motion of trucks, and the electric language of their capped drivers. Restaurants and saloons that deny the sun and stand defiantly on the corner and shout, "Just try me, buddy." The Louvre of the common man who appreciates art with his stomach.

Europe in Chicago? Yes, and so much of it still to be found in our ethnic neighborhoods which slowly are losing ground. Here, very readily, Chicagoans can experience a taste of Italy, Bohemia, France, Poland, Russia, Sweden, Yugoslavia . . .

Germany is no exception. My Germany can be found in the old neighborhood on the North Side of Chicago.

Qualities of the German village are fixed firmly in the area surrounding St. Alphonsus church [1429 Wellington Ave.]. This is a neighborhood of kind people, shingled homes, wooden steps, the red dump truck of the Andrew Kunz Coal company and children sometimes dressed in lederhosen.

At night the church has an overpowering aura of a cathedral. The white face, high in the steeple, is a harvest moon clock to preserve the time of night. Standing beneath, I am again in Cologne at 2 in the morning.

The Mediterranean in the Windy City? Yes, partly in our Greek neighborhood. Their groceries and restaurants are rich in an ancient heritage.

The Coffeehouse Panhellenic stands on Halsted street and admits only Greek hearts. I look through the windows at night, I study the faces in smoke; the faces of old men who sit alone staring into a time and place of a taverna by the sea.

I stare too, and I am with the Greeks. The owner of a Greek restaurant invites me into his kitchen. He swirls the contents of his uncovered pots with the air of a man proud of his art. He encourages me to taste the octopus and lemon soup. I sit outside in the white-white sun, by the blue-blue water, drink violent red wine, and partake in the most satisfying meal of my life. This is the way gods must dine.

Parks are sacred to Europeans. They understand them. They delight in the green quiet that only a park provides for city men.

Chicago parks are very European in layout and atmosphere. Columbus park, for one, could be St. James' in London—if the day has the right touch of mist, if the ducks are out, and if the flowers are in bloom.

Lincoln park is the most cosmopolitan park in the city. Foreigners are drawn to this place. At times, one can hear four or five different languages in the air. What a delicious sound—a language I cannot understand. Something about this park draws the newcomers.

It must be the ancient stone buildings, the benches and fences of green; trees just tall enough not to offend the sky, old fashioned lamp posts, and bridges that are fun to cross because they are bridges. And the pigeons that shower down at the least suggestion of food. And, of course, in the sun of Sunday, a balloon man takes flight and rainbows the wind for children.

The more I look, the more I see bits of Europe in Chicago. There is so much here that can set off the heart of the traveler, the poet, the lover, the man alive.

In my own Bohemian neighborhood, the Card Players—a scene out of Cezanne. Only here at night, framed in a white basement window and lace curtain, two gray-haired men, one in shirtsleeves, the other in underclothing and suspenders, rest their pinochle hands on worn oilcloth. Two glasses are half filled with amber. A brown quart bottle stands within easy reach. I have witnessed this scene before throughout central Europe—the elderly and their game of cards. Perhaps a good and graceful way for men to grow old.

Even a ride on the Douglas Park elevated train brings thoughts of another land. Between Kedzie and California Avenues, churches make their presence felt much as they do in Europe—the green domes of St. Casimir on Whipple Street, the black steeple of St. Marks on California. Coming into view with all the pomp and magnificence of a cathedral in Bavaria, the twin piercing spires of St. Paul's on Hoyne avenue—an inspiration for any man.

No, Chicago is not Europe. Perhaps it doesn't have to be. Perhaps it can stand tall as the American Beauty it is. But we are a hybrid people, and if we are not careful, soon the best of our colorful heritage will vanish. We are forever building a great city, but we are forgetting the people and the importance of human touches which must remain. Chicago's tradition can be so much more than crime and concrete. We have a real woman here, but we don't romance her enough.

Where are the street vendors to roast chestnuts and sell flowers on every corner? Why only one great fountain? Why aren't there more church bells to ring out the hours, Tivoli parks for men and children to forget their age, and sidewalk cafes up and down Michigan avenue?

Then the sea, the Chicago sea—Lake Michigan. Only here do men at last find true peace.

Port Chicago draws me two, three, sometimes seven days a week. I have been conditioning my son to the lore and lure of the sea. He is at the stage now where we can stand together above the cargo ships flying flags of Japan, Yugoslavia, Ireland, Sweden, Germany, Norway, and watch the cranes swoop like giant birds—loading, unloading barrels, boxes, burlap bags.

We watch together: he absorbed in the action of cargo and crane; and I anchored at the railing, standing in a hundred different ports, sailing the Atlantic, the Irish sea, the North sea, the Baltic, the Adriatic, the Ionian, the Aegean. Sailing on big and little ships, at all hours of the day and night; in sunshine and gale.

Cook County Hospital:
The Confidence of Competence

If you grew up in Cook County, there were always certain institutions wrapped in legend and packed with superstition. One, of course, was City Hall. Others were the County Jail, the County Morgue, the Juvenile Home and the most fearful of all: County Hospital.

Among the ethnics, the greatest tragedy that could befall a man was to be down and out with nowhere to turn for help but Cook County Hospital. One had to work hard and save one's money to avoid such a fate. Stories of overcrowding, neglect, nonsurvival (fly-swatters in the operating room) were common among working persons who would do all in their power to afford private physicians and good hospitals.

"You'll end up in County Hospital," was one of the strongest threats an old-fashioned father could mete out to an unreliable member of the family. It was the poorhouse, the end of the line and hell all rolled into one. If you had a relative ailing there, you kept quiet about it. He was "in the hospital." That's all.

Approaching the office of Dr. James G. Haughton, executive director of the Health and Hospitals Governing Commission of Cook County, at 1900 W. Polk, all this bad history is in mind, mixed in with the contemporary knowledge that Haughton is completing his fifth year at County, as controversy continues to surround his every move.

After being led courteously through a maze of outer and inner offices, I finally stepped into a room to find Haughton seated behind his desk. He rose and shook hands, and it was immediately evident that the task of depicting the personal presence of the man in such a classic Chicago setting of power, politics and public works, would be an overwhelming one.

He big, black, Impressive. The office he represents is immense, immeasurable, almost intangible in some areas. The proposed budget for 1976 alone, $167.8 million, is likely to be incomprehensible to the average Cook County resident.

But it's possible to talk statistics about the 1976 budget, perhaps foresee an-

61

other financial crisis, but never come close to the man or comprehend the complexities of his office. He can recite a litany of statistics available to his lightening-quick mind. He can deal expertly with every accusation that has been made against him and the hospital.

One doesn't go to bed as a child and dream of becoming the executive director of the Health and Hospitals Governing Commission of Cook County, though as a child, born in Panama City in 1925, Haughton admitted, "I always wanted to be a doctor. My father said I said so when I was four years old."

Dr. Haughton came to Chicago in 1970 to take over direction of Cook County Hospital after having served as first deputy administrator of the Health Services Administration of New York City since 1966.

The real administrative power governing Cook County Hospital, however, was in the hands of the Cook County Board of Commissioners, which was responsible for much of the mess and the terrible conditions that plagued the hospital: patronage, poor facilities, power factions among doctors in the hospital, inept administrators. Probationary accreditation threatened the existence of County.

In 1969, the Health and Hospitals Governing Commission was created to manage Cook County Hospital, Oak Forest Hospital and Cermak Memorial, which provides services to the Cook County Jail and the House of Correction.

Problems persisted. For the most part the problem was money—or control of the budget, which still remained in the hands of the County Board. The governing commission hired Haughton in October, 1970. And he, along with the chairman of the commission, Edwin L. Brashears Jr., began to exert strong leadership, which gradually and dramatically would turn County Hospital and the board around.

Haughton, in particular, reached a verbal agreement with the County Board that he would be in full control of the commission with the members' complete backing.

His feelings at that time were, he said, "I would have their full and complete support. If they were not prepared to delegate that type of authority, I would not come. I cannot depend on nine people who aren't here. I didn't come here under contract because I don't want a contract. My position was: 'If you are dissatisfied with my function, I want you to have the right to get rid of me. If I'm dissatisfied with your backing, I'm going to walk out, and I don't want any contracts tying me down.' "

Haughton, unconservatively dressed in a casual tan suit (the jacket draped around the chair), tieless, wearing a brown-and-white, polka dot shirt with epaulets and a necklace, clasped his hands, heavily ringed in silver, behind his neck, stretched and listened, unsmilingly at first, but with concern.

On October 1, 1970, he had set out a number of goals for himself and the commission, and he had said he was not coming to Chicago primarily to run Cook County Hospital. He did, however, expect to lead the commission in "planning the health services for all the people in Cook County."

He was sure, he said then, that the commission would end patronage (and it has). He also planned to introduce politicians to some of the problems.

"I'm not one of those who consider politicians the enemy," he said. "In fact, some of the most important decisions affecting health care, such as budgetary decisions, are made by politicians. I have found that politicians need to be made aware of the issues and the problems of health care and that they are very helpful."

Money, and the control of it by the County Board President, George W. Dunne, was perhaps the name of the game in the beginning, though, Haughton said, "I don't think money is the major problem in the health field. Most institutions have more money than they need to spend. The flexibility to use the money effectively is much more important than the amount . . . to eliminate unnecessary jobs and purchase expeditiously and use the money to improve the care of the poor."

His first move, though, would be to get County Hospital into better shape. The administration was a shambles.

"The most dramatic changes took place the first eight months," Haughton said. "The place was filthy. And cleaning up the hospital—just plain ordinary housekeeping—resulted in giving the employees a tremendous boost in morale."

The staff itself had to be revitalized by "building the medical staff with senior physicians to supervise the teaching of resident physicians." So County was to remain a training ground for doctors but a more effective and balanced one than ever before.

"We began to attract doctors as we were able to tell them that they would get a decent salary," Haughton continued. "And, too, they would see the new equipment, which always had a positive effect on a nursing staff. The whole flow of new equipment and supplies coming into the hospital brought new hope to the employees."

Haughton, in his dark-rimmed glasses, the gray, lambchop sideburns . . . the dualism here of physician/politician, administrator/humanist, conservative/radical, is not easy to define.

His knowledge of hospital administration is unquestionable. His conversation, laced with facts, flows smoothly and convincingly. He knows his work, understands the responsibilities of power and loves it. What's more, he is conscious of, and seems to relish, the thin line that separates the politico from the servant of the people.

"You have to work with them [politicians]," he admitted. "I work very closely with the Legislature. They need professional advice. Yet I've never tried to tell any politician how to vote on anything. Only guidance . . . what bills to vote on, based on the issues. The only problem I have with the County Board is at budget time. In between those sessions I get nothing but cooperation from the County Board, especially George Dunne."

Haughton turned County Hospital around, almost anyone will tell you. He exudes confidence. But just who is James Haughton?

The credentials are all there: "I took all my elementary and half my secondary education in Panama, the other half in Costa Rica. Then I came to this country to college (Pacific Union College) at the age of 17. My parents were both Seventh Day Adventists, so I went to that school in California."

He received a B.A. in 1947 and entered Loma Linda University, also in California, where he received an M.D. in 1950 and then went on to New York University's post-graduate medical school.

"I had an internship at Unity Hospital in Brooklyn and then a four-year fellowship there in surgery," Haughton said. "I started practice in 1952."

He served in the U.S. Naval Reserve Medical Corps from 1956-1958, where he became interested in the administration of health care. Later he enrolled in Columbia University for study of public health and administrative medicine, where he received a master's degree in 1962.

His experience, prior to coming to Cook County in 1970, is encompassing and impressive: private practice of obstetrics and abdominal surgery, 1952-66, and child-health clinician, 1958-60; resident public health physician, 1960-62; assistant to the executive director of medical-care services, 1962-63, and director of medical-care services to the indigent and medically indigent aged, 1963-65, all with the New York City Health Department, and first deputy administrator of the New York City Health Services Administration, 1966-70.

During many of those years he also served in similar capacities with New York City's Welfare Department.

His private practice was in the Bedford-Stuyvesant area of New York City, where he became acquainted with the inadequate hospital care for the poor. He said:

"If I saw a patient in my office [who needed hospital care], my only recourse was to refer him to an agency. I was never able to present proper care to those people. I can remember sending a man out of my office with a temperature of 105. They had refused to admit him to the hospital, and I had to take care of him at home somehow."

What he learned under those conditions was important to how he feels now: "Private practice could not serve a poor community well."

It was while in the service that Haughton began his unique blend of medicine and administration, explaining, "When I got to my base, I discovered I was to be in the medical administration office. That was my first experience in the field. So for two years I ran the administration. I learned two things from that: No. 1, I had the temperament for administration; No. 2, good organization would increase the productivity of the medical enterprise. In 1960 I started administrative training at Columbia University."

But what of his private practice, the Blacks and Latinos who needed his help? He said, "I missed taking care of my patients. I didn't give them up until 1966, when I became first deputy in New York."

In his job today, he said, "I'm up at 5 a.m. It's hard for me to get any paperwork done here so I take a big, fat briefcase home every night and work at home three or four hours each morning. I'm here 9:30, 10, till whenever. I am not a night worker."

For physical exercise "I swim. There are two pools in the building where I live. I work out every morning with my weights . . . ride my 10-speed racer."

Health foods? "I'm not a faddist. I think very few people need special diets. They need to control their intake.

"I love music and play the piano . . . classical piano. I studied it for ten years. I like progressive jazz, too.

"I have an excellent library. I love history. Absolutely hated history in school, but I've grown to enjoy it. Right now I'm reading Churchill's history of the Second World War. I do some lighter reading, too . . . all of Sherlock Holmes."

Medical programs on television? "No," he said with a laugh. "They're not real, man.

"I go to the opera . . . a season's ticket every year. Also the Goodman Theater. I like Tennessee Williams."

He spoke of his Seventh Day Adventist background, saying, "I went to church every week for 25 years. I don't regret my religious upbringing. I think I got a lot of important values from that. But I don't need the ritual."

One minus in his life is his divorce, but, he said, "I have two lovely children and a two-year-old grandson. Children live their own lives very quickly. Yet I am a family kind of person, and I regret that my family broke up. One of my great regrets at the moment is that my grandson is growing up in another city."

What of the criticisms that he is an arrogant man and probably draws the highest salary—$74,544 yearly—of any health executive in the country?

He smiled and framed a reply: "If arrogant means having confidence in my own judgement, doing what I think needs to be done, then I'm arrogant.

"If I were running a $150 million corporation [which is what he is doing on a public health basis], what do you think my salary would be? A piddling $74 thousand? No way!"

And what is the feedback from patients in County Hospital? How aware are they that Haughton is in charge? He said:

"I walk through the wards . . . I talk to patients. I find out from them what kind of care they're getting. Most of them have a lot of nice things to say. They make a lot of comments about the attitudes of the employees . . . how much things have improved. Family, ministers, chaplains all tell me what a difference they see."

A professional journal for medical students named eight Chicagoans among fifty men and women as the biggest movers and shakers in U.S. medicine, and Haughton was one of them.

"I'm not sure why," he said. "I don't consider myself a shaker or mover at all."

"Oh, I'm happy here. Actually, by completing my fifth year here, this is the longest I've held any position. I'd like to see some additional neighborhood centers develop around the county. And I would like to see a new hospital here. A new, smaller Cook County Hospital. About 800 beds instead of 1,600. A very sophisticated operation. To decentralize, though. Decentralizing and developing partnerships with the private sectors . . . doing things together with them."

Fred and the Chocolate Factory

Fred Paillon is a chocolate maker, a kind of Willy Wonka, Chicago-style, who runs a place called Rahmig's House of Fine Chocolates at 3109 N. Broadway, a neighborhood sort of place among New Town's quick-change shops. He bought the store from his father-in-law, Willy Rahmig, four years ago. Willy ran a fine House of Chocolate for sixteen years. Then Fred moved in with bigger and better ideas for pastries, cakes, and candies for chocolate lovers. So Willy moved over, while Fred began melting and shaping chocolate in his own inimitable way. Stand back while Fred dumps a ten-pound bar of chocolate into the chocolate melting machine that can turn 500 pounds of chocolate into a river of ecstasy, Willy Wonka style. . . .

First, Fred, the German chocolate maker, age 40, is standing in the chocolate kitchen, working on a Bar Mitzvah Basket Cake . . . chocolate, of course. The outside of it, of all his chocolate cakes, is a special kind of shiny frosting called "ganache," actually whipped cream and chocolate cooked together. He is decorating it in a kind of basket weave of yellow butter cream, bending, squeezing, adding 17 flowers, then spelling the name Jon. Now he grabs a little spray gun of food coloring and highlights the whole creation in gold.

"How much?" I ask.

"$25. It will feed about 50 people. Also for Bar Mitzvah I make a Bible cake, a temple cake, a Torah cake and a star cake. The temple cake is the most expensive, about $60. Hey, you want something to eat? Some coffee? Some bakery?"

Yes. Yes, of course.

"Go in the shop. Tell Betty what you want."

I greet Betty in the front store and tell her I am hankering for an almond crescent, for openers.

The House of Fine Chocolates is a house of really fine, dark continental chocolates. "We buy the best grades of chocolate; we use maybe four or five different kinds, plus cocoa butter to make it even richer." But the House of Fine Chocolates is more than just chocolate. It is also a bakery, a cake shop, a candy shop which caters, in a small way, to street trade but in an even greater way to caterers and outside orders. Part of the operation also includes a Kosher baking section under rabbinical supervision where Paillon makes all of the usual items. (The Kosher part is "strictly by order only; not over the counter.")

"The store itself, unfortunately, is the smallest part of our operation," says Fred. "For one reason or another, Broadway has never been much for street trade."

Betty runs the shop all alone quite nicely, and handles most of the phone orders. Fred seems to handle the big stuff: Bar Mitzvah cakes for hotels, birthday cakes, wedding cakes, sweet table assortments of fantastic Viennese pastries and those continental candies.

Candy. Chocolate-covered candy . . . more than fifty varieties. "This is the candy machine," says Fred in a sort of staccato German-American blend of precise pronunciation. "I bought it in Germany."

He explains how the fruit or nut or marzipan fillings are arranged on the machine, how the chocolate is added and cooled. How the chocolate and candy center meet and become one . . . a neat machine.

We move then to a long table filled with wooden trays of various chocolate candies.

"Here, try this one," he says. "Good?"

"Delicious. What is it?"

"Nougatine with a candied hazelnut on top. Here, some fruit candies. This here is a *kroknt*: butter, sugar, almonds, diced orange, and chocolate. Here, some marzipan . . . a mixture of almond paste and sugar. This is ginger marzipan. It comes from the Far East . . . crystalized ginger. It can be chopped up in all kinds of candy. This, see, candied orange and pears . . . comes from Australia. Cut it up in pieces, cover with chocolate.

I'm belly-up in chocolate and a true believer. Chocolate for breakfast is a first for me.

"Here, after-dinner mints." (Pink, white, yellow, blue . . .) "Taste. Ah, you haven't seen nothing yet. Wait till I show you about chocolate."

I leave Fred while he puts a few more finishing touches on the basket cake and move through the bakery section, headed by Louie Hausman, and into the cake department, where two men, Herbert Berthold and Andre Rimbaud, are up to their ears in cakes and Viennese pastries. It's Herb for cakes, Rimbaud for pastries.

Herb is working on a ten-inch chocolate birthday cake, chocolate chip filling, fudge frosting . . . HAPPY BIRTHDAY LISA. Now some fancy work with the whippy decorating tubes, around and around, up and down, psssssssssh . . . plunking down a few colored flowers.

Herb, topped to the teeth in a German accent, smiles and makes it quite obvious that he's a man in charge (22 years of service), and happy in his work.

"This is my department," he explains. "I fill all the cakes and decorate them."

Andre Rimbaud—a great name for a French pastry chef—is a quiet man in his seventies and an artist in soft sculpture. Right now he's fooling with a bowl of pink frosting.

Herb takes over. "That's Rimbaud. In France they called him an artist. He comes here and has to start all over again," he laughs. Rimbaud only smiles, and coaxes the pink frosting.

Pastries, sweet soft pastries. Their very names, poetry enough for a Rimbaud. Victoria boats, *fuerst pueckier,* Victoria fruit-tarlettes, macaroon *rolleaux,* goa squares, Dusseldorfer puffs, orange chocolate, lemon chocolate, *saboyan.* Black Forest cherry torte, Dobosh torte, Napoleon slices. . . .

Fred returns to share his insights about pastries: "Assorted pastries, 30 different kinds we make for the Sweet Table; $1.45 a dozen to $2.45 a dozen. We sell maybe 300 to 400 dozen this weekend. But in June or July . . . 1,200 dozen a weekend."

Rimbaud is into the Viennese pastry now, dazzling the pink layers, the pink frosting, with a touch of bright red.

Yet, claims Fred as he watches the artistry of Andre Rimbaud, "What I'm trying to stay away from is too much goo. Is the main thing wrong with American pastry."

I follow him into a walk-in freezer as he divulges his philosophy of pastry, his secret of the oh so Sweet Table. "After the meal, you know, after the big dinner, you want to hit every taste bud! So, the Sweet Table."

The freezer is a veritable cache of pastry, towering shelves of pastel goodies, gobs of butter cream, sheets of chocolate-topped cakes, soft pounds of passionate pastry damned near winking at a man, whispering, "Try me, try me."

Fred grabs a cake that looks as if it's going to float away. "This is a German specialty called 'Bienenstich' . . . a yeast dough, honey, almonds put on top. Baked, then split and filled with a Bavarian cream, a mixture of whipped cream and custard."

It sells for $1.75 and looks like a giant hamburger bun stuffed with about four inches of whipped cream instead of hamburger. The depths of pastry are staggering.

The Willy Wonka side of Fred Paillon is a fascination with inventions to make the Sweet Life even sweeter and faster and easier for Fred, pastry people, and chocolate-chosen people everywhere.

He has invented something called "the brandy spray" which his cake man, Herb, uses between the layers of cake to keep them moist.

And now Fred shows me a sheet of chocolate mousse. Its top layer is an extravaganza of intricate designs in chocolate. Fred cast them there from a rubber mold—his own patent. He has learned to cast chocolate as other people cast plaster of Paris. Now he is working on a way to spray chocolate like paint.

"The purists in our profession may not agree. They will argue that this is too mechanical, that the pastry chef and his decorating tube is the only way. But, after all, no one is going to pay me 50 bucks for all the extra time. And I never cheat on the ingredients. You've got to give people their money's worth. It costs just as much labor to make garbage as to make something good. If you start with garbage, you come out with garbage."

Back in the chocolate room, Fred grabs a pot and dips it into the chocolate melting machine. "The average baker today doesn't even know how to work with chocolate. Too cold, it gets gray and streaky. Too hot, it gets gray and streaky. Chocolate doesn't refrigerate too well, and it also doesn't freeze. It's melted down between 125 and 140 degrees. I go through six or seven hundred pounds of chocolate a week."

Fred pours the pot of hot chocolate on a marble slab, and then begins working it (tempering it, he calls it) with a spatula.

"This is the whole secret, you know . . . tempering. One degree makes a hell of a difference. The correct temperature is between 87 and 89 degrees. 89 is already the limit. There's no additives, no preservatives. Chocolate's touchy, period."

I have never seen such a pool of melted chocolate before. Fred seldom lets his arm rest. He's continually slapping it around, stirring it, shaping it, conjuring it, bringing the temperature down with the precise control only artists and craftsmen understand . . . sight, touch, taste.

"Here," he says, handing me a spoonful of melted chocolate. "Try for temperature . . . just touch to your lips."

I lip-test it, but my mustache is in the way. Perfect . . . another Fred Paillon original! A chocolate mustache!

He tests the temperature himself . . . "almost." A few more swipes of the spatula and he says, "I make some Easter eggs. Watch." He goes for the egg molds and some water.

"See. The more cold water I pour in the chocolate, the stiffer it gets."

He reaches for an ordinary paint brush and begins brushing the chocolate into the molds, a thin layer at a time. "Now I just pop these in the ice box about five minutes; then they have to be brushed once more with chocolate. You see about chocolate? You're only limited by your own imagination. And you can't learn it out of books. Come in the office a minute."

I like Fred's office. There's an air of carelessness about it . . . a couple of bread knives on the desk, notes, old orders, even a sheaf of old thank you notes, one a long poem praising a Torah cake, many of them just a few words of gratitude. . . . "Mr. Paillon, the cake was magnificent and truly a work of art. It tasted as good as it looked—even better." Behind him is a little table with a bottle of Puerto Rican Rum and a bottle of Bols maraschino liquer. This is a working man's office . . . a chocolate-maker's haunt.

On the wall are photographs of his father-in-law, Willy Rahmig (who still comes in almost everyday to look things over), and various awards and cake creations. Willy came over from Germany in 1923 and was one of the youngest pastry chefs in New York City. In 1941 he came to Chicago and became pastry chef at the Bismarck Hotel. Then in 1946 he started his own business around Addison and Broadway. He moved to the present location in 1952, where Fred began working for him four years later.

But it was in Willy Rahmig's House of Chocolates where Fred met and wooed and married Willy's daughter, Patricia. Love in the Chocolate House . . . one can only wonder. Fred bought the old man out in 1969 and the world's been coming up chocolate ever since.

We move out toward the Easter eggs once again. After the second brushing of chocolate in the molds, plus another brief refrigeration period, the egg shells are ready. They slip easily out of the molds, each of them actually one half of a hollow egg, waiting for its mate.

"Look," he hands me a chocolate egg shell. "See how smooth. No marks. Perfect. Now we got to put feet on them so they can stand. Then we fill them with candy, decorate the top with more chocolate, some flowers, and tie it up with a ribbon."

He takes another pot of hot chocolate from the big chocolate melting machine and places it on the table where he will work on the eggs.

"Now let me show you again what happens when I add plain cold water to the pot. Now you would think the chocolate would get thinner, no? Look . . . look how thick it gets. I can't tell you why this happens . . . it just happens. Now I use this chocolate for the designs on top of the eggs."

Fred begins decorating an egg, first with fancy border swirls, laying the chocolate in there in wave and curlicues. He removes more shells from the mold, examining each of them.

"This means it's good, the shine in the chocolate. Some of the 'shoemakers' who work with chocolate put a lacquer on it to make it shine."

He calls for Andre Rimbaud to show him about making feet for the chocolate eggs to rest upon. "Andre, come here. You want to know how to make feet for the eggs, you said. Look, I show you." Rimbaud watches intently.

"The Easter eggs sell for $2.75 to $12.50, decorated, filled with candy, tied with a ribbon and put in a box." He is interrupted by Betty, who tells him that so and so is on the phone.

While Fred's handling the caller, I return to the boys in the back room to see what they're up to. Herb is up to here with a chocolate wedding cake. A stunning hymn to chocolate with a shiny dark ganache frosting, chocolate chips inside, chocolate butter cream decoration, even chocolate flowers. With weddings and birthdays . . . in a rush . . . Herb figures he can knock off an average of 25 to 30 cakes in a day.

Rimbaud is engaged in a lemony yellow licky-sticky-whippy frosting right now. Such intensity in the old man. I try to pull a few words out of him.

"I was the pastry chef in the old Morrison Hotel," he says. "I learned about pastry in France . . . I'm going to be 72," he smiles. "I'd rather be working than anything. I'm more healthy this way."

Fred steps up with a big smile and points to Rimbaud. "He's my old pastry chef," says Fred. "I used to work for him. He's the only guy who taught me anything."

Fred is called to the phone again, and another man passes slowly by me carrying empty pans and cake sheets. He's got a reddish-brown mustache and something like a permanent smile on his face. He stops and studies me and I study Herb's chocolate wedding cake.

Who are you? I ask.

"Milton," he says. "Milton J. Brown. I clean up around here. I'm a baker's helper. Looks good, huh, don't it?" he nods toward the cake. "But," inching closer to me, whispering, "it's very rich."

Louie Hausman, the baker, makes the cakes for Herb to decorate and for Rimbauld to transform into pastries. Now he's working on some cherry cheese cakes.

"Nothing too glamorous to being a baker," he says. "You don't see them standing in line to be bakers these days like they stand in line to be electricians."

I return to Fred's office to take up the chocolate works once again. Fred, I'm convinced, could make the Civic Center out of chocolate. Or maybe the whole Chicago skyline. There is a chocolate mania about him.

He takes out some photographs. "See, a camera in chocolate for some photographer. Look, all chocolate wedding cakes. More than half my cakes are made of chocolate, white or dark. See this; I once blew a vase out of sugar and then brushed chocolate on it. Here, you know what this is? A chocolate church . . . Mayor Daley's own church. He donated it to some orphanage, I think. I've even made a cake for McDonald's Hamburgers, yellow arches and all. And here, you see, chocolate houses, thin layers I cut and then cement together with chocolate."

"I once shipped a spun sugar wedding cake to West Berlin on Lufthansa. I put it on Wednesday to Frankfort, from there to Berlin, and on Saturday was the wedding. Spun sugar is not well known in Germany. The cake was going to be just for show, you know. But those Germans . . . they polished it all off."

"I've even shipped a cake to the South Pole." Chocolate has gotten hold of him now.

"For Easter I make this special Easter wagon for the front window. A big chocolate egg with wheels and four running rabbits. Some fellow used to come in here and buy it for an orphanage every Easter. But for the last few years he has not shown up. I don't know who he was."

Time passes in a chocolate way.

Louie, the baker, is checking his cheese cakes.

Betty is selling a birthday cake.

Rimbaud is working up a new easel of frostings.

Leo is packing pastries.

And Fred Paillon, the chocolate maker, is decorating a Bar Mitzvah cake as big as a Bible. A chocolate Bible cake, indeed, that will feed at least 75 people: a huge chocolate book almost three feet across with lemon-yellow butter cream scroll work. The very pages are butter cream—squeezed from the tube, then sprayed in a gold gilt sort of way. A wide ribbon page marker is laid across the center of the open book of chocolate. On the left, a Jewish star. And on the right . . . "Now I put down the Ten Commandments . . . in Hebrew." The artistry is incredible.

On the table behind him rest a couple dozen chocolate Easter egg shells, waiting for their day. And who knows how many pounds of Easter bunnies running around the chocolate machine, waiting for Fred to make them a wagon.

Bill Stipe: Invisible Artist

It's all a beginning and ending with Stipe, every snatch of conversation. You can start anywhere with him because Stipe is nowhere. Begin with a quote, his or somebody else's. Which is one of the ways Bill Stipe, the copy machine artist, shares his vision:

I HAVE NOTHING TO SAY AND I AM SAYING IT AS I NEED IT AND THAT IS POETRY.   —John Cage

Which is printed on one side of a Xerox artwork of Stipe's. On the other side is a single panel from Peanuts which shows a perplexed Snoopy at his typewriter with Lucy reading a page of the manuscript: "That's the dumbest thing ever written!" she says.

And that's it. Another Bill Stipe, dated, unnumbered, "colored" in the characterisitc gray tones of copy prints. And if you'd like one, he'd be glad to run off an original for you. For as long as Stipe is where he's at today ("I can average better than a new idea every week."), it's a thrill to supply the world with his originals.

The copy machine has discovered Bill Stipe, or Bill Stipe has discovered the copy machine. Or, to quote Stipe from another of his Xerox orignals:

EVERYTHING IS THERE BEFORE YOU DISCOVER IT.

"In one sense, everything that we discover is already there, according to J. Bornowski," explains Bill Stipe. "He meant that in terms of Michelangelo's efforts as well as Galileo's discoveries. But mine is a little different. I mean discovering what is already within yourself . . . and always there is more."

Stipe, in ever-present cap and work clothes, sits in his magnificently cluttered apartment in Rogers Park and could pass as the maintenance man to the building. He seems so serene amidst the artifacts of his life shouting to be seen, heard, touched, read, that one begins to question himself rather than Stipe's vision.

75

He is a small man in stature, ageless, rather hard-edged in the face lines, with the mischievous child almost visible. Something in Bill Stipe is always laughing at you, the world, Bill Stipe himself. The artist as clown? Partly. But the artist as innovator, speculator, philosopher, teacher, student, poet, ever-changing.

For one, Bill Stipe is concerned about nothing. Nothing bothers him. Nothing but the real truth. It refer to his CB (check book or copy book) of June 10, 1975, "The Second Clearing" which consists of nine pages (copy machine prints) fastened together like traveller's checks, but a little larger in size. The third page/print reads and looks like this:

> Why is orange juice orange?
>   because it ain't.
>   My mother
>   said it was orange
> but — it's really
>   yellow juice!
> "Have some orange juice, dear.
>   You'll like it,
> especially since it's made
>   from real orange oranges."

On the fourth and fifth pages, he gets right down to it with: "13 Pieces of Misinformation": 1. the earth is not flat 2. the sun doesn't rise or set 3. we don't see everything right side up 4. the flag doesn't wave 5. in a rearview mirror the guy behind you is driving on the wrong side of the road 6. almost everybody knocks on wood wrong 7. yellow juice isn't orange 8. the middle stop light isn't yellow 9. you don't eat up your food 10. it doesn't rain 11. moonlight doesn't exist 12. waves do not travel 13. a shooting star isn't shot and it isn't a star WS

But an artist of the Bill Stipe type didn't come from nowhere to nothing overnight. (He didn't Xerox his ear last year just to top Van Gogh.) All journies into the self, especially the artist's, are solitary one-way streets of no final promises with only the possibility of discoveries along the way. "I think Marcel [Duchamp] would say there isn't anything that isn't art. Maybe that's what I got from him."

Stipe, born in Clarinda, Iowa, discovered something about himself at an early age. "I did art because I wasn't good at anything else. They didn't have art in high school, but I kept on doing it. I got into solid geometry and got A's because I could do all the drawings. Any subject I could draw was alright."

He received his B.A. and M.A. degrees from the University of Iowa. "Grant Wood was there. I studied with him. He was one of the lousiest teachers I ever had. An artist named McCray was there too, and he was good because he was the first teacher who wouldn't answer any of my questions. That was something new."

After Iowa he attended the Museum School of Fine Arts in Boston where he studied under Karl Zerbe. "They put me in a beginning drawing class, which was humiliating. But that's where I belonged. They never taught me to draw at Iowa. But at Boston I learned how to draw. Personally, I got under the influence of Bemelmans [Ludwig] . . . you can draw anything you love to draw."

It's difficult to keep Stipe and his conversation in any semblance of order, especially chronological. He attended the Institute of Design in Chicago in 1947; he was in the New Horizons show in Chicago in 1976; he won the Pauline Palmer Prize (2nd) at the Art Institute 59th Annual Show in 1956; he did a wall painting, 6' X 80', "Davis 'L' Bus Stop," which was commissioned by the Evanston Chamber of Commerce in 1971; he is in museums and private collections; but most importantly, he is Stipe who will not be stopped. He just keeps on doing it. Picking up on anything which might lead to yet another discovery within or without—a life defined by art, an art defined by life.

"I got to Paris when I was in the army and met Gertrude Stein," he says without the slightest intention of impressing anyone. "She talked beautifully. Quite an intellect. I can't remember wht she talked about. All I remember is she had a crewcut and Alice [Toklas] had a mustache."

At the Insitute of Design in Chicago, after WWII, "I learned something about design, which was a good thing. I learned the philosophy that design could be the basis for everything." And then he began teaching at Northwestern University in 1947, where he was an associate professor of art (until his retirement in 1985).

"I came out of Boston thinking I was a watercolorist. John Marin was my big gun, so I was very free. But I got tired of watercolor and started doing collage about 1953, and that started what happened ever since. I took them down to galleries, and no one liked them. So then I started to paint the collage. That was a little better. I went to New York (a one-man show at the Ruth White Gallery in 1957), but it took me four years to get a one-man show here in Chicago, and that wasn't until a year after I won 2nd prize at the Annual Chicago Show. About that time I also became interested in titles. I was always interested in writing."

For many artists, especially Midwestern, the one-man show in New York could be the giant step to success. Not so with Stipe, who has been singularly unsuccessful with his work, if one measures success by dollars and New York. He remains one of the great unknowns in the Chicago art world. Yet there is no bitterness of defeat in the man, only humor as he laughingly recalls: "After the New York show—nothing. Nobody of any importance came to the gallery to see it."

Not unlike his mural, "Davis 'L' Bus Stop," which has all but disappeared in Evanston.

"It's all covered over except for the last section which fortunately has my

MARCEL DUCHAMP IS DEAD!

   GOODBYE marcel - a lot of dead people
are with you...and not just the ones who
raised questions about your show, but also
the ones who thought they knew the
answers.
   NOBODY seems to know that you were
really raising questions - not giving
                                answers.
   NOBODY seems to realize that it was
not a put on - that there actually
                were no answers.
   NOBODY saw the King with the invis-
ible clothes.
                Very regretfully,
                signed_____

WS

78

name on it. The rest is wiped out. 'Invisible' in more ways than one, between the graffiti and the posters. As the posters get torn off it, then it gets nice and textural.

"I don't think anything is permanent. It takes great effort for an artist's work to be permanent anyway. I still think there's a very great, invisible mystery about Van Gogh. Why did they save all his paintings? He was crazy when he died. So then, what do you do with a crazy guy's work? In those days, it hadn't been too long before that when crazy people were put in jail. They were just as bad as burglars and robbers and rapists and everything. It's a miracle when anything is preserved, when anything does last.

"And as for who's to judge that anything's a work of art . . . well, you know, that's quicksand. It's constantly changing. Sure, it's one of the reasons why some artists go crazy, why some are so insecure. They need reaffirmation. Thousands of invisible artists are not in galleries. There's a whole mess of them. Most artists don't have the courage, or what do you call it, fortitude, just doing it on their own. That's rare. That's the French attitude."

Throughout the early '60s, Stipe continued to do work, which others called pop art, but which he called "realism": "I called it realism because I tried to copy just what I saw. Then I discovered I couldn't copy it. In the 1960s I got into more or less free-form painting. But in '68 we had a show at Northwestern on concrete poetry, and I got real excited. For me, that was a breakthrough. About a year later I started this "initial" poetry. It just looks like a whole lot of initials, but then you find you can read it. And now I'm finding out that other people are doing it. But I finally got into the word business that way."

```
THE     SNO
EAR     TFL
THI     AT!
```

So words got a hold on Stipe. And an artist's first words can lead to strange discoveries. "What do we really mean with words? What do words mean? ("Words don't describe anything—words are ideas," J. Boronowski.) ETSA came out of this. The sun doesn't rise, and the sun doesn't set. There is only ETSA—Earth Turning Sun Appearing. "And I decided that there are a whole lot of things we talk about wrong, are named wrong. ETSA instead of sunrise. ETE—Everything Turns East. All the planets turn east. Everything turns east. That's our world, the world we live in."

"I think it's all a matter of orientation. I ask people which way the moon moves. They think it moves west. They're just uninvolved. I've also discovered that most people don't care. They accept all their illusions. I don't know how important this is, but every once in a while people do change some things."

```
WHA   TIS   ESS   ENT   IAL   ISI   NVI   SIB   LETO   THE
EYE          —the Little Prince
```

Somewhere around 1973, 1974, words and pictures and nothing but the truth (according to Stipe . . . via McLuhan's message, and the discovery of Xerox) began to come together with the result of a lithograph called, "the und/pun."

Stipe explains: "In 1920, Kurt Schwitters said, 'The expression of a picture cannot be put into words, any more than the expressing of a word 'and' for example, can be painted.' " So Bill Stipe created the und (German for "and") pun:

und

(turn the word upsidedown and you can see Stipe smiling.)

"The next big thing that came around was using Xerox or copy machines in 1973, '74," says Stipe . . . characteristically unchronologically. He has this thing with clocks and calendars which leads one to suspect that time does not exist for him. (There's an old clock sitting on top the radiator in his apartment. The hands move entirely by air currents, and mostly in winter.)

"June, 1974, is the exact date I got into Xerox. That's when I discovered I wasn't copying; I was making original prints. So then I began to sign and date them. I Xeroxed everything I felt would say something. I even sent my ear over a telephone (telecopier) and decided that had some meaning."

Stipe also attended a workshop at the Art Institute in the fall of '74 under the direction of Sonia Sheridan. "It was a Generative Systems Workshop. Actually, I just got some reenforcement there. When you start with these things, you need all the reenforcement you can get. The philosophy was that my machine (system) can be used as art, whether it's a machine or a system in your head."

The UPC (universal price code on packaging) caught Stipe's eye in the spring of '75 and became part of his imagination for some time. The lines, the form, the symbols, the image . . . all of it makes Bill Stipe smile.

"It's on everything!" he throws his hands up in abandonment. "It's a sign. I don't think of words as letters. They're signs; they're not even words. I began to collect UPCs right from the start. I stuck them on everything. Xeroxed them. Incidentally, that one there's Campbell's Chunky Sirloin Beef Soup.

"The same month UPCs began to interest me, I went on a ski trip and had to get some traveller's checks. That's when I got the idea of combining several Xerox prints together and making a check book. There are things you can say with several that you can't say with one. I'm even dropping the name 'Xerox.' I'm calling them CB—check book or copy book.

"This is another series I began: Fon Books. The sounds of words. How you put down sounds of words . . . signs for sounds."

pes   on   urth
u   bloo   it!
—WS

"I'm always trying to find funny signs and things like that."

Stop
sin

The artist as teacher, the teacher as artist, Stipe floats in the midst of it, playing down his professional image to the point of invisibility. It's difficult to imagine a Professor William Stipe on the hallowed grounds of Northwestern University. He just doesn't look the part.

"I have a standard assignment for a beginning painting class. I have them all do a good painting and a bad painting, and then we discuss them. You find some people whose bad stuff is really good. I'm trying to find out what they think is bad and good, and then we can start from there.

"I also have them do a one-minute drawing. I've saved those through the years. That's going to be a book someday. What would you draw if you only had one minute?" He holds a drawing that looks like a peak of a mountain or a crest of a wave. "This is one of the best." On the drawing the student has written: "I'm not good at decisions. Too many to make in 60 seconds." "Isn't that great?" says Stipe. "And I never saw her again. She dropped the course right after."

"I try all kinds of things. I'll give them a test on which way is north. Out of 40 people, I'll only have two or three who will even come close." (Stipe usually wears a compass on his wrist.) "It's more important to raise questions than give answers."

What does all this have to do with art? "I think it's orientation. If art has anything at all, it's orientation—knowing where you're at and who you are. There's nothing easy about knowing who you are. It's a continual thing you work on all your life."

As for Northwestern itself: "They never questioned what I did. I could run the classes the way I wanted to. There was never any conflict. So I loved teaching. I liked the students. I didn't impress Northwestern. I never made it beyond Associate Assistant Professor. But that's alright too. After all, I'm invisible."

As for Chicago: "It's a good place in one way. You're not in the center of things. You can be yourself here. In another way it's bad because you can't sell your things. You can be a good starving artist in Chicago. Most of them are.

"But Chicago isn't my place. I've got to get out. If I get recognition, it'll probably be from somewhere else. It could even be New York. I've gotten more recognition from New York than from Chicago. I think every artist has to find his place. Picasso wasn't that important until he got to Paris, and then, bang! Away he went."

Though the response to Stipe's work has been underwhelming at best, he harbors no bitterness, no agony. "You just wait. Maybe that's all you can do. What did Buckminster Fuller say? 'Give people 20 years to understand my ideas'? When you first start doing something, you want a little reassurance. I've been ignored for years now. I haven't been in the Art Institute shows. Northwestern ignores me. I haven't sold any prints. I don't have a gallery. I don't see how it could be any worse!" he laughs. "I think I sold one book [CB]. I got a fan letter in April. My first one. So I sent him a CB and told him he could do it too."

Mr. Stipe

In school I had to write about
a famous person I wrote about you.
I think you are a kind person and
a great artist. When I grow up I
want to be a great artist like you.
I wish you good health. Bless you and
your family. My teacher said you are
too busy to read or answer my letter.

> from Edward Cabral
> age 9 years
> New Bedford Mass 02740 USA

"I'm content with myself. It's all new. It's all exciting. And with print-making, I'm starting over again. I like what I'm doing. I took a course in Chinese cooking once. Once of the greatest classes I ever took. We each prepared three dishes, and at the end, everyone got to share the food. And I thought, gosh, if you could only do that in class! I like to teach a class where everybody gets something.

"I think I've had more freedom since I got into the copy machine thing because I found I could make something to give away. More things should be like that." (Many of Stipe's students throw his gift of copy machine art in the waste-basket.)

"I think we're 'thing' possessed. The UPC is a labeling thing. The students throw my work away because it's just a 'thing.' If art has any value, it's not because it's a thing but because it does have value as an idea. When you buy something from an artist, you're not buying a thing. You're paying the artist to continue his work."

What you receive then from Stipe is a refreshing sense of spirit, a questioning of everything, an acceptance of even nothingness that is rare these days, especially in the hustle of the art world. Stipe, I am certain, awakens every day to wonder. And then pursues it.

"I can't talk about unknowns. That's what I'm working with. I'm learning how to pronounce. I'm fascinated with the signs. I'm working with unknowns. I like learning, going back to school. I went down to the Planetarium to learn everything I could about astronomy. That's when I discovered everything turns east. I'm a biker . . . a slow one. I like to look around. I ski in winter. It's *all* art. It's either all art or nothing is art.

"This past winter I skied right across the middle of a down-hill ski run up in

Michigan. No one had ever done it before! First you ask, why hasn't anyone done it? Then you ask, why not me? I'll be the first! I like the Guinness Book of World Records and all those crazy firsts."

Yet a comparison to one of the most influential artists of the 20th century, Marcel Duchamp, persists. There is a lot of Duchamp in Stipe. A lot of Stipe in Duchamp.

"He was a good publicity man," admits Stipe, somewhat brushing away the comparison at first. "He was wonderful. I don't know how he could be any better. If there's any comparison, though, I may be a little closer to Vermeer. He just painted his pictures in the backend of an art supply store or something. Almost nobody knew him. I don't know how the word got around. It was all underground, grapevine. Maybe you sent a man out to go get a painting. He wasn't in demand. And now . . . there are only about 34 Vermeers left. And yet, look how famous he is. No dealers, no galleries, no museums . . . maybe just beginning a collection and that was it."

But Stipe does share Duchamp's ideas about art?

"Absolutely. His complete acceptance that it's nothing definite. Nothing permanent. It could all disappear tomorrow, and that included his notoriety and everything. And yet, of course, he liked it. He certainly didn't object to it. I thought he was as secure as you can get. His humor was absolutely wonderful. That's one of his trademarks. Anything could be funny, whether it was words, events or things, or pieces of things. He could see. Even when his glass paintings cracked . . . he thought that was alright. He liked the cracks. Anybody else would say, Geez! Their masterpieces, cracked up! But he could accept almost anything, even 'invizm'."

Invizm is another Stipe art concept he discovered was always there. "This is my 3,500th day of being invisible," he said to me on October 6, 1987.

"What's the difference between minimalism and invizm?" he asks. "And the answer is, invizm is invisible. That's it. Meant to be that way. And it might be minimal but at the same time it's definitely invisible, with some invisible meaning or aspect to it. You know the old saying, 'As plain as the nose on your face'? You never see your nose. If you're going to get serious, what are you going to talk about, religion? That's full of invizm. Science? Look at all the things they don't know yet. And what else, politics? Who's going to become the next president? He sure is invisible. Nuclear threats? Boy, are they invisible. You don't even want to think about it. You keep wanting to talk about peace, which is certainly invisible.

"Mona Lisa's smile? That wasn't what was invisible. What was invisible with her were her eyebrows. Only a few years back I learned that Picasso's old man with a guitar had an invisible woman in it. If you get the right angle you can see the under-painting bleeding through. The woman was on the panel first, and then he painted her out, painting the old man with the guitar over her.

"What's beauty? That's one of the most invisible things of all. The whole art world is invisible. It's all a big mystery.

"And in the end, who are you? You're invisible."

Stipe has faded in and out of my life the past fifteen years. Months of silence, of nothing, then suddenly, some wonderful new concept, some miraculous little work of art appears in my mailbox. I save everything, though much of his older Xerox copy art has begun to fade. Whole pages have disappeared in a gray sameness.

At times I wonder where he is, today, both physically and in the world of art. I try tracking him down at his old Chicago address. Nothing. Bill Stipe doesn't live here anymore. His phone has been disconnected. "Nothing is just a direction," he once said.

Now in his 70s, somewhere in the Midwest? Somewhere in America? The artist is creating his ultimate masterpiece: the invisible Bill Stipe.

Max Zimmerman:
I Can Drink It For You Wholesale

Zimmerman's, the world's largest cut rate liquor store, sitting in the Loop, on the relatively unexciting corner of Randolph and Franklin, right here in the Second City . . . it's impressive. Whether you like booze or not, Max has an institution going here. Max the Hat himself will tell you, "It's a Chicago landmark."

You enter those doors at 240 W. Randolph and you're immediately immersed in an amber land of glass and warm golden liquid . . . scotch, bourbon, brandy, cognac, rum, sweet technicolored cordials, and the soft garnet and white wonder of wine. You can almost, but not quite, taste it. You're here, anyway, to reacquaint your taste buds with the tangy miracles of alcohol, for the night, the weekend, the month.

Enough of the aesthetics. This is a cut rate liquor house. You come to Zimmerman's for bargains. Nobody, but nobody, in Chicago, in the world, undersells Zimmerman. If you don't believe it, just ask Max the Hat. You say you can get the same gin at Walgreen's for $3.89? "Give it to him for $3.79," says Max. And so the people pour in, especially on weekends.

Max the Hat's employees, in light blue jackets, are everywhere—behind counters, ringing up sales, filling shelves, answering phones, helping customers select the proper wines, writing orders, pushing flat trucks of booze, bending, reaching, walking, scurrying down the aisles, around the counters, in the offices, upstairs, downstairs, all around Zimmerman land. And where's Max the Hat?

Right in the thick of it. Selling a shopping cart full of Rhine wine to two Michigan teachers who drove in this morning to stock up on German wine . . . $76 worth. How do you find him? Look for the western-styled brown felt hat he's been wearing in the store for over twenty years. (The original has been cast in bronze.) Nobody else who works for Max wears such a hat. "I see to that," says Max.

Historically speaking, Max is into his fortieth anniversary year. He is a

Horatio Alger story, like most successful old-time businessmen. Max came out of the West Side of Chicago (Ashland and Roosevelt), hawking newspapers from 1917 to 1923 in the same area where his World's Largest Liquor Store now stands. "I was practically born and raised in this spot." He sold shopping bags, 3 cents apiece, on Maxwell Street. He was a fruit peddler on the corner of Halstead and Madison. He drove a cab for awhile in the early '30s.

The repeal of Prohibition came along and Max had the foresight to capitalize on a peculiar thirst in people. He opened a tiny liquor store in 1933—"about 12 feet wide"—and began with the only two brands of whiskey to be had: Crab Orchard and Snug Harbor, 59 cents a pint.

Max rolled with the times, moving to larger quarters, always increasing his volume, building the present store in 1959, catering always to a public that grows thirstier every day. He's a neat little man. Immaculate, twinkling eyes. Always smiling. Nothing "Western" about him, except the hat, which of course is just a gimmick, now bordering on a legend. And when he hangs up his hat in the office, sits behind the desk, answers phone calls, takes orders, chats with customers (his door is always open) discusses problems with his staff, wheels and deals in whiskey, talks wordily of wines, you realize that the hat means nothing at all. Max is a super salesman; his business just happens to be booze. He could probably make a fortune, hatless, selling paper airplanes. But booze is his stock in trade, his life, his art.

What kind of drinkers are we today?

"The oldest bourbon brand is a whiskey named Golden Wedding," says Max the Hat. "It came out of the repeal. It's still around in certain parts of the country. It was a straight whiskey. Most were straight whiskies right after the repeal. Well, bourbon was a man's drink at the time. They thought a blend of 86 proof would be what the new drinkers would like. Before that, only 100 proof was available."

So with the blending, a lighter whiskey, a softer whiskey, a new taste was cultivated. But blends sell in only certain parts of the country. The East is a blend market; Chicago and the West is bourbon.

"The war, you see, caused us to stretch what we had; the blending began right after the '40s. From then on, bourbon stayed popular and blends were coming up a little. Then Canadian and Scotch whiskies and vodkas started to take a hold. This was after the war; a lot of people wanted to get into sophisticated drinking. They went to restaurants and clubs and saw others getting different drinks.

"Vodka became a rage. You could do anything with it. What the hell, whoever heard of orange juice and spirits before? The reason for vodka's popularity is simple. It's odorless. You could drink and not be detected. Today vodka is outselling gin. And vodka keeps getting bigger and bigger. Gin is just holding its own. Bourbon has slipped tremendously, especially the 100 proof. The lighter bourbons, 88 proof, are holding. Canadian whiskey is big.

"Coming up fast are specialty items like this, Apricot Sours. Personally, I wouldn't drink the stuff. The Harvey Wallbanger, strictly a gimmick by the Galliano people. Harvey Wallbanger sweatshirts, you know. . . . "

Soft whiskey? Hard whiskey? What's it all about?

"It costs more money to age a straight whiskey than a bourbon . . . 6 years old, 10 years old . . . a distillery's money is tied up for all that time. The tax is based on a 100-proof gallon . . . $10.50. Government law sets this $10.50 a gallon tax based on 100 proof spirits. So now you find much of your whiskey is 80 proof: that's 20 per cent less. For example, Gordon's Gin was always 90 proof gin. So it's a case of raising the price to cover costs, or reducing the proof of this gin from 90 to 86 proof. This is to avoid increasing the price of their product. So now the government gets less tax and they [the distilleries] don't have to raise the price of their gin. I don't think there'll be much resentment about this from the public."

Inside the store itself, a late Saturday-morning momentum is developing, a steady stream of liquor-conscious people flowing in, filling shopping carts. Hardly anyone walks around with only one bottle in hand. It's either an armful or a shopping cart tingling with Old Fitz, Seagrams, Chivas Regal, Smirnoff's; fifths, quarts, half gallons, and gallons. Wines of every label. The sales are staggering . . . $26, $43, $26, $154. People must be tuning in to Max's sign on the marquee outside: "Save your energy, use ours."

Max the Hat ponders the ethics of his business: a little soul searching of America's alcohol mystique. Are we a country coming together or falling apart? What is this tremendous craving for booze doing to our heads? What's the difference between a man dealing in liquid spirits and a kid on a corner dealing drugs?

"I always preach moderation," says Max. "Personally I hate to see a sloppy customer walk in. If somebody comes in here who looks like he's had too much, I refuse to sell him. I preach moderation. I don't need bums that bad, not in this business. The exploited drinker is a drunk who doesn't care what the hell you charge him for a half pint of booze. You'll always have the habitual drunkards, but I don't think today it's as big as it seems. I think most of the whiskey we sell is strictly social drinking. I don't see the drug thing, even legalization of marijuana as any threat to me. The liquor business has been nothing but up every year since the repeal."

The youth market is interesting: it's been always kind of a beer market, but now the liquor companies seem out to get them with new sensations.

"Pop wines," says Max; "all the young ones, all the kids are drinking this stuff. But it's all junk. There's no sophistication in it. Cold Beer, Cold Duck, Apple Wine, Jug Wine. But you take a pop wine that you can sell for 75 cents with 12 per cent alcohol and compare that to beer with 4 per cent and you can see why pop wine is big."

And what's the sophisticated drinker into these days?

"Number one, Scotch. Number two, Canadians . . . light whiskies. Then, vodka. Another thing that's getting very big is cordials, liqueurs in homes. People are buying more rum these days . . . that's getting phenomenal. People are travelling more; they get into some exotic drinking."

I sense a parched throat for Max the Hat. He's been doing a lot of talking. I feel a sudden thirst coming on myself. What's your own favorite drink, I ask Max. He smiles, pushes an intercom button, asks for one of his employees to rinse some glasses, instructs another employee to bring him a bottle, and sooner than you can say, Max the Hat, he plunks down a bottle of cognac before me: Jacques Arnoul V.S.O.P. going for close to ten bucks a bottle. He breaks it open, pours two brandy snifters, does a tiny ritual of swirling, inhaling the essence of fine cognac, tastes, pours, swallows, and smiles. "A great cognac, reasonably priced, very smooth." I agree, and we continue with our business, talking, laughing, quietly putting an end to Jacque Arnoul, a fine man, whoever the hell he is or was.

"For outside drinking, Scotch is my drink. Dewar's White Label, my favorite. Wine? I'm a great wine drinker. I drink wine when I'm out for dinner. I may start out with a cocktail . . . a drink or two will not hurt, in any way, the wine taste. At home, we always have wine. My wife, she has a hell of a palate. I favor reds, Bordeaux. I do like some whites, a good white Chablis."

This business of wine. It's a big thing at Zimmerman's. "Hell, I do over $5 million in wine here a year. There are 70,000 cases of wine in the warehouse. One third of our business is wine."

Where does a neophyte wino begin? What does he buy? How much should he spend? What's the way to wine connoiseurdom?

"Always start from the bottom, not the top," advises Max. "Start out in the $2 range. Move slowly up. Buy by taste, not by price. If you can concentrate and remember tastes, you can develop, remembering what you discovered with each bottle. This is the way to develop your palate, become a little bit of an expert."

Braced with another snifter of cognac, Max the Hat is even more eloquent on the subject of wine. He's into determining factors of fine wine: "The roundness of the wine, the softness the wine developed. A wine with a little harshness to it, a little roughness, didn't get enough sun, or there was too much rain, too much wind, too much sun. All this can determine the character of the wine. And wine *lives* in a bottle! Remember that. Why do you think they keep wine for 10, 12 years? Wine lives and matures in the bottle. You take a '70 vintage, drink it now and 10 years from now, and you'll find a real difference. By tasting, you can tell what a wine's potential is.

"German wines? The Rhine wines are medium dry. Mosel is the driest. You can get a damn good German wine in a $2 range. Sweet wines are sold mainly to women. Occasionally you'll sell a port wine to someone who knows how to serve it—with cheese. American wines . . . most are no good. And the ones that are good are so damned high-priced that they're getting more for them than the good high-priced French wines."

Max is interrupted by a phone call; his service is personal. "There's always a Zimmerman in the store." If not Max, then brother Ben or brother Hyman or one of three sons, Jack, Donald or Arnold. "It's on the truck," says Max to the phone. "You want to place another order now? Sure, I'll take care of it. How many cases you want? Four cases, okay . . . take the Calvert's. We have a sale, $7.09 a half gallon. What else? How about some vermouth for those martinis? Four vermouths . . . Okay, buddy, see ya, thanks."

He takes another sip of Jacques Arnoul. "I'm up every morning, traditionally, at 5 o'clock. I'm here at 7:30 opening the door. I'm not a nightclub person;

all I've ever done all my life is work. And I love my business. This I think is the biggest factor why I've been successful—I enjoy being on the floor meeting people."

Once again Max is interrupted, this time by a customer who claims a conflict in the price of wine. Max dons his hat, steps out into the wine aisle and handles himself admirably. A customer's wife claims she can get Pommard somewhere else at a better price. Max smiles knowingly, explaining how there are over 40 Pommard wines, and this one, Pierre Chevalier, is something special—only Max has it. It can't even be sold elsewhere.

The husband is on Max's side, and then he clinches it: "We'll take six bottles." The end? Not quite. Max the Hat adjusts his brim carefully, flashes a Gary cooper smile and goes into some really fancy shooting.

"Now may I sell you one bottle I especially like? This is a 1945 vintage, decanted in 1964." He's got him, her, everybody. Don't ever complain to Max the Hat about a price, or you'll find yourself buying an additional case of something else you never intended to get all the while thanking him for his kind help.

The Zimmerman scene on a late Saturday afternoon is almost bizarre. Where have all these people come from? (All over the city, especially the North Side, and the suburbs.) How can one store possibly move so much booze?

Shopping carts, counters full of wine. More sales of $50 and up. The men in the blue jackets are everywhere in a blur. Max, too, fading into the scene. Look for the hat! Max is at the counter soft-selling a young, blond-bearded man. This customer knows what he wants. Max is just a medium making a record of products and prices, with occasional, almost off-handed, suggestions.

"Give me two gins and two vodkas," says the blond beard.

"That's $10.98 a half gallon [gin] and $6.79 a half gallon of Vodka," says Max. "Why don't you take 3 of each?"

"Okay. "

"Hey Tony!" yells Max, keeping his eyes and ears and hands in control of the whole scene, "bring three cases of that Brazilian wine out here."

The cash registers hum: $42.50, $84.29, $112.37.

Max breaks out a bottle of Spanish brandy for his blond-bearded customer. "This is the only way to drink cognac that's neat," says Max. "Straight with a cognac glass. You hold it in your hand like this, like Winston Churchill used to hold it. Now look at this." Max holds it up to the light. "Look how it clings to the glass."

Max sells the blond beard a bottle of Spanish brandy. He adds that to a flat truck load of booze. A big party, I presume?

"No," says the blond beard. "I like to keep a little stock around . . . people always passing by." Grand total, $203.60. Without a flinch. Another customer, a neat older man, breathes down Max's neck. "What's your best in red table wine? I drink the stuff like water."

"I've got everything," says Max. "How about a case of Spanish burgundy?"

The man nods.

"I got a case of Spanish burgundy coming down here," yells Max to the boys in the backroom. "Bring it out here . . . $43.08, sir."

Max has the basement and second floor of the store stocked with booze.

Max has a warehouse down the street with over 50,000 cases of wine at perfect temperature, and his stock is down because of inventory.

Max has La Fite Rothschild, 1959, for $1,400 a case. A Romanee-Conti Grands Echezeaux, 1955, for $150 a bottle, a collector's item. And La Fite, 1966, for $500 a case: "We sold two cases yesterday." Max once sold $9,000 worth of liquor in a single shot.

"Max, how much you think you might pull in on an average day like today, Saturday, at the Zimmerman corral in Chicago?"

"I'd say today will be maybe a $50,000 day."

Max takes a bead on a stranger wandering aimlessly down a bourboned trail, cuts him off at the pass with a smile, and leads him disarmingly down a winey canyon, his hat fading away into a sunset of Scotch and brandy.

Nik Klein:
The Man Who Made Rocking Horses

They stare at me through the window of the shop at 2934 N. Lincoln as I approach. Horses. Corralled behind a window pane. Pintos, black and white, brown and white. And there's a big fellow in there almost as tall as me, a chestnut beauty.

"Nik Klein . . . Rocking Horses," says the sign on the front window.

But Nik is nowhere in sight. Only these rocking horses in the window staring out at me and the passing scene. A smile . . . my reflection in the window. So simple a thing as a rocking horse does this. Gives a man pause.

You can walk through city streets all day feeling like hell, nobody acknowledging you exist, nobody caring, and then you walk into a window herd of rocking horses, and you suddenly smile.

Chalk one up for a man, Nik Klein, making rocking horses in the midst of all the unpleasantness a city can smother you with. Chalk one up for humanity, still making its steady, quiet move in place. Much like a rocking horse, I would imagine.

A small sign on the front door says to try the upstairs bell, second floor. So I saunter down the long gangway toward the yard, find a door but no bell, and so continue on the trail until off in the distance, along a backyard fence, a string of seven horses studies my approach.

Nik is in the center of the yard, washing the herd down with a hose. He wears a funny little fedora and a long apron. I wave. We smile, shake hands, and try to put together this whole business of a man making rocking horses.

It is an almost impossible conversation at best. Nik speaks hardly any English, and my knowledge of German is confined to those very few words and phrases almost everyone knows. Yet almost any handicap can prove beneficial in the long run. And Nik seems to understand some of my questions and manages to get part of the answer in English before fading into German, and then finally resorting to gestures . . . leading me to one place or another, pointing, making motions, making things understood with his hands.

Nik takes me from the yard through a small work area in the back of the shop and on into the front of the store, which serves as kind of a showroom for those rocking horses that stare out into the street day and night. He gestures for me to look around, while he stands quietly in the background. The silence begins to get you in a room full of rocking horses.

Well, if you've seen one, you've seen them all. Now what? I try to figure my next move in this frozen ambush of 20 or 30 rocking horses of various sizes with flared nostrils, open mouths, and painted white teeth too pretty to bite. I walk up to the big chestnut beauty I had seen before through the window. A man-size rocking horse!

"Who the hell is this for?" I try to ask Nik. "A grown man? Someone like me? Do grown men come in and buy rocking horses for themselves?" I have visions of a captain of industry on Michigan Avenue riding a big rocking horse in his plush office. But Nik doesn't understand, so I let it pass and rest content with my illusion that maybe a man is never too old for a rocking horse.

I notice myself looking into the horse's eyes and petting his long neck. Nik's rocking horses do strange things to a man. I would like to tell him about this too, but I realize that I'm even more than just lost for words. I'm plain lost. What else is there to say about an old man who makes rocking horses except that I'm delighted to know that such an artist exists in Chicago and that he deserves a citizen's award of some sort in the Civic Center. The particulars are easy enough to get at. Nikolaus Klein, age 77, came to America in 1952 from Stuttgart, Germany. He started making rocking horses over there just a few years before he came here. He was a harness maker before that. These things I'm able to pull out of him with a few words and gestures.

The prices? They start at $85 for a small one, and go as high as $400 for that big baby over there that I'd like to have and keep in my living room merely as a conversation piece. Once in a while I'd let kids try it out. But most of the time I'd just let it stare out the window at the people who pass.

"They're beautiful," I tell him. And Nik smiles. He knows they're beautiful, or why would he have been putting so much of himself in them for over twenty years?

"You ought to have a show," I tell him. "If contemporary museums of modern art can exhibit junk sculpture and even hire an artist to wrap up a building as a work of art, then certainly there must be a museum of a gallery ready for rocking horse art." He doesn't understand that either.

"Who buys them, Nik? buys . . . money. Do people just come in off the street and buy a $235 handmade rocking horse with a genuine leather saddle just like that? Buys . . . who?"

"Stores," he says. "Marshall Field's . . . but no this year. Other times."

"Other stores?"

"Oh, other stores . . . New York, California . . . privates . . . "

"Privates?"

"Peoples."

"You mean regular people. Private parties."

"Yes, privates."

"But how do they know about you, Nik? How do people from different parts of the country know that there's a neat old man in Chicago making rocking horses by hand?"

Nik smiles. He doesn't understand the question.

I smile. And go up and pet my $400 rocking horse again . . . "Nice horsey."

Silence in the stable while I make my rounds to the other horses, chucking them under the chin, brushing their manes, setting them off on their rocking runs.

"What do you think about plastic horses, Nik? Plastic horses on chrome stands with spring action? Or those monstrous electric horses that go up and down and around and around about five times for a dime in shopping plazas? Any good?"

Nik smiles. I try again.

"Plastic? Bounce, bounce, bounce, springs? Good? No Good? Plastic?"

"No, no plastic. Wood. Real Hide. All handmade, see?" He gestures as if he's stitching something together, sawing wood, carving wood, hammering nails. "No plastic. This mine. Me handmade."

"How do you make a rocking horse, Nik? Where do you begin?"

"How?"

"Make horse, how? Start with head? Head first? Saw? Carve? Legs?

95

Hide? Where begin?" I pull out all stops with my gestures waving my arms in the air, hammering, stitching, pointing to my leg, his head, and finally the body of a nearby rocking horse.

He gestures for me to follow him, and so I do, into the garage where I am quickly overwhelmed by the smell of genuine hides, some stacked in piles, others soaking in a barrel.

How do you make a real rocking horse? You start with a real hide, of course. but I'm still concerned as to the inner flesh and bones of the critters.

"What next? What else? Head, body, how?"

And so we go from the garage, through the backyard pasture with the line of clean rocking horses grazing along the fence, and then up one, two, three flights of stairs. We come to an attic door with a padlock on it. Nik opens the door, and we walk about 20 feet into the long dark attic until he reaches around in the darkness, in the center of things, and pulls on a light bulb.

Horses! Dead and alive! In various parts of completion. A veritable parts factory for rocking horses. Some without eyes. Over there, about 50 heads. The basic design in wood. Some a little more shaped and painted with nostrils, teeth, and eyes. Over here, maybe another twenty creatures, just the beginning carpentry of the grand design . . . the anatomy of a wooden horse, a 2 by 4 for a backbone, a plywood neck, carved forelegs, a hank of hair . . . a skeletal wonder awaiting flesh. On one side of me, a pile of tails. On the other, a bundle of manes.

"Real?" I ask Nik.

"Is all real . . . hide, tail, hair."

A little beyond the center of the attic under the slanted roof tops where final stages, the frames now fleshed out, formed in burlap, stuffed with wood shavings and sawdust. And at the very front of the attic, near the only window, somber ranks of another fifty, complete but for a saddle and their runners for rocking.

It's an eerie sensation, a scene mostly of deep shadows, refracted light, strange shapes. The lair of the rocking horse maker. A dry old attic under slanted roof tops where real rocking horses come to be. Those open painted mouths. Those teeth, those eyes fixed to such infinite horizons. Prancing motion arrested for the time being, destined to move someday only in the mind of the rider.

The real question. Why? Why does a man make rocking horses? Nik could never answer that.

"Did you have a rocking horse when you were a child?" I ask and gesture for size, pointing to him and a nearby horse.

The old man laughs, points to himself, and says, in effect, "Me? No, no," as if he never had time for such foolishness as a child.

But that explains a good deal, and gives reasons to his work, his art. Hasn't the artist always been a child at heart? The man intent on creating something he never possessed or fully comprehends?

So I leave the maker of rocking horses to his own silent landscape, his own secret source, and slowly descend the steps.

Wasn't there the mystery of D.H. Lawrence's "The Rocking Horse Winner," who won but lost? Wasn't there a song about a rocking horse that ran away? Haven't toys from the beginning of time always taken men out of themselves for the instant and placed them in pure pastures of pleasure? The rocking horse knows the way.

Didn't I have one named Tony, stabled under the kitchen table, and didn't I ride? Didn't I buy a rocking horse for my children, and. . . . "

No! They've never had one! How could I have been so thoughtless, so negligent as a father? Everything but a rocking horse!

Maybe the boy's too big already, but maybe the girl can still squeeze in under the age of rocking horse riders. But even if they are too big, what an heirloom, what a family treasure to pass down from one generation to another. A real rocking horse made by Nik Klein! It should last forever.

I can see my future grandson one day explaining to his friends as they look 'way up at that chestnut beauty of a real rocking horse. "This is my grandpa's old rocking horse. He bought it when he was over 30 years old. Hello, Grandpa, can I have a ride?"

"Hold your horses, son. Just hold your horses."

Travels with Royko
or The Kid Who Scattered Pigeons

Mike Royko, the hottest newspaper columnist in town, has been called many things. Fire Commissioner Quinn calls him a Muckraker. The boys at City Hall call him a dirty liar. The crime syndicate bosses say he is a gentleman. Even his mother has been heard to say he's a bad boy. In his defense, Chicagoland has decided now is the time for all good editors to come to the aid of their compatriot. Here—if there is such a person—is the real Royko.

And so we start slowly, in daylight yet in dark, at the Billy Goat Inn, a kind of underground taverna. The heavy red door with the invitation (challenge?)—"Butt Inn, Billy Goat." A more symbolic place to find Mike Royko? A more "neighborly" restaurant, considering the quality of life and restaurants above—high-rises continually sprouting with blueprint parkways, people, and restaurants?

In the Billy Goat we get down to earth again. Down to good conversation and coffee and drink. Down to elevator starters, doormen, drivers, pressmen, and reporters. Down to *Up Against It*—Royko, who is already seated at a back table with Billy Goat Sianis himself.

Royko does not look like Royko. He must be someone else. Royko is dressed like Many-Man from above (slick black-frame glasses, adman suit, regulation shirt and tie) on the way up, watching the floor, anticipating the next level.

But it is all a disguise. The photo in the column and the man in the Billy Goat are two different people—"I like that photo," he says. "I'm seldom recognized." The adman costume and the real man are only distant relatives. Royko becomes an individual aware of heights in buildings and people. A neighborhood man, feet on the ground, who feels it isn't an especially true or natural view from way up there.

So to his office in the *Daily News*, his corner of the city room overlooking the Wrigley building, the river, the bridge, the lake. Royko puts his back to the view, faces the action of the room, answers the phone (a tip about some gypsies moving into Old Town), and seems anxious to get out into the street.

His office library reflects little about Royko except a newspaperman's interest in facts, and a compassionate concern for the setting he has inherited: Kogan and Wendt's *Chicago, a Pictorial History,* and Ade's *Chicago Sketches* stand out.

Preparing to leave, to head first for the Park district where arrangements for the First Annual Mongrel Dog Show are to be checked, and then to his old neighborhood, I point to the Italian destroyer, the *San Giorgio,* docked at the Michigan Avenue bridge, and suggest many stories (all romantic) that must be found there. Today the girls, the women, would be there again, waiting, waving to their men of the sea. Would Royko write about it, I wondered? "What gets me," he said, "is the Italian navy. What the hell is the Italian navy?" Pow! The Royko cut. And true. So very true. Precisely the kind of angle Royko, a man on the ground, would see, while every other newspaper in Chicago would play up romance and the *San Giorgio.* And I should have known. After all, didn't he write "The Young Man and the Sea"?

In transit, now, on East Lake Street, bending around the Prudential building, coming to a stop at Randolph, his route temporarily upset by a portable sign warning "NO LEFT TURN Except C.T.A. Buses & Taxi Cabs." This sign upsets him because sometimes it's there and sometimes it isn't. It wasn't there yesterday. He uses the same route whenever he takes the Drive south, and the damn sign makes less and less sense. It seems almost unnecessary. Besides, to obey it could mean going around in right turns for hours. Royko takes a left.

In three or four minutes he is pulled to the side of Lake Shore Drive and forced to answer the inevitable, "Didn't you see the . . . ?" Yes, Royko saw it, but he doesn't understand the game. And what's more, he is tired of playing "Now you see it, now you don't." He is a reporter, he explains, on a story.

And he will be saved, I feel. Show him, Mike. Show him who you are. Flash your press card or something. Say you're the *Daily News.* Say at least, "I'm Mike Royko!" But he doesn't. He plays it Citizen Chicago all the way.

The cop, agreeing that the sign does move (will, in fact, be removed at 10:30—5 more minutes), asks for the driver's license, and Royko turns it over. Now, I think; now you'll see. Wait till you read that name!

Nothing. Nothing. This cop does not read the *Daily News.* He is a conversation dropout, or else he plays it smart and never lets on. In the end, Royko is glad the cop did not recognize him. "It's better this way. It would have put him in a tough spot."

So Royko gets the ticket and is just a little bit angry. But it's not the ticket, it's the kind of violation, the illogical aspect of it. "Look at the headlines . . . 3 NEW ATTACKS IN EL STATIONS. That's where he's needed. Not here."

Another column, I think.

A week later, in one of his letter columns, I see the fruits of a ticket for a

NO LEFT TURN . . . "As a matter of fact, yes," he answers a reader concerned about police protection. "You must understand that many policemen are busy meeting their ticket quotas. This provides the city administration with millions of dollars in revenue. If every policeman who is assigned to giving tickets for non-dangerous violations were switched to subway and elevated duty, you could safely ride a train at midnight with your arms full of gold bars." Royko down to earth again. Swinging. A home run.

He remains a neighborhood kid from the Northwest Side, and like most neighborhood kids, he cannot forget those years; he will never forget that time, that sense of proportion where boundaries are invisible but respected, where manhood is determined by how long a ball you can hit, how loud you can holler, and, in time, how well you can hold your beer.

Royko and Chicago. The Northwest Side. Royko—his real name—part Polish, with a questionable touch of either Ukrainian or Hungarian. These were his neighborhoods:

Damen and Thomas. Where the Urban Grocery & Meat Market still stands: "Your Taste Will Tell Urban Sausage Is the Best." "That's where I go for all my homemade Polish sausage," he confesses. 2012 W. Thomas, Royko's house at one time. FOR SALE, the sign reads now.

A neighborhood. The kind of neighborhood where catalpa trees (of Indian cigars) and locust trees (of coffee beans) still grow (dirty trees, suburbia says). Where the front porches are wooden and usually painted grey (sometimes with holes bored into the steps to drain off the rain water); with fancy iron railings (painted silver) and wooden front doors painted ochre or black (so the dirt won't show); of knee-high, iron rail fences (some fancy; most, plain pipe painted green or black) bordering tiny but healthy green lawns. Of houses commonly distinctive, windows shining, curtains crisp, brick facades painted red, the stone sills and decorations highlighted in white. "Look at the paint job on that one. Look at the work he put into it. And the garden in front. The flowers. You don't see this kind of thing in suburbia. There are no trees there. And this neighborhood is in trouble. It's a shame."

The old people have left, most of them. The new generation has abandoned the walks, the alleys, the prairies. The owners live "somewhere else"—the first step to a broken neighborhood. The Puerto Ricans do not have the money to buy the houses, to stave off the coming high-rises. Says Royko, "You can't put people in high-rises. High-rises don't solve anything. The self-contained neighborhood is what we need."

And the neighborhood is Division and Wolcott. Another house, Wolcott and Potomac, where his parents owned a cleaning store. Where Max's tavern sat on the corner and sold beer by the bucket. A house, a building, an entire way of life in ruins. "When I lived in this neighborhood, all the old men had mustaches and looked like Joe Stalin."

And the neighborhood is Wicker Park. "Just look at the park. One of the most beautiful little neighborhood parks in the city. And where are the kids? Hardly any kids here anymore." Wicker Park. A patch of green peace—baseball, basketball, benches, picnic tables, and old men undisturbed by the sudden flight of flocks of sparrows and pigeons. Horseshoes, swings, concrete fountains, and a pool with a sprinkler, enjoyed now by one sun-kissed Puerto Rican child.

Across the street, a prairie wild in weed, and the inevitable El tracks (indigenous backdrop of so much Chicago fiction) breaking up the sun into shadows and strips of light.

And the neighborhood is Armitage and Point. All his neighborhoods, always hugging that life-line of Northwest Chicago: Milwaukee Avenue, a kind of Polish Michigan Avenue, where produce and flowers are still sold on the walks. "This is what I call a neighborhood. A grocery store, a gas station, a cleaners, a tavern," he points them out.

We stop at the tavern, no longer owned by the family Royko remembered, but still inhabited by Royko people: a bartender who knows when to listen and when to talk, a customer in wilted white tee shirt, another in tattoos.

Royko handles Christian Brothers like an old convert. Who is Slats Grobnik? I ask. "I knew a Slats Grobnik. This neighborhood is full of Slats Grobniks. Two of them are at the bar."

McLuhan would say you're looking at the present through a rear-view mirror, I suggest. "No," he says at first. Then, "Yes, maybe so. In principle I oppose expressways, but when I need them, I'm glad they're there. But I'm for the self-contained neighborhood, the gas station, the tavern, the store, the empty lot. I guess I'm even for the neighborhood school."

In time, we leave the tavern. Royko points ecstatically across the street: "That was the biggest prairie in Chicago. They shrunk it!" And passing the red fortress of Soloman Chase School (his grammar school), he leans over the iron fence, stares at the broken asphalt playground, "What the hell do they have to pave everything for? You know, I once hit a home run that flew across the street and scattered the pigeons in the loft at the back of the house . . . the pigeon loft's gone."

We are back in the car, and Royko is talking about short streets in a neighborhood. The variety. The crazy patterns. Streets and alleys jutting into each other at odd angles or NO OUTLETS. Chanay Street, almost half a block long. Unexpected turns (bends) like Francis Place. Imaginative streets where grown men may get lost, but kids find direction.

The neighborhood is changing. "The times they are a-changin'." "What was once a Polish drugstore is now Hernando's Tacos, or something."

Off now to another part of Chicago. With the old neighborhood at our backs, we merge with the momentum and madness of expressways. The talk too is suddenly faster and fractured: the column, the reactions, the excitement of writing. Where is it?

"Hitting a good idea and having it come easy, one paragraph after another, just the way you want. It maybe happens once a year."

He doesn't really write the first time, just let's go—no organization or spelling or structure. "Just get it down. Then write it, penciling in the extras. Then rewrite it one or two more times till I get it what I want it to be." His own deadline, 7 o'clock the night before. Theoretically, he has as late as 6:30 a.m.

He likes a feeling of competition. When he first started the column, he felt a strong competition with Mabley. "I was unknown. Writing under the gun. I like it that way."

As for form, "Whatever tells it best." He tries to avoid it. "You can't write a daily column and sustain a style. Buchwald is a good example. He's backed himself into a corner."

Is it sometimes hard to find humor in a difficult situation? "Yes. I sometimes use humor as an outlet. Work it off. I was awfully mad at Selma, for example. Awfully scared, being followed by a tribe of rednecks. Later I did a piece on it in a chillingly funny way."

About that punch line at the end of each column. Deliberate? "Always end with a sentence to bring them back tomorrow."

Has he ever read *Miss Lonelyhearts*? Has he ever felt that way? "Sometimes, as a matter of fact, I've thought exactly like that. I get mail where I can't possibly do anything for them. Maybe jump out the window in a sense of protest. I couldn't do that type of column regularly. People with so many awful problems."

The story is the key to his choice of subject. "Is it a good story?" He doesn't feel he's a man with a mission. He doesn't feel obligated to stand up for every underdog. There are limits to what he feels he can handle well in a column, to what he believes in. "I wouldn't go to bat for any little man who's pushing hardcore pornography, then gets busted by the cops and yells censorship. I'm a liberal. I read Baldwin's *Another Country* and I stood up for it because I thought it was a good book."

Reactions to the column? His readers? "A good range. I get mail from saloon customers, neighborhood people, suburban kids. My own interests are wide, so I'm bound to hit a lot of people. I'm agreed with more than disagreed with. Some say they like forty per cent of what I say and tolerate the rest of me."

Mayor Daley? "He just glares at me."

Quinn? "Quinn hates my guts, and I can't blame him. If anybody wrote about me the way I write about Quinn, I'd hate his guts too."

The mail ran 3-to-1 in Royko's favor during the Howard Miller melee. "Miller's supporters were the kind of people who said things like, 'You would be a better person if you would wave the flag once in a while.' His devoted following, I would gather, is very stupid."

Lunch time. Southwest of the Loop. Royko explaining, "I never eat inside the El tracks. The food is bad and expensive. Service is lousy." So it's Gennaro's on Taylor Street. Another neighborhood, Italian, now going urban renewal. Gennaro's, a Royko 5 ***** star restaurant, where food and family are one, and the red wine provokes warmth and conversation that can only be called homemade.

Royko in the spotlight. A columnist, an author, a man with a following. Royko with a taste of power. How does it feel? Is he a leader?

"I doubt that I am. I don't think I could alter the outcome of an election for dog catcher. I possibly have some influence . . . but the cop gave me a ticket, didn't he?"

As for constant praise and recognition, "I have my own standards. Nothing that anyone says about a column is going to change my way of thinking. What's important is that it satisfies me."

Pour the wine to that.

Success. In Mauldin's warm and wise introduction to *Up Against It*, he speaks like a man who has experienced the danger of success and ends with an almost Roykian touch on the subject of corruption. Is Royko prepared for big success? Is he corruptible?

"I love success. The money end of it is just great. Success means I can eat at Gennaro's as often as I want to. I love not having to worry about money. I just like being able to have a beer when I want it. Freedom. Having enough dough to live on. I haven't changed. I live the same way I lived ten years ago except that I have a lot more money. Success to me is knowing John Gennaro, where I did not know him before. Being able to sit down and drink and shoot the breeze with Algren and Studs. That's the real benefit of fame."

We drink to that.

Reaching now for talk even closer to home. Chicago itself. Chicago today. Is it a good place to live? An exciting time? "Yes, I think so. I haven't the slightest idea of what's going to happen to it. The city will get as good as it can within the limits of its political structure. This city can move fast. I would guess that if any lake can be saved, it will be this one. There's a respect for opinion in this city. Chicago represents the right to stand up and blow off at the mouth!"

Mayor Daley, again. Always good for a laugh, no? "Nothing is as good at public works than a dictatorship. And that's what we've got. That's great. He's ineffective as far as human relations are concerned. He's a follower like all politicians. He reacts. He responds. But the more I see of him, in terms of public works projects, he is effective. A fantastic public works man."

Religion. (Religion? Must be the wine.) "I like religion. All religions. I think they're the marijuana of the masses."

Cody. He carries a hell of a lot of weight in this city, doesn't he? "The Dick Daley of the Catholics. He's good at getting what he wants."

Chicago and style. New York and style. Is there such a thing as a Chicago style? "Lack of style is the Chicago style. Look how important style is to Lindsay. That guy breathes style. He's always leaping around the place. And here in Chicago we have a little fat guy mayor who couldn't pass Speech I. In New York you have style. In Daley, lack of style is the dramatic and startling thing. New York worries about style."

Talk of New York makes him mad. He continues: "Take authors. I read *In Cold Blood*. I don't know that Capote really warrants the national adulation. I don't really know it [*In Cold Blood*] warranted the tremendous publicity it got. I really think New York's a bum influence. Who needs it? No, I wouldn't go there. They offered me a TV job doing my column. We didn't even get to the negotiating stages. I said, no. I don't feel I have to go to New York to do what I want to do.

"Look at Nelson. Anybody who tells me that Truman Capote is a better writer than Algren is mad! Algren is a better human being, a better man. Algren is happy in Chicago. He's happy playing poker here. I'm happy here. I can write just the same here. Besides, there aren't as many rubes from Iowa in Chicago as there are in New York. This is a Chicagoan's city. Chicago doesn't care about New York.

"I was at a party once, and some New Yorker asked me about this second city business. I represented the smelly arm pit, I guess. So I told him I don't give a damn about New York. He couldn't believe this. People in Chicago aren't interested in New York! Guys here think about their mortgages, their jobs, their hemorrhoids. They don't give a damn about New York. This is not a second city!"

In the end we return to the beginning, the Billy Goat. And Royko is off to find out what he can about that gypsy invasion of Old Town. Royko is off to scatter more pigeons.

But not yet. Not before the parting shot, the Royko punch line.

"Say," he stops me momentarily. "I've always wanted to be able to ask this: 'You're not going to write me up, are you?'"

105

Riverview—

A merry-go-round horse peeks from under a

canvas cover as dismantling begins at River-

view Park.

The Bare

The water has been drained from the pond into

which the Chutes carried fun-seekers.

Bones

Are

Autumn's leaves tumble along the

ghost town amusement park streets.

Showing

Aladdin seems to be taking a farewell

look over his domain.

Paint My Body, Color Your Mind

It is a day to investigate once again the unsung pleasures of my city. A day of sun and sky and pleasant temperatures, and though Chicago is never quite ready for reform, it is periodically quite ripe for investigation. It's a city made for the poetic eye. Look. Seek and you shall find. Everything. In Chicago.

It is a day when the attractions of the "I will" city cry out again for interpretation. A day of Gary Steelmill Sun and Commonwealth Edison Sky which—despite the sulphur dioxide level .9, carbon monoxide, 7 ppm, ozone .004 ppm—give a poet's tired feet and bad heart a moment of pause and reflection . . . *under the smoke, dust all over his mouth, laughing with white teeth. . . .*

It's a city made for rose-colored glasses. I polish mine against my coat sleeve and put them on to face the day and look where I am going. Seek and you shall find everything—no matter how dark or foreboding. Walk softly and carry a rolled newspaper, just in case.

I bite my fingernails, check the poetic license in my breast pocket, and saunter down Sandburg territory, the North Side.

They tell me you are wicked and I believe them, for I have seen your painted women under the gas lamps luring the farm boys. . . .

An Undesirable Character approaches me on Lincoln Ave., weaving into my investigatory path. Poetic-rhetorical decision: roll my morning newspaper into a tighter weapon? Bite my fingernails with a hangnail of fear?

A sleuth's solution: hide behind the front page, chew my fingernails, and check the weather report . . . partly cloudy with a high in the mid-60s. . . . Check details on page 118. I flip to Amusements by mistake: COMPLETELY NUDE, EXCITING YOUNG WOMEN . . . MANICURES . . . BODY PAINTING . . . TIFFANY'S, 2512 N. Lincoln. . . .

If you look hard enough or hide long enough, answers of all sorts will be revealed to you on the streets of Chicago. I peer over the top of the page and discover my potential assailant has disappeared. I succor a bloody hangnail and hotfoot it over to TIFFANY'S to have my fingers looked at, to investigate the newsy nudity of manicure parlors in the city of the big shoulders.

I first check the windows through my rose-colored glasses and see only what appears to be a Mercurochrome void. Ah, I have it: a false front operation. The door, however, is open a crack so I cast a mean glance inside just to document the possibility of a body around, COMPLETELY NUDE or not.

I angle one foot inside, and find myself sinking fast and softly into quicksand carpeting. The place is done up right: a kind of contemporary beauty parlor modern. Everything seems black and white and shiny enough to slip right out of your hands—desk, lamp, telephone. It looks like another ephemeral business enterprise to which Chicago is prone, with its Old Towns and Up Towns and New Towns . . . places with infinite possibilities and short histories.

From out of a hidden doorway comes a long tall dude stepping suddenly into the scene. I reach immediately inside my coat pocket for my piece but grab my poetic license instead and a spiral notebook of free verse. Even worse, I jab my sore, hangnailed finger into the sharp point of my Dixon Ticonderoga #2 Soft pencil and react immediately in pain by putting my finger in my mouth to stop the blood.

"Can I help you?" he says.

I show him my finger. He seems to understand and leads me quietly to the desk, like one of the walking wounded you see up and down the old streets of Chicago.

"Would you like to take your glasses off?" he smiles.

"It won't help. My eyes hurt, too. I can't stand to see things in real light."

"Certainly. Now would you like the manicure for 15 minutes and $15, or the body painting for 20 minutes and $20?"

I check the ad in the paper again to see if I'm in the right place. The price of service is not mentioned, of course. Chicago knows better than to show its hand.

"Pardon me," I turn around to check by billfold. I have $20 in five spots. That's it. And my finger is hurting, and this guy is intimidating me by his very size. It's the old vise game. What's more, I have the sneaking suspicion that if I don't go at least for the manicure, I may walk out with less than ten fingers.

I flip him three 5's with a disgusted "Here," and instinctively move to soften my approach. "Weather's kind of strange out there today. There's a high pressure area situated over Butte, Montana . . . partly cloudy . . . but it all looks like a rosy little picture to me."

"Um," he replies. He's not interested in weather reports. He writes something down and hands me a ticket like a beer chip at a fireman's picnic. Then the phone rings and he answers with the authority of the desk man at the Ambassador East, plus all smiles and courtesies. I watch him record a name in his appointment book for a few hours from now . . . S-m-i-t-h. A good name.

While he's still talking on the phone, real professional like, he waves a hand toward that mysterious doorway and in steps an EXCITING YOUNG WOMAN who has been chosen to give my fingers a professional job.

I don't know how EXCITING she is yet, but she's dark haired and pretty and looks as if she's in need of some rest . . . about two weeks sleep would do it.

She puts her hand out for my ticket, and I press it into the sweaty little palm of her hand like a kid going to a matinee movie. "This way," she says.

"Let me tell you about this finger," I try to spark a conversation. But she won't listen, so I keep following. We pass through a sort of waiting room where there are no customers but plenty of Exciting Young Women just lounging around, fixing their nails, and staring at themselves in mirrors.

I give them a poetic wave of the hand and my best investigative Chicago nod, but they don't buy any of it. Hard women. They just seem bored as hell in their own little glass menagerie, waiting for some gentlemen callers.

My Exciting Young Woman opens a door into a small room that seems to be painted mostly black with a touch of white here and there. A deep rug, an easy chair, something like a hassock, and a tiny table full of bottles and junk with a lamp hanging down makes up the whole setting. She leads me to the easy chair and then closes the door.

I try to whip out my spiral notebook behind her back and capture a few images, but she's too fast for me. Besides, I have a feeling that I am in a scene for the moment that is totally anti-investigatory. To put it bluntly, she (or her friend at the main desk) just might do unnatural things to me and my notebook. They're not used to poets on the premises. Poets cannot afford manicures. And I cannot afford to blow my cover-up operation.

"Hi," she says, leaning into the closed door.

"Hi," I reply. "I'm Carl Sandburg. You probably never heard of me before."

"Nope," she answers, edging her way toward the hassock. On the back of the door I discover another sign of the times, a revelation of the Chicago Fine Art of Con: TIPPING IS CUSTOMARY.

"Alright," she says, without a smile on her face or a hint of happiness in her work. "I'll explain the rules."

"Rules, Ma'am? I didn't come to play bingo or write a sonnet."

"I undress completely, but there's no touching beneath the waist. Remember that. Did you come for a manicure or a body painting?"

"Well, you see, I've got this bad finger here plus all these other ones I keep nibbling on. . . . "

"OK. You have fifteen minutes."

"For what?"

She smiles and proceeds to tell me what else a body can do with itself while she's disrobing, dismantling . . . if a body cared to.

I peer over Seattle, where it's 56 and raining, flip up my rose-colored glasses momentarily, and discover before me a thin, pale, Chicago Venus perched upon a hassock.

I could write a poem about you this way, I think. Vulnerable and sad. Instead, I reset my glasses and go into my man-about-town routine.

"I can see all there is to see. Is this all I get for fifteen bucks?"

"I'm afraid that's all. And a manicure."

So I thrust my right hand out and say, "Exciting Young Woman, do your stuff. Take care now, these are sensitive fingers. The hands of a surgeon, I've been told."

"Are you a doctor?"

"No, a sleuth."

"What's that?"

"Someone always looking for inspiration."

"You're not law and order are you?"

"That is a beautiful question. No, whatever gave you that idea? Listen, are you sure this is all I get for my money?"

"That's all, baby. Some of the girls gave a little too much and lost their jobs a few days ago."

"And you don't care to join the ranks of the unemployed, right?"

"Right. What did you do to your finger here?"

"That's a hangnail. Haven't you ever seen a hangnail before?"

"Oh yeah."

"OUCH! Gentle, gentle, please." But my Exciting Young Woman keeps bearing down on my nails with something like a screwdriver, just picking and jabbing away, drawing mostly pain and blood.

"How long you been manicuring for a living?"

"Just a few days."

"Don't you have to be certified or something?"

"Nope. All you need is the tools and a small room. Don't you want to do anything else?"

"Not unless I can do what you say I can't do. I'd like to check the rest of the weather map, though."

She smiles.

"Look at this. There's a moonrise at 6:05 p.m. today. Ever seen a moonrise over Lake Michigan?"

"Nope."

"Exciting Young Woman, where's all the poetry in you? There's just a few natural beautiful things left to investigate in Chicago. One of them's a moonrise, and the other is a sunrise over the lake. And let's see . . . haze today: 48 coefficient of haze per 1,000 linear feet (COH). Normal reading is .75 . . . so unless things change by late this afternoon, Chicago's good for mooning tonight."

"You want to paint me?"

"Paint you? How? With what? Why?"

"Here's some brushes and some paint over here. Twenty dollars. Give me your other hand."

"You mean guys really come in here and just . . . OUCH! That's enough! You mean just paint you up?"

"Yeah, I been painted twice today already. Yesterday I was painted ten times."

"Tell me, where do they begin?"

"Sometimes they try to paint. . . ."

"No? It's a strange life, isn't it?"

"You want to try it?"

"No. I'm just a paint-by-number man myself. Does it tickle? What does is feel like?"

"Oh, nothing."

"What do they paint on you?"

"All kinds of crazy things. Mostly just a bunch of shit."

"Like what? Ever get any real talent in here? A Chicago Rembrandt or something?"

"Most of them can't paint. One guy painted me all over with birds and flowers."

"That was nice."

"Another guy painted me full of dirty sayings in foreign languages, front and back. I never knew what they meant."

"Incredible. Chicago and suburbs would be surprised to know how many frustrated artists walk these streets just looking for an opportunity to bare their souls."

"That same guy painted the Ten Commandments up and down my legs."

"Exciting Young Woman, are you pulling my leg? The Ten Commandments! All up and down those pretty little legs of yours? I don't care to discover anymore. That revelation alone puts chills up and down my spine. How much is the 'customary tip'? I must be off."

"Your time's not up."

"Exciting Young Woman, a time comes in a sleuth's life when there's nothing left to look for. You've seen and heard it all. You've got everything right here in your hands. What's a fair tip?"

"Most men tip about $10."

"I'm not most men. And it's not fair. A five's all I've got. But if I could, I'd give you ten or even fifteen. Not just because I feel sorry for you. You and me and Chicago and street people in general are above all that. Truthfully, my heart goes out for the guy who has to come in here and paint the Ten Commandments on your body. There are some things even a poet doesn't care to discover in his own city. Some things, exciting, bizarre as they may be for some people, that make no sense at all to investigate and might best be kept in the dark for those creatures who must make their way in the night. Not to deny them this, but to understand their needs. . . . "

"I don't know what you're talking about."

"Get yourself some rose-colored glasses, woman. Check the moon tonight. You know what you need? A good sunburn. Look here, it's 79 in Albuquerque, 85 in Miami . . . can you imagine how bright it might be in Greece tomorrow? Yet, as dark as it may seem here, you're probably all the necessary warmth and inspiration some men may need."

"Are you through, Mister?"

And having answered so, I turn once more to those who sneer at this my city, and I give them back the sneer and say to them:

Come and show me another city with lifted head singing so proud to be alive and coarse and strong and cunning.

Hoke Norris
and the Quiet Night of the Soul

So what's he like?

Who?

Hoke Norris.

He's a nice guy.

What the hell does that mean?

Woman, you will drive a good man mad. Get me a beer.

Everybody you meet is a nice guy. Is Hoke his real name?

Yes. Southern. Used as both a first name and last name. He said his grand-
father called his first son Hoke.

So what about him? Don't you have any facts?

Damn it, woman, facts don't interest me. You know that by now. Facts do
not make Hoke Norris or anybody else. So he was born and raised in North Car-
olina. So he has a Bachelor's degree from Wake Forest College, Graduate stud-
ies—University of North Carolina, Harvard (Nieman Fellow), and University of
Chicago (Ford Foundation Fellowship). So he has worked on newspapers and
for Associated Press before joining the staff of the *Sun-Times* in 1955 and its
literary critic since 1958. So? So? So what?

So, that's something.

That's nothing. That's not Hoke.

What's he look like?

Kind of a middle-aged Huck Finn.

So is that Hoke Norris, a middle-aged Huck Finn up North?

No, but that's a beginning.

He's quiet. Very quiet. Almost anonymously quiet. That's what I mean
about a nice guy . . . a quiet guy . . . a good guy. Even the Burns body guard in
the lobby of the *Sun-Times* didn't know who Hoke was. "Who?" he said.
"Hoke?" If I had said Kup, he would have probably stopped the presses. And he
couldn't even get him on the house phone. Took him ten minutes to find the
right number. That's anonymity. When I found his office, it wasn't an office at
all. A closet, a cell with a solid wooden door that said "Book Week." No glass.

113

No name. And the strange thing is, when we were leaving the building, and I was trying to break the ice, and I asked him about Herman Kogan and if Kogan wasn't playing a kind of behind the scenes role as the new editor of *Book Week* and wouldn't he maybe begin writing a column of his own soon and Hoke said, "He hasn't shown any interest in it so far. But you can't keep a writer anonymous very long. A writer gets damn tired of anonymity." And he was talking about Kogan, but I was thinking about Hoke.

So he's humble. Arthur Godfrey's humble, but what's Norris like?

I'm getting to that, I'm getting to that. He published a novel in 1956, *All The Kingdoms Of Earth*. A very nice novel, a very good novel . . .

You mean like Hoke?

Yes, of course. Now you're catching on . . . a very little novel, a very quiet novel like *Maud Martha*. A novel that just does its stuff to you, and when you're finished it stays with you and maybe changes you in very small ways. The kind of novel nobody writes any more. The kind that New York publishers can't afford to print.

No sex?

Quiet sex. It's about the South. It's about a couple of generations of poor Negroes who live in a place called Crooked Creek. It's about their living and their dying and, as Hoke says, "It showed some of the sources and resources of the Negro people. They do have a remarkable record of survival . . . to develop their own philosophy, their own wit; to have survived in a period when survival was their greatest problem." He started the book at Harvard. "It was the outgrowth of two things: a creative writing course taught by Ted Morrison and a philosophy course where he studied Job. It seemed to me Job was full of themes." How did it sell? "2,500 copies. Enough to cover the advance." It was well received. "A pretty good critical reception. Oddly enough a fellow from North Carolina reviewed it for the *New York Times* and didn't like it. But just the other day I heard from the Syracuse Public Library that they had listed it as one of the fifty best books. It's still in print." Oh yes, I said it was about poor Negroes. But Hoke said, "It doesn't apply to Negroes only. Anyone calling for help."

That's Job.

That's Hoke. Get me another beer. Things are beginning to clear up. His father was a Southern Baptist preacher.

What does that mean?

I don't know. Just thought I'd throw it in. But it means a hell of a lot, I'm sure. There's this great preacher in his book, Preacher Prescott, who is faced with the moral dilemma of preaching a funeral service for a bad man. He tries in vain to find someone who can remember something good about this man. In the end, he handles the service in such a neat way and still saves his own soul. "Brothers and Sisters," he said, "you knowed Charlie. I knowed Charlie. Let's bury him." I asked him how he thought the book might be received today. "I suppose there are Negroes who would call Preacher Prescott an Uncle Tom. He would not condone violence. But you do not have to accept everything."

What else has he written?

We Dissent, non-fiction. And short stories. A lot of them. *Take Her Up Tenderly,* from Prairie Schooner, was his first story and was reprinted in Foley's *Best American Short Stories* 1950.

That's good.

Yes, but I'll get back to that later. The South. You know why he left the South?

"To take a better job."

Well, some people are interested in working.

Very subtle, but that's not the point. A man writes a novel twelve years ago and something happens, and nothing happens. Maybe he writes a few more or is still writing them. I'm talking about a writer here and a heritage. I'm talking about silence, about not giving up and, and, and all kinds of things I can't possibly discuss on two beers. "I go back about once a year," he says. Has it changed? "Of course the South had further to go but it's moved further than the North has. Then, fifteen years ago you would say it was impossible for the things to happen that have happened—desegregation in schools, eating places, public halls—things that I thought wouldn't happen for a very long time. Of course, it would not have happened if the Negro hadn't become militant in his approach. Nothing would have happened if someone hadn't done something to push." It sounds like the place where a born Southerner, a writer, would want to be now, doesn't it? He said in his introduction to *We Dissent,* "It is easy, and tempting, to be virtuous if your virtue is never tested. It is a challenge of a man's fiber and guts if in being brotherly, and courageous, he risks economic, social or political disadvantage, if not destruction." He was talking about Northern liberals four years ago. But I'm thinking of someone else now. Do you see what I'm getting at?

No.

And the Negro writers, I asked. Are they all speaking from the North? Isn't anyone down there at all? "He could live there and write as he damn well pleased," Hoke said, "and no one would touch him. It's just that he feels better away from the South. The Negro writers all have lived long enough in the North to be considered natives of the North." The young ones? "They've been so busy with other things, they haven't had time to develop." The white liberal? "I don't know how he gets along now. It used to be pretty lonesome. There are some who have done good work for a long time. Ralph McGill is one." And then I asked him the big one . . . Isn't there a novel of this new South just waiting to be written? Just waiting for him? "I'd have to go back and live there for awhile. I've been away too long."

So?

So why doesn't he?

115

He has a good job here. He has responsibilities. He's a critic.

All right, all right. I asked him about that too. The conflict. What does he consider himself, a novelist or a critic? "It's rather confusing to work both sides of the street, but not as confusing as you think." He likes the *Sun-Times*. He says it's hospitable. It has to be. Any place than can house Father, Blessed-are-the-righteous-for-they-shall-censor, Molloy and Roger Up-underground Ebert under the same roof must be hospitable. Not only that, they just hired a poet as a reporter. I can't wait till he covers his first fire. "It's a hospitable place, the *Sun-Times* is, for originality, for individual expression. About as good a place as I can work. I have been able to do my own work in my own way through the generosity of management. I couldn't make a living as a full-time novelist. Very few can."

Well, he's truthful.

Of course he's truthful. That's Hoke. That's what bothers me.

What?

I don't know, I don't know. I guess that the guy who works both sides of the street doesn't dare enough. Some of these things I couldn't ask. I was afraid to ask. Some of these things a writer must ask himself and answer himself and never spread the word around. Take the collection *Best American Short Stories of 1950*. You know who's in there with him? Do you know? Saul Bellow, George P. Elliott, Leslie Fiedler, Peter Taylor, Paul Bowles!

Great company.

Yeah, but you know who else? Sanora Babb, Clay Putman, Romona Stewart, Speed Lamkin.

Who?

Precisely. Give me another beer with a short one for the heart.

So what does he say about this?

I didn't ask him. The really important things are what I didn't ask and what he didn't tell me. Then we talked about his column. I asked him about the old Hoke Norris who was really the young Hoke Norris. I showed him all the clippings of five years ago when he was fighting Chicago censorship, defending Miller's *Tropic Of Cancer*.

Well, censorship's dead.

Yes, exactly what he said. And thanks in a large measure to him, which he didn't say. But there were other causes too, not the least of which was championing the writer—whether he was discussing the state of the short story, slick magazines, satirizing New York publishers . . . "Dear Mr. Melville: We have read your manuscript with great interest. However, we do not feel that it is suitable to our list at this time. While much of it is compelling and even awesome, it is our consensus that the long passages devoted to philosophical discussion and to biological consideration of the whale too often interrupt the flow of the narrative. With these elements eliminated, we believe that it might make a fine adventure book for boys." Or on non-books: " Mr. Publisher, please don't call them books. Just face it. I don't know what they are, but I know that they aren't books." Oh hell, I could go on, but the point is he was fighting, he was giving writing and young writers attention. Maybe he was hurting too. But he was coming through strong. And no one else in Chicago newspapers, except for Kogan, was doing this. Everyone else was interested in finding 'gold in your attic' or Harry Mark Petrakis. I don't even have an attic. and Petrakis is now in quest of the Golden Fleece off the shores of Hollywood.

And now?

And now I seldom see him fighting any more. Maybe all the causes are dead. Now he often sounds too much like New York. Now it's too much history. History is for tired men. Is "mellowing" the word?

Yes. Did you ask him?

Sort of.

And what did he think?

He said he wasn't aware of it. But then he looked over the columns, and I had the feeling he was concerned. I pointed out one column in particular, "Fat On The Soul" in which he was discussing security in academia, but I was thinking of something else . . . 'I've seen it happen dozens of times,' said my friend, a writer and university professor. 'A teacher in a college or university works very hard for years. He publishes, he teaches, he travels—he is a promising man. He will do much. And then they make a full professor of him, and he slows down. Sometimes he comes to a complete halt. He stops publishing. His teaching loses something—freshness, firmness, aliveness. He's got tenure—security— and he stops running. He starts sitting.'"

So now what?

I don't know. Maybe he'll light out for the territory like Huck. He's still writing fiction. And he mentioned he had something coming out on Bill Witherspoon, so perhaps capital punishment will be his cause. He's going to do something on McCormick and the *New American Review #2*. And he still has great faith in little magazines, little presses, and independent publishers. He gave *Anaconda* a mention even though he didn't like it. That's still more than any other reviewer did in Chicago. He talked about a lot of these things, things I hope he'll write about. And he said, "If a young writer will come up with a novel, I'll be delighted to review it. But something isn't automatically published because it's written by somebody. You have to serve a seven-year apprenticeship to be a plumber. And writing is a far more demanding profession than plumbing. You have to learn to write before you can publish. And even after you serve an apprenticeship there may be no one to publish you."

Is he married?

I knew you'd ask that.

I knew you wouldn't.

So did he, but he told me anyway. His wife's name is Edna and his daughter, Marion, is "13 going on 18" and attends the Latin School.

117

Well, you never ask things like that.

He sees Chicago writing "all over the place. And there are people who are working quietly and somewhat obscurely who might break out. It's not really done in Bohemia. Wells Street will never produce a writer, a painter. It's not done with conspicuous behavior. It's done in the quiet night of the soul. You never know where it will come from. You attend a literary party with all these people performing, and it's always a little fellow in the corner that you overlook." There, that's Hoke Norris. Oh, and I asked him about a city, a newspaper having some responsibility toward its writers.

You weren't looking for work, were you?

Smart, smart. Get some more beer. No, he said he didn't see why a newspaper should show any more responsibility toward its writers than it did toward its teachers or anybody else. But as far as the government is concerned, since it's taking care of everyone else, he thinks the writers ought to get their share and they're not. "Writing's the biggest one-man self-help project there is." He likes the idea of writers maybe reviewing or something for the newspapers . . . "But there again, you're paying a writer to do everything but write a book. That's the problem with these foundations who will give money to writers to do everything but write—teaching, research, committee work. What a writer really needs is a wad of money to go away and write his damn book." I'm afraid I talked too much.

Why?

There was so much to say. He was such a nice guy he even asked for my name and address. And I gave it to him.

So what?

So I should have acted anonymously or said my name was Slats Grobnik.

You mean nice anonymous guys finish last?

No, they aren't even in the race. But they survive, and maybe that's victory enough.

That's a moral.

I hate morals. They're nothing but soft facts. Let me get you a beer with a short one.

Here's to . . . who?

Right. And the quiet night of the soul.

Leaving the Big Bulls to Him for Whom
the Bell Tolls on the Hour: J. Robert Nash

Hello, America, this is Hunkie Hassock looking, as usual, for a place to begin. We'll leave endings, if there are any, till later.

Oh, I could tell you stories about him that you wouldn't believe.

One thing about writers and poets, bullfighters and soldiers, gangsters and old Chicago newspapermen: they celebrate their madness either openly (the whole body, hands, feet, head swinging) or locked inside somewhere behind the eyeballs. They're all hell-bent for private or public destruction.

Now take Lionoel O'Roaragon (a k a J.R. Nash). Inside and outside, every word of his mouth (triggered to the written word of his hand) is an invitation to death. Death, he says, come to the party. He's the only writer I know who works the keys of the typewriter with both fists, a clean fighter who keeps the action out in the open, always. And whether he's writing about War or Peace, for the public or posterity, his only message is (quote from his weekly literary report, *WAR*), "Line up, gentlemen, one punch to a customer."

Death, what else? But note the quality of the challenge, the dignity of the man: 'gentlemen' he calls the black bull who waits at the end of the long alley.

Take me, your storyteller, Hassock. I know all about these things. But with me everything was always locked inside, getting more and more crowded like popcorn in those tinfoil fry pans that keep ballooning with heat. Then I met Liono.

Oh, I had read about him before, heard about him, even talked about him. He was where the action was. I know because I saw it all in *WAR*, and I was a conscientious neighborhood objector. Damn, there were guerrilla-goings-on, hand-to-hand combat, raids, invasions, landings, sabotage and bombings. All right here in the city. Right here in Chicago, one of the major fronts. And Liono was leading one of (not one of!) the best crack company artists any city could muster. They fought alongside him. They believed him. They threw worded grenades. Many were lost, but some were chosen. And only he, O'Roaragon, knew who the enemy really was!

119

Some quotes now. You'll see, you'll see what I mean: "Writers, scattered in unwanted seclusion, drift with the younger painters and sculptors toward the Old-town district where the fight is—the War is with the Successful, the Institution-alized--knowing the enemy as only the sycophant who is called artist and who is not, who has defamed the arts through faked popularity and bogus achievement."

See! See! He fights on all fronts, even the artistic. And his constant battle is the Battle of the New Renaissance: "Strange, diversified and unpredictable, a RENAISSANCE, a second coming of the artist—the whole artist, be he painter, writer, poet or critic—has happened in Chicago. Due to the traditional ignorance of an opulent society, of economically purged minorities desperately clinging to their flagging nationalities, of trite, staid pre-gimmicked newspapers, of useless causes ending in a forgotten chant dirged in the darkness of anachronistic bug-house square, the artist exists."

Where's my banner? Hassock, where the hell's your banner? How could a man not rally to a call like that? Damned coward that I am. Where the hell's your red badge, where? I sit back. I let him fight the wars. How should I know the enemy was surrounding me?

(Hassock, get on with the story! You met Liono finally, didn't you?)

No, no. I heard about him first. I talked about him with one of his enemies at that time, Hans Hogan—one of the newspapermen of the old school. A hell of a good man, whatever my words are worth. But how was I to know that he was the "enemy" at that time?

"Do you know this guy, O'Roaragon?" he asked.

"No, but I read *WAR*. Seems like he's against everyone."

Hogan laughed, "He is. He's paranoic. He's got this sinister scowl on his face all the time. I think he's the illegitimate son of Ben Hecht."

I laughed; what else could I do? But I said, "I'll probably meet him some-time. I just have a feeling someday we'll meet."

And we did. By pure accident. I was having a tooth fixed by a rotten dentist in a condemned building on the north side, and he says to me in between the HUMMM . . . BIZZZZ, "So you do some writing, huh?"

"Ouch, sometimes. OHOOOOOO Yes, I guess HELP, I write."

"Then you know Liono in the next office? GRRRRR . . . BIZZZZ"

"Lionoel? O'Roaragon? AHHHHHHHHH"

"Yeah, the nut who publishes *WAR*. Spit it out."

So I stumbled into *WAR*'s office bleeding from the mouth.

"A writer! Sit down, I'll get my first aid kit. Brought it all the way back from the Spanish front. I was an ambulance driver then, me and the rest of them. Can you write a book review? I need book reviews for the next issue of *WAR*. War! Do you know what that means? The literary lifeblood of this whole rotten city, that's what it means! The establishment! There are enough cretins in the Chicago establishment, but it's nothing compared to New York. Nothing! See that, over there by the wall? Twenty unpublished novels. I wrote my guts out in those books. But unpublished. Why? New York, that's why. They're afraid to publish anything with guts in it. The whole Midwest is dung to them. We got too many men here. They want homosexuals to write their novels. But I'll show 'em! We'll show them! I always said I'll give myself till forty, and if I haven't published a book by then, I'll do two things—first I'll be-come an insurance man, then I'll kill myself. Here, you want some more crap to review? Stacks and stacks of half-baked New York nothings—religious, diatribe, cookbooks. Cookbooks! That's all the hell they publish today. Chicago a sec-ond city, ha! Nobody knows what the hell's going on here. Nobody cares . . . (time for another quote from *WAR*) . . . 'One sagging and sycophantic sage of ambiguity, William Murray, wind-passing in *Holiday* magazine, delivered a high-pitched diatribe about Chicago's literary life. Waxing his stupidity in the putt-putting of a cretin unworthy of indictment in Berloiz's *Evenings with an Orchestra*, Murray ignorantly stated, 'The saddest aspect of the city's [Chicago] cultural life is the almost total absence of local publications open to native writ-ing.' Untrue, Boobis Americanus!"

Oh, Hassock is breaking up right here on the page. You got to meet O'Roaragon someday to really appreciate what I'm saying.

Anyway, we met. And we became friends. And I wouldn't be writing this about him now, if I didn't like the guy and think he was necessary for all of us. You too. That's one thing that still separates me from O'Roaragon, though: I write about the things I like, but he writes about the things he hates.

(Will you end the story, Hassock, already?)

Okay, okay. But I don't know where to begin. Because this is not an artsy story, and I'm writing it for him. If this were an artsy story, I'd be slipping you

121

the theme by now. So, why slip it? Right, Liono? Right! "Tell it with guts!" Ladies and gentlemen, I will not present the theme of this story. Here, take it in the guts!

All of you literati in Chicago and New York and everyplace, it's time to stop making fun of this man! Someday, you out there in Chicago on the newspapers and in the universities, someday too late you're going to recognize what a writer you've got here and what he did for everybody! Yeah! Before I met O'Roaragon, I used to think I was a writer. But O'Roaragon makes you feel like a writer, and he tells you, you are one! (Editor, please print that in bold type. Repeat: **O'ROARAGON MAKES YOU FEEL LIKE A WRITER!**)

That's all. That's it. What else should I tell you? Should I tell you about how many men he killed in the war? (What war? Now really, are numbers and names necessary any longer?) He killed at least twenty men. Ask him sometime when he's drunk. He has medals to prove it. And wounds. No, I haven't seen any of this, and I don't want to. I know he's been there. And to tell me this isn't true would hurt me—and maybe him. Besides, we wouldn't believe you anyway.

Should I tell you of the delicious nights of drunkenness? Where O'Roaragon roosts in O'Brian's Pub? Where he's been known to have pummeled (Sorry Liono) PUNCHED! PUNCHED! PUNCHED! ten dilettantes in a row at the bar?

Or the time a piper walked and moaned and wailed "Garry Owen" over and over again for O'Roaragon?

Or how he can walk into a northside bar and whisper to you out of the corner of his mouth, "There are at least six guys in here who would like to kill me."

How about the time he had it out with Algren?

Or the tears he's wept for Conroy, Farrell, Fitzgerald—oh, the troubles and the Irish and all. . . .

What do you want to know? What do you want to hear? What do you think of the three of us—O'Roaragon, Loneson, and Hassock—gone out to a roadhouse one night. (That's right, roadhouse. When you're with O'Roaragon, there are only pubs, speakeasys, and roadhouses.) So we went to this roadhouse on the outskirts of town to hear some real Dixieland. Bix was playing, only his name was Kimm and he played a clarinet. But it was Bix up there. O'Roaragon said so. He kept ordering VO & beer, and you're damn right it was Bix up there. And O'Roaragon kept calling out all the great Bix numbers and Kimm, Bix, kept playing them. The whole roadhouse was stomping down the highway. Liono was standing on a table holding it down. "Gimme a horn!" he kept yelling, "Gimme a horn!" And later that morning we moved the whole roadhouse to Bix's home where we listened to 78s of Bix and Spike Jones and all the really great ones. "Gimme a horn! Gimme a horn!" he kept yelling. Bix reeled around the living room with a stack of old 78s asking, "Where did you find this guy? He's an original, a real original. He even looks like Bix," that's what Kimm, I mean Bix said.

"Glimme a horn!" So Kimm's, I mean Bix's wife, pulled an antique horn off the wall and handed it to him, "Here, you crazy nut. Here's your damn horn. Now go outside and blow."

And he went quietly. He left all the noise on the inside and went out into the dark street of what, I guess, was suburbia and started playing. Started blowing long, sorrowful false sounds. Started blowing and blaring into the night till someone remembered where the hell he was and went outside to rescue him from whatever suburbia had in store for a solo horn player in the early hours of the morning.

"Get in here," some gray-haired guy threatened him. "You'll get the cops after us. Who the hell is this guy, anyway?"

"He's the last of the great Chicago-Irish writers!" I yelled into the darkness. "The drinkers! The singers! The fighters! The madmen! Don't touch him! He'll kill you! And he must be preserved!"

"Come here with that horn"; the gray-haired man moved toward O'Roaragon.

"Go away. I've got to find the sound. The sound that was Bix!"

The party began to move outside. O'Roaragon's horn kept blaring and blaring through the trees, around the windows, over the lawns.

"I'm going to write a great novel about you, Bix! Do you hear me, Bix? A great novel!"

The gray-haired man continued to pester him, began to hold his arms.

"Get away from me old man, Mr. Death. Get away! You're dying. You're too old to fight."

"Gimme that horn." Liono dropped him with one punch, all the while holding on to the horn.

"Death! Death! Death! Death! I'll play you a dirge!"

Me and Loneson finally got him under control, got him to give up the horn. "I've lost my lip, I've lost my lip," he kept saying in the car as we glided down the sidestreets without headlights till we reached the expressway for Chicago.

"You're good writers," O'Roaragon hoarsely whispered to Loneson and me from the back seat, "but you'll never be great. Just leave the big bulls for me."

123

Marshall Field's

You begin with that Big Green Clock on the corner of State and Randolph, if Marshall Field's shopping is any part of your day downtown. That's the landmark, the pole star. So it's under the Big Green Clock and into the main doorway—137—to which all other doorways seem like exits.

Once, maybe twice around the revolving door, and into a half-acre of Cosmetics, where it is always eternal spring. Maybe a new scent for the woman? the wife? (the old lady?) Glass showcases, counters tiered with Smell for Sale. (For what? For whom?) For love's sake. Pass the old aphrodisiacs.

"The Wholesome Face" beckons . . . and what about the possibilities of something called "Youth Dew"? A guy in a yellow hardhat says to the salewoman, "Mmmmm, I like that. What'd you say it was called?"

"Youth Dew," the woman exudes. The hard hat softens a little.

Cosmetic women alone are worth a Field's trip, worth all the gawking you can give them. They thrive on the forever beautiful. Tired women, plain women, even pretty women hang on the counters imagining new faces.

I approach a salesperson, readying her counter for new faces. She's arranging bottles, checking the reserves, tidying up.

"Excuse me, I'd like some information about women and cosmetics . . . the attraction, the relationship, the need."

"I'm sorry. I'm very busy as you can see. We have a lot to do, and I really can't take the time to answer your questions. Why don't you talk to Miss Murphy: She's the Manager. I'm sure she can take care of you."

Shot down by a Cosmo Woman.

Nevertheless, I like them. They always make me smile. There's an air of circus and cabaret about them . . . or maybe it's the Cosmos. Scented scenes and conversation:

"Have you ever tried Moon Drops?"

"How about New Slipper Lip Licks by Yardley?"

Miss Murphy is young and cool and sharp and distant and not all that heavy into Cosmetics like some of her women. She seems willing enough to talk, but suspicious of a man's motives.

125

She assures me that her department is probably the largest cosmetic department on State Street and probably all of Chicago.

"But isn't there a movement away from all this? I mean among the young people . . . to be themselves?"

"I don't know what you're referring to, but for those who want the natural look, we do carry all the natural creams and lotions."

I drift unnaturally away on a sea of sweet smells and sight my first Un-Cola, Un-Cosmo woman behind a counter, a simply natural, youthful, long-haired creature who will, no doubt, never need an excuse for false eyelashes.

"What's the latest scent?" I ask.

"Musk Oil," she whispers serenely. "It brings out the animal."

From such Elysian fields, past the Pharmacy (with a distinct odor of its own . . . anti-aphrodisiac), it's once across the main floor (State Street side) to see if the world of Field's is still in order. It is. Buttons, belts, blouses, bags and a bouquet of umbrellas, worthy of a poem, a story, a book, a film. Field's leads a man's soul to such inspiration. Up to 7 now for some breakfast.

Field's is a mansion of many moods. For an unhurried and elegant sense of dining, there is the Walnut Room on 7. A shopper tends to gear down in such an atmosphere.

Maybe it's the wood and carpeting that does it (as opposed to the flashiness of Formica, Naugahyde and chrome). But certainly it's the touch of the past, when even time was a pleasure to consume. That certain elegance . . . the shine and tinkle of silver and crystal . . . a pitcher of water, a bouquet of flowers, a real white tablecloth and napkin. People deserve the sanity of such dining. And Field's seems to understand.

Even Ellis treats you like her own honored guest. I've been watching Ellis for years now. She's an extraordinary hostess, a person of smiles, well wishes, concern and just plain humanism in a day when most people find it fashionable to either distrust or disown others.

When Ellis smiles and says, "Good morning," it is . . . whether you feel like hell or not. She could lead you to the worst table in the room, the darkest corner, and you'd take it without flinching, knowing that Ellis is probably giving you the only table that's open, and she's doing her best. She's black . . . she's beautiful . . . and when people today, and since the time of man, talk about *soul* . . . they mean Ellis.

"I'll get you some coffee," she says. And a waitress appears almost immediately with a silver coffeepot. "Have a nice breakfast," Ellis says as she heads for a party of four. She knows many customers by name and seems always concerned about everyone's welfare.

"Do you feel better today?"

"He's in the hospital? I didn't know that. I'll have to send him a card."

She approaches a child; "Is your daddy coming today?"

I settle down to the pot of hot coffee and some grapefruit juice, and order a beautiful breakfast of country eggs scrambled in cream, served with tomato wedges and a sprig of parsley. Toasted homemade bread and thick strawberry preserves sets it all off.

It's just a nice place and way to enjoy breakfast. I hate to get up. But all of Marshall Field's keeps urging me on.

Elevators, escalators pointing Up. But Down's my next destination. Field's bargain basement. There's something lower-class about basements. Field's doesn't even call it that by name. It's their Budget Floor.

Even the shoppers look different down here, something about their clothes, their shopping bags, their attitude. Neighborhood people, not the Lake Shore nifties on most of the other floors.

I ask a woman investigating a piece of costume jewelry, "Is this stuff any cheaper down here?"

"I don't know. It's supposed to be," she laughs. "It's the Budget Floor."

Wandering into Women's Sportswear I come across a trio of manager-type women discussing the disposition of a somewhat dusty mannikin. "Just look at her," one says in jest. "After all," another smiles, "this is Marshall Field's!"

When they break, I sidle up to one and learn that she is Jandy Widler, a manager of Women's Sportswear. Expecting another Cosmo-Lady type, I am happy to discover she is just a neat young woman, happy in her work, and another credit to the Field's establishment.

As for whether or not there are any real basement bargains, Jandy Widler claims that, at least in her department, the prices tend to overlap. Some merchandise higher, some lower than merchandise on the other floors.

"But it's the best budget floor downtown," she says loyally. "And the budget shoppers are definitely different from other shoppers in Field's. Why, there are some women shoppers who wouldn't *dare* think of shopping budget."

"You mean some who would even never set foot down here?"

"Absolutely. And there are even differences among shoppers on the other floors, differences among other sections of the women's fashions. In Budget, though, you notice women checking prices. Still, we handle no irregular merchandise here. There is just no comparison between the quality of our merchandise and that of discount stores."

Right next door, and still in the basement, I saunter in Misses' Dresses, perhaps a present for the wife, and riffle a rack of incomprehensible sizes, looking for something more colorful than anything else. I find it. A wild, flowered print. A dress, I think, about as long as a blouse. A beloved bargain to boot.

I rip it right from the rack, beating out the nearest bargaineer, and rush to the safety of the nearest counter, where a pleasant black woman, Ms. Phillips on her name tag, waits on me.

"You mean women's lib has even struck Marshall Field's, Miz Phillips?"

"Oh, I don't know," she laughs, "but it's coming I guess. At least that's what the name tag says. My, this is a pretty dress. And only $12? Where'd you find this?"

"Right over there. Don't tell anybody. Maybe it's mismarked."

"You got the right size?"

"Instinctively, I can't be too far off. It looks about the same size as the blouse I once bought her."

"Oh, you got good taste for a man. Your woman's gonna like this."

"Thank you, Miz Phillips. You're a great saleswoman. Field's should be proud of you. Saleswomen, as a rule, tend to have the disposition of dragons."

I elevator up to 1 this time, from the basement of the Men's Store Annex, attempt a jaywalk across Washington but settle for the sanity of the corner stoplight instead . . . then enter the main store again at the only other exit I will acknowledge: 102 N. Wabash. Because of the clocks, the silver, the aura of pomp and circumstance that dwells over this particular domain of Field's. Even with only $10 in my pocket, I have a feeling I'm in the right place.

I observe a man buying a diamond bracelet for his wife. I notice the careful clerk displaying the item like his every gesture is worth a cool thousand. One thing at a time. Precision salesmanship in jewels.

I ask another salesman about grandfather clocks. I want one. I'm directed to Mr. Kaplan, the clock man, whose first reaction to me is as if I'm not worth the time of day. I mention to him that I had noticed a grandmother's clock on the floor a few weeks ago, French antique, circa 1800 . . . $1,250. "What's the grandmother's clock, by the way?"

"A grandmother's clock is about six feet tall, while a grandfather's is seven feet. The important thing, though, in these clocks is the inner works. All our clocks are authenticated."

"What about shipping one up all the way to Northern Wisconsin somewhere, someday?"

"No problem. We shipped one to Hawaii the other day."

Shuffling through Silver, soothed in all the reflections . . . counters, showcases, rooms of incredible ornateness and shining intensity, I hear a woman say to a man, "I could buy all of it, everything here . . . I love it," while the man whisks her away in wonder toward the Washington exit, without once blinking back.

Pipes, barometers, telescopes, sun glasses, luggage . . . just ahead looms games and cards and typewriters and candy. A taste for Field's Famous Chocolate Covered Frango Mints takes hold of me. "Later, later," I promise myself. My God, it's time for the Magic Man!

It's up the nearest escalator to 4, a dash through Toys, and there at the entrance to Crafts and Hobbies . . . the Magic Man.

He has been peddling magic at the same stand for as long as I can remember, though he never seems to change, never looks any different. He's usually dressed in a brown baggy suit, a sport shirt, and an old-fashioned tie. A little heavyset, with a short haircut neatly combed in 1940 style, the man casts a mysterious air of magician about him. And that's exactly what he is.

One is almost afraid to probe into the secrecy of his own personal life lest he should pull a disappearing act with the first question. One is just happy that here is a real, live professional magician employed as a magic clerk.

He's describing a Magic Card Case trick to a kid at the moment, while counseling a woman on the merits of purchasing a gyroscope for a child.

"It's not magic," he tells her. "It's an entirely scientific toy, but kids love it. Watch." (Who says the universe isn't magic?)

So he has the gyroscope going and has confused the kid with the Magic Card Case trick, and now he's digging around for the Magic Egg Bag. He shows you the egg, puts it in the bag and, of course, it isn't in the bag at all, either inside or out. Where is it? Where is it? It's under his arm . . . or in one of the pockets of his baggy brown suit. No. This time it's behind his collar!

A crowd of a dozen people have slowly gathered around him, oohing and ahhing, and giving him a real polite round of applause. He is a real person indeed Joe Zering by name, who has been with Marshall Field's for eighteen years. "Zeringo is the name I go by professionally," he says.

"And how's the magic business, Joe?"

"Here, at the store, pretty good. But around the city, most of the professional magic shops have gone."

He has just sold a kid $13.95 worth of magic, and throws in a little bit of his own professionalism to boot:

"Don't forget," he tells the kid, "first and foremost you must be a good entertainer. You must practice before you perform the tricks before others. I practice everyday. You've got to keep your hands in it all the time or else you go rusty. And *never* tell the secret to anyone."

I ponder the lesson just as the first hunger pangs make themselves felt. Jogging around Field's all morning eventually gets to me before noon.

The closest distance between hunger on a lower floor and the restaurants on 7 is a quick diagonal toward an elevator and a sharp right around a corner to a slumbering escalator. In the process, fragments of conversation, broken poems, department store dramas of no beginnings or ends.

Two clerks, a young man who looks as if he still listens to the Four Freshmen, circa the '50s, and a young woman of shimmering long hair who looks as if she might be as far advanced as Musk Oil, plot a liaison amongst a thicket of lamps.

(Shades of modern drama, ala Becket . . . off-on . . . darkness-light. . . .)

"How about later?" Click, on.

"I'll have to see." Click, off.

"Tonight? . . . in Candy." Click, on.

Then, inching my way up on moving stairs, a surreal fragment floating up

from the floor below—
"I've lost two firetrucks . . . "

There are five restaurants on 7, each a little different: The Buffet Cafeteria, the English Room, the Narcissus Room, the Veranda and, of course, the Walnut Room. But the best buy in the building is the Veranda.

Lunch at the Veranda. A line, as usual. There is always this line of paired-off old ladies waiting for a table. Going in as a single is a dangerous game. The hostess seems deadset against seating any singles. So either you wait till starvation sets in or accept the proposition, made ever so sweetly, "Would you mind sharing your table?"

I have never been left alone with a meal in the Veranda. Worse than that, I have never been granted a table on the Veranda itself (something like Booth 1 in the Pump Room). Instead of sitting up there along the banister, in the lime-light, I inevitably find myself lost in the yard of the center floor . . . no esteem whatsoever.

Nursing a deep premonition this time, I follow the hostess to a tiny table on the Veranda itself! I take a seat with quiet dignity and cast a tired glance at the envious eaters in the yard commons below. I await my dinner companion.

She's a gray-haired woman who acknowledges my presence with a smile and a nod. Followed, it seems, by an interminable silence while we both seek the anonymity of the menu, studying the possibilities, marking the choices with a pencil.

There's chicken fricasse on a Holland rusk and spiced fruit; there's a fresh vegatable salad bowl with blue cheese; there's batter-fried halibut, tartar sauce, buttered green beans . . . a couple of lesser treats. But there's Field's famous fresh apple pie for dessert, plus a damned good cup of coffee. I settle for chicken-fric, apple pie, and coffee. All this for only $1.60 "including tax and gratuity" as it says on the menu.

A waitress gathers our score cards, reads aloud the orders and suggests something not on the menu.

"Hard or soft what?" I gently reprimand her terse attitude. Gratuity or not, I'm dining on the Veranda today!

"Hard or soft roll."

"Oh, I'd like a nice soft roll."

Silence at the dinner table as my partner and I stare off into the distance, make mental notes of each other and attempt the usual banal conversation concerning the weather. Without weather, most Americans would be mutes.

I have a feeling she may be afraid of me . . . that I may indeed be the fearsome Mugger all Chicago has been warned of. So I bend over backward convincing her I'm just an average shopper who's been carrying on this love affair with Marshall Field's for years. And this shifts our conversation into high gear. Our food comes, but there's hardly time to eat.

130

"Oh, this is such a wonderful store," she says. "I always try to get down here at least once a year. I live in Des Plaines now but years ago I lived closer to the city, and I would come shopping down here all the time."

"Well, there are all those shopping plazas in the suburbs now, beautiful places like Oak Brook, Old Orchard, Woodfield, but you can't forget downtown, you know. You can't dismiss it just like that . . . just because of all the bad things you hear. I hate to see people desert State Street and all the great stores, especially this grand old queen, Marshall Field's, just because they've heard so many rumors that the city is dangerous and falling apart. That's one of the good things about Daley. He has great faith in this city.

"The people will be back, I'm sure of that. It's turning already . . . but very slowly. One of these days shopping downtown will again be the only thing to do. There's a climate, an intimacy, a joy of shopping in a State Street department store this huge and exciting that can't be equalled in any suburban shopping center, where things seem a little too pre-planned and accessible."

It's a good lunch shared by two strangers. In time, I bid my table partner good-by and ride the elevator down to 2 for an after-dinner affair with Art. Maybe it's lunch or just the afternoon that sets me on a loftier course . . . a strangely placid mood where I seem to be fighting time (the oncoming rush hour) yet tend to glide even more slowly through all my favorite departments.

Field's art gallery never fails to satisfy me. You may not get the currently *in* artists, and though serious artists may downgrade this as *department store art*, or *interior decorating*, there are hundreds of paintings here that please me. And probably fifty, at the moment, that I wouldn't mind hanging on my walls.

I'm in the mood for a little more rest, and so it's down to 3 and the comforts of the Waiting Room. Maybe I can catch a ten-minute nap, if I can find a comfortable chair. I beat an old woman burdened with bundles to a seat near my second favorite Field's clock, and study it into somnolence. It's 12:55 in Chicago. 12:50 in Calcutta, 8:55 in Stalingrad, 1:40 in Paris.

"Where are you from?" I hear a woman across from me.

"Indiana," replies the woman beside her. "I come here on the train once a week to shop."

I drift off . . . and awake with a start in fifteen minutes, a bit refreshed, and set off through the rest of 3 . . . through Lingerie, where two men are sizing up a blue negligee, each saying to the other: "I don't think it will fit her." Who knows? Maybe they're buying it for their sister?

Through Women's Robes, where I come to rest momentarily, find a chair, and watch a tall man with a knitted hat, mustache and beard shop for a lounging robe. He holds the saleslady spellbound with his desires.

"I'm looking for a lounging robe that works both aesthetically and mechanically," he says. (You don't find distinctive customers like this in Shopper's World.)

I decide to make a complete circuit of 3, winding my way from Robes to

131

Foundation Garments, where two saleswomen and their manager are going at it with all the heavy equipment they can muster.

"She is too making more money than me!"

"That's not so."

"Well, I saw what she makes."

"You don't know what you're talking about."

"Don't tell me I don't know what I'm talking about!"

It's late. I'm losing time. Field's is just too full of wonders. How about Toys? No, I would waste a good hour there . . . but maybe a few minutes . . . up to 4!

Stuffed animals . . . puppets. Four kids holding an impromptu puppet show in a little theater they've taken off the counter. "I'm the Wolf," says one. "I'm the King," says another. "I'm Big Bird," says a third. Sounds like a great show. I wish I could catch the whole act.

The Magic Man is still at it, with a couple of cronies around him now. Good friends, it seems, and fellow magicians. A lot of inside magic and kidding going around . . . much to the delight of shoppers.

"These are two famous magicians here," Joe tells the shoppers. A black kid walks up to one of them and asks, "Say, are you a real magician?"

"Yeah, after a fashion," says the magician. "After about three old fashioneds!" he laughs.

The Magic Man, caught up in the general good feeling of the occasion, injects a little humor of his own. "You guys stick around," he says. "Because after I sell all my magic, I'm going to start selling magicians."

I discover, always to my dismay, there's not enough time for all the floors I want to visit. Another rest stop on 3? Five and 6 hold no wonders for me . . . millinery, shoes, coats, bridal woes and maternity meanderings. Seven pulls the hardest . . . food . . . gourmet specials!

I discuss these rich tastes with Linda of the afro hairdo, a pleasant enough girl, indeed, to handle the delicacies of gourmet people.

"Do you really sell much of this caviar? Do people really plunk down this kind of money?"

"Oh sure," she says. "People just love caviar. They buy it for other people, for gifts."

This is the land of surreal stomachs . . . Wild Boar Fillets with Foie Gras and Truffles, $27.45. Cooked Cured Lamb Tongues, 9 ounces, $1.79. Bombay Duck, $1.75.

Tea? Everything from Keemun to Hibiscus.

Coffee? Costa Rican Bucara, Maracaibo, Java Bogota.

And maybe a bar of Dutch Chocolate to keep it all down.

Up to 8, furniture. Down to 3 again, past twenty telephones and directories to all the United States plus Canada and England . . . a travel bureau, a quarter acre of tired shoppers, and not an empty chair to be had.

I lean against the Punch Bowl and order a stiff shot of refreshing Coconut Milk for 35 cents.

It's 4:10 in Calcutta . . . they're sleeping in Stalingrad . . . Paris must be reeling at this hour. . . .

I wing it down to 1, Wabash side, pick up a few pounds of Field's Famous Frango Mints, push into perfume, breathe deep, check the chick still meditating in Musk Oil, then bid Field's, the Grande Dame, a fond adieu, ducking out under and beyond the Big Green Clock, popping Frango Mints all the way home in a magical sort of way.

A Man on a Bench

At four every morning Innocenzo Bonelli is up, partly because of the pain, partly because a ninety-year-old man does not sleep long. He eats in his room at the Wells Grand ("Men Only, No Transients") and usually by six heads for a bench in Grant Park.

All men are not bench sitters. Young people, especially, seem to have no use for the furniture of city parks and small-town courthouse squares. It takes an Innocenzo Bonelli, a classic bench sitter, to give the pastime the grace it deserves. The buses roll by him down Michigan Avenue, the early morning traffic is ponderous, but he has the grass, the pigeons, a newspaper, and his bench. He is a study in tranquility.

"I come down here just to pass the time," he says. "I don't do nothing. I go home eleven o'clock and make something to eat. Afternoon I take nap, or I read some books . . . any book I find. Sometimes I walk down to the lake and watch somebody catch the fish. I like to be by myself."

Bonelli, a retired baker, has lived in Chicago almost seventy years. "I come from Italy in 1910," he says. "Never was back. No want to. I don't care for the old country. It's pretty good here." There are long pauses in the conversation. To bench sitters, what is said is not important. You do not find a bench for yourself in the park to converse. But should a stranger come by and share your time and bench, you may make small talk.

"I get $184 from Social Security," Bonelli says, rubbing his chin. "For me, is enough. I cook, I wash my own clothes, I cut my hair. Sixty dollars for rent. The landlady is nice."

Bonelli has never married and has been in bad health most of his life. "Every month I go to the doctor to take blood pressure," he says. "I can't sleep only three or four hours a night. I had an operation here," pointing, "by nose . . . here, by ear . . . and down here, prostate. I get medicine. But about six weeks ago they tell me they pay too much already. Last hospital bill, $3,000."

Pigeons flutter around him. The sun is getting higher, and he pulls down his cap to protect his eyes.

Some coffee, Innocenzo? Some breakfast? On me.

"I don't want nothing from nobody," he smiles, opening his newspaper. "I just say thank you." Then he disappears into the silence of his art.

Max Marek: The Antique Dealer Who Beat Joe Louis

It's an old, stained, red-brick building at the corner of Sheffield and Grace, a building highlighted by a cheap white trim around the windows, across the doors and entrances. It's Max Marek's Sat-Sun Antique Shop.

In a cinder parking lot across the street, one derelict car, fallen flat on its wheels, rusts in peace. Horace Greeley School stands like a stage-set on the other corner, with the El throttling close behind. It's a classic Chicago setting of has-beens who battle, flat-footed, to function with some sense of dignity—to stave off the wrecker, the ropes, the canvas, and the final count of ten.

It's a quiet Sunday afternoon. Max Marek, once rated among the world's ten best heavyweights, former United States amateur champion, "the man who beat Joe Louis," sits behind a desk in the dark of his antique shop and nods a welcome.

He's sixty. And he fits the place, looking like a beat-up bust of Buddha in bronze that three exhausted men deposited on top of a desk. But Max is real enough, bundled in a huge overcoat, wearing a leathery black hat, brown tinted glasses, and smoking a pipe that disappears in a fist the size of a five-pound ham. A tired, devoted Dalmatian sits beside him and cries.

"Hello," says Max. "What's old?"

I return his nod with a smile, shrug my shoulders, but leave the old boxer-turned-antique-dealer to his Sunday reveries for the moment and take a walk through the warehouse, where Max also has a furniture-refinishing business. Max seems fond of his handmade signs, carefully scattered amid the antiques. Humor sometimes tells more about human nature than anybody cares to know. And signs, when they are effective, can hit a man right between the eyes with a sudden truth.

PROMOTE MENTAL HEALTH*
*commit yourself

Max has some antique barber poles for sale, $150 each. A 24-foot gondola oar, $150; a barber's chair, $150; then a paean to the past: rolltop desks, round oak tables, Tiffany lamps, school clocks, church pews, iron stoves, stained-glass windows, old paintings, wine presses, hand wringers. And the bizarre: a doctor's old examining table, $100; a wooden coffin, a bird cage that might hold a pair of eagles, a broken wooden wheelchair.

Enter a customer: "Hey, Max. What do you want for that lion hanging up there?"

Max moves out of a dark corner and begins the sale by bemoaning the state of his business. "You know, that small place I had on Clybourn and Fullerton, that place did fantastic business on Sunday afternoon. There was all this walk-about business. I averaged $400 and better on Sunday afternoon. Now I have this big place and nobody's around."

"What do you want for the lion, Max?"

"Well, I'll give you a rock-bottom price. The Frame cost me. . . . "

"I don't want the frame. Keep the frame, Max. I want the lion."

"Ohhhhh, don't tell me that. I'm going to get $20 for that thing, but you want just the picture! What are you, nuts about lions or something? You mean I gotta take that nice lion out of that beautiful frame?"

No sale.

On his way out, the guy comes over like he's letting me in on a big secret. "It's hard to find pictures of lions like that these days," he says. I shrug. It's a time of shortages across America.

That crazy Dalmatian keeps following Max around, whimpering at his heels. He sounds hungry. Max pauses against a rolltop desk. The Dalmatian drops his whole head on a chair, looks up to his master with sorrowfully sad eyes, and whimpers once again.

"Sam, Sam, Sam," says Max to his dog. "What are you always crying for, Sam?"

WANTED
DALMATIAN DOG, SQUARE BLACK SPOTS.
WILL BREED AND MAKE FORTUNE SELLING
TO CHESS PLAYERS & RACING BUFFS

Silence once again pervades the shop, a silence of ticking clocks, a car passing by, and Sam's whimpering. From off in a distant corner, perhaps under a stained-glass window, you hear a faint, gruff whisper: "Now, Sam, you don't have to keep crying. I'm with you, Sam."

Another customer enters, this one looking for a wooden cabinet for his stereo. Max bumps around an aisle deep in old furniture and comes up with one. "Five bucks and you're all set," he says. Then he launches into a lecture on Tiffany lamps.

"I'll take down that old Tiffany if you want to buy it, and I'll stand on top of it, and it won't break. That's the difference in lamps today." The customer seems impressed. "See that lamp hanging there?" Max continues. "That's a re-

138

production of the original Tiffany peacock lamp, which is worth $6,000. I'm selling that one for $500."

Slowly the Sat-Sun Antique Shop is coming alive with the "walking-in peoples" Max is waiting for. One has a huge armload of wooden spindles.

"Gee whiz, those are beautiful," says Max. "Where did you find them?"

Then, to a young couple: "Gee, you're just in time. I only got a few thousand things left."

Max somewhat contradicts the legend of the old punchy boxer with the bells ringing in his head. There's a tiredness about him, a nose broken too many times, and those fists hang out from that overcoat like clubs. He has a tendency to slur over some words and enunciate others almost too perfectly. A punch-drunk boxer he's not, but an old battler, weaving pretty surely in place, he could be.

Max went to Notre Dame from 1932 to 1935. "I was majoring in pre-med," he says. "But then I found out I could make good money boxing."

He's been married to June Alpha Martin for eight years. She's a painter—"a women's-lib nut," in Max's words—who's trying to make it in the art world without his help. He says her portrait of Jack Dempsey is the best study he has ever seen of the true Dempsey viciousness. "People don't know what a cruel animal Jack was in the ring. It's a wonder he didn't kill a dozen men."

There was a previous marriage . . . "when I was in my prime as a fighter," says Max. "And, oh, lots of women, innumerable women who stayed for maybe four or five years, then they want to get married, and you know, you know . . . I've got a daughter in California and four grandchildren. I don't do much in my spare time, a little reading. Once or twice a week I may go to one of the Old Town bars with my wife. She likes to talk. She's a woman of a few thousand words. I just sit there and listen to her. I like to listen to her."

His private history of boxing goes back to the '30s and '40s. He was a Golden Gloves champ, a CYO champ, and in 1933 he beat Joe Louis for the United States Amateur Championship in Boston. You do something like that once in your life, and you hang on to it. You've got a remembrance that increases in value through your falling years like a rare antique.

Louis went on to become the Brown Bomber and, from 1937 to 1949, the heavyweight champion of the world. And Max Marek? Max moved beyond the ropes to coaching, then in again to wrestle in the '50s. He still has the whole history of fighting in his head, and he'll dust it off for you at the drop of a name: Barney Ross, Bob Fitzsimmons. . . .

Now Max stands tall, slightly dazed, under a skylight ringed around and around with old wooden chairs and the Sunday afternoon light pouring down upon him. "I had fifteen peanut machines," he says. "And I had to make thirteen keys for them. I taped all the keys to the machines, and in a few weeks all the keys were gone. Now what the hell do people want to steal peanut keys for?"

PLEASE
DON'T THROW CIGARETTE BUTTS
ON THE FLOOR.
OUR COCKROACHES ARE GETTING CANCER.

Customers continue to drift in and out, some buying, many "just looking." Max keeps weaving around, musing on the way things were, the way things are.

"I love this business," he'd written in a handful of "notes" he places before me, "for the same reason as most of the dealers in the Junkque and Antique Business: We are like gold prospectors, hoping to hit a gold mine to make us rich. That is, to find a 'sleeper,' a Rembrandt, a Tiffany, from some attic or 'picker' who is dumber than we are.

"All of us do have the 'instinctive' intuition of the beauty or craftsmanship of an article, and thus we latch onto it and make wild guesses at price. Besides having an eye for the 'something different' item, like a human skull, a camel saddle, a gondola oar, wood coffin, telephone booth, I like to 'create' interesting items out of junk, like taking a singer sewing machine, removing the machine, and adding a top to the cast-iron base to make a 'conversation piece' table. Candelabras out of thick, turned table legs are always good sellers.

"Then there was this casket-maker who moved to larger quarters, leaving behind a few old wooden coffins, which I bought. I stole the idea out of *Playboy* to make a phone booth out of one. Then one of my employees, Will Gibson, said, 'Let me fill one up with wine racks and make a casket-wine cellar."

People are always after something different, and Max picks up on this and rolls with the punches. "There's a big demand for church pews now . . . 4 to 5-foot benches. This is still going strong."

Whimpering Sam is at it again, so Max digs out a couple of cans of Ken-L-Ration, which set Sam off in a delirium of tail-wagging and heavy breathing. But a customer seems interested in the barber's chair, and Max discusses the possibilities of reupholstery with her while Sam drops his head once again to the chair, looks up at the dog food on the desk, and barely holds back the tears.

Sam reminds me so much of the faithful old RCA dog looking into the horn of His Master's Voice that I am startled by the sight of the real thing. There in the window sits the very 3 or 4-foot dog I am thinking of, minus the horn. Who else would have this dog in his shop?

"That's Nipper," Max says. "A friend of mine had him over on the South Side. Nipper and the Morning Glory Horn. I paid a $100 for Nipper and $100 for the horn. There are only five guys in Chicago who own a Nipper, and none of 'em want to sell. I'm trying to get permission from RCA to make some new ones. They'll sell like crazy.

"There's a guy in California who makes them out of plaster, but that's too delicate. The originals were made of papier-mache. I'm thinking I'll get them made out of a hard rubber."

The Morning Glory Horn, though, is missing. One morning a helper opened the shop and sold the horn to someone for $80, a figure he found written on the bottom. "I been looking all over Chicago for that horn," says Max forlornly. And so Nipper sits alone, a part of his past gone, looking somewhere across Sheffield for his master's voice.

Near the main entrance, a few feet behind Max's desk, stands a huge monster. Max notices my stare and tosses over another one of his signs to explain the mystery.

WHAT'S IN A NAME?

This was Murgatroyd. Born 1945 of normal parents, led a normal life until he was 12, with only shock after shock from fellow children who taunted him for his name, Murgatroyd. Murgy took up body-building with a vengeance, over-developed his pituitary, thyroid, and other glands, and became a terror, a monster in size, and feared by everyone. He died at 25 from an enlarged athletic heart.

His parents being Irish had an open-house wake, where everybody stayed drunk for three days and nights with music, food and liquor. Everyone enjoyed themselves so much that at the suggestion of one of the drunken relatives ("Such a grand wake, Mrs. Murphy. You should have the body stuffed and keep the wake going for a week.") they had Murgatroyd stuffed. The police finally shut down the gala but morbid celebration and Max Marek bought the body.

What's in a name? It can ruin a boy's life.

Max, memorialist of monsters, assumes his Buddha position behind the desk, engulfs the pipe with his fist, and reaches down to pat Sam. "Now, Sam, stop that crying . . . I'll get something to feed you.

"In '55 I got fat," he says all of a sudden. "I got fat drinking in the saloons. I was putting down a bottle a day. And one day my girl friend showed me a picture of us at the beach. 'Who's that big fat guy?' I said. 'That's you,' she said. 'Me? Well then, I'm going to wrestle.'

"So I called up Fred Kohler at Marigold Gardens and told him I wanted to become a wrestler. I was so out of shape it took me five months to get ready. I wrestled under the name of Polish Pride. I had this long mustache, this major-domo hat, and a cape. And I used to go into the ring with this midget under my cape, hanging by a strap. All the fans used to wait for that. I'd say, 'Okay, Eddie,' that would be the signal, and then the midget would drop to the floor.

"It was a gimmick, you know. It was a hell of a lot of fun. But the midget took the whole business too seriously. I used to sell $1000 worth of tickets a week for Kohler, ten per cent for me. So you know, every time I wrestled, I won! I used to promote these things. But that damned midget wasn't hep to the phoniness of the thing. I was fighting Gardini once, going at him with these resounding whacks across the chest, waiting for him to fall to the floor, which is what he was supposed to do. But this time he didn't go down, which had me confused. All of a sudden Gardini motions, pointing to the back of him with his thumb. And there's Eddie, holding Gardini by the hair so he can't go down. 'You better get rid of that goddam midget,' Kohler told me."

Max breaks into laughter now, recalling those times. "Once I was walking up to ringside with Eddie hanging from that strap under my cape. And the ring, you know, is about five feet above the floor. So I step up there to the corner, along the edge but not inside the ropes, when all of a sudden I see a friend of mine at ringside. So I turn around and yell, 'Hi, Kelly!' and the midget, thinking I gave him the signal, lets go of the strap and drops five feet to the floor! 'You sonofabitch!' he yells at me."

He's interrupted again by a customer, this time a sale. The woman has just bought the old barber's chair, an old stove, and a few other items. A knockout total of $265. Much easier that flashing your fists for a living.

"Oh, it's a young man's game," admits Max. "I don't miss it. Actually, there's no pain in boxing. You get tough and immune to those blows, till they're like water off a duck's back. There actually isn't any pain, only momentarily.

"How's my boy, Sam? Oh, such a baby, always crying, crying. . . . "

But at the age of sixty, Max Marek is not finished fighting for good.

"I've got a few little projects I'm working on. I'm trying to get the ecological offices of the United States to spend some money on a rat-elimination system I've worked out . . . ferrets. They used to use ferrets to control the rat population. Now, when the government is spending millions on rat elimination, I can't get them to spend $1000 on this experiment. The bureaucracy and red tape is incredible," says Max as he digs out three file folders—his correspondence on ferrets to the newspapers, agencies, and universities.

"Ferrets are becoming obsolete in this country," he explains. "The cases of rat bites are figured at 46,000 a year, and who knows how many are unreported. Also, there are millions of dollars of foodstuffs, cheese, meat, wheat, being destroyed by rats. So what's a few thousand for me to try this experiment?

"I suggest: Raise ferrets. Release only the male ferret. Thus you do not create another parasite. In other words, their longevity is only six years, and they should do a pretty good job in that time.

"The black-footed ferret, which is about twelve inches long and seven inches tall, is big enough and mean enough to tackle any goddam big rat. And there are rats in Chicago as big as alley cats. . . . "

Again Max is interrupted by a customer:

"Say, you got a child's coffin back there. What do you want for it?"

"Twenty-five bucks."

"Let me think about it."

"So you train these ferrets," resumes Max in a shadow-boxing soliloquy.

"Train 'em to eat at 6 p.m. Say you ring the bell at 6 p.m. and feed them. Now, each day that you put that ferret in the building, you have all the cages set up and then at 6 o'clock you ring the bell and get them back in the cages.

"Do you know what a rat does when it sees a ferret? There was this rat walking around in a basement, and suddenly this ferret was let out. The rat shook with palsy, actually stood up on its hind feet in fear of that ferret! There was this plank set up, leading to a furnace. This rat actually ran up that plank and engulfed himself in the fiery furnace!

"But you know what I think the real problem might be? I think the ferrets might be too effective. They might actually hurt the rat-exterminating business."

Sam is slumped in total resignation by now, whimpering in his sleep. A customer is eyeing that gondola oar, and I'm almost afraid he might buy it. Max goes down slowly in his chair, leading with that right fist for an empty pipe.

"If I had my life to lead over again," he says, "I wish I could."

Chicago's Unforgettable Newsies:
They Come with the Corner

In early morning, State and Randolph is an intersection possessed by neon and night. Vapor lights, Field's clock, silence. Stoplights with nothing to stop except an occasional CTA bus, empty but for a driver and two passengers. On the northeast corner, a man bends over a bundle of papers at the news stand, pulls one out, throws a dime on the shelf, and crosses the street.

Nine bundles of morning papers are heaped near the stand, tossed from the trucks minutes ago. And now, down Randolph, comes Tony. A giant of a man dressed in blue jacket and navy watch cap. He moves quickly in halting steps. "Gotta get here before six or they start stealing the papers."

No one seems to know or care where the news vendors come from, so rarely are they seen coming or going. They are just there everyday, a part of the news stand, a piece of the corner. And nobody knows their names.

It is cold this morning and wet. Tony carefully sets old newspapers down in the entrance way to Walgreen's, then begins lugging and stacking the bundles there so people will not complain about wet papers.

By 6 a.m., more people gradually appear, and Tony greets them all. He collects whatever small change has been left on the stand by early customers, and hopes the amount is correct. It seldom is.

The stand itself, gray metal like a piece of office furniture, is almost indistinguishable from the other gray metal news stands on every corner in the Loop. It is, in fact, like every other "hard" news stand [the latest Chicago papers, some scratch sheets, little else] except for one thing—Tony. From 6 a.m. to 7 p.m., six days a week, he lends his own personality with each paper, his own style to news vending. And in the evening, if you listen carefully, you will even hear him "hawk" the news—"Papers! Get your latest papers!"—a lost street song in our time.

Tony never tires. He is a man at peace with work and people. "They're swell to me. I love people. They're like teachers—you learn so much from them. It's a school right here on this corner. They tell me about their jobs, about how they live. Been here since '57. I learn all the time. Kay Loring comes here. And Norman Ross. And lots of great people."

The nature of the stand [and even the news vendor] seems determined by the setting. As neon and streetlights give way to day, thousands of people descend upon State and Randolph, then fan out across the Loop, every one hungry for news . . . the latest news. At times, Tony almost spins with papers—hands behind his back, hands at both sides, hands outstretched with dimes and quarters and dollar bills [so difficult to change in the rush hours]. The faces are familiar, many of them, but the names usually a mystery. There is never enough time, at this time, this place. Yet everyone is welcome.

Even the weather. "Love all kinds of weather. It don't bother me. No, never. Never at all. I was right in the thick of it in the the snowstorm last year. Froze my thumb, that's all."

Seven o'clock, 8 o'clock, 8:45 a.m., people on their way, trying to make the store, the office, the appointment. Buses parade with standing passengers. Stoplights wink a halt for pedestrians. A cop whistles to the wind. Everyone wants a newspaper. Tony's hands are black from ink.

"Nobody here gives me a hard time 'cept this mailman here," Tony grins. They greet each other with a laugh, a jab, a punch in the arm. "He tried to give me a knuckle sandwich the other day," Tony says, all the while selling papers, greeting other customers, thanking them, and losing track of the mailman who disappears in the crowd with a wave of an arm. "Hey, where's State and Randolph?" someone yells in Tony's ear. Another wise guy, this time a neighbor of his.

Patience, good service, call it what you will, Tony displays an abundance of it when suddenly, in the midst of this morning madness, the inevitable crotchety old woman approaches the stand, peers over the papers, studies the headlines, the editions, blocks out the other customers, and selfishly goes about giving orders. "Mister, I want the *Tribune*, the *Times*, and the *American*. No, not the top ones. Wait, somebody looked at that one; it's all wrinkled." Tony pulls out fresh copies from the bottom, "Thirty cents, Ma'am."

She sets down her shopping bag, opens her purse, sorts through the change for two dimes, a nickel, and five pennies while Tony thanks her, folds the papers, and attempts to place them under her arm.

"No," she scolds him, "don't bend them. Put them in my shopping bag straight or else you'll tear them."

And still he smiles. And still he accepts everyone, even punks.

Tony handles his money with only one free hand. He works out of a bulging canvas apron but finds it faster and easier to keep loose change on the stand. He is ready in an instant to change a dime, a quarter, a dollar bill. "Yeah, but these kids work together. Two of 'em. One will start banging the stand on this side and when I move around to see what's going on, another comes around the other side, scoops up all the change. I can't chase 'em."

Tony will never work anywhere else. "Worked in a laundry before this. For twenty years. This has the laundry all beat. This is the greatest. You know, I sold 1,900 papers myself when Kennedy was killed. Nineteen hundred. Had my picture in the paper standing here holding the papers up like this. I was even on TV."

In midmorning at Harrison and Central, in snow and freezing rain, an old man sits hunched on a wooden box before a news stand, watching his fire and the empty streets.

He has been here since 5 a.m. Each morning he comes by bus, crosses Central with the aid of a broomstick cane, and opens the shack. One bundle of papers waits for him.

At 5 a.m. the huge Shell sign across the street neither glows nor turns. At 5 a.m. the Greek church stands quietly on guard behind him. Only the sign, "Louie's Snack Shop" is lit far down on Harrison, too far for him to even see. CTA buses hum at the terminal across the street. Trucks growl along Congress expressway, high up and a block away.

When you are seventy-five years old and have been selling newspapers since 1932, mornings like this mean nothing. You are here again to make what you can of the day. Work. The same work. Opening the stand. Moving all the wooden boxes, the milk cases, the concrete doorstops so that the shack is finally free and the lock can be touched and opened.

The enemy is still the weather [and now, age]. Today the sharp wind fights from the north. So you build a small barricade of sorts, a barricade of boxes and

planks. Every day, like a child, you build and destroy a new fort for yourself.

Now for fire. The rusty drum, knee-high, is stuffed with old newspapers and wood—orange crates he collects from the Greek grocers near by. Then suddenly in the darkness of that corner, there is light and warmth.

The old man opens the one bundle of papers and sets them down on the curb with a rock. There is no room for them on the stand. The stand is filled with wood, sticks, wire, twine, rags, old papers, bags, cigar boxes. "All for the fire," he explains. "All kindling." He pulls a wooden box next to the fire and waits.

He is always waiting. Waiting for something to happen down Harrison, a street that dead-ends into Central and Columbus Park. Waiting perhaps for the 10 o'clock truck. Or waiting for people. Or death.

His name is Charley. "Most people call me that. Though most people don't know me."

Most people don't know him. Most people can hardly see him at the stand. For even in daylight, the shack gradually emerging in all its hopeless dereliction, Charley fades into the setting with his own protective coloring.

His head is bowed, almost permanently now with time. His hands are hardly there. An old red hunting cap lends what little color there is in the scene.

Where does he live? "Rent's too high here. I tell people I got a room at the

Morrison hotel. But they see through that right away."

The weather? "Can't pay much attention to it anymore," he says. "This winter's the first time my right hand has bothered me. Can't count the money out for paper trucks and pay the boys when they come to collect."

Charley has the time to talk, but no one to talk to. Regular customers, he says, "come for a while. Then they move. They get a new job. There ain't very many of them I ever learned their first names. I never see them anywhere else but here."

Charley sets out a cigar box for money, gradually moves to the east side of the stand, and pulls out an old green wagon. Then, with painfully slow steps, he starts across the street, in search of more firewood. By the time he returns, the fire will be down, and the cigar box probably still empty.

He has no regrets. "If I could have gotten acquainted with somebody who had a good job and could have cleaned off a desk for me in City Hall or the Board of Health or the CTA, that might have been better. But I don't know people. I don't know people. You just can't walk into an office an' say, 'How do you do, I'm Charley.'"

Returning to the stand with more wooden boxes, he crosses the street like a toy mechanical man [the motor running down, the steps pulling]. A car slows, then stops to let him pass [the driver gasping at such a sight, such a man alive]. Charley moves alone and can be seen now in daylight, apart from the stand, as the man he really is.

A scarecrow of a man. A man in gym shoes. A man of patches and safety pins and string. A rag-doll of a man. An old, old man who battles cold and freezing rain today in the strangest of get-ups—a second pair of pants hitched up with safety pins to his money apron, knee-high like cowboy chaps. An old, old man of thick gray hair sticking out in clumps over his shoulder like the feathered neck of a wet bird.

A man who has but one eye left for watching.

A man with only one arm left for working. The empty coat sleeve is tied up with newspaper twine to keep out the wind and cold.

A man whose clean white handkerchief is the cover sheet from the bundle of morning newspapers.

He sits now at the fire, turns his head, watches and waits for noon.

At 4 o'clock in the afternoon on the northeast corner of Cermak and Oak Park, the "regulars" begin to assemble around Jerry's neighborhood news stand and wait for finals.

If the weather is mild, they will stand outside against the windows of the corner restaurant, face the kelly green stand and discuss the headlines, the weather, the people passing, and eventually the ups and downs of the stock market. They will look through the long, colorful rack of magazines, study the front page of the latest *Enquirer* [10 YEAR OLD GIRL MOTHER OF 5 LB. BOY] or watch

149

the tiny American flag on top of the stand whip around in the wind. They will wait.

The final edition is worth waiting for. Other editions were only just beginning to tell the news, but the final edition, the FINAL, has everything all wrapped up with THE END. And nothing, nothing at all "new" can happen . . . till tomorrow morning.

In a short time, if the finals have not arrived, the regulars will begin their finals-are-late ritual of estimating how far away the paper truck is and how much longer they must wait. Sometimes they will wager.

Jerry steps lively through it all, getting rid of as many late editions as possible. But at this hour of the afternoon, only the really desperate will take a "late" when the Final lurks somewhere around the corner and down the street. Jerry collects money from the waiting regulars and remembers their faces. When the truck arrives, he will snap open the first bundle, and these people will help themselves while he handles the curb service.

When you work a neighborhood news stand ten hours a day, week after week, year after year, you become a part of everyone's life. You match newspapers and magazines to faces and usually names. You welcome the old-timers who are happy to get out of the house and come to the stand to talk. You welcome the housewife coming for her magazines, the kids for their comic books, the Bohemians for their "Hlasatels"—The Only Czechoslovak Daily in Chicago and Suburbs, 5 cents.

Jerry begins his day at 9 a.m., relieving the morning man who has handled most of the rush of working people. At 10:15 the *News* and *American* come. The trade is usually sidewalk trade in these hours—shoppers heading for the stores along Cermak road. The late morning and early afternoon trade is seldom heavy. "Up until 3:30 is the deadest time. I'll grab a sandwich around 2:30 or 3:00, if I can find somebody to take the stand. Usually there's always somebody around to watch it, except when the weather's really bad. Nobody hangs around then. I'll miss my dinner and have to go through the whole afternoon with nothing to eat."

In the early afternoon, before the final rush, there is still plenty to do—getting the magazines in order, sweeping around the stand, counting returns. A kind of housekeeping.

"You're busier in the winter time, so it works out real good. When you're busy, you keep warm. The worst is the triple blow—strong wind, cold, and blowing snow. Wind is bad all the time. You gotta keep watching the papers to see that they all don't blow down the street when some guy helps himself and forgets to put the weight back."

Automatic paper boxes he regards as just a pain in the neck. "They don't get the latest papers," he says. "And most of the time the people don't know how to work them. They put their money in and they don't get their papers. They lose.

They come back to the news stand."

During rush hour, the curb service customers command most of his attention. He must keep them moving fast for there is only enough room for two cars. Here he begins to match paper to car. "Most of them are regulars. I know the cars, the kind of paper each one gets. If the guy was walking, I probably wouldn't know who he was."

Sometimes someone gives Jerry pennies, and that means trouble. "You're trying to hold on to 'em or count 'em with gloves on, and the guy behind gets nervous and starts blowing his horn." [And then the light changes on Cermak and the buses can't move, and the cars behind the buses start blowing their horns, and the people coming home from work can't cross the street, and everybody is just a bit peeved, including Jerry who has just dropped a few pennies.]

"Why does everyone think they have to unload their pennies at the news stand?" he asks. "This lady comes up to me with a handful of change and she's pickin' out ten damned pennies for me! Can you imagine that? A handful of change, and it's so damned cold and the cars are waitin' and she's standin' there pickin' out these pennies. So I just threw them at the stand, and they went rolling all over the ground. There's another one there. The hell with it."

It is now 4:05, the finals nowhere in sight, and Wes, one of the regulars, agrees to watch the stand while Jerry checks his anti-freeze for the evening rush. He walks down two doors away from the stand, enters the House of Cole, and orders a boilermaker. "Here comes Jerry the Bohemian," says Lyle, the innkeeper. And so begins another loud round of "look-who's-calling-who-a-Bohemian" till eventually Wes sticks his head in and yells, "Jerry, I'm freezing," and Jerry signals O.K., pulls on his gloves, kills the beer, pockets a few pretzels, yells, "So long, you Bohemian," and returns to his stand, now almost empty of papers. "Thanks, Wes." He gathers the coins from the shelf and feeds them into the changer which hangs from two eye hooks screwed into the front of his thick navy jacket.

Wes and the regulars have assembled in the heated, glass-enclosed entrance way of the corner restaurant and continue their vigil. It is already 4:35. The driver is late.

The talk today is war, as the men shuffle around the radiator.

"Still say we ought to go in there and bomb the hell out of them."

"What gets me is how a little puny country can pick on the U.S."

"Check the truck, will you, Wes?"

Jerry is running back and forth to the curb, placating his customers, shouting and hand-signalling "no papers," telling them to take another turn around the block. "They should be here any minute."

"That's what you said the last time I went around," a driver replies.

Wes rejoins the boys in the entrance way, "Nowhere in sight."

"Must be a new driver."

151

"Yeah, it's a new driver."

"Probably doesn't have a helper."

"It's cold today. That holds him up."

"It was cold yesterday and he was here at 4:14."

"It's those little corner machines. That holds them up. Monkeying with five papers."

Jerry's getting a workout. He's out of everything now. "Frank, check the truck."

Frank hits the windy corner, holds onto his collar and hat, struggles through the onrush of people and traffic, and signals to the boys behind the glass that he's spotted the truck. In he comes. "He's coming up on Ridgeland."

"Ah, go on, you can't see that far."

"Yeah, yeah, sure. He's coming."

Roy's turn. He goes out, peers straight down Cermak, waves to Jerry and hollers, "Ridgeland, Jerry!"

Back inside, "See, I told you he was coming."

"Yeah, but you couldn't see him at no Lombard."

"Here he is, fellas."

A steady stream of bundled men file out of the doorway and head for the stand at precisely the time the paper truck, front end angled like a charging bull, rounds the corner with a roar, the helper jumping off with a weird bundle of finals, the truck never seeming to stop but only hovering there for an instant. "A hundred and eighty," the driver calls out as Jerry frees the finals with a snip, the helper throwing the bundles to the pavement with a splat! splat! splat! "That sounds like a good number," Jerry shouts, "no returns."

"What took you so long?" yells one of the blue-chip regulars.

"I got ears but you don't see me running, do you?" the driver cracks as he tears away from the stand, the helper barely making it through the door on time.

It is all over in minutes. The regulars, once a cluster, fold the final markets under their arms, separate with hardly a farewell, and silently return home.

Jerry is left alone, busy with the curb service. The cars will keep coming now for hours. Soon it will be dark. Headlights will approach the curb, the windows on the restaurant will glow, and Jerry will flick on a small light for the stand. At 7 o'clock he will turn it all over to Nick, the night man, and get into his car and drive home in the neighborhood to wife and family.

On State and Randolph, Tony, the last of the hawkers, will call out his final "Papers! Get your latest papers!" and prepare to catch the Illinois Central for a quiet suburb and dinner with his sister.

And on Harrison and Central, the old man's stand, locked and barricaded for hours, disappears in the night. The finals are in vending boxes chained to a pole. No one stops. Charley sits alone in a room on skid row and waits for morning.

Chicago's Public Library

A man's home is his own castle, he remembered reading somewhere. And Carp Diem called the Chicago Public Library home. Who knows where he came from, or why he suddenly plunged into such darkness, a fugitive in his own castle? These kinds of questions Carp kept trying to find answers for at 78 E. Washington—home.

One morning, exploring his own castle, Carp picked up one of the new free brochures at the Randolph Street information desk. "Your Public Library is open to serve you from 9:00 a.m. to 9:00 p.m., Monday through Friday, and 9:00 a.m. to 5:30 p.m. on Saturday. It is a tax supported institution, and its services are free to all people."

Those were the kinds of words Carp liked to read. Words conducive to his own lifestyle: "your," "serve you," "free to all people." He didn't like the way they passed over Sunday all so quickly. Sundays were hell for Carp. For one thing he found himself out on the street with a whole day to kill. "Some freedom," Carp could often be heard mumbling to himself as he circled the library all day Sunday. "A man locked out of his own castle."

Early the next morning he'd be there, though, waiting at the Randolph Street entrance for the drawbridge to go down. He'd be anxious, after a day spent stalking the deserted Loop without a word to read, after a night under Wacker, inside a Madison Street mission, or between a couple of Grant Park bushes. He, and a handful of other cronies who had discovered that books could open doors would be standing around the entrance with their paper sacks and used shopping bags in various classic poses of crosslegged anxiety.

The second the drawbridge came down, the doors swung open (9:00 a.m. sharp!), Carp and his fellow travelers made a painful dash past the lending desk, the popular library, and into the waiting elevators. Carp, the fastest reader in the first floor dash, would always manage to get possession of the west elevator all to himself—in fact, take a reader's delight in hitting the "close door" button just as a crony's hand reached into the hissing doors.

Books and doors, openings and closings . . . these were certainly symbolic things for a lover of libraries to ponder as the elevator ground up and up to the third floor where Carp, once again beating his cronies in the east elevator, was the first man to run safely home free into the men's washroom screaming: "Sanctuary! Sanctuary! Sanctuary!" all the way.

A day in the castle always began this way. Safe inside the confines of the free toilet, perched upon his throne, Carp would contemplate the contents of his very limp paper sack. The razor was there, the comb with 13 missing teeth, the assorted memorabilia of a man on the move, king of his own castle.

He chewed an old pencil stub to a crude point, rummaged through his bag for a torn piece of paper, and inscribed upon his marble walls the line he came across last week in the Humanities Department, third floor, Randolph Street side: "You are a King by your own fireside, as much as any Monarch in his Throne." . . . Carp Diem. Carp was always stealing somebody else's ideas. But, "What the hell," he'd say. "It's my library."

And it is. Or was. Carp made it his home, a morning, a noon, a night at a time—except on Sundays. After completing his early morning toilet, clean shaven, hair slicked back with free, green liquid soap and combed with visible gaps because of the thirteen missing teeth, Carp would begin his daily life in the library. Carp, the keeper of the word.

Starting from where he was on the third floor men's room, there was no place else to go. Third Floor North was a veritable dead end. Much to Carp's confusion, the architect of the old Chicago Public Library must have been a genius in the strategy and structure of ancient fortresses. Depending on which entrance an unsuspecting reader approached, should he aspire to higher levels or confrontations of sorts at the opposite end of the castle, he could inexplicably run into a blank marble wall, a stairway leading to oblivion, or a corridor of containment.

In the early days, there were times when Carp met himself coming and going. He once spent an entire week as hostage in the Civil War Museum, Second Floor North, trying his damnedest to break through to Second Floor South. He finally surmised that the shortest distance between two points was a broken line which involved a jump from the window of the north courtyard; a dash across the yard; and a climbing attack to the south courtyard window. This left only the problem of distinguishing windows from walls.

"Who the hell built this place?" Carp was heard to have said as he found himself wandering one afternoon lost in the fiction stacks, staring down at the floor into the foggy glass blocks glowing in some obvious life below that was going on, on still another level of secrecy. "Kafka," a voice replied from another aisle. "Well tell Kafka, Carp says he's a damned poor architect."

Carp, however, was free. Free to read anything that held his attention. Free to vanish in sections of the library that suddenly imprisoned him. Free to spend his late morning in the reading room, going through all the newspapers. Free to spend his afternoons at a lecture in the Auditorium, Randolph Street, 12:15 p.m. . . . "Mrs. Henry Marks, the Ikenobo School of Japanese Flower Arrangement;"

or listen to music, "Eisenhower High School, Blue Island: Pep Band, directed by Peter Bertuca;" or free-see a movie.

According to his free monthly calendar of events, next Monday evening was a banner night. Marlene Dietrich in "The Blue Angel." For a horny old guy like Carp who couldn't afford a skin flick, what more could a man desire than Dietrich and that Gotterdammerung of legs in his own castle?

Well, you can't judge a book by its covers, as Carp was soon to learn. And when the day of reckoning comes, brother, will you be saved?

It happened on a Monday, as Carp recalled. He had spent the entire Sunday as a moving target for hostile pigeons in Grant Park. They had no respect for an old man who said he was King of the Castle across the street. Carp made it that Monday to the third floor men's room in record time. He dashed out of his private elevator for the door which, like books, he learned, led to pleasure, only to be stopped dead in his tracks by a blue uniformed guard.

"Where are you going?"

"In there," said Carp.

"What for?"

"To sit on the throne."

"Why?"

"Because I am in need of it."

"Are you a smart guy?"

"No. But books are the windows to knowledge, and I am a slow learner."

"What's your name?"

"Mr. Diem."

"Let's see your library card."

"I don't have one. I've never had any need for one. Libraries are free."

"Then what do you come here for?"

"Please, can I go first and answer later?"

"You must be one of the guys we're getting complaints about. You look like the kind of guy who writes obscenities on marble walls, makes crude advances toward our motherly, matronly librarians, follows unsuspecting girls into the stacks, steals books."

"No, no. On my word. Believe me. This is my temple, this is my castle. The library has been put here for the good of all men, like me. And I am a good man."

"Then how come you don't have a library card?"

"I don't know."

"Well, you can't use the john unless you have a library card."

"Then you are about to witness a grown man have an accident."

"Take off!"

And Carp flew. To the fourth floor men's room, Washington Street entrance.

155

Carp spent the next couple of days hiding out in the Applied Science & Technology Department, pondering his plight. He liked this particular department because of the view it had overlooking the flower stall on Garland Court. He had napped many sunny afternoons there. But now he had to get down to some serious plans. He was beginning to be recognized. Carp adjusted his false mustache and thought deeply.

Not only guarded washrooms, but freelance knights in plain clothes were passing through every floor, every level of his castle.

Carp was in a sweat. He thumbed through his free brochure looking for an answer. "Although its resources are vast, every effort is made to make it easy for you to use the library's riches." Nothing. "Transients and temporary residents may borrow books on a Cash Deposit Card." He was a transient without a cash deposit. "Public Washrooms: For Men—Third Floor-North, Fourth Floor—Southeast." Carp could not go home again. "You must have a Library Card in order to borrow books from the Chicago Public Library."

Of course. That was the answer. A library card maketh a free man! With a library card, once again he could become a nonentity, entitled to all the privileges of the men's room, etc. So Carp filled out the application with no trouble at all until he reached the line which asked for his address. How could he tell them he lived at 78 E. Washington Street? But he did. And they believed him—for castles thrive on illusion. Carp was now an official man in his own castle.

And so Carp continued to thrive in his ambiguity till still another Monday when a final coup of sorts was staged. Carp passed easily into the Randolph Street entrance that morning, not in the least confused by the presence of a chrome turnstile. It was, after all, a logical and more organized way to admit the rush of readers into the castle. There would be no more pushing and shoving now. To every man his turn. Nice, one at a time. Carp first. First into the elevator, into the men's room, safe inside the castle. Only later that afternoon, as he prepared to exit on the Washington side for a brief stroll in Grant Park, did Carp realize what a fish he had been.

At the exit entrance stood another guard.

"Open your paper sack," he said to Carp. "Book Check."

Behind him, in front of him, people of all ages were lined up against the walls, emptying shopping bags, purses, briefcases, packages, pockets. Anything that could possibly conceal a book was open to scrutiny. And what was in Carp's paper sack? A razor, a comb with 13 missing teeth, assorted memorabilia of a man on the move, and . . . and?

"Open the sack," he said to Carp.

"But there's nothing in it except a few personal belongings."

"If there's nothing in it, then you got nothing to hide."

"But that's not the point," countered Carp. "Do you know your own library? Do you know the quotation up there on the staircase . . . A LIBRARY IMPLIES AN ACT OF FAITH WHICH GENERATIONS STILL IN DARK-

NESS HID SIGN IN THEIR NIGHT IN WITNESS OF THE DAWN—Carp Diem?"

"You act like a book thief," coughed the guard.

Which immediately caused Carp to panic, flee into the hissing doors of an empty elevator mysteriously headed DOWN, screaming all the way, "THE CHICAGO PUBLIC LIBRARY IS UNDER SIEGE! UP THE PEOPLE! UP THE REVOLUTION! UP THE GUARDS! UP THE CASTLE! CHECKMATE!"

Carp had never been in the basement before. It was not on his floor plan of the library. It was a new world. Maybe this was what he was looking at through the foggy glass-tiled floor of the fiction stacks. Maybe this was what that word "Labyrinth" meant that he found in the dictionary last week. Maybe here guards feared to tread. Carp would carry on his private subversions from the lower levels. "UP KAFKA!" he was heard to yell just before disappearing into a damp corridor of darkness.

School for Brewmasters

No, it's not I.I.T. but S.I.T. (the Siebel Institute of Technology) situated in a rather unimposing office building at 4055 W. Peterson, headquarters in Chicago for J. E. Siebel Sons' Co., Marshall Division, Miles Laboratories, Inc., which includes the Institute. Through these portals pass some of the heroes of folk history—brewmasters.

Aside from neighborhood ne'er-do-wells who occasionally retreated to the basements of bungalows to research the secrets of home brew, I met only one real brewmaster in my life, Ted Eisch, of the Joseph Huber Brewing Co. in Monroe, Wisconsin. Brewing for over forty years, Eisch, a man of many secrets, could make the very kettles sing in his presence. He revealed only two secrets of the brewmaster's life to me:

"I used to be a bootlegger in my younger days. That's where I learned it." And, "I studied brewing at the Siebel Institute of Technology in Chicago."

That remained with me to this very day. A school for brewmasters? In Chicago?

Oh, to be a brewmaster! I conjure visions of rollicking old German brewmasters in magical Black Forest breweries tapping kegs of amber, wiping creamy foam from their walrus mustaches. Or mad monks dashing around candlelit caves, the lust for lager upon them!

With "How do I become a brewmaster?" on my mind, I enter the Siebel Institute of Technology to see just what it takes to get ahead in beer.

A young Mr. William R. Siebel (third generation) leads me to his private office (nary a touch of an old brewmaster about him) explaining how, as far as the school is concerned, he's the whole administration rolled into one.

"The company began in 1872," he explains, "and the school was started in 1900 by my grandfather, J. E. Siebel Sr. He came over in the 1860s. He was basically a scientist, a chemist—University of Berlin. He was interested in brewing when he came over here and started the First Western Scientific Station for Brewing. He was one of the early workers on refrigeration.

"In the past, people learned the art of brewing through experience, through a brewmaster. A lot of Germans got the breweries going. They brought that with them when they came to this country. So did the English. In 1912 there were 53 breweries in Chicago. But most of the brewing that goes on here came from the German tradition—a lager beer. People had developed their own method of brewing beer, and then the scientist came along and explained why things happened the way they did . . . how to control things . . . what to do to come up with the final result."

And what about the old fashioned brewmaster who worked with a gut feeling for a gusto brew? (I taste strong and bitter, therefore I am real brew.) And what genuine old brewmaster, in or out of his cups, would come up with an insult called Light Beer?

"There is still a lot of art left in it," explains Bill. "A good feeling for what needs to be done, but also how to control it . . . how to prevent problems from developing."

Where does brewing begin for a trainee in the art of brewmastering?

"Basically, you start with barley. You put that into a process called malting, where it starts growing on its own. You steep it in water. Internal changes go on in the seed itself, converting the starches and proteins into other substances. This is controlled. Then the process is heated at a point, stopped, killed . . . warmed and dried. It is now malt.

"This is typically the stage where the brewers buy it. Then the malt is ground, put into the mash with water, and heated to different temperature stops which will permit more of the substances—sugars and proteins—to develop, which will become the basic substances that become the beer.

"It's still the mash, which is then filtered through the grain bed. The liquid filters through there, comes out relatively clear, and goes into kettles at which stage it is boiled and then the hops are added. It is now called wort.

"Hops gives it more of a beer flavor. The wort concentrates it somewhat and settles out protein that coagulates during the boil. The wort next goes through the cooler, then it's typically placed in large fermentation tanks and yeast is added. It's now called the fermentation process, which usually takes about 5 days. Technology helps control the temperature and the amount of yeast added.

"Then there is the drawing of samples on it as it goes through the fermentation process . . . taking what time is needed to cool it down. It is now called 'ruh' beer, which basically means 'into storage.' It's cooled down to the low 30s."

The mystery of hops?

"It's a plant, a vine. Actually, it's the cone that grows out of it really—kind of the flower of the plant. The Germans, I think, were really the first who added the hops. Some German probably had a hop cone in his hand, tossed it in, and thought the beer tasted very good. Without hops, really the flavoring substance, you'd have a sweeter drink . . . pretty much a grain flavor."

And yeast? Yeast was always a strange and magic taste sensation for me. As a kid I ate packages of it like candy.

160

"Yeast has the job of converting starches and sugars into carbon dioxide and alcohol. It's a living organism. Most brewers keep their own culture of yeast going so they are sure they will always have their own strain.

"The whole process of brewing takes several weeks. At least ten days for the first storage—but in the past, several weeks to two months. Then a second stage from three weeks to a month. And at about his stage any beer would be ready for consumption. In modern breweries, ten days to three weeks. Beer is a perishable product. It should be kept refrigerated."

I still wonder about J. E. Siebel himself, the founder of the company and the school. "He was once Chief Chemist for the city of Chicago," explains the grandson. "Although he was a scientist, he was a little more on the business side. He came up with different products like corrective water salt, chill proof beer. He was interested in flavor stability, age stability . . . so the beer could be duplicated. So it will hold up better when it reaches the consumer."

One question lingers: can a guy like me walk into Siebel school with no more than an appreciation for good brew and a desire to become a brewmaster?

"Very rarely do we have people come in off the street. I don't really know of anyone who applied after the basic interest stage. Our main function is to provide technically competent people for the brewing industry. Almost to a last man these people are sponsored by breweries.

"You need at least two years' experience in a brewery and in as many departments of a brewery as possible. You would need at least the equivalent of a year in college, a background in chemistry, math, physics, biology. . . . And you would need the recommendation of the brewmaster who you're serving under."

I meet almost none of these requirements. I'm heartbroken. There's no room for an apprentice brewmaster with a background in poetry and on a continued quest for great brew. Furthermore, I loathe chemistry and physics and would like to think there is still a place in this world for the improvisational brewmaster.

"There are about 45 different brewing organizations in the country," continues Bill Siebel, "and about 95 brewmasters. In the larger companies, the brewmaster might be called the Vice President of Production. In the larger plants you might have brewmasters and assistant brewmaster. In the smaller breweries, there is only one brewmaster on the whole."

And no chance at all for an amateur to get his hands in the hops?

"No. We wouldn't want someone coming in without experience. It would slow the class down. And we wouldn't have the room. If we had openings . . . well, you'd still need some kind of background. A college graduate . . . chemistry, biochemistry, engineering . . . possibly someone like that might qualify, but he still wouldn't get the same thing out of the courses as people with experience. I guess if we had space, it would be a possibility. But it really hasn't occurred."

Besides, I couldn't get into the Siebel Institute of Technology at the moment no matter how hard I tried. School won't be in session again until next year.

"Our schedule is eleven weeks, every two years. There is a short course (five days) in the off year, but it is more a long seminar than the regular course. The short course is intended for basically a different audience—men specifically working in quality control or microbiology.

"Our last class consisted of 48 people. We try to house everyone together in a couple of hotels by Lincoln and Peterson. They spend more time together and have a better start. We help as much as we can with any problems they have.

"The average student is usually anywhere from 23 to 48 years old, out of college, often with an advanced degree. Maybe two or three per course don't have a full college education, but they have at least chemistry and math equivalent to the first year of college. The average student has been brewing five to seven years. They come here because they know it will be good for their career.

"Typically, they're paid while they're here—basically an expense account— and the company is paying their tuition (over $2,000) and their way here. A few of them pay their own way.

"They are more flexible at getting jobs elsewhere when they get back. We also act as an informal placement service if they [the company or the employee] will let us know."

What profits it a man to be a brewmaster?

"Usually in a few years [after Siebel] they'll move up the line. $17,000 to $19,000 base salary for those who come here. With overtime, perhaps $24,000. Breweries pay pretty good. My own guess--$30,000 to $40,000 for a top brewmaster or vice president of production."

With brewmasters becoming vice presidents of production in brewing bureaucracy these days plus the dying of small breweries everywhere, the future would appear dim for young brewers.

"There are less brewing companies, but more beer is being produced all the time. Production is more consolidated, but there will be a continued need for brewmasters. True, more of the smaller companies are going to close down, but there is no reason why some of the smaller ones can't make it.

"What still needs to be done—and brewmasters are a big part of this—is to learn more about the beer market for today: brew beer with a longer flavor stability, improve the shelf life so that beer retains its taste and brilliancy longer.

"We work with the small breweries. We provide an outside testing facility for them and send people out for in-plant inspection and to make recommendations for improving things for their benefit."

As for brewmasters themselves, in these technological days, doing any experimenting on their own, Bill Siebel explains, "In the old days, yes, brewmasters would try different things. But now the marketing people control this."

What's to become of our tastebuds, one wonders, in the country fast being overrun by technologists and marketing people telling us what we should have? Has brewmastering itself been reduced to a type person these days?

"Well, the technical training these people have today, almost down to the

162

last man, is incredible. They are bright people, and getting better all the time. The competition is fierce. But these people have a real feeling and love for the business too. They like beer. They love the industry. There's a lot of exchange of scientific knowledge to continually improve the brewing process."

But no contact with the old art of brewing?

"Aside from our staff we do have occasional guest lecturers."

How about an old German brewmaster?

"Not now. There aren't that many anymore."

Ted Konis enters the office, a technical service representative for the J. E. Siebel Sons' Co., also a former assistant brewmaster at Carling Brewing Co., a graduate of Carnegie Institute of Medical Technology, a B.S. from Kent State, and post-graduate work in biochemistry at Marquette University. Also a faculty member of Siebel Institute, he explains, "I just finished a course last year. I do mostly brewing materials, brewing, seller processing and management. Brewing materials are malt, hops, and adjuncts.

"I've got a lot of hours in brew house calculations. I think the systematic formula and practical use of calculations in brewing is very important—tank and bin computations, the complete derivation of a brew through mathematical calculations. In other words, if you want to do this on a brew—how much?"

And there you have the modern brewmaster. Ted's feelings about the foreign students who come to Siebel's for training?

"They're good. We had two students from Japan, for example. Very good. They come with a purpose. We give them a complete picture of brewing, from basic malting to the retail shelf, which leaves them open for managerial positions in their own companies.

"Every student has his company's beer shipped here. The local brewers ship kegs. Those from overseas fly in two or three cases a week. These we use for classes and the bierstube.

"The students are trained to detect defects, know what they are, what causes them, what measures to take."

Bill Siebel begins to show me around the Institute, beginning with the J. E. Siebel Library on brewing. (The room is reminiscent of those I used to find tucked away in the upper floors of the old Chicago library. Nobody quite knew what they contained or what went on there, but occasionally the bent figure of an old man might surface and hover momentarily above some ancient volume.)

The library is empty, a bit cluttered with odds and ends, some very old books on brewing, a few shelves of magazines, and a bust of the founder himself, to whom Bill refers reverently as, "Old J.E."

"The students are often assigned different topics," explains Bill. "And they must do a short presentation, a five to ten-minute speech. They come here and do a little research in the library. This gives them some group work experience, they learn to use the library, and they learn how to make a short presentation."

Periodicals in the library range from the *Harvard Business Review* to *Der*

Weihenftephoner. The books all seem very old. "Not many new books come out," says Bill. A book such as *Handbuch der Spiritusfabrikation* looks like something that might interest an alchemist. Another book credits Anton Schwartz and J.E. Siebel as "Pioneers of brewing science in America." Down a long hall is a gallery of Siebel Instittute graduation portraits, class photographs which end with last year and date back to the first class, 1900-1901, with four students and nine faculty. (The faculty today averages ten people.)

The main classroom is about the size of the average science lab in any public school. The classes—mostly straight lecture but also a microbiology lab and a taste panel—cover 370 hours of classroom study (almost the equivalent of a full year of college) on topics such as raw materials (barley selection, malting process, enzymes, etc.) the chemistry of hop constituents, the composition of various brewing waters; brewhouse theory and practice; fermentation; storage and finishing; packaging; quality control; microscopy (techniques in the examination of beer sediments); taste panel; engineering production management.

Classes run 9 a.m. to 4 p.m., five days a week, one hour for lunch. Final exams are given. A diploma is issued to signify successful completion of the course. No one has ever flunked out.

The taste panel intrigues me, and I accompany Bill Siebel down to the Taste Panel Lab, a room sectioned into areas like phone booths with a red glass in each one. (There is also much banging and smashing of empty beer bottles in a refuse container, and, ah . . . finally the aroma of beer.)

The company runs regular tests here for various breweries—some on a regular basis. And during the time the Institute runs classes, students use these facilities once a week for about two hours.

The man in charge of Taste is a company man named George Skocic, chief chemist, who describes his particular role with Siebel as "Let George do it."

"One 12-ounce bottle goes to five glasses, evenly spaced," he explains. "I really don't know what the samples are." (Each brand is coded.)

The proper way to taste beer?

"The person who is tasting . . . his buds should be in a fairly neutral state. No smoking. No residue food from breakfast or lunch. No cold. No stress. A fairly neutral state. His taste buds should be in prime condition.

"He should first check the aroma of all the samples because it's a good indication of what the beer is going to taste like. He should taste the strongest aromas last. You try to taste the milder ones first.

"You taste with your tongue, like this, but your olfactory system has an influence on flavor. There are only four basic tastes: sweet, sour, salty, and bitter. Most of the things you taste in beer are all the other things, and all the other flavors that have nothing to do with taste.

"Most people like beer with a mild hop character, a little bit estery, and a little bit sweet."

Upstairs again, across the hall from the classroom-lab is another learning center of the Siebel Institute of Technology: the bierstube. As fine and comfortable a bar, with German neighborhood tavern overtones,as can be found in any Chicago office or school complex. Oh to be an apprentice brewmaster cracking the brew books in the on-campus bierstube just down the hall!

"For the Taste Panel," explains Bill, "students get a lecture at the bar here and then go down to the taste panel for the actual tastinga lab style class. Usually, by the way, each class donates something to leave behind. The last class donated the most practical thing—these bar stools."

I try out the class donation while Bill Siebel slowly slips behind the bar and draws one for me . . . the brand a secret, but my unsophisticated taste buds would guess it to be Stroh's, which is real fine with me.

The bierstube, sort of the student union of the Siebel Institute, is a place for students to hold meetings, get together. "They also have their meals here. We put them in charge of everything. They usually have a caterer bring in food. Oh, they might have pizza or something. There's a kitchen back there too. Occasionally one of them may want to cook."

It's a great old bar, a real find on the premises. Some old mugs decorate the shelves . . . mugs, in most cases, donated by former students. Cut-off ties hang on one wall. "The last class session," explains Bill, "is an evening of cutting off everyone's tie and hanging it on the wall." (Ah, these modern brewmasters: there might be some hope for them yet.)

CLASS OF '75 . . . GOOD FOR ONE FREE DRINK AT THE HIDDEN COVE PUB, 5338 N. Lincoln reads another annoucement on the wall. "A favorite hangout," says Bill.

With the heavy class schedule each day at the Institute, one would not expect the future brewmasters of the world to have much time to put down more than a glass of beer or two at the in-school bierstube, with "night classes" at the Hidden Cove Pub being something else entirely.

Bill Stiebel pauses . . . "Oh, I think the last class we averaged a half a barrel a day here. Yeah, brewmasters are pretty good drinkers. They really love beer."

I feel sad I'll never make it as a student of the Siebel Institute of Chicago and the bierstube itself is as good a place and time as any to cry in my beer.

The old brewmasters are gone. They will never be the same. Science, research, marketing, the beer business itself marches on, reminding us we only go around once in life . . . as if any true beer lover need be reminded. That's why he got into beer in the first place! But the times, they are certainly changing.

"The last course, we finally had our first woman in it," confesses Bill.

My god . . . a brewperson! I consider the possibility of drowning in my beer.

"The old German brewmasters didn't want women in the plant," explains Bill. "They felt they carried wild yeast with them and would affect the beer."

Beautiful, beautiful. Here's to the old German brewmasters! Here's to brew! Ah, hell, here's to wild yeast, wild women, and all the brewmistresses to come!

Jovan Trboyevic: Restaurateur

I am to meet him at Le Perroquet, 70 E. Walton, and check his story out. The entrance is neither suggestive nor deceiving. A touch of nondescript elegance inside the foyer, a hint of privacy and shadows.

I share a small, old fashioned elevator to the third floor with a man fashionably dressed as a first class French waiter. "Please," he says as the elevator comes to a halt, the door opens, and he directs me to the anteroom of Le Perroquet . . . a few chairs, a reservation desk, a small bar.

I have come to see Jovan Trboyevic. They seem to sense this. I take a chair momentarily, but within seconds I am ushered to a quiet corner in the dining room with attentiveness, graciousness, and much table pulling and arranging.

Though the room is only moderate in size and partially filled with luncheon diners at the moment, there is an engaging sense of quiet repose about the place. I sit back comfortable amidst a multitude of large, tapestry pillows. A strain of soft music . . . violins . . . gypsy?

Whatever, a touch of East European, definitely, a bit of Budapest here . . . a touch of a three-star Michelin French restaurant . . . and more than a touch of fine dining a la Ljublijana, Zagreb, Dubrovnik. Once again I'm beset by plush red velvet memories of all night journeys on the Simplon-Orient Express.

I slowly extricate a cigarette from my breast pocket, tap it a few times on the table, and quietly marvel at the instantaneous response of a waiter hovering over me, nestling flame in his hand. Mon Dieu! Such attention! It sure beats counter service at Walgreen's.

Wrapped in a cough and a cloud of my own smoke, I carefully grasp my cigarette continental-style, cradling the lighted end in the palm of my hand, and ponder the questioning of Trboyevic. . . .

"Mr. Trboyevic, vere are your papers, please?"

Casting a secretive eye around the room, assured no one is paying any attention to me, I peruse the surroundings more carefully, picking up dishes, feeling the table cloth . . . all my Slavic ethics coming home to roost. Fresh flowers on the table, plush red upholstery . . . dishes, hand-painted, French . . . a delicate little table lamp . . . a bottle of Mountain Valley water. The tablecloth is white

167

with an orange and green stripe running down each side plus a pattern of little green parrots, two at a time, running down the center.

Le Perroquet is neither dark nor light. It is subdued. Quite perfect for a rendezvous, or the quiet pursuit of personal history between two strangers. I manage to light a second cigarette myself, though a bus boy immediately descends upon the table from nowhere and empties the ash tray of a single charred match.

With a retinue of waiters and bus boys about him, a tall man, impeccably attired in a dark suit, white shirt and tie, approaches the table. He extends his hand and his apologies. The table is pulled out for him with a flourish. He questions my preference of wine (I'm noncommittal), and he proceeds to order a fine Meursault, in French.

Trboyevic has arrived.

Seated, he is still a big man. He's careful, precise. His gestures are minimal. I'm not quite sure of him yet, but he's obviously the most refined Yugoslav I have ever met. We play the traditional mind game of Who came from Where, a beginning which only a true ethnic understands.

My grandmother was born in Croatia, I explain. Koncanica . . . not far from Daruvar . . . near Zagreb. But she was really Czech.

"I was born in Zagreb (Croatia)," says Trboyevic. "It should make me a Croatian, but both my parents were Serbs. It's like an Irishman born in London."

Ah, common ground . . . so we proceed, with caution. His speech baffles me. Expecting harsh, Slavic overtones, I hear instead a very sophisticated English with overtones of French phrasing and with only occasional long lost thrusts of his muscular Slavic heritage.

Austro-Hungarian, I detect . . . Peter Lorre? Theo Bikel? Something of each in his presence plus all the character actors who exude the mystique of the Balkans—the brooder, the melancholic. A man apt to risk his life for a cause, or suffer his dark nature in silence. And there is laughter, too, humanity, and a sense of mission about his life.

"My father was a lawyer . . . on and off a member of Parliament," he continues. "I had a classical high school education. As a boy I spent my summer vacations in France and Austria. I did speak French, German, and English by the time I was fifteen.

"My father was a gourmet. I grew up in a family of gourmets. I had an amazing father. He would entertain, you know, and he would have a poor man bring fresh oysters and lobsters from the Adriatic. It would take him thirty hours by horse and wagon.

"Yugoslavian restaurants before the war were extremely interesting . . . all the way up to '39. You had influences of French, Italian, Turkish, Russian, North African, Austrian. So with all this, you always had something interesting. In those days restaurants were a way of life . . . you could afford it."

Both our wine goblets are continually and unobtrusively replenished. Trboy-

168

evic sits back, grasps his glass in both hands like a chalice, in one instance, remains completely still for a moment, and then picks up his story.

"I left Yugoslavia on a submarine that mutineed, and joined the British first in Crete and then in Egypt . . . that was April, 1941. I was 21.

"April 16, 1941. This was before Russia or America were in the war. Greece was collapsing and Yugoslavia falling . . . all the rest had already been occupied by the Nazis . . . Europe was lost."

Trboyevic sits even taller at the table now as he recounts the escape from his homeland by submarine. He was a member of the Yugoslav Royal Navy at the time, and under orders to surrender the sub to the Italians who controlled the Adriatic.

"The submarine," he laughs, "was made in England in 1916 . . . the oldest commissioned submarine in the world. Some of us decided not to surrender to the Italians. We mutineed. We lined the rest up on the front of the sub with machine guns and explained that we were going to escape with the sub, and those who wanted to join us could do so, and those who cared to remain could do so too. Fourteen stayed out of forty-four. We got the commander out on the dinghy.

"From there on we took all kinds of passengers who wanted to get the hell out of the country; some were air force, one cabinet member, one priest."

On a submarine that normally held a crew of forty-five, Trboyevic explains, "We took on seventy. And out of the seventy, only twenty were submariners. I was the youngest man on board. We had four hours training in diving procedures for the non-submariners, how to surface, things like that, and then we were ready. Our new commander was another submarine commander without a ship. We left Kotor, I remember, at 6 p.m. on April 27, 1941, in rain and snow.

"I haven't thought about it much, but it seems humorous now. We had one guy who said, 'Let's take it (the sub) to Argentina, sell it, and take the money.' Another, a communist, wanted us to take it to Russia. But we all had one thing in common: We were against the Nazis."

Some of the humor but mostly the danger dominates the journey as Trboyevic describes the submergence of the vessel off the coast of his homeland, now enemy waters with the Italian fleet all about.

"How did we avoid them? We went right under them," he says. "We moved under the Italian fleet, out of the Adriatic and into the Mediterranean. We had to be careful of mine fields. How we made it was sheer luck. It would be like closing your eyes and trying to walk across the Kennedy Expressway.

"We had to surface every night for three hours to recharge our batteries, in the moonless time of night. It took us four days to reach the Greek island of Kefallinia, south of Corfu. We got into the Bay of Argostolion and our periscope established that the Germans were not there yet. We surfaced and immediately established ourselves so as not to be shot at. And the Greeks told us, 'Don't move. You're in the middle of our mine field.' There was no plan to their minefield. They had to send some fishermen out to get us through.

"We gave them lots of Yugoslav money for souvenirs, and the Greeks gave us a dinghy full of oranges. Then from Crete, to Alexandria, Egypt . . . about three days. Do you really want to know more about this? Shall we have some more wine? Or would you like something to eat?"

I nod my approval of the conversation, the wine, the mere suggestion of food, while Trboyevic gestures with a nod of the head to a waiter who has been diligently keeping a part of his entire being trained to our table. Andre stands beside Jovan and begins to recite a litany of food in French. I don't understand a word of it but for the English translations, yet it sounds so magnificent that I want to taste it all.

For lunch at Le Perroquet ($9.50 per person) there are fourteen appetizers such as La Truffe du Perigord en Feinllete, Tour aux Champignons, Gazpacho Andalou, Pate's Assortis, Mousse de Saumon, sauce verte . . . For entrees, a choice of twelve, such specialties as Ris de Veau a l'Orange; Souffle de Crabe; Tripes Basquaise; "Lamp Chops" au poivre Vert; L'Escalopines de Veau au Citron; Entrecote Minute; Confit d'Oie, Pommes Sarladaise, Les Poissons du Jour; and Nos Plats du Jour.

At Jovan's suggestion, I go for the pate and the fresh blue fish, from the North Atlantic. I am not disappointed. My taste buds are suddenly revitalized after too many days of franchised food and instant coffee. By God, I can't remember fish tasting this perfect since . . . since . . . since the Dalmatic coast of Yugoslavia . . . since the South of France.

Dinner at Le Perroquet seems even more compelling with entrees of Dodine de Pigeon; Le Caneton Roti "Maison"; Steak Moutarde; Le Carre d'Agneau Poele ($19.50 per person).

An hour passes, maybe two . . . who knows? Who cares at Le Perroquet? The food, the wine, the room, the service, the conversation . . . Trboyevic, that submarine—did it have a name? What the hell ever became of it?

"It was called the 'Fearless' (at which point I almost choke on a mouthful of wine) and is now, I think, in some naval museum in Yugoslavia, which is probably where it belonged before we got on it.

"The British decommissioned the sub in Alexandria, and the men scattered. I was with the British then for a few months on special assignment, which included training in Palestine for commando and paratroop work. And after that it was back to Yugoslavia for infiltration work to establish connections with the resisting Yugoslavians. I parachuted in at Montenegro. There were four of us. Two were killed in the parachute drop. We were flown in on Liberators (American b-24 bombers) by a bunch of Canadians. It's amazing. I slept all the way there. They had to wake me up for the jump. Today, I don't sleep well.

"This was September, 1942. It took us five days to find the resisters without falling into the hands of the Germans or Italians. We brought a wireless set, and we had codes and ciphers. And we found General Draja Mikhailovich, who was in Montenegro."

Yugoslavia, at this time, was a bouillabaisse of factions—those still loyal to King Peter II (who fled the country upon the invasion of German, Hungarian, Italian, and Bulgarian forces on April 6, 1941) which included General Mikhailovich and his Serbian guerrilla forces (the Chetniks), who soon found themselves engaged in a civil war as well as against partisan forces led by Marshall Tito, a communist.

And now, enter Trboyevic, recently escaped to Egypt on a mutineer-commanded submarine, trained by the British in Palestine, and now parachuted into Montenegro to establish contact with Mikhailovich.

"Shortly after, I decided that my country was not only occupied but involved in a civil war. I was saddled with a battalion of orphans in the middle of Bosnia. I was father, priest, commanding officer of 300 men through the winter of 1942 until May, 1943. I was then disassigned from that, given forged papers and instructions to penetrate northern Italy and set up a wireless operation to keep the British supplied with information.

"With a gun, papers, money, wrong name, I travelled by train and boat to Italy . . . between Rijeka, Split, Trieste, Milan . . . I would translate to Mikhailovich headquarters and from there was relayed to the British. Some of us were caught and executed. I got jaundice. And I ran out of everything else, so I went to Switzerland . . . curing a jaundice. More wine?'

I nod an affirmative while trying to put together the puzzle of Trboyevic on the move, now in Switzerland, next in London, face to face with King Peter II himself.

"I wanted to meet King Peter and tell him what was going on. Peter was a twenty-year-old boy . . . I was 23 or 24 . . . I couldn't give him much advice, just how I divined the country really was. No one had any ideas except the communists as to what to do with the country after the war. He [King Peter] believed the British and the Americans would prevail . . . free elections. I went back to Switzerland to rally various nationalistic forces.

"Money was really no problem. I had gold on me from Egypt. I had my full military pay being deposited in a London account. So I was decommissioned in London in 1944 and returned to Switzerland where I had to supplement my livelihood by working in restaurants. Eventually I went to the hotel school in Lausanne. I took three courses of six months each, one in chef's school, one in dining room service, and one in administration.

"I really liked this. I liked the food, I liked the wine. I worked everything in restaurants from humble jobs to assistant manager. Then I gave up on the whole thing. I came to America in 1954. I have not been back to Yugoslavia since 1943. It is still not safe for me to return. How about some dessert?"

Both Trboyevic and I are feeling the wine, I sense. Hours, years, a whole Slavic history has passed before us, but why end it now? Or here, in Le Perroquet? Jovan Trboyevic in America. What does that lead to?

"I was living in a suitcase. I wanted to belong to a society. I was too long in total anarchy. I am rather . . . well, what I think I wanted ultimately was for a person to have his own politics. Frankly, I think I'm an anarchist.

"I hate 'prisoners,' I think eighty per cent of prisoners should not become prisoners. For a man to become prisoner is a pretty sad thing in a society. To me America was the last trench of freedom, democracy.

"How did I plan to make a living here? It never crossed my mind. I really couldn't care less what I would do. I knew I could find something. In New York I worked at Sardi's as a captain, also the 21 Club. And I opened a restaurant in Larchmont called Cafe Continental. I had it for five years. I served a sophisticated food.

"Eventually I got involved with Burton Brown, who hired me to set up his New York and Washington D.C. clubs. In 1967 he brought me to Chicago. He wanted me to open up a restaurant as part of his Gaslight Club, but then he changed his mind about that. 'Burton,' I said to him, 'do you mind if I open a restaurant across the street from the Gaslight?' 'No, it will be good for my business,' he said, 'but it won't work.' So I opened Jovan's (16 E. Huron) in 1967. When he saw it worked, he opened his restaurant. He asked me to set up the kitchen for him, and I did."

Which brings us finally, to Le Perroquet, with Trboyevic reflecting upon everything, including himself and life in general.

"Well, Jovan's, you see, is more of a bistro. Le Perroquet, something special. I opened it in 1972."

Where does an ex-Serbian guerilla fighter and chetnik get enough gold to open a place as fine as this?

Trboyevic laughs. "Gordon Bent and his friends, they helped me open Jovan's. One of the most important things in life is contacts, the friends you make. Jovan's was so successful that we had people who were even more demanding, people who wanted only one sitting.

"So Le Perroquet is more luxurious in every way. Open Monday through Friday for lunch, Monday through Saturday for dinner. Lunch at 12, dinner at 6. Last dinner order out by 10 o'clock. Closed by midnight."

I asked him for his own feelings about Le Perroquet, about the good taste evidenced everywhere in the room (which he credits to the artistry of a young woman, Maggie Abbott.)

"There are ways that I would brag about this room," he confesses. "Very often the critics bypass their sense of smell. There should be lots of oxygen, fresh air to a room. You don't want any smell of burnt onions when you dine. The kitchen and dining room have to be separated.

"Most of this is not money-making, but where luxury is concerned, this is a very small thing. Acoustics, too . . . and not only of the room. Also, you have noticed, the help is very quiet. The crashes of unbreakable plates in some restaurants is something incredible. But it's a matter of training. We have to house-

172

break each new busboy and waiter.

"Ah . . . tables. Tables, you see, are well spaced. Important. This room seats eighty-five, about as many as you can handle in this style, and still respect privacy.

"Decor ought not to be gimmicky. I personally hate it. It should not be the dominant thing . . . but to make it fresh. I cannot understand, for example, why so many restaurants reflect a medieval theme. If anything, Le Perroquet is the 1930s. In the '30s we really got away from ornateness, and we went for comfort without being outright lazy. Simplicity, elegance . . . yes.

"Crystal, china . . . now we're speaking money for a room . . . and you want it to be luxurious. The only cut glass we use is for water. Everything else, crystal. A French plate . . . Limoges. This vase, Italian."

The food, though, what sets it apart? What is elegant dining all about?

"Lightness of food. You avoid flour, avoid fat, avoid starch. Use fresh vegetables, herbs, spices . . . everything always undercooked. Even chicken should be a little pink. I'm absolutely happy with the new wave of French cuisine. It's an absolute fit to civilization, a gift to our senses. The new wave is concerned with the raw material—how good, how noble, how fresh it is. You have to be dedicated to feel this . . . it's anti-moneymaking.

"You order every day, everything you need, every bit. It's a constant battle for freshness, trueness. Very often I go to South Water Market myself in the morning.

"You try to cook without obliterating it. And you don't do anything gimmicky like making flowers out of radishes. A radish is a radish! Simplicity. Sauces cannot tolerate unnecessary fat . . . starch. Everything that cannot be itemized will cost more money."

What's wrong with American restaurants?

"They cook the hell out of everything. And they don't fight the suppliers. In truth, I don't make much money here. This is terribly challenging . . . to tell a customer I have only one salad dressing, I hardly serve potatoes here. I try to do something that the man does not get at home regularly. I want to give them something that would take his wife two days to prepare. I don't think in two and a half years we have had a combined waiting time here of sixty minutes.

"Time is important. You pay for it everywhere, even the parking meter. But there is no rush here. It's up to the people. They want to pay for this or they don't. The most expensive wine, we don't even list. We have 150 wines at least. The average customer pays $16 to $18 for a bottle of wine.

"A nice person is a big shot. We try to give equal treatment to everybody. Of course, people patronize us for our food. This is not a restaurant to be seen at. It is a restaurant to enjoy yourself with friends."

Trboyevic is unwinding now. I sense it. I know the natural melancholic state of the Slavs. And I almost welcome it now after the superb dining, the fine wine, the natural storytelling. We are countrymen, I suspect, in more ways than we supposed hours ago.

"I prefer nervous, tense people, to the after-golf, two-martini crowd. I'm a frustrated, nervous man myself and understand these people. I like melancholy city people as opposed to the healthy countryset people. I prefer to make happy a melancholy executive as opposed to a happy suburban couple who have been playing tennis all day.

"I didn't know what a sense of insecurity was. I developed it in America by some kind of feeling of carrying a tremendous overhead when I get out of bed. Between getting out of bed and brushing my teeth, I think I owe somebody $100. From then till 6 p.m. it's all uphill. Then at midnight I will have my nightcap, and I will see if I made my day or didn't."

And why the name, Le Perroquet?

"I like parrots. I'm very fond of them. I like the color. I used to drink at a Le Perroquet in Switzerland, in Montreux, outside of Lausanne. And there are some other, ill-fared Perroquets . . . clandestine. It is almost the '30s again.

"I'm a very bad mixer. Call me a restaurateur. I'm also an anonymous host here. I spend more and more of my time at Le Perroquet. Actually, I'm quite bored at this stage in life.

"My best years were when I was socially and nationally weightless. That is when you become introverted, when you become acquainted with yourself, when you are dissociated. When I had only myself to decide what was right or wrong.

"I'm not this, and I'm not that. I'm free. I'm a weird little species that is totally alone."

And now that you know who you are, Jovan Trboyevic, you'd rather not know?

"Probably. . . ."

The Great Hot Dog Quest

It begins innocently enoug—a sort of hot dog hunger. If you're a hot dog person, you understand the feeling that comes upon you about three hours after supper, or maybe in the middle of the day, or maybe whenever you see the sign HOT DOG. Suddenly there's this insatiable craving for a dog with "the works."

I have never given serious consideration to hot dog lore, but this, I suddenly realize, is one of the chief characteristics of hot dog people: hot doggers are the easiest people in the world to satisfy. They don't have much taste as far as good and bad dogs are concerned. If it looks like a hot dog and is stuck in a bun, the trimmings will take care of the rest.

Is there such a thing as a great hot dog? And in the crowded hot dog environs of Chicago? And what in frankfurt's name could possibly distinguish a good hot dog from a great one?

At least a million or two hot dogs must be sold in Chicago each day. Where does the search begin?

I'm on the outskirts of the city, in the Arlington Heights area, feeling kind of hot doggy, when out of the darkness appears a trailer at the junction of Rand Road and Thomas. PEEP'S HOT DOGS. Immediately I like the name, PEEP, and know, even before tasting, that Peep will put out a good dog.

Peep's place is a common, second-hand house trailer. He has hauled this unbecoming structure into the franchise restaurant land of suburbia and established himself in the homey business of selling hot dogs face-to-face. You step inside and find him cooking in one end of the trailer; the other end is reserved for stand-up eating. Nothing special—which is pretty much the kind of comforts hot doggers are accustomed to. "One dog with the works," I say in a typical hot doguese. Peep puts a kind of small dog on a nice warm bun, adds the standard trimmings, (but no fries—"The machine ain't working yet."), wraps it tight in a napkin, and drops it in a brown No. 6 brown paper bag, all for 35 cents.

In my car, I devour it in three good bites, wipe the mustard from my mustache and conclude that Peep has a good dog—not a great one. But then again, as a lifetime hot dogger, I'm not easily given to comparisons. Gooder than what? Greater than whose?

Half an hour later in Des Plaines, on 83 and 62, I read LUM'S FAMOUS

HOT DOG [STEAMED IN BEER] 40 cents. Maybe this is the great hot dog?

To make this taste a fresh start, I chew one pack of gum and smoke a small cigar. Then, convinced that Peep's dog and its onions are only a memory, I find a table at Lum's and study the menu. But something is wrong. These are not the classic hot dog surroundings: red carpet, red globe ceiling lights, red ash tray, red menu, red waitress in a red apron, red vests on the men behind the counter, red coffee cup, red spoon. "I"ll have a red hot with the works," I tell the waitress. She returns a few minutes later with a beautiful red hot in a red plastic basket.

The dog is a rather hefty handful—pickles, raw onion, sliced tomato. A pretty fat dog on a pretty fair bun. And a respectable clump of french fries [35 cents extra], all in uniform gold [with a faint red cast] and not a burnt one in the bunch. Still, the surroundings bother me. It's a little like eating a hot dog in the Pump Room. The table. It must be the table. Hot doggers are not table eaters. There's something sacreligious about sitting down at a table and eating a hot dog, almost as bad as eating a hot dog at home.

I have devoured the last piece of my Lum's famous hot dog and stuffed myself with french fries before I realize that I have recorded not the slightest taste sensation of steamed beer. So I order a large schooner to alleviate the matter, and conclude that the Lum hot dog is a very good hot dog—not much better than Peep's except that Peep has that trailer going for him.

Next morning I'm on State Street, next to the Chicago Theater, in a place called Bob Elfman's. The menu plastered outside says it's been on State for over forty years, which is less than my lifetime. I can still remember seeing stage shows at the Chicago with Frank Sinatra and Jane Russell and a cast of thousands, but I cannot recall ever entering Bob Elfman's right next door.

Elfman's I like as soon as I find an empty stool at the bar. It's like a Paris Bistro! The service is swift, almost too swift. I've hardly begun to try twirling myself around on the bar stool before I am attacked on both fronts: Kitty, the waitress, asking me what I want (and then slapping at me for my ignorance), then the bartender with his gruff, "What'll you have?"

"A beer," I meekly reply.

The Red Hot Special (90 cents), served on a plate by Kitty, is some hot dog: half a kosher pickle; half a sweet green pepper; succulent, soft french fries; a paper cup of chopped raw onion; and the greenest picadilli I've ever seen.

My companions at the bar include a postman who is reading comic books and also hot-dogging it, a theater usher in full dress, and any number of common urban heroes trying to sort things out over their lunch. I nurse my beer (the bartender is ready to pounce for a refill) and stall for time by chewing the dog slowly and sorting out the fries according to size.

This is the best hot dog I have eaten today, I tell myself, holding back on the "great" designation since I still have miles to eat. I gesture "the end" to the bartender (who immediately looks upon me as the enemy) while Kitty comes from nowhere, whips out the check, and still hovers, I feel, somewhere behind me waiting for any final action. I make a gesture to light my pipe, and the bartender (for an encore) magically strikes two matches simultaneously.

"You need two for a pipe," he smiles.

I see the light: I've been trapped by waitress and bartender in the famous tip squeeze. Tips, I conclude, are alien to hot doggers: no hot dogger in his right mind would ever tip a hot dog man. But this is not a hot dog man confrontation. This is a restaurant. I slide from my stool and lay a quarter on the bar. Before my back is turned, I hear the sound of two hands slapping the bar.

"I'll take that!" says Kitty to the bartender. "I've had enough of your tricks."

"He was at the bar," says the man.

"He was my hot dog," says Kitty.

I have never been called a hot dog before.

Later that afternoon, my stomach tells me a hot dog and a beer for breakfast is not a good idea.

On 26th Street near Trumbull I find a hot dog place called Julio's. Twenty-Sixth Street was once solidly Slavic, a hot bed for hot doggers, but Hispanics have added their flavor to the neighborhood, so Julio's is now also hot on tacos. What I like right away about Julio's is that the windows are colorfully painted in that kind of chalky poster paint you can rub off with your fingers. The outside wears a cheap paint job with somebody's leftover quart of cerulean blue. One window is broken and taped, and the other has a painted picture of a foot-long hot dog for only 38 cents (with fries).

Inside there's sawdust on the floor, signs ("*Haga Su Pedido Aqui Pague Al Recibirlo*"—"Please Pay When Served"), a bullfighting tapestry, a couple of tables and a stand-up arrangement for hot doggers to lean into. Behind the counter a Spanish-speaking woman raves away to herself, probably wondering how she ended up a hot dog lady on 26th Street, Chicago. She speaks about two incomprehensible words of English. She must take orders by intution.

"Not a hamburger!" screams a teenager at the woman. "I said hot dog!"

The woman vents a few more Spanish expletives and then looks at me as if I'm a stranger to tacos.

"Hot dog," I say, almost lip-syncing the words to her. "Hot dog . . . hot dog . . . hot dog."

"Uno? Dos? Tres???"

"No, no, one . . . uno dogo, uno," I gesture. I raise a finger. I try to pacify her with my best high school Spanish. I am quickly handed a foot-long dog and a few interesting words as well. I have an inner dislike, however, for the foot-long dog. I have a sneaky suspicion it's the same as the regular dog, only stretched out by some sadist. Julio's is certainly worth 38 cents, but it is not a great dog. Mucho atmosphere, however.

Down the street I spot another *Red Hot* sign. I'm headed toward it, when suddenly I remember the hot dog man—the guy who pushed a cart. Those were the great hot dogs! Where are all the hot dog men? I hop into my car and spend a few hours cruising various neighborhoods in search of the old hot dog man. Nothing. The hot dog man has gone the way of most vendors, I conclude, just like the organ grinder and his monkey, the balloon man, the guy who came down the alley to sharpen scissors, the rag man with his horse.

There's got to be a hot dog man left in this city, I tell myself. For my kid's sake! He's got to experience eating food on the street! When you come right down to it, that's what a hot dog really is, street food! It's getting outside in the sunshine, taking a bite, dribbling mustard and onion and tomato down your chin. Nostalgic? Hell! Essential? Yes!

Somebody must have declared the hot dog man unsanitary! Some politician! I begin to yell aloud in the car. How many people ever died from a dirty hot dog? I see myself screaming at Mayor Daley, YOU TAKE OUR HOT DOG MEN AWAY AND LEAVE US WITH CTA BUS FUMES INSTEAD!

You can't fight City Hall, they say, but I stop at the first phone booth and dial City Hall, 744-4000. "I want to talk to someone about hot dog men." I am shuffled around from one clerk to another till a guy in the collection department says, "You mean peddlers?" And I say, "Yes, peddlers!" thinking to myself about what a great word "peddler" is and too bad it's almost extinct.

"I want to know where the hell all the hot dog peddlers are in the city."

"There's no such thing as a hot dog peddler anymore," he says. "No push carts. You got to have hot and cold running water. It has to be a trailer or a storefront." He hangs up.

I return to 26th Street to investigate that *Red Hot* sign I saw a few blocks from Julio's, around 3900 West. That's another thing about hot dogging it in the city: you never have to travel far. The places have a tendency to bunch up together. Often they're right next door to each other, trying to put out a better hot dog than the next guy for maybe a penny's difference—which is all the difference in the world to a true hot dogger.

Stepping up closer to Jumbo Steaks Red Hots (its real name is Ben's Stand, and that, too, seems to be the earmark of a real hot dogger place—no fancy names; better yet, no name at all—just HOT DOGS) I am taken aback by its size. It's a gangway, that's all, an enclosed gangway between two real storefronts. Nifty! Only a hot dogger would see the charm in such a place. There's no entrance. You get your hot dog from a window facing the sidewalk. And you are reminded by a sign: SORRY NO CHANGE FOR BUS. DON'T ASK. [That's the way hot doggers are used to being treated.]

I'm studying the menu posted on the window, something called the Garden Hot Dog going for 42 cents with mustard, catsup, relish, onion, cole slaw, tomato, pickle and pepper [hot]. A "garden" hot dog! "One garden," I tell the man at the window. Finally a touch of the poet among hot doggers. That's another

178

thing that's been bugging me—the lack of imagination in hot dog men. Maybe all hot dogs were made to taste pretty much alike, but occasionally a hot dogger wants a change, a touch of the exotic, the bizarre . . . even if it's only in name. A hot dogger in Western Springs once told me that thirty-five years ago in Minneapolis a guy sold a great hot dog covered with Rice Krispies. That's the artistry I'm looking for in this city! Is there no sense of the avant garde among hot dog men? Are there no experiments other than a chili dog?

"One garden!" I hear, and a bag is thrust at me through the window. I want to stand on the sidewalk and eat, but I can't manage the bag, bottle of soda and the dog without dropping everything on the pavement. So I retreat to my car, unwrap my garden of earthly delight, take special note of the full, ripe, juicy tomatoes, and make one delicious attack after another. The garden is bursting forth in my hands, on my lap, the steering wheel, the seat, the floor . . . I have tomato seeds on my shoes. No matter. The true hot dogger has a touch of the slob about him. This is the closest I've come to the great hot dog!

By my third morning I figure if I don't eat another hot dog until the next circus comes to town, I will survive.

Maxwell Street. It's still alive. There is a strange aroma in the air, food being cooked almost right on the street. I haven't smelled that since Mexico, since Greece, since Germany, where I am sure the great hot dog still thrives. My nose directs me to the northwest corner of Maxwell and Halsted, and I am astounded by the sight of the wildest hot dog stand I have yet found in the city. No name. A place like this doesn't need a name: a long green stand with all the windows wide open. And inside, a bunch of good-looking mustachioed Greeks working wonders at the grill.

Their knockout Polish sausage just begs to be eaten. Piles of raw onion, actual piles about six inches high, slowly brown on the grill. Twenty, maybe thirty pork chops sizzle and simmer and smoke. I see a man buy a "Polish" that is damned near buried in stringy grilled onions. I see a woman buy a pork chop sandwich that sets my stomach panting. I buy a hot dog with the works and discover that it is only pretty good. But my judgment has been impaired by the Polish and the pork chop. So I follow the hot dog with one of each and come to a rash conclusion: the greatest Polish/pork chop on top of a hot dog I have ever eaten!

The search continues: there is still Milwaukee Avenue. Milwaukee Avenue's got movement—people, bushels of fruit and vegetables sold on the sidewalk, a sense of life that most Chicago streets used to have but have lost to the canned excitement of suburban shopping plazas. This street was born for hot dogging.

On Damen and Milwaukee I spot a sign, *G & D Red Hots, 29 cents with all the trimmings.* This is the most rock-bottom, discount dog I've come across in all my wanderings. And G & D's interior does not disappoint me: a sterile Halloween motif of orange and black that keeps coming.

179

What kind of dog will 29 cents buy? A bargain beauty. A damned fine dog covered with trimmings, especially tomatoes. Most hot dog men kind of parcel out their thin, pale slices of tomatoes one, two, maybe three to a bun. This guy, though, knows his tomatoes and keeps dropping them on.

G&D's is full of real hot doggers—one guy who demolishes three of these red, dripping beauties in less than ten minutes; two Milwaukee Avenue business men types in wrinkled corduroy carcoats, faded Rex Harrison hats and shiny ga-bardine slacks, bantering economic prognostications like "I think maybe this guy's doing a land office business, huh?"; and a hot dogger beside me with a stuffed mouth mumbling away to me in friendly conversation, while I nod and mumble back like I really understand what the hell we're talking about.

Outside again, on the corner of Milwaukee and Damen, I walk into a woman leaning against the building, smoking a cigar. I feel that I've now found hot dog land.

I should walk Milwaukee Avenue, walk off some of this excess hot doggish-ness I've been carrying around with me. Instead, I head for the comfortable con-fines of the car and catnap my parking-meter-time away. A few minutes later, still somewhat dazed from dogs, I start the car and head slowly down Milwaukee Avenue, trying hard to recover my senses. Somehow the only sense that regis-ters is onions. Raw onions.

Suddenly, I find myself slamming on the brakes, damn near squashing a hot dog peddler who has just darted in front of me, pushcart and all! Quick! A park-ing place! That's him! I found him! No hot and cold water plumbing in sight!

I turn the corner around Paulina, ditch the car, and start hopping down Mil-waukee, laughing to myself and making obscene gestures to City Hall for all their self-righteousness in putting down the hot dog peddler. I find my man on Milwaukee and Mautene Court, one of those strange Chicago streets that run wild for a distance of half a block. And there, right in the middle of it all, red and white pushcart complete, is my outlaw hot dog man bigger than . . . all the clerks in City Hall lined end on end. And on the front of his cart he's got paint-ed (in pure, human freehand) HOT DO G 35c. I especially like the space be-tween the O and G.

He's wearing a trooper's hat, a little askew, in true hot dog fashion, and he's got this white apron wrapped around him with pockets for making change. There's a full basket of red tomatoes on his cart, and he seems to be squinting at them there in the sun. I walk right up, pat him on the back and say, "One hot dog with everything." He smiles and nods and carefully prepares the feast. He understands the handling of hot dogs, this man. His whole life is hot dogs.

Standing there in the midst of Milwaukee, eating a hot dog at the curb, watching the people, enjoying, enjoying the whole scene, I begin talking to the hot dog man. He is Spanish. Lazos is his name, as near as I can decipher it. And Lazos is a beautiful name for a hot dog peddler. "Five years I be here," he

180

says. "Yesterday only 'leven dollar." He shrugs his shoulders. "Sometimes too cold for hot dogs. Too many people no work."

The sun is high now over Milwaukee Avenue. Not the hot sun that Lazos knew as a native, I'm sure, but an overworked Chicago sun trying its damnedest to filter a little light and warmth on the street. A pigeon flies from one building to another, and then down the entire length of the block.

Soon, Lazos and I are wrapped in deep discussion, one of those hot dog conversations where the ideas, the words never quite meet but veer off into space; yet the feelings are understood.

"Lazos," I say, trying to grapple with the essential metaphysics of hot dogs, "pretty soon, warmer. Hot dog weather."

Lazos smiles. "Five years I be here."

"You can fight City Hall, Lazos. You got as much right to be here as Picasso."

"Yesterday, 'leven dollar. Other time, too cold."

"This was great luck, Lazos, finding you. Maybe you're the last of the hot dog men? Maybe the next time I come looking for you with my kid, you'll be gone. But Milwaukee's a long street, huh, Lazos? I'll find you."

"Too many people no work. Nothing."

"This is a great hot dog, Lazos because this is a great moment for the human spirit."

"Tomatoes," he says. "Thirty-nine, pound."

Dr. Preston Bradley: Amazing Grace

He smiles upon entering his study. "If talk would settle the problems of the world, I would have settled them years ago," he says. Lighting his pipe, settling himself comfortably behind the desk in a book-crammed room of an apartment overlooking Lincoln Park and the lake, his voice instantly triggers memories of radio, and all the good and bad guys I could only imagine. Dr. Bradley was a good guy . . . he just sounded that way.

He wears a gray suit, vest, white shirt and bow tie. His long gray hair ("I have always had long hair. I was the first hippie") curls up over his collar. He looks like an etching of a gentle doctor selling a patent medicine in an old magazine. He belongs on an early *Saturday Evening Post* cover painted by Norman Rockwell. He's a sepia photograph of a serene grandfather in a velvet-covered family album gathering dust in the attic.

Yet he is as much a part of today, Chicago, the country, the world, as any man alive involved with the human condition. (He's planning another trip around the world this summer.) There is very little that he has not examined. "I'll be 88 my next birthday," says Dr. Preston Bradley. "The 18th of August. Oh yes, I'm a Leo. I don't put a great deal of faith in astrology, but I'm a true Leo," he chuckles. "I certainly am."

The Sunday following my visit with him, I find myself driving west through Chicago and at 11 o'clock tuning in Dr. Bradley and the People's Church just to double-check the timelessness of his message. "Have You Met You?" he announces the sermon for the morning. Right on, Good Doctor, I smile. He's into the whole business of self-awareness these days.

"We are not accidents in the cosmos," his voice comes through strong, and as dramatic as ever. "There are no accidents . . . Personality is not a gift, it is an achievement . . . Man is the sovereign, not the victim. The greatest opportunity in life is the unfoldment of your own personality . . . Religion is that faculty of the human spirit that brings out the best in a person . . . No man need be a failure until he admits it . . . To live life under the influence of goodness, truth and beauty is to live the virtuous. The real test will be found in what you are out there in the world of men. Let me see you there, and I can have an adequate appraisal of your religion!"

Goosebumps . . . take care of that man, I echo a refrain. Great spirit, preserve him. In a city that gave us a Frank Lloyd Wright, a Carl Sandburg, may we hold onto a Preston Bradley as long as we can.

In these days of Jesus Freaks, gurus, Billy Grahams and Reverend Moons, new awareness and old awareness devotees, the good Doctor Preston Bradley of the People's Church, Lawrence Ave. at Sheridan Rd., remains pretty much where he began, down-to-earth and still making a hell of a lot of sense.

Going on 88, older than even the maharashi, and probably wiser, no cult as such has ever developed around Bradley. His whole life has been, simply, a "people's" church. "The good, the true, the beautiful, our only creed." Religion stripped down to the bare essentials. Something a lot of people can live with, and do, by literally tuning him in on WAIT at 11 a.m. each Sunday.

"Radio?" he returns the question with a warm smile, "I started it! I'm the oldest program in American radio. This is the 64th year of the People's Church, and I've been the pastor the whole time. I was the first radio preacher. It was quite an opportunity, radio."

Though my family is Catholic, I can still see my father on Sunday mornings after mass, tuning in the old Majestic radio on the refrigerator to WJJD (in those days) and Preston Bradley. The radio was buzz and hum, then the organ would play, and soon the sonorous voice of Preston Bradley would fill the entire kitchen. I pictured him as old then (twenty-five years ago) with gray hair, a long beard, and sounding much like God.

When I reached the age of questioning, I confronted my father once with the moral implications of a good Catholic (my own father!) listening to a Protestant preacher. But my father simply replied, "He's good. Listen to him. He makes a lot of sense."

To this day, side by side on my father's dresser, are two contributory envelopes: one for the local parish, and one which he posts to the People's Church. He has never seen Bradley, or ever attended his church. Most likely, he never will. But he carries a lot of Bradley's humorous stories in his head, and much of the Doctor's goodness in his own life.

"Our first congregation was 34 people," explains Dr. Bradley, "and we've grown to a membership of over 4,000—the largest liberal, independent church in the country. You can be independent and not liberal, you know."

Born in Michigan, he refers frequently to his summer home in Blackduck, Minnesota, "The only place that's home to me. I have always been a lover of the outdoors. I will never stay indoors if I can be outdoors.

"I've been three times around the world, visited every country on this globe, but I've never found a place that I've loved more or has been better to me than Chicago. I love Chicago," and once more I pick up the fervor, the tremolo of the man's voice and feel goose pimples on my neck.

"I think Chicago has its problems. But it hasn't one for which there isn't a solution. We have to meet the challenge of a wide diversity of people. I'm aware of it [problems of race, crime, violence . . . apathy and depression] more than ever in my lifetime here; but Chicago has a great future. We've got everything to become a truly great city.

"You must start in the schools with education. If I could, I would change the curriculum of much of the study that's given to youngsters before the twelfth grade. We have generations growing up that haven't even the remotest idea of this country's history."

In spite of everything you've lived through, I ask him, and in spite of all the recent horrors this country has experienced, you still believe that man is good?

"If you give up on man," he looks me straight in the eye, "you might as well put a torch to the whole business, and let it go!"

The People's Church of Chicago ironically finds itself in the boundaries of Uptown these days, a 'bad-news' part of the city that receives a tremendous amount of negative attention. Outsiders find it a ripe and ready place to hustle to death because nobody gives a damn. Those residents and clergy who must live in the midst of it find the challenge of making Uptown work more worthy of attention.

"Every city has a community just like Uptown," says Bradley. "There's nothing unique about it. It's part of a city's growth and development. It was once the finest residential district in the city of Chicago.

"The church, in a sociological role, tends to get bigoted. 'My way is the only way, and if you don't go my way, you're wrong.' No one church has got the whole truth.

"There are some good, wholesome influences in Uptown—the Kiwanis, for one—but they don't live there, they are not a part of the people. The People's Church . . . well, we're trying to set an example. Those do-good organizations usually wind up in a fight. My congregation is a cross-section of Chicago life—rich people, to people on relief.

"Diversity, that's part of the problem in Uptown. And that in itself presents a challenge. And each racial unit tries to exist by their culture and habits of living that they have brought with them and are not interested in changing. No, it's not good. I want to see any new truth that's discovered. If we could all try to find a creative, constructive attempt in our relations with each other, it would be a different world in a year."

Uptown is not the world, but then again, maybe it is, from Dr. Bradley's perspective of the way we live in America today. There is despair in the country, he acknowledges that . . . "It's more indicative in a national election year." He has known many of the leaders of the world, including U.S. Presidents. "I grew up not too far from Jerry [Ford]. I know him very well. Personally, I would be happy if we could have our future depend upon the character and quality of our national leadership."

185

And as for morality, "The basic morality is undisturbed. I think there is a basic reality about the American ideal, the American dream, but it will have to meet the challenge every day in these times by fortifying it with an unimpeachable morality."

Your message, Dr. Bradley . . . what is it, really? Can it possibly be summed up in a few words? Has it changed at all in sixty-four years?

"Not one bit. I'm preaching the same sermon today as when I began. People were surprised at my type of message at first, when I came on the radio. I have a little poem, and it says it all as far as I'm concerned. I don't know who wrote it . . .

So many gods
So many creeds
So many paths that wind and wind
But just the art of being kind
Is all this sad world needs.

That's my message."

Do you know Kurt Vonnegut's work I ask him (*Slaughterhouse Five, God Bless You Mr. Rosewater*, etc.). "Yes, yes," he replies. Well, he has a modern version of that message, if you'll pardon the expression. "Go ahead," he gestures. Vonnegut says, 'Goddam it, you've got to be kind.' Bradley throws his head back and laughs. "Oh, I like that. I like that."

And who have Bradley's influences been?

"Being adventurous in your thinking, you never run out of ideas," he explains. "I have been influenced by two people more than any other: Ralph Waldo Emerson and Thoreau. I've never paid much attention to professional theologians. I don't think I've ever preached a sermon where I haven't paid tribute to nature.

"Jefferson's Bible, I like that too. Do you know what he did? He took out everything in the New Testament that Jesus said, and that became his bible—the pure, unadulterated words of Jesus. Jefferson did that! Not the creeds, not the dogma. I could never accept a creed. There's a formality about people with creeds as if they spoke the last truth."

There is this openness, then, about Bradley, his faith, his way of considering all manner of men and beliefs. Nothing escapes him—science, mysticism, even the West's tendency these days to look toward the East for spiritual guidance.

"I think the great interest in Eastern religion is proof in itself that religion is of no primary concern these days. When a man says, 'I have no religion,' that's his religion, isn't it?

"I've been a mystic all my life. I don't think you can have any religion without mysticism. Mysticism is a process, it isn't a final, set thing.

"I don't think science was ever more united than it is today. Most of the scientists that I know are very serious-minded people. Psychiatry and organized religion . . . it's going to make religion rethink itself. That's hope. I think that

186

when God created man, and he did, he wasn't toying or playing. He had a purpose. Being born a human being and turned loose in the world is a great opportunity."

The pretty and warm-hearted Mrs. Bradley enters the study, and I fear I have overstayed my welcome. The dinner hour draws near, and I have badgered the Good Doctor long enough, perhaps worn him to a frazzle. Mrs. Bradley seems so lovingly protective of the old man, and I want to respect that.

But no, there is no hurry, she says. They are going out to dinner, but there is plenty of time. "We'll be married twenty-four years in June," Dr. Bradley smiles, "and people said it wouldn't last six months. She's a pretty good wife," he kids her. "I've known her since she was fifteen years old. She and my first wife, Grace (who died) were like twin sisters."

Of all the things we've discussed, Dr. Bradley, never once has the word "love" come up in our conversation.

"Love . . . that's in back of the whole business, isn't it? Most people don't use it with the connotation that's involved. Love is an acknowledgement of the validity of our differences."

I like that. I want to keep that as a souvenir from Dr. Bradley. I thank him and Mrs. Bradley for the time, and apologize for running into their dinner hour. (And just where would the Good Doctor and his wife be going for dinner, I wondered? A fine, French restaurant perhaps. Something definitely elegant.)

"We're going out for pizza," says Mrs. Bradley. "Down to the Home Run Inn to see Nick," says Dr. Bradley. "Do you know him, Nick Perrino? What a wonderful human being. He works with the Boys Club. He gives so much . . . I never saw so much adoration."

Dr. Preston Bradley and the Home Run Inn for pizza. A wild combination, but not the least bit out of character for the People's Preacher.

At the door, bidding good-bye to Mrs. Bradley, I listen to her recount an incident concerning a talk Dr. Bradley gave to some young people in Michigan.

"One of the boys came up to me after the talk, he had long hair down to here and tears in his eyes. 'Take care of him, Mrs. Bradley,' he said."

Take care of him.

Mornings at Pixley's

It was Monday morning at Pixley's near the library, a time, just before nine, to get things cleared up. A time to finish the last cup of coffee, put away the cigarettes, stare at the last page of the newspaper where there would be pictures and very little to read. Pictures do not take as much time as hard news. With pictures there is no real story, nothing to think about. Time disappears and he could make his own stories.

The man and the woman sat at the other end of his table near the window. The man sat with his back to the outside, facing her and all the confusion of a restaurant in the morning—people finding tables, moving chairs, turning newspapers, asking others to please pass the sugar. He was a business man, from the cool cut of his wrinkled clothes to the silent movement of his wristwatch, at which he would glance when he was sure she was not looking. He was a business man not quite prepared for a Monday morning. He needed a shave.

She had eyes only for the window, the outside. Beautiful eyes of such magnetism that most of the eyes on the outside—the men, the women, the students—were caught by them. One man stopped dead, looked at her intensely, then gave up when she would not let go with a smile or a motion.

"What are you looking at?"

"Nothing."

"Do you want some more coffee?" He checked his watch.

"No."

Close up she was not a beautiful woman. She was a satisfactory one—a woman whose hair needed more brushing, a woman who flicked cigarette ashes to the floor, a woman whose face seemed more used to crying than laughing. A woman who attracted men because there was something sorry about her.

The man bent down to tie his shoe. He looked again at the time. It was almost nine.

"Do you have your ticket?" he asked.

"Yes. Where did you say I catch the train?"

"Over there," he pointed. "Across the street. Downstairs. The 9:15. Maybe we better be going."

188

"Are you late for work?"

"No, that's all right. It doesn't matter. I don't have to punch in or anything. It doesn't matter."

"I should have taken the bus earlier this morning."

"Why should you take a bus? The train's much faster. It's more comfortable. I hate bus depots."

"Oh, I don't mind them. Once you're on the bus, it's okay."

"Do you want more coffee? Half a cup?"

"No."

She opened a heavy overnight case on the chair beside her—the kind of common sense luggage a parent might give a daughter upon graduation from high school—took out a comb and brush and began to fix herself up. She stubbed out her cigarette in the saucer.

The man pushed his chair on an angle so he could look out the window. The clock on the building across the street said 9:05, and there were not as many people walking as there were when he first came in. Even the traffic was lighter, although there seemed to be no end to the green busses and yellow cabs going back and forth. There were flowers for sale in buckets on the corner. He had never noticed that before. All the time he had come here every day to the city, and he had never noticed that flower stand. Wasn't there a birthday at the office just last week? Didn't someone mention flowers? Get some flowers for the desk. But no one knew where to go. Well, he would have to remember this place next time and buy some roses or something in a matter of minutes. Maybe he should buy some for her. Maybe that would be nice. Those yellow ones.

He turned around to ask her if she would like some flowers to take with her, but she had already gone outside, on the other side of the window, the green coat rushing past the buckets of flowers, through the line of yellow cabs, and disappearing down, down the stairs.

Chanoyu in Uptown Chicago

From the east, heading west down Montrose, crossing Broadway; north on Racine . . . tension, confusion, futility . . . men out of place and running amuck. Crossing Wilson Avenue . . . sirens . . . a man curled up on a sidewalk . . . a group of men and women, a grim hardness to their faces, lined up in a way suggesting force, revealing weakness . . . passing a bottle in their own shadows while an afternoon sun settles behind their shoulders.

Second floor, third floor windows, windows on both sides of the street open to emptiness, open to dark voids . . . voices hollering, screaming hates, wants, misunderstandings, false hopes. "YOU WERE . . . " "NO!" People preparing to violate one another, once again.

At the corner of Racine and Leland Avenues (1151 W. Leland, 4645 N. Racine) rest the Buddhist Educational Center and the Buddhist Temple of Chicago. Sirens and the silence of sunlight on leafy vines.

> Drinking a bowl of
> green tea
> I stopped
> the war
> —reps

Tea is why I am here. Chanoyu—"hot water for tea." Chado: the Way of Tea.

Inside the temple, Gyomay M. Kubose, head minister, explains some of the elements of Buddhism to a visiting group of students from Northwestern University and their teacher, a Buddhist monk from Ceylon. The Buddhist monk, enveloped in an orange robe, is wrapped in a sunset.

Gyomay Kubose sings in his talk, a rhythm of inflections, reducing metaphysics to common sense . . . swiftly, simply, gently. "Oneness not twoness," he teaches. "No worship or prayers, but meditation. There is not sin in Buddhism, only ignorance." A statue of the Amida Buddha, the ideal Buddha, glows from the altar behind him.

191

The nut-brown monk smiles serenely.

Gyomay Kubose explains incense, candlelight, then strikes a gong—a symbol and aid in meditation: "When a beautiful sound is heard, we listen to its resonance through to the soundless sound upon which depends the meditation."

Racine and Leland Avenues do not exist.

It's tea time.

Led by the monk, the group moves to the meditation room. I follow Reverend Kubose through many doors: from the temple through the educational center, to the outdoors, through a locked door of the rectory, and up the stairs. Outside the entrance to his own living quarters, we remove our shoes.

Minnie Kubose, his wife, gracious hostess—instructor in Chanoyu, dressed in blue and white kimono—bows, smiles, accepts my awkward Western handshake, and guides us through the tea room for the moment, to a balcony outdoors in the sun. A balcony which is, for all purposes, a Japanese garden, alive with plants, water, design . . . a quiet, floating somewhere above Racine Avenue and the street-life below.

A Lipton Tea-man on occasion, a coffee drinker by habit, I am ignorant of the rites of tea. Lover, though, of Japanese art and self-proclaimed student of Eastern religion, I am prepared to discover beauty, mystery, and peace in much that is done, not done . . . said, unsaid. Including tea.

"For Teaism is the art of concealing beauty that you may discover it, of suggesting what you dare not reveal."—Okakura Kakuzo, *The Book of Tea*

I know that (think I know it) for openers.

I know, too, the feeling of Lotung, a Tang Poet:

> The first cup moistens my lips and throat, the second cup breaks my loneliness, the third cup searches my barren entrail but to find therein some five thousand volumes of odd ideographs. The fourth cup raises a slight perspiration——all the wrong of life passes away through my pores. At the fifth cup I am purified; the sixth cup calls me to the· realms of immortals. The seventh cup—ah, but I could take no more! I only feel the breath of cool wind that rises in my sleeves. Where is Horaisan [heaven]? Let me ride on this sweet breeze and waft away thither.

I know too that Reverend Kubose knows, but he's not talking tea . . . yet. He's explaining that he founded the Buddhist Temple of Chicago in 1944. He's passing very quickly over the fact that after returning from Japan in 1941 (where he went for further study after receiving his B.A. from the University of California at Berkeley), he was sent to a war relocation camp in Wyoming. After two years there, he and his family came to Chicago.

He's explaining that his temple has a congregation of 600 paid members and how, as a community center, cultural programs are also provided. "As a result, we have 7,000 people passing through here a month." From Boy Scouts to Buddhism students.

Two red fire engines whine down the street below. But I do not hear the sirens. Minnie Kubose places a dish of sweets and two tall glasses of ice tea before us—"Lipton's," she laughs—while I absorb the gentle talk and teaching of the man, Gyomay (bright dawn), occassionally letting my mind wander to the ginko tree behind him, tracing a fan-shaped leaf. A man is hollering on a corner in the distance. I cannot make out his words.

"When I came here twenty years ago [he was in Hyde Park for twelve years], it was different from now. Ten years ago, people from the South, Puerto Ricans, started moving in. The general standard was degraded. These people never lived in cities . . . they have to learn. They're getting better. I came to Chicago from the camp . . . 20,000 of us came here. East of the Rockies, we could go anywhere. Now we have 5,000 American Indians. This is very cosmopolitan here," he smiles.

The Buddhist Educational Center offers beginning and advanced courses in Buddhism each fall, winter, and spring . . . ten weeks per term, $30 per course. There is also instruction in Sanskrit, Japanese, literature, and history. For aesthetics, there are courses in calligraphy, brush painting, flower arranging, Bonsai, and the tea ceremony.

Minnie Kubose sits in silence beside me; Gyomay, at an angle, across from me. The sun is warm and in my eyes. The glass of tea, cool in my hands.

"The Japanese tea ceremony," he explains, "gradually developed over the past four hundred years. It came out of the Zen school. Sen Rikyu was the founder of the formal Zen tea ceremony. He was a Zen priest, son of a rich merchant, interested in doing the tea. Way of Zen, Way of Tea . . . together. You cannot separate. Zen comes first, then the tea. Sen Rikyu developed, formalized the Way of Tea."

Long before Rikyu's time, tea was drunk in China among Zen priests and monks to keep them from falling asleep during meditation. Japanese priests, in search of the philosophy of Buddha in southern China, brought "tea" back to Japan. "First the tea cake from China, then the seeds, which were planted," explains Gyomay. And with the tea itself came the association of meditation . . . simplicity . . . peace. "Everything started in China," says Gyomay.

"Way of Tea," he says, "teaches patience, serenity, concentration. In essence, it is meditation."

"To prepare the tea," explains Minnie Kubose, "you need so much concentration. If you are not serene, you make a mistake."

"Tea Way teaches self-less," he counters.

All of which sounds ethereal . . . elusive as a Zen koan:

A professor commuted from Tokyo to Nanin's temple in Kamkura many Sunday mornings to learn Zen. One morning Nanin served

him tea. He poured the professor's cup full—and kept on pouring. The professor watched until he could restrain himself no longer. "Sensei!" he protested, "it is overflowing!" Master Nanin said, "Like this cup, you are so full of opinions and speculations that there is no room for anything further."
—*Zen Koans*, Gyomay Kubose (Regnery, 1973)

"Riyku also formalized the tea room," continues Gyomay. "He built the first tea house with a graden next to the house. He said a 4 1/2 mat tea room was the ideal size, 9x9. One mat is 3x6. The smallest is 1 1/2 or 2 mat. This room is 8 mat. Tea room always has an alcove (tokonoma) to hang the scroll (usually Zen calligraphy) and to place a simple flower in the middle. Also to burn incense."

The flower can be anything, placed in the container as naturally as it might be found growing, and in harmony with the season. "But never a rose," cautions Gyomay. "It has a thorn. Beautiful—but a thorn."

Minnie Kubose softly interjects that the school of tea she practices (and teaches) is called Urasenke. "Ura, meaning back; senke, meaning house of the Sen family. It all goes back to Sen Rikyu. The present Grand Tea Master, Sen Soshitsu, is the fifteenth generation descendant from Sen Rikyu."

Sen Rikyu not only formalized the tea room and emphasized the aesthetics, he also introduced the four basic principles of Chado, the Way of Tea: Wa, Kei, Sei, Jaku.

"Wa," explains Gyomay, "Harmony. One with nature. Harmony as to nature and the season. Harmony too between hostess and guest, between guests, between guests and utensils. Kei . . . Respect. Humility. Unless you attain humility you cannot respect others. Not only people, utensils. Respect . . . humility. A teacher is a teacher, a student a student, but there is respect, humility. Like maternal respect . . . equal value. Each utensil has its own uniqueness and value. Respect each other. When you enter the tea room, you respect the room. You enter, then you bow. A bow is respect."

Though the formal tea ceremony has not begun, the principles of Urasenke Chanoyu, as Reverend Kubose and his wife carefully, gently explain, seem already in evidence around me. The balcony garden . . . the harmony and respect of these two people . . . the peacefulness of the moment.

"Sei," he continues, "Purity. Simplicity . . . unreserved . . . beautiful, refreshing. Unpretentious. Things as they are. In a formal tea ceremony, before entering the tea house, the guests pass through the garden where there is a water basin. "We rinse our hands there, rinse our mouth . . . to prepare ourselves spiritually before we enter the ceremony. Jaku . . . Serenity. Tranquility. Inner peace . . . undisturbed. Satisfied. Contentment. Poetic spirit. Real inner peace from meditation."

Gyomay pauses, takes a sip of ice tea. Sets the glass down. Takes one piece of candy between his fingers. Studies it. "Respects" it. Tastes it.

"Those are the four principles that the ceremony is based on," he continues. "All in all, it is a discipline of one's life. To make a life beautiful . . . simple. To be aware. It's teaching of awareness . . . fully aware of life . . . appreciating it."

Before I enter the tea room for the ceremony itself, Minnie Kubose explains more of the details of a very formal ceremony. "Three is the ideal number to serve. Five is all right. If you have help in the kitchen, you can serve ten."

The regular ceremony begins with a light dinner served on individual trays. "Dinner would consist of fish rolled thin, rice, soup, all served on a beautiful laquered tray."

A short break follows the dinner as the guests retire to the garden. "When you come in again, you are served a thick tea, which is as thick as pea soup." This is followed by the serving of usucha, thin tea, which is frothy. The entire ceremony lasts between three and a half and four hours. Usucha, often performed alone, takes an hour or less.

The tea ceremony today (usucha) will be an informal/formal one, I suggest to my hostess. "Yes," she nods and laughs. Are the guests allowed to talk during the ceremony?

"They can converse with each other, but no gossip," she says. "No politics," adds Gyomay. "To enjoy the moment itself," counters Minnie. "Talk usually of things related to tea, . . . to life," says Gyomay. "Until the thick tea is made—no conversation. Strict rule. Timing is very important, so that things go smoothly."

And if I should drop the tea bowl, do something utterly out of harmony with the service? "If things don't go smoothly, one must learn to cope with them," explains Minnie. "If you become disturbed, I'm going to feel bad." (I like that, respect that.) To master whatever the circumstances . . . to keep things going as smoothly as possible. Mutual cooperation, consideration for each other.

"Always the deep consideration for others. I like that part of the ceremony," adds Reverend Kubose. "Control, but natural. Control is forgotten, but natural and free." (Which brings us back to Zen.)

So I enter the room with Reverend Kubose and his wife to partake of the formalities (and my own informalities) of Chanoyu. In a typical setting, the guests would assemble in a waiting room, then be led down the garden path by the host toward the tea room. The ritual of purity (physical and spiritual) would be performed at a stone basin on the way, the guests bending low to accomplish this— Rikyu's idea to bring a man closer to nature.

The tea room is traditionally small so that guests must humble themselves by crawling through. (Wa, Kei, Sei, Jaku immediately setting the tone of the tea ceremony from waiting room to garden path to tearoom.)

I am the honored guest, explains Minnie, handing me two cushions to kneel/ sit upon. But before taking my honored position in the room, I "respect" the

195

room, as Gyomay teaches.

(How does one "respect" a room? Why hasn't Western culture ever "respected" a room? We decorate them. We use them. We redecorate them, remodel them. But do we "respect" them?)

I respect the tokonoma, the alcove, and study the sprig of tiny white flowers in the vase. Simplicity, beauty . . . these words, these symbols roll around in my head. I look at the scroll. Though I cannot read it, there is nevertheless a mysterious serenity about the characters. Respect the room . . . yes. The stark nakedness, bone barrenness . . . utter emptiness of it all. Emptiness . . . it begins working on you. Time . . . now or the past? The same.

Then the hearth or the brazier where the tea is to be prepared. There are these "objects" to a formal tea ceremony, these "utensils." There is a tea bowl, a tea caddy, a bamboo tea whisk and a bamboo spoon. There is a wooden dipper, a kettle, even a stand for the cover of the kettle, and a receptacle for waste water.

And all of these utensils are beautiful, chosen with care, often valuable art objects in themselves. What's more, they "speak" of harmony in what they are, in how one uses them. "One 'respects' the utensils," teaches Gyomay. That too casts a whole different aura on the partaking of tea, raising dining, if you will, to a level of reverence.

We take our seats (the honored guest nearest the hostess, the Reverend Kubose beside me), exchange greetings and respect with the hostess and the guests, and become aware of the respect, harmony, and tranquility in the air as we silently watch the hostess prepare the thin green tea.

Ritual, drama, reverence . . . what is it all about? It is here though. Zen teaches: This is It! I see, for maybe only the second or third time in my life, what it all means. Paradox, yes. I can't really explain it.

There is an expression in Zen, in Chado: wabi. Untranslatable. Solitariness . . . aloneness . . . the feeling came out of the Zen monasteries. It is not a negative thing though. When the solitariness of things (nature, man, life) is expressed creatively, artistically, that is wabi. Such an experience invokes serenity, tranquility. The beauty in the ordinary . . . things being what they are.

> Harvest moon:
> around the pond I wander
> and the night is gone.
> —Basho

Wabi. The feeling experienced in observing the hostess kneeling, preparing to make tea. The care, the precision in each gesture. A dish of sweets is set before me—to heighten the taste of tea. Timing . . . the Reverend Kubose reminding me, "The candy should be consumed at the precise moment the tea bowl is served to you."

But I am not prepared, inwardly, for Chanoyu. Instead of observing and ab-

196

sorbing the artistry, the peace, I am too consciously studying every aspect of the ritual. First comes this, then comes that. I am "separating." I am asking questions aloud. Instead of the creative emptiness of a tea cup, I am overflowing. (Bad "tea".) Still, I am a "student" in a way. And to the hostess, I am an honored guest. It would make her feel bad to know that my mind is running in a thousand directions during the tea ceremony . . . she covers for me beautifully. She keeps it all flowing smoothly.

Order . . . precision . . . features almost stylized. The manner in which she wipes the caddy and spoon with a small cloth (purity), washes the whisk in a bowl of hot water . . . every utensil handled with beauty and grace, every utensil, when not in use, resting alone, alone in the simple beauty of what it is. "It is what it does." Pure design. Pure aesthetics. "Soiled" water is placed in another bowl.

The making of tea. Lifting the caddy and the tea spoon with delicacy, putting 2, 2 1/2 spoonfuls of matcha (powdered green tea) into the bowl. Handling the wooden dipper like a wand, gently filling it from the kettle, pouring about a third of it into the tea bowl and returning the rest to the kettle. Putting down the dipper, running her fingers over and under the handle . . . placing it at a precise angle of rest. Picking up the bamboo whisk, whipping the tea into a green froth, "froth of the liquid jade," finally placing it for the honored guest (who has consumed his last sweet at the exact moment) who is now ready to move on his knees to pick up the bowl of tea.

Wa, Kei, Sei, Jaku . . . these principles evident but unspoken, inseparable. The honored gueat bowing, showing respect to the other guests, then handling the bowl with reverence, placing it in the palm of the left hand ("You're left hand becomes a saucer," explains Gyomay) and grasping one side of the bowl with the right hand. And infinity of tiny, perfect gestures (ritual cleansing of the bowl, where lips have touched, on the part of hostess and guest) to be performed with the grace of artistry. To list each move would be to choreograph a ballet, a bullfight, a mass. And there would still be those spaces in between.

Taking the first sip . . . praising the taste . . . (no comparisons: it is not like any other tea, it is matcha.) Taking two and a half more sips. "There are three and a half sips to the bowl," says Gyomay. Then placing the empty bowl before you, bending down, your arms resting upon your thighs, to admire, to pay respect to the bowl itself. You feel it . . . the glaze, the form. You are absorbed by its color. "You respect not only the bowl," teaches Gyomay, "but the man who made it."

(Something in the emptiness inside me wants to say, "This is the way men were meant to be. This is the way life is supposed to be lived.")

Returning the bowl to the hostess . . . the rite of purity once again . . . the preparing of tea for the next guest ("Only the sound of boiling water should be heard," whispers Gyomay), as Gyomay now begins the taste of sweets, as all partake of the ceremony until each has been served, until all are aware of the

197

tranquility and the act itself unbroken . . . one.

"Our life in this society becomes more materialistic, mechanized," explains Reverend Kubose. "People are seeking more serenity in life. Some have turned to meditation. But tea is much more than meditation. Perhaps in the next ten years or so, Tea will be more popularized. After Zen and meditation, they will want to learn the Tea."

I take a last look at the scroll . . . " 'Empty mind, straight joints, that is my teacher,' " explains Minnie. "It was written by Kyoto Daikakuji, head minister."

" 'My teacher is like straight bamboo,' " interprets Gyomay. "Empty mind is not empty mind, you know. Empty mind means full mind."

And after the Way of Tea?

"Beyond Tea," smile Gyomay Kubose, "ordinary life . . . but a different spirit. We know everything but ordinary life."

I cannot return to the confusion of Racine Avenue. I do not know the depths of Chado and can never explain it. I know the sun is setting across these crazy streets, that the vines clinging to the temple wall glow the color of matcha, and that there is beauty even in dereliction. I know that Okakura Kakuzo calls it the cup of humanity:

Meanwhile, let us have a sip of tea. The afternoon glow is brightening the bamboos, the fountains are bubbling with delight, the sighing of the pines is heard in our kettle. Let us dream of evanescence, and linger in the beautiful foolishness of things.

I turn the corner and follow the sound of a red fire engine.

The Headhunter: Dr. A. R. Schwartz

He's a headhunter, he'll tell you, with probably the only Jewish voodoo altar in the world in his living room. "Dr. A. R. Schwartz, Middle Management Recruiting-Consulting," reads his card. He has a suite on Sheridan road, plus an office he shares with Bryant Associates in the John Hancock Center.

I first heard of him in a response to an article I did for *Midwest* concerning neighborhood games, past and present. It must have set something off in Dr. Schwartz because he fired off eight wild, hand-written pages, cataloging his own childhood in Detroit (many of the games unprintable), throwing in chunks of autobiography and philosophy along the way:

"By the way, whatever happened to 'aggies' and mibs? My best friend cried when I cheated him out of his whole bag of aggies. I'm still cheating. I'm now a legal thief, con man and cheater. I steal executives from here and deliver them there, and I am paid handsomely to boot by clients too cowardly to do their own 'body-snatching.'"

Dr. Schwartz seemed to be a promising story, and I found myself phoning him one day, making an appointment. That's when he told me about the Jewish voodoo center in his living room. That's when I realized I might be heading into dangerous territory.

But after all, he's a doctor, I kept telling myself all the way up the elevator to his suite. He was waiting for me when the door opened. First off, he hit me with a six-page, 20-stanza poem he had written in longhand for me. The first stanza being

Norbert Blei's come to ask me why?
I'm zany as I yam;
"Why?" he'll ask, "Do youse remember your past?"
So I'm telling him, ala-ka-zam!

Dr. Schwartz, I presume you're crazy? Which he readily admits. He's been back and forth a few times. Having thus established the ground rules, we proceed with a long day's journey into the jungle life of a headhunter.

"See, I'm a doctor," he says, pointing to his license hanging on the wall. "But I lie a little. I'm a doctor of Podiatry." A foot doctor . . . fully accredited, and currently licensed to practice by the state of Illinois.

All right. So I have a crazy, Jewish foot doctor who actually headhunts executives for a living. "I'm licensed, but I don't practice. I've even got my little black bag. I can cut from your feet, all the way up to your. . . . " No, thank you, Dr. Schwartz.

The suite is his apartment, with is something basic and rare. There's an organized emptiness about it, punctuated in places with definite appointments a la Dr. Schwartz. Like the many upturned whiskey bottles on the windowsills, the floor, the dresser, filled with a green liquid that looks like Scope; the chrome motorcycle exhaust pipes which he sees as vases or modern sculpture; the magic mirror near his desk, and the voodoo altar.

He seems pretty serious about the altar, which is actually his chartreuse sofa ("Don't sit there!"), some Oriental art work on the wall, a tapestry of animals on the backrest ("Voodoo, you sacrifice animals, right? My animals . . . "), a piece of wampum, a cocktail table of candles and two symbolic red and white kneeling rugs, which Dr. Schwartz demonstrates by kneeling down and explaining: "Red is for blood, and white . . . I'm looking for a virgin. None of this stuff I bought. All of this stuff came from the boiler room in the building. What people throw away."

Schwartz is a small man with glasses perched down on his nose (he is forever looking over them) and hardly any teeth in his mouth at present. He's fighting some enemies down the street—a health center which he does not feel is on the up-and-up. They have his teeth there, but he is not going to pay for them. Money is not the object. The guy who runs the center is a crook, says Schwartz, and he can wear Schwartz's teeth himself for all that Schwartz cares.

About this time I begin to suspect that Dr. Schwartz is not so crazy, after all. A fighter with no teeth is a hell of a fighter indeed.

One other area of the room stands out like a Schwartz Mission Control Center which reflects his business, middle management recruiting (headhunting). The desk and wall above it are covered with notes, memos, letters and a telephone. His lifeline. His weapon. His spear, if you will. Without a phone, Schwartz would be dead. This headhunter lives by his mouth, not by his hands.

He talks, scatter-gun style, about the whole business of finding particular people to fit particular positions. (Schwartz's mind moves so quickly from topic to topic, that it would be unnatural to organize his ideas in any other way.)

"It was just starting after the Korean War. I've been twenty years in the business. Companies were saying, 'Hey, I need people!' Business tripled after the war. It was a great time. This country went crazy with new business. They needed the managers and executives to run them. Go out and get them! That's where I came in.

"Twenty-four years married . . . broke up. A little testimony from my wife put me in the nuthouse for a month. I suffer from depression. I don't mind talking about it. It's a chemical thing, very common. I was a foot doctor until then. After Elgin, I started in an employment agency. We don't charge the individuals, only the corporations. And we charge plenty. Average, $200,000 a year in service fees over the past twenty years. If I placed one every day, I'd be on my yacht.

"I broke in with a joint run by a guy named John Greene. He taught me the business. A real character. He taught me how to handle the phone, how to talk to people. If you're afraid of the phone, you can't be in this business.

"I'm a damn good Ph. D. when it comes to psychoanalyzing people, though. I'm an industrial consultant . . . I also have a B.S. in psychology."

What is middle management recruiting? "The big corporations. I find the people for them. Middle management is the most important crew a big company has. The jobs run from $18,000 to $30,000 and will eventually lead to executive positions.

"If the company will pay, we'll test them. I'm a pretty good analyzer. I can analyze you pretty well. You're a pipe smoker. Nobody would hire you. You spend too damned much time lighting the thing. The mustache, you've got to trim. You're twenty-five pounds overweight.

"The bastard that kills us dead is the interview. If the guy can't sell himself to the company, that's the heartache. So I try to teach the cat how to interview. Number one: companies like you to know they exist; two, dress, cut your hair, trim the mustache or else get the hell out of my office and never come back. You don't go for an interview without a tie. Three: top grades in accounting and engineering. I don't handle nothing but degrees, mostly M.B.A's.

"The young kid, 6-feet-2, eyes of blue, he's the beautiful candidate. That's what the chairman likes to see running around his office. Ethnic groups? Ah, it's quiet, but it's there. Finally: The company will ask: 'How much money do you want?' You say, 'I'm making $20,000. I'd like to make more.' Once you get an offer, I take over. I do the bargaining. Whatever you think I can do best for you, that's what I want to do."

Throughout the conversation, Schwartz sits in a chair, stands up, parades around the room, fiddles with his glasses, interjects dirty stories, plays with the telephone—actually calls up people to inform them that he has a writer in his apartment, interviewing him! "Yeah, me! Can you imagine that? He must be crazier that me. Bye." Bang! the phone goes down.

A headhunter's salary? "25 to 50 grand without even trying. 200 grand, tops. Even the dope can make 15 grand. A good headhunter needs intelligence, balls, imagination and you gotta be a good talker. You have to sell on the telphone. That's difficult as hell. You have to make the client drool . . . 'Just talk to him for five minutes. You can't lose.'

"We only bullshit to get the interview. The longer the first interview in time, the better. If he's there ten minutes, forget it. If he's there an hour, forget it. If he's invited for lunch . . . good omen. Immediately after the interview we want the guy to call us. What did you say? What did they say? Then we tell him how well he did. If they don't hire fast, it's not too good."

Morals . . . ethics . . . what have you, Schwartz? You say you cheat, you say you lie. How do you sleep nights peddling human cargo the way you do?

He doesn't sleep nights . . . suffers from insomnia.

"I'm 85 per cent honest," he says, moving to the telephone to ring a secretary to the president of a large corporation (another voice on the other end of the line he has never met . . . Schwartz remains a physical anonymity over the phone) to tell her he is being interviewed (he protects my name) and convinces me to talk to her to verify my reality. What do you think of this guy? I ask her. "He's quite a fascinating individual," she tells me. "I enjoy talking to him."

Schwartz takes the phone out of my hand and begins explaining his love life to her. "I got a new one . . . I got three now . . . They are all screwballs because they see anything worthwhile in me . . . Okay . . . goodbye . . . I gotta hang up."

"I'd like to meet her someday. But she's married. I'm what you call a character," he picks up on one of our many loose trains of thought. "This is a good business, I'm good at it, and I wish to die in San Diego. That's my town. You know why Nixon went to China? He sold the United States for 400 million bucks, but the bill won't be presented for five years.

"Moral implications . . . yeah, I'm a legal thief. What do I do for a living? I cause live bodies to move from here to there. Many companies tell me, for example: 'I want Norbert Blei . . . Forget the price. Get him, and we'll take good care of you.' They hire me to do their dirty work. It's not a question of morality . . . it's business."

Nevertheless, the basic morality is there in Schwartz, down-to-earth-Jewish and therefore, historically compassionate, Schwartz. "The goddam country is going to the dogs. Why don't they—the big corporations so fond of the stereotype, safe human commodity—6 ft. 2, eyes of blue, hire the oddballs, the unhireables? How do I help unhireables get a job? I've pushed unhireables all my life. I've busted my ass for them. If I didn't spend so much time trying to help them, I'd really be rich.

"Who are the unhireables? People physically deformed . . . people who can't interview worth a crap. Age . . . 34 is *too old* for a trainee! Ethnic groups. If you're 6-feet-2, eyes of blue, you've got to be something. I sent four Jews to a big Chicago company. Top grades, ambitious. Why didn't they hire one of them?"

His Jewishness haunts Schwartz, though I suspect it's something that has held him together, despite a family split to pieces, which has torn him apart. (Schwartz, an unhireable himself? Very possibly.)

"My son is dead." (He is alive but no longer speaking to his father.) "The old Jews, you know how they would mourn the loss of a son?" (Scwartz grabs his shirt . . . there are tears in his eyes.) "They tear a piece of their clothing like

202

this! My son is dead. Grandchildren, I hardly see. Look, I've seen her only once . . . beautiful, eh? Two things I've always wanted to do: be a writer, be a comedian. I've been a comedian all my life. My family thinks I'm nuts.

"You know, when you suffer a little bit, you begin to think you're a clown. But isn't it better to cause laughter in the world? And isn't it better at your own expense? I'm not afraid to make an ass of myself. Most people are. I prefer to be a clown. Laughter and chicken soup will cure anything. It'll put the doctors out of business, and that'll be a damned good thing. You know, Lazarus was raised from the dead once, and what the hell did he do? Nothing. I was raised four times. What do I do?" Schwartz gets up, laughs, throws his arms above his head, and begins whirling around the room. . . .

"I dance! I'm a good dancer . . . I dance very well. So, big deal . . . I am also a good crier."

Inside Chicago's Foreign Banks

I enter Banca Commerciale Italiana cautiously. Tucked away on a secluded upper floor, the place looks more like an Italian designer's studio than a bank: white on white walls, Op Art paintings and congenial receptionist (not Italian looking) with a copy of the popular fem novel, *Jane*, on her desk.

"Can I help you?"

I would like to ask her what became of the bank. Instead I explain that I'm interested in foreign banking operations in Chicago and would like to talk to a genuine Italian banker. I'm asked to take a seat, and do so, sinking softly to the very inner depths of a plush red sofa.

It seems they can't find a genuine Italian bank officer for me at the moment, so I am placed in the hands of a junior American bank officer, a nice guy who smiles a lot, loves his work, knows his stuff, and is afraid to give me his name. That's one thing about being a junior anything . . . fear.

He can explain the function of his bank, though: "basically to service Italian firms located in this area and American firms who have subsidiaries in Italy."

What about little old Chicago Italians with a bankroll, yearning for the old country, who might want to open an account with a mother bank?

"We're a full service bank; we can do it. But obviously up here where we're located not many people are going to find us. We can do it, but we don't actually solicit it. Local banks can do it much better."

Of nineteen employees, four are genuine Italians. I can't find any Italian touch to the place, unless it be the ultra-modern interior design: no cup of espresso, no Italian flag, nothing to conjure up days and nights in sunny Italy. Not even a whiff of garlic.

The junior officer gives me a quick tour of the place, but it still strikes me as more a movie set for *Business, Modern Italian Style* than a bank. Leaving, I hear the receptionist purring Italian on the telephone. Ah, I think, finally a touch of Italy.

As I'm about to leave, the junior officer discloses, "By the way, we have absolutely no money here except what we carry in our wallets."

"Ciao," I smile. A banking operation even the Godfather would admire.

Except for Scandinavia, Germany, Switzerland and England, what I recall most about banks overseas is confusion compounded semi-hourly by language problems and red tape. Everything needs ten signatures and twenty-five rubber stamp marks. Spanish clerks in particular must sleep at night with a rubber stamp in each hand, pounding away at the wall. A Turkish bank is Kafka's Castle with minarets.

As for Far East banking, I know nothing. So it is with some sense of adventure that I enter the Sanwa Bank, LTD., 39 So. LaSalle Street, just a stone's throw from Osaka.

Old building . . . marble, marble, everywhere, like some Eastern shrine. Then art work in the corridor leading to the main entrance . . . kind of abstract expressionistic sumi brush strokes (East gives the West the brush, I ponder).

I see mostly imperial green with ivory: modern, with a suggestion of strong tradition. Quiet, very quiet, though at least fifteen people are seated at desks or engaged in various phases of Far Eastern banking.

I explain my presence to a young woman, who quickly and politely tells me that Mr. Hideo Shiozaki will see me. She takes my scruffy coat, almost a sacrilege amidst this splendor, and leads me to a conference room? parlor? suite? tea room? where Mr. Shiozaki approaches, shakes hands, and directs me to a green velvet sofa.

Style . . . this place has style. Only the Japanese express it so well, so unexpressedly. No wonder capitalism adapted so perfectly to the Japanese climate. It was the perfect match of raw power and technical know-how reduced to inner beauty, with all the power still intact but unnoticeable. You give Japan the financial backing to manufacture and market a monster Muntz TV, and they hand you back something beautfiul like a Sony which you can hold in your hand like a piece of fruit.

Hideo Shiozaki proudly explains his role in Chicago: "The Midwest does a lot of banking in Japan. And we are here primarily to assist both sides. We have more representatives. We have a little more knowledge of the country. We have the largest individual accounts in Japan. We are called the People's Bank, or, 'Your Bank.'

"We will help to make Chicago and the Midwest more international. We are here and most happy to help anyone who needs our services. This branch office can do anything. And we don't discourage retail banking. We assume we can do anything you want, and we try. We should be a U.S. bank, even though we come from Japan. We, too, use things 'Made in U.S.A.' "

There are more than fifteen foreign banks in Chicago, and their number grows: France, England, Italy, the Netherlands, Germany, Israel, Greece, and even a Banque de L'Indochine, whose whereabouts must be Top Secret, since it keeps disappearing from me this morning. I'd probably get in trouble there, anyway, trying to discover precisely what America's investment is in that part of the world, and the rate of return.

So I slide into the Banque Nationale de Paris, 33 N. Dearborn St., remembering all the trite Parisian scenes from Utrillo to the Champs Elysees.

The bank itself hovers on the twenty-first floor and is worth every bit of the ride up. I haven't seen a more dramatic entrance since Versailles. French and American flags greet you at the entrance to the corridor, and I am almost certain that the ghost of De Gualle awaits me at the end, Legion of Honor in hand.

Yet the Plexiglas, stainless-steel-kitchen-sink sheen to the place might make an automaton feel at home, but make this human being a bit uncertain. Then a pleasant receptionist and a lovely-sounding French secretary intercept me, and it's vive la France all over again.

While awaiting an appointment with Mr. Paul Henderson, executive vice president, I peruse the Banque Nationale de Paris' brochure, entitled *The Art of Money*. Leave it to the French to view it as an art. . . .

"As the design of coins and other instruments is an art, so the management of money is an equally challenging art. . . . "

I meet Mr. Henderson in a spacious modern corner office with an exhilarating view of Chicago, though I still feel boxed in a smoke-tinted Plexiglas cube. He comes on as a knowledgeable international banker (twenty-four years of overseas banking), a Scotsman, who has served in Australia and West Africa, and speaks French "and a smattering of Persian."

He seems impressed that his bank services many major U.S. corporations in the Midwest. "Being in sixty-two countries of the world, we can assist them in speedy transfers around the world. Our aim in the future is to expand this to the less developed countries. Our main effort is to help middle-range corporations."

He sees the presence of the Banque Nationale de Paris in Chicago as positive and mutually beneficial. "It adds a new dimension to the Midwest. No longer is it necessary to turn to New York for large problems of major investments in overseas countries. Now there will be a greater tendency to handle this business right here, in Chicago."

Basking in this growing, cosmopolitan Chicago consciousness, I speed to the Swiss Bank Corporation, 150 S. Wacker Drive, to see just what my chances might be for a Swiss numbered account.

Once again I enter a setting out of *2001*, in this case a street operation rather than the highrise nest these banks seem to prefer.

The whole scene is guarded openness: a receptionist asks me to fill out an appointment card, directs me to a seat, and probably runs a check on me.

Ensconced in a soft red chair beside an indoor garden of poinsettia and ivy, I pick up the magazine *Der Monat* and study the cover illustration of a 1929 thunder cloud with the caption *"Weltwirtschaftskvise Gespents Oder Realitat?"* It scares hell out of me: I don't appreciate the Germanic sense of economic humor, especially that thunder cloud.

Nor do I enjoy being kept waiting in such an atmosphere of ominous silence. A man at a desk stares when he thinks I'm not looking, a woman at another desk looks at me when she thinks I'm not staring, and the lady with my appointment card keeps going in and out some huge red doors, where I am sure some kind of financial doom awaits me.

Silence, silence, silence. I get the feeling that if I dropped a coin, the Swiss franc would take a disastrous plunge. Where are all the customers? Why the hell are there no people in all these foreign banks? They talk about retail banking. I'd like to take these guys to Cermak Road and the Mid-American Savings & Loan some Saturday morning, show them the neighborhood people drinking free coffee, eating, gossiping, lined up at the tellers with their shopping bags and passbooks, waiting to make another $1,000 deposit or get their interest put in the book for the day!

But suddenly I am hailed and led, behind closed doors, through a maze of red carpeting and white walls into a small room with a desk, a chair, and two lights beaming down on me. "Mr. Hugentobler will be with you shortly."

I continue to wait, feeling a little like a character out of *Darkness at Noon* or an old fashioned police story where I'm about to be worked over in the lights.

Mr. Peter H. Hugentobler, vice president, enters . . . pin-striped suit, every hair in place, a touch of the burgermeister about him. As he begins to speak, I realize why Swiss banking is a philosophy rather than an institution: there is not a question in either international or domestic banking that Peter H. Hugentobler can't field with statistics, common sense, and a touch of metaphysics.

"Our bank is one of the three large Swiss banks. We have been in existence since 1872. We have traditionally had corporate clients in Chicago . . . the individual people who would tap the Swiss capital market with bond issues in Swiss banks, whenever, of course, it would be in their favor . . . people like Sears Roebuck, Borg Warner.

"We have operated in this country since 1939 in New York. We have over 500 people there, also an agency in San Fransisco and a representative office in L.A. Two years ago we decided to open a representative office here in the Midwest, which I opened in 1973. We changed from representative to branch office in 1974 when the Illinois law was changed. So our status is now the same as any local bank that has the same charter.

"We have checking accounts, sure," he explains, "but a minimum balance requirement of $5,000. And we have savings accounts with a minimum deposit of $500. The accounts are not covered by FDIC, however."

No insurance? The Swiss bank would never get the Bohemian trade, I guess.

"The Swiss bank doesn't need insurance," he laughs. "Though I wouldn't say that. But we feel that way."

And as for the fabled Swiss bank accounts, they can be opened here in Chicago. "We do the paper work here, establish the identity, get signature cards and general information. We take [a customer's] check in dollars, convert it here to Swiss francs, and then send it to Switzerland. From that point on, though, he must deal with the Swiss bank directly. He can add to his account here, but he cannot withdraw. That he must handle himself with the bank in Switzerland."

There are other stipulations which one must understand, since banking is the major industry of Switzerland. There is a thirty per cent holding tax on any interest earned, for example. And as Peter H. Hugentobler explains, "There is a big myth about secret accounts. Here, of course, in Chicago we operate under state laws." And so there would be no secrecy should the government wish to check the books and see the accounting.

"But in Switzerland," he explains, "privacy is upheld unless there are criminal charges involved. In other words . . . no fishing expeditions."

From Switzerland, I bounce to merry old England . . . Barclays Bank International, Ltd., 208 S. LaSalle St. Barclays seems quite inviting from the street level, and does, in fact, go all out for retail trade. It's the first foreign bank I've found with actual real live people inside, doing some banking business.

I meet Mary at the head desk, a very engaging woman who admits a deep love affair with her work at Barclays. "I worked in a suburban bank before. This is much more exciting." She quickly lines me up for a converstaion with Mr. Robin W.A. Parr.

Instead of a tweedy old Englishman opining on the pound sterling, I find a really quick and fascinating young bank officer with more enthusiasm for the bloody business of banking than I ever suspected in one man.

"We were the first full service foreign bank to come here," he says, "in October, 1973. We've always chosen around the world to go for street trade. We've found, being on the street level, a lot of people just plain discover we're here! We see our importance here mainly to assist the smaller businesses. We can help the guy who's got a good product, wants to go overseas, but doesn't quite know how to go about it. We often find each other on the street level, you see.

"For example, there's a man who's got a very fine weighing device. He's anxious to market it in various parts of the world. We can help find the market and perhaps loan him the money to establish himself overseas.

"The role of the international banker in Chicago is to facilitate trade between the Middle West and the rest of the world. Visiting foreign businessmen come to this city, and if you're on the street level and you're visible, maybe they'll come and find you and we can do business. Most Europeans think New York does all the banking. Our first few months of operation here, led by Barclays, has brought $225 millions worth of new money in the Chicago market place."

Robin Parr, of all the foreign bankers, seems to have certainly found a home here. He is constantly impressed by the friendly reception he receives throughout the city. A rhododendron man himself, he has recently been accepted with open arms by Chicago's flower people. He is a personable man, with a passion for personal banking. . . .

"We even look after the foreign students who come to this country. Many of them remember us from their own countries perhaps. We speak over twenty languages in this office, three Chinese dialects, a Yugoslav, a Pole, a German, an

Egyptian, two Jamacians. . . . I've actually lent money here in Swahili, which I speak, to a young man who was interested in importing East African handbags and opening a business on the North Side."

With Robin Parr and Barclays, I have just about brought foreign banking into focus for myself. I like his style and his whole philosophy of open banking on the foreign scene. If I decide to market Bohemian dumplings, I'm going to see him.

Foreign banking in Chicago will have only a negligible influence, if any, upon me, but it puts Chicago on the world money map. And Chicago's about the center of the universe for me, right now, except for Greece.

Greece . . . I wonder what the drachma-dollar rate is today: How goes the economy now that the junta is gone? Could I still afford to live there? I syrtaki it over to the new National Bank of Greece, 168 N. Michigan, find the bank managers, George K. Kostis and Vasilios A. Skouras, and wonder aloud.

Plush, plush, plush, is my first reaction. This is the kind of a layout they have in Athens and on Rhodes to cater to all that Scandinavian, West German, and American currency. This is the Parthenon open for banking.

It's Vasilios, first, and then Kostis who make Greek banking come alive. Vasilios (co-manager) comes forth with a warm handshake and a friendly back slap to lead me, a perfect stranger, on a grand tour of the premises. (George Kostis, manager, is entertaining a friend or customer at the moment.)

We discuss mutual Greek friends in Chicago, Greek politics and the country itself. "All you need now is the account of the Cafe Diana, and you're in business," I tell him, jokingly. "We've got it," he smiles.

He dodges into the office momentarily, rattles some Greek to the manager, and suddenly I'm ushered into the presence of George K. Kostis, who sits in a black leather chair, wears a black, pin-striped suit, and looks for all the world like a smiling Greek godfather figure.

"Sit down, pull up a chair . . . how's your Greek?"

We're supposed to be talking foreign banking, and though we manage to hit upon it here and there, all of life is open for discussion when you're in the company of a Greek. They may not be Swiss bankers, but they're fun and relaxing to do business with.

"The main reason we are here is retail banking," says George. "So we have the door open for everybody, especially the Greek. 50 per cent Greek, 50 per cent American, eh? About 300,000 Greeks in Chicago. We give special service. We speak the language. We personalize our business. Also, we provide services in Greece, my country. We have branches all over the world. We make loans to everybody."

"Say," says Kostis, the bank manager, "You have lunch? How about some Greek food?"

Eat! Did you say, Eat! I am ready to exchange all my dollars for drachmas. This is what I call foreign banking in Chicago.

A Warm Conversation With Burr

Oliver J. Dragon, where are you? I think about you and all the Kuklapolitans while walking through Chicago's near North Side, on the way to meet your maker, Burr Tillstrom. I miss those expressions of astonishment, wonder, joie de vivre, and pathos that radiated from your crazy-tooth dragon face. The way you could rest your head on Fran, or turn it around upside down if you felt like it.

I miss all the Kuklapolitans and the way we were in the '50s. The distance between us grows greater everyday. Call it nostalgia or maybe just the loss of innocence; it happens to us all. But Kukla, Fran, and Ollie were an important part of my growing up. Then all of a sudden they were gone, or I had left, and it's never been the same.

When my own kids were born in the '60s, the Kuklapolitans had all but disappeared from TV except for occasional guest shots. I was hoping for some kind of rebirth for them, for my kids, for all of us. But then Sesame Street and the Muppets began to dominate our imaginations.

Though I admire the Cookie Monster and Kermit the Frog, I sure wish Oliver J. Dragon was around each afternoon to make the kids laugh and wonder about themselves. I know he'd make the evening news more palatable for me these days.

The master puppeteer Burr Tillstrom is still boyish for his 58 years. He lives in a rather tastefully done bachelor apartment with a living room that in some way reflects the elegance of a New York salon. On top of a grand piano rest two of his three Emmy awards (he gave one to Fran): Kukla, Fran, and Ollie as a show—953; the Berlin Wall Hand Ballet—1964-1965; Burr Tillstrom as a performer—Kukla, Fran, and Ollie—1971.

Sitting with his dog, Emily, at his feet, Tillstrom starts to talk about his own childhood in Chicago. "There was not much known about puppetry, at least to me. A friend and I built a puppet theater out of orange crates. He did the lighting, I did the curtain. You must remember, there were no books available to me. There was actually very little information about puppetry.

"It was rather a private art . . . traditions of the puppeteers from Europe . . . these secrets were handed down from family to family. And this lasted even all the way into the 1950s when the famous Salzburg Marionettes from Europe were here. I went backstage to greet them, and they wouldn't let me in. The tradition of secrecy still existed.

"I always followed my intuition . . . the best thing to do. Puppetry was strictly my own; it just came to me. I think the influences in particular were early movies, the movie itself and the stage show that went with it. Also, my father and mother were interested in theater. My father was a natural clown, a physical clown. He was a natural dancer.

"I had these miniature teddy bears, and I would be in the front parlor and put on a show. I used the window shade as a kind of curtain. I was six or seven at the time. I think back to when I learned how to construct a pulley system for draw drapes—what a marvelous event that was for me. I still feel the moment of a curtain in a great theater is one of the most exciting to experience.

"I used to get little dolls' heads," he says. "It was just terrifying for me to go to the store and buy a doll. Today . . . what a long way we've come. There's no thought of penalizing someone for liking gentle things. So my dad would buy them for me, and I would cut the heads off and attach them to a body that I'd made out of scraps of wood. I still have some of these. They bring you back to earth."

When he finally learned to make a marionette, with the help of a neighbor who was an arts and crafts teacher, he made a clown—"the smartest thing to make when you're first starting out. The clown is abstract. You don't have to worry about realistic features. Also, in manipulating it, you can get away with less skill."

In the fall of 1935, Tillstrom went to work for the Chicago Park District, which had formed a puppet theater under the auspices of the WPA. Though it lasted for only eighteen months, Tillstrom earned $85 a month as a nonrelief worker. The money was good for the times, but the experience was even more valuable.

Forsaking a half-scholarship at the University of Chicago for puppetry with pay (academia bored him), Tillstrom came away with a profession, an art, a way of life.

Kukla was born of WPA days with the park district. In 1936 the group was invited to attend the First American Puppet Festival in Detroit, and there Tillstrom saw puppets other than marionettes for the first time. "The hand puppets I saw were directly responsible for my making Kukla. I went back to basic cloth construction that I knew, and I made a clown. I used to stuff him in my overcoat pocket. We had a touring season that fall, and we would often go to a restaurant. Somewhere along the line I would get down behind a chair and bring out Kukla.

"He would comment on the people in our group. He would kid them. He's

very wise, Kukla. But he would never ridicule. He would tease about things we knew about each other . . . 'How come you do Shakespeare with a Polish accent?' But it would always be kindly, and Kukla always included himself . . . he picks on the whole human picture, laughing at himself at the same time.

For almost six months Tillstrom worked the puppet without a name gradually developing his character. But it was a ballerina, Tamara Toumanova, who bestowed the name Kukla upon the puppet. "I was backstage once, and I brought the puppet out of my pocket. Toumanova was looking in a mirror, and I put him over her shoulder. She looked up and said, 'Ah, Kukla,' which means doll. It's a term of endearment in Russian, also in Greek."

RCA was Tillstrom's first sponsor when he went on commercial television with the Kuklapolitans in 1947. They were on from 4 to 5 p.m. the first year, later moving to the 6 to 6:30 p.m. time slot, which would become their home for ten years. Those were the years I met Kukla, Ollie, Fran, Beulah Witch, Fletcher Rabbit, Cecil Bill, and the whole gang.

What was their charm? It could have been Kukla's concern for every living thing. It could have been the raspy voice, the zaniness of ugly but somehow beautiful Beulah Witch. Or it could have been overly confident Oliver J. Dragon, maybe all excited about a secret he couldn't keep. Ollie's antics alone—plopping his head down on the stage so forlornly, nudging Kukla with his tooth, stretching his neck so haughtily—projected a kind of friendship and trust that made being human both understandable and fun. And Fran . . . well, I was probably in love with Fran, who had enough sympathy for the whole world in her voice. You could do no wrong in her eyes.

"My reasons for creating characters were unconscious, based upon the need for creating a show," says Tillstrom. "Television is responsible for creating a concept of communal living. Before that time, the characters were created for a single performance. But when television came, I was forced to create their lives . . . they lived on television. The great affection that existed among us came about because the audience was in on their growth. They shared it with me. It went from characters in a play to living people. And this is the basic affection, friendship, and dependence that people have on the Kuklapolitans.

"The response from the audience was what taught me. I found that Kukla and Ollie were responsible for influencing people's lives. Once, Kukla blew his nose in the curtain and a whole bunch of handkerchiefs were sent in."

And much of this was Fran's influence as well. If you found it hard to believe in puppets, Fran was always there to bridge the gap between reality and illusion.

"She was responsible many times for turning my imagination on," says Tillstrom. "I would come up with some outrageous stories about Fletcher Rabbit's life that would just break her up. She laughed, she sympathized . . . loved them, sang songs to them. She became their big sister, favorite teacher, baby sitter, girlfriend, mother . . . all the lovely, ideal qualities we associate with them.

"Fran, you know . . . " and Burr begins to chuckle in fondness for her. "I don't mean it this way, but she was really totally out of it. She never knew what time is was. And she never went backstage. She never looked at the puppets when they weren't performing. She just didn't want to see them that way. She thought of them as real people. I never want to show them that way either, exhibit them, make copies of them. I see no reason to destroy the illusion I worked so hard to create."

To compare the Kuklapolitan World to Sesame Street would perhaps be unfair. It's a different TV time-span entirely, even though it was pioneered by the puppetry of Tillstrom.

"There are no boundaries to time and place," Tillstrom says. "We can be anywhere. We don't have these boundaries in thought. I kept it simple. No sets, conceptual art. I like it when Kukla and Ollie come up with a table and a pot and say, 'This is a kitchen.' I think it's important to give the audience a chance to fill something in. A good artist never tells the whole story. Television tells too much today. You've got to see everything! It's just a very talkative, literal society.

"They [the Kuklapolitans] are definitely theater people who have banded together. They live together like my old WPA troupe. When they go down to the workshop, or down to the mailroom, you don't see that. I don't know where all that stuff is myself, but it was there. We all believed it, didn't we?"

"I'm what you call a one-man show, a one-man puppeteer. Jim Henson, creator of the Muppets, tends to go for the big finish, while I tend to go for the quiet finish. He's one of the most brilliant puppeteers around. His innovations in puppetry are great, marvelous, very funny. So much of puppetry has been freed by him. He came into puppetry in the age of television. Many times the freedom of manipulation and the construction of his puppets are determined by how they might look and act on TV. I could not go into the free form that Jim did.

"It's not valid to compare us just because we're puppeteers. I'm interested in story and the history of my characters. If I'm part of any teaching process, I hope only to instill the possibilities of imagination and love."

Which brings us back again to the puppets, Kukla and Ollie . . . the extensions of the man himself, the artist, Burr Tillstrom. Yet he still hides behind his creations:

"Kukla's Everyman. He's the immortal of the troupe. The only one without a history, a personal history. He's an essence. Very wise. Knows a lot more than anybody tells . . . very seldom ventures an opinion. I don't think of them as puppets. I think of them as characters. I'm the puppeteer. I pick them to tell my story.

"Ollie's lovable, brash, romantic . . . very, if you can use the word, human. He's undaunted. Very self-oriented, but not in a disturbing way. He makes all the mistakes we do, and a few more. He's a great dreamer. He's vain. He has sex appeal. I don't know why he does, but the audience says he does.

"He's very classic, in the tradition of a classic type of hand puppet. The crocodile (only don't call him a crocodile . . . he'd be very upset . . . he's a dragon), opposition of thumb and fingers . . . the mouth that opens. I didn't want him to appear frightening so I made him of soft materials—instead of giving him a lot of teeth, which are frightening to a child, think of 'Jaws.' One tooth is not a threat. The idea is not to terrify but to entertain. A gentle dragon, but still a dragon.

"I can still give examples of the small lessons in life. Kukla and Ollie can show this . . . people can live together."

The Kuklapolitans still host the Children's Film Festival on CBS, though their weekly TV show on NBC was dropped.

"They wanted a preschool show to satisfy their obligations to the FCC," says Tillstrom. "I was very upset when the show was broken into by other shows, which destroyed the story. And once we were preempted. My feeling is, that was probably the last time I will attempt to do Kukla, Fran, and Ollie other than in a special.

"TV today just isn't fun anymore," he continues. "The race for ratings, the greed motive. We take the pulse of the nation and say, 'Let's fit that.' We don't say, 'Let's make it better.' TV has lost some of the quality of just going on and visiting.

"I don't have any big ambitions. My ambition is not to get the highest rating. My ambition is not to be a big television star. My ambition has always been to entertain. I must say I'm not driven as I once was. I love to play for a small audience. I'd love to go back for the fun of playing without the enormous strain of time. The problem with being an artist in this country is that you have to be a commodity. An artist has to be marketable. He has to have a gimmick."

I think of asking Tillstrom to do Ollie, or possibly even show him to me. But then I recall Fran, and how she never wanted to see the puppets that way. She's right. Ollie and the others are too real. It would destroy something in me to see them lying in a suitcase or a box.

I am reminded of Tillstrom's famous hand ballet concerning the Berlin Wall. How he conveyed a feeling, celebrated a theme in the tradition of great dramatic literature known throughout the world. And he used only his two bare hands: "The ridiculous attempt by man to wall off communications between mankind," he described it.

Petting his dog, Burr Tillstrom reminisces over the spontaneity of early television and the Kuklapolitan World. No script, improvisation, the picking up of the story wherever you were, carrying it, shaping it, making it out of yourself in the way only an artist lets happen. . . .

216

Scavenger City

At 6:40 a.m. on a dark and damp Saturday morning, young Jim Boer of the B. Boer & Son Scavengers at 6840 W. 16th St. in Berwyn opens the door to the garage and begins jockeying six massive trucks around. "This one's got problems . . . . a bad solenoid," he says, clearing a space for the truck he will use on this morning's route. Jim Boer, the son, third generation scavenger, blond-haired, somewhat distant at first . . . a Dutchman.

We called them the woodenheads . . . woodenshoes . . . the scavengers. And they were, in truth, the Dutchmen. They lived on the north side of Cicero, concentrated between 16th Street and 12th Street, Austin and Central. They had their own schools, their own churches. They were extremely clannish.

They were difficult to get to know, almost impossible to develop as close friends. They were noted for cleanliness and Christianity. There was always something clandestine about them, which might have had something to do with the scavenger business. But they didn't *look* like garbage men: none of the unpleasantries one associates with garbage seemed in any way related to them.

We met them rarely in the neighborhood, but always on the softball field in spring. While our team was a crazy-quilt mixture of nationalities, tempers, physical abilities and characters, the Dutchmen (at least half of them big, blond and silent) came to the game with a sense of solidarity and purpose to their play. They were one of the few teams, I recall, in which every player had a uniform. They had names like Hockstra, Buikema, Vandermolen. When they approached the ballfield like a small army, we knew our work was cut out for us. "Here come the woodenheads!" we shouted in a false sense of bravado. (It was our field, after all.) "Goddam scavengers," mumbled one of our more fearless pitchers. "They're gonna clean us up." And they usually did.

Today, there are only three drivers left in this, one of the last of the small, family-owned scavenger businesses: Polish Tom, Silent Eddie, and Jim, the son. His father, Art Boer, semi-retired, pretty much runs the operation from a small office in the garage.

"We pick up restaurants, grocery stores, apartment buildings," explains Jim, kicking the tires of the truck. "With the rain and everything, you get behind."

Notices on the wall of the office read:

ALL DRIVERS . . . Kick tires before going to dump also when leaving. If you ruin a tire riding it flat, you just bought it. Art.

ALL B. BOER DRIVERS: Any driver driving on the expressway with our trucks, unless empty, will be subject to immediate dismissal. Arthur Boer.

DRIVERS: Don't start early and be quiet as possible. Cops are issuing tickets. Art.

Jim continues kicking the tires of the brown and white #7 Diamond Reo with a Leach compactor unit attached, and then prepares to start it. "This truck's probably got a load of garbage in the cab because the driver doesn't care." He climbs down again, leaving it rumbling in place, and steps into the office where he meets another driver, Tom, the Polish Wonder, who has brought some containers of hot coffee. They express a few feelings concerning the day's work. Jim pulls on a pair of galoshes, puts on an old jacket and says, "Let's go."

The day begins chugging, puffing, jerking, pulling away in this big garbage truck, west down 16th Street, turning north down Harlem and on to the expressway, in the cold darkness of another morning.

They got into the scavenger business about thirty years ago. "My dad and my grandfather bought a route from the de Boer brothers." But times are not the same. Everybody's hurting these days, even the scavengers . . . especially the small outfits. There are no set rates, it seems. "The bigger guys are always outbidding us."

A good truck nowadays will cost 45 to 50 thousand, Jim will tell you. "And you're always repairing something. The little guy doesn't have a chance. We bid on a school on the north side of Berwyn. I gave them a fair price, but the other guys got it for a few bucks less. And there's no way, no way they can make any money on it. This is the only business I know where the prices are the same or even less that they were ten years ago, yet we're hauling more."

At 7:15 a.m., Jim Boer backs into his first stop, the Little Chef Grill on Division and Kostner. He tips a few barrels into the trough of the truck, flings cardboard and wooden boxes, grabs handfuls of old vegetables littering the ground. His day begins this way, his hands in garbage. "The city is not supposed to pick up commercial stops," he explains.

Back in the truck, Jim points to a corner business as we pass by. "There's a stop we lost. Had them for years. But another guy got them for $10 less." He pulls up into a Kentucky Fried Chicken at Lawndale and Division where a large container called a "trip saver" awaits him.

"People like to steal them. Especially the small ones, going at $150 a

218

crack. The big ones like this come out to $400. They stole eight containers on one guy one night."

Moving past a block of brick houses still wrapped in sleep and streetlights, Jim turns left turn down a narrow alley crusted with early-March ice, stopping to empty a container behind an apartment building. A small container on wheels, it is nevertheless a test of strength to shove it somewhere within range of the hoist. Lifting the cover, Jim jumps back as a dark form leaps out. "Watch out!" he yells. "There goes a big one!" A rat, the length of a man's arm, jumps, hits the ground, and scurries off.

"Haven't seen one around here in a long time," he says. "Actually, the city's much cleaner than it used to be."

The cold begins to cut into me. The constant jumping in and out of the cab renders a heater useless. The feet go first. A numbness sets in. I empathize with scavengers everywhere . . . the energy they expend driving, walking, pushing, pulling, lifting . . . especially in cold weather. A helper is paid slightly under $7 an hour for this work. A driver gets $7.02. It is not easy money.

He jumps out at another stop, the cold air rushes into the cab again, and I roll out behind him. "The idea here is that they got a new dishwasher, and he thinks he should put a little garbage in both containers rather than filling up one at a time." A sense of organization about this scavenger as he shifts garbage from one container to the other, pushing it out into the alley, lining it up with the truck.

Noise of the hoist screaming, rumble and whine of the truck. The revving of the compactor, moaning in steely pressure while doing its job. . . . "I'm just trying to exist, to get along. Not make noise," he says. But the noise is clear to me.

Alleys in the winter and early spring, in snow and ice and rain and slush, can be insufferable for any man trying to maneuver his way out into the street. Doubly so, triply so for the scavenger, though he can make a path through it all with the machinery of sheer force. The hazards, the obstacles, the real work lies beyond the machine. It's the slippery, the numb, the bruising hand-to-hand combat with garbage and containers that wearies a scavenger's soul.

"If we had another snowstorm like '67, I think I'd just walk away. You just couldn't, couldn't get through those alleys for days."

And what of garbage picking, that favorite pastime of neighborhood people? Do scavengers garbage-pick, or is there no time for such foolishness these days with the mechanism of compactors and containers?

"Oh, once in a while, if you see something good, like copper. Here in the city, the people beat you to it. I've had it in some place like the National, where you have to beat the people . . . arguing with you, swearing at you, trying to get the left-over bread and stuff. How you gonna tell them I'm just doing my job? A lot of people got funny ideas about us . . . a garbage man . . . a muscle-bound dummy who gets in the truck and loads garbage, they think."

219

At ten minutes to eight I am cold, I am hungry. The rattling cab of the truck provides little comfort. Finally, at Belmont and Central he pulls the truck into an alley and we stop for coffee.

I cup my hands around the hot coffee, inhaling the steam, clearing my head, thawing my whole body. There's something almost sacramental about coffee at this time in the morning, under these conditions. Even feelings begin to thaw. Jim rubs his hand against his chin. "Forgot to shave this morning. My wife don't like that. She doesn't like this old jacket either. I always tell my wife, the garbage don't care what I look like."

Even a scavenger dreams the American dream. Nobody, it seems, wants to be fixed in place anymore, not even a Dutchman with the traditional ties of family and home.

"I'll be thirty years old soon. In ten years I'll be forty. That's too old to try something different. I want to find something different in Arizona. My wife hates the winters here."

The darkness, the twilight zone of early morning scavenging is over. We move out of the restaurant into a new day . . . a gray and cold day, but a recognizable morning now, with people and traffic moving about, mechanical and human sounds of a city's energy once again exerting itself. Yet, barrelling down Milwakuee Boulevard, pulling behind a restaurant for a pick up, the quality of the day does not really affect the conditions of the scavenger. If anything, the pace seems to intensify, while the work grows almost more gargantuan for man and machine.

One container is unmovable, welded into the ice. Jim chips at it with a shovel, tries to get a bite on it with the wench, tugs and finally pulls it free with his own hands. And dreams aloud of Arizona. "I've had enough of this. I can take some sun and dry heat for awhile. It'll be good for my son, too. He's got asthma."

What about accidents? "Stuff comes flying out of the hopper," he says. "I got hit by a board last summer. Then there are always sprained ankles, sprained backs, broken fingers, broken toes. It's pretty dangerous, really. I have trouble with my back all the time."

Scavengers take pride in their strength and hard labor. Jim frequently mentions Tom, the Polish Wonder, as a particularly strong and dedicated worker. "I never thought he would make it, but he's tough. Some guys don't even last a day. But even to this day Tom can carry a can and roll another at the same time. Some of the guys in the business are almost inhuman in strength. My dad had a guy working for him who used to lift a barrel of watermelons and put it on the truck."

Scavengers make an average of fifty to sixty stops a day, and work an average of ten or eleven hours, from 5 a.m. to 2 or 4 in the afternoon. And pay is not high. Jim figures it might run about $30 a month to pick up a six- or eight-flat apartment building with one small container and two stops a week,

220

He scoffs about Chicago's operation: up to four men operate one city truck. "Someone should try to figure out what they would save with less men. The gravy part of the city job is the driver. He doesn't do anything. He just drives. I'd go nuts sittin' there like that all the time."

We move into the Lawernce and Western area, behind the Delphi Restaurant and Food Market, where three overloaded containers of frozen garbage await him down a long passageway packed with snow. "They better give me a hand here," he mumbles under his breath.

The containers will not budge. Jim goes for a shovel, the owner goes back inside for more help. Pretty soon the cook joins them, the dishwasher, the waiter . . . everybody trying to get the garbage moving. Another shovel appears; first one, then the other containers are dislodged and moved inch by inch toward the truck. "One of these days I'm going to just take the empty containers and not come back."

They are painstakingly lined up at the hoist and raised, but only part of the garbage spills out of the container. The rest remains frozen inside. Jim takes the shovel and a board to the back of the container and begins banging it to free the stuff. Finally the garbage falls out in chunks.

There's something regal about a garbage truck, despite all its groveling with lowlife and waste in the back alleys. There's something powerful in its presence, as men, women, and children stop dead in their tracks to watch.

Jim compresses everything in one final squeeze. He opens a side door to check the capacity. "I should have more room . . . well, there's a little space left, but I better get to the dump." Crawling down Milwaukee Avenue, and other traffic-packed Saturday streets in Chicago, Jim deadheads for the dump, filling in the details of growing up Dutch and scavenging for a living.

"This is a business that was ninety percent Dutch and Swede at one time. But then the big outfits began buying them out. All this within the last three years. The old Dutch—most of them just sold out. The young aren't interested. No one sold out in fear, though. It was nothing like that. A lot of them work for the big outfits now. Some of them just moved away."

"The Dutch people are mostly hard working, clean people. I don't know too many of them who sit on their ass and collect welfare. I'm sure that we have some lazy ones too, but I don't know them. If the Dutch got money, they like to enjoy it . . . summer homes, Cadillacs, furs, vacations.

"It's changing, though. I had to sneak to a movie when I was growing up. If you wanted to watch TV, all you could watch was *Lassie* on Sunday night. But there's no more right or wrong with them than any other nationality. The Dutch are not supposed to be drinkers. I had a buddy who married an Italian. Her father wouldn't talk to her for six months. At the wedding, the woodenshoes drank the Italians under the table."

Day ends at the dump for the scavenger. We pull in at 1:45, sign a dump ticket ("They charge over $30 a load," says Jim), and head for wherever the bulldozer happens to be.

We back into a pile of every conceivable kind of trash. King of the Garbage Hill, I smile. Jim pulls some levers. The back end of the truck goes up while all the compacted garbage is automatically eased out, dumping the whole history of our day, the lettuce, the bread, the bottles, cans, boxes, food, doors, glass, film. . . .

I walk upon the surface for the first time and feel a strangeness, an unsteadiness about my limbs. The eeriest sensation of all. Something to save, to take back, to scavage from the day: the new earth moves, even trembles beneath my feet.

Jim waves me on back to the empty truck and the long ride to the garage in Berwyn. He's in a hurry. He and his wife will leave by plane this evening for Arizona to check on the possibilities of a new way of life for an ex-scavenger. He wants to throw away winter, a bad back, a whole tradition of work which has become meaningless in his generation.

Meanwhile, I mull over the sensation of a hollow earth, still moving beneath my feet . . . a world not as solid as I once believed.

Gene Sage: Party Man

Gene Sage is throwing a party tonight. Actually, there are two parties going simultaneously at two of his restaurants, Eugene's and Mon Petit, which happen to be separate, unique, and just across the hall from each other at 1255 N. State Parkway. So it is the same party, in a way . . .with all the earmarks of a daily double celebration. Confusing? Perhaps. But typical Sage-o-mania.

I arrive at 5 p.m., an invitation in my shirt pocket and confused. One side of the invitation reads, "Eugene's invites you to its 1st Anniversary Procrastinator's Party." The other side reads, "You are cordially invited to celebrate the new and complete Sage's Mon Petit, champagne & hors doeuvres."

I have never eaten in a Gene Sage restaurant before, and checking the beautiful people stepping out of taxis and long black cars, I have a distinct feeling I'm underdressed, lack pizzaz, and am very probably out of place.

My connection, a man named Mort, will lead me to Sage. "Hey, who and where is Mort?" I ask the bartender. "Mort's across the hall in Mon Petit," he says. "He's got bushy hair and he's wearing a blue suit."

I'm surrounded by bushy haired guys wearing blue suits in the dimness. I'm surrounded by Damon Runyon dolls that sure do come together in Eugene's. I decide to reserve my standing-room-only spot at the bar and hunt for the hors d'oeuvres. Let the Mort come to me. "Tell him I'm here," I tell the bartender, who nods as if he really recognizes who I am. As for Sage on Sage, somewhere he once said, "You lend your presence to the place. That's ninety percent of our game." Given the present circumstances of eternal champagne and plates of tasties floating by me, I figure I understand maybe fifty percent of the man already. The balance of his presence will surely be revealed in time.

Hors d'oeuvres! Does the Sage call these hors d'oeuvres? These tables veritably groaning under the weight of such delicacies as Oysters Rockefeller, Clams Casino, fresh shrimp, cheese, crab legs, chicken breasts, fruit, bacon wrapped around dates? I settle in my anonymity for awhile, methodically (shrimp, clams, oysters . . . oysters, clams, shrimp) overindulging in the repast.

Later, I move across the hall to the elegance of Mon Petit, and a semi-serious search for my connection to Sage. At the bar I spy a busy head of hair, a

223

blue suit, surrounded by dolls and dolls . . . maybe the man, Mort? It is. We exchange pleasantries. He leads me to Sage in the plush dining room, holding another hundred or more hungry people, Sage enthusiasts all, standing shoulder to shoulder, balancing food, drink, and their own sense of presence.

I shake hands with Sage, small in stature, who later invites me to an empty table as the bash begins to unwind at the appointed hour and tables are set for dinner. Sage, fashionably dressed, an impish flash in his eye, taking in everything, everybody in the room. He does, indeed, have an air of showbiz about him . . . a promoter extraordinaire, but more than that, a definite presence. You feel that he is always somewhere on the scene; you know you are in good hands; and he knows he has you, on way or another. He is never the odd man out.

"What do you figure this bash cost you?"

"Aside from the two hundred parking tickets we'll have to pay for . . . we went through sixteen cases of champagne . . . then, of course, I decided to open the bar the last minute . . . the food, everything . . . about $1,500. But this is Monday, a slow night. And many of these people will stay on for dinner. So part of that is back already. Besides, I think we made a lot of people happy."

His real scene is Sage's East, 181 E. Lake Shore Dr., where I meet him the next morning and where he seems most at home. Sage's East is very, very English in tone, mixing the elegance of Olde England with a touch of the friendly pub.

There's the Downing Street Dining Room and the Wimbledon Bar. And a menu (in dollars and pounds) of inspired mother country dishes such as Le Boeuf Marlborough; Veal in the Manner of the Virgin Queen; Chyken Livers, Alfred Lord Tennyson; Sole, Samuel Hoare.

Picking up the pieces of last night's conversation on cost, Sage comes up with some Tuesday morning statistics on the art of promotion. "As opposed to doing $3,000 or so for a Monday, we did $5,000."

Returning to roots, though, the man as opposed to the restaurateur. "I was born and raised here . . . the North Side. Senn High School. Went to Riverside Military Academy, prep school, where I learned to lie, steal and cheat. It was terrible. Majored in liberal arts at Northwestern. Received a masters degree in political science from UCLA." While on his way from California to Boston to attend law school, he stopped in Chicago to give his father a helping hand in the restaurant he had opened—Alex's, at 35 W. Adams. Sage, twenty-two years old at the time, never got out.

Eventually he opened his own place on LaSalle, Sage's 1 North, in 1959. He admits, "I didn't get the desire until about five years after I was at La Salle. All the while I had this feeling of being trapped."

"This was a very large place on two floors that had gone bankrupt. We acquired it. I met a man who has been very influential in my life, Howard Arvey (Jake Arvey's son). He helped me make the deal.

"I remodeled a downstairs bar and called it the Chambers. I still think it's the

224

prettiest room I ever built . . . beamed . . . red and plush . . . a fireplace. La Salle St. at that time was a forerunner of what goes on now at the singles bars. We catered to wealthy lawyers, politicians. About that time I began to get interested. We did a tremendous business.

"I determined that we were going to become part of the legal community. And we became, in a very short time, an institution on La Salle St. At that point we were the only real restaurant there. Truthfully, I think we were the first singles bar in the country. It started on a Friday night. All of a sudden we got to be known as a meeting place on Friday nights for lawyers, insurance men, secretaries. It was wonderful. It was almost embarrassing, and I don't know how it happened.

"We opened another room, called it the Cloak and Dagger, and made it a key club for our distinguished lawyers and judges. When we opened up, the menus were bound in mystery books.

"We'd have Richard Ogilvie sitting there in one booth when he was sheriff, and somebody with a case against him in another booth. A strange mixture of people . . . anybody on trial . . . deals being made. The FBI would be there. Bobby Kennedy was there once . . . Adlai II. Most of the federal judges used to eat there at one time or another. During that time (the early '60s) there wasn't a politician in the state of Illinois who didn't eat there, who I didn't know."

One can see at the outset how Sage the restaurateur and Sage the promoter began to blend a unique style of Chicago dining. Setting had become very important to the man.

"I felt you had to have a motif. If you weren't where the foot traffic was, you had to have something going for you. Eating out is an experience; it's dining more than eating. The successful restaurant today puts together an entertainment package no matter how you look at it."

So, the "entertainment" he discovered and pursued on N. La Salle was law and mystery. "Our membership cards had nothing on them till you held them to the light." Gimmicky? To a certain degree, perhaps. But Sage was just getting into the act, the art of promotion. "And good, good food. We had an old German cook, Marie Luelsdorf, who made the best brown sauce I've ever eaten in my life. She was a great cook, a great chef."

Most of his help has always stayed with him. "My big problem in starting a new restaurant is getting the crew together and making it cohesive. Our food, our service, our atmosphere is our entertainment."

As for Sage's East, where we now sit, "I did it British. I was an Anglophile . . . until I went to England. But this was to be a second place that would give a little more income. We opened it eleven years ago . . . an instant success. Mayor Daley came in three or four months after I opened it, just to help me out. 'Would you like me to go through the bar, Gene?' he said. Daley came in at La Salle, too. Never a steady customer, though. Never saw the man take a drink. Anyway, there was a need in this area (the Gold Coast) for this kind of restaurant—the plushest neighborhood tavern around!"

What happened to his first restaurant, his first love? "I sold it for a lot of money. I cried like a baby when I sold it. It was home. It was where I found out I enjoyed what I was doing rather than being stuck in it." The personality of the promoter, however, seems to dominate the Sage presence, perhaps diminishing the sophisticated image of the restaurateur. Sage may just have found the delicate balance. Not a soft sell, nor a hard sell, but a Sage sell marked with imagination, honesty and humor.

But not all of his promotions have been successful. "My biggest flop was a nine-hole pitch-and-putt golf course that nobody came to. I thought we'd have about four hundred people. Nine people showed up. And I had fifteen trophies to give away."

We get into the whole Chicago/New York restaurant scene for a moment, just to see where the Sage sympathies lie. "We abandoned the Loop before the Loop abandoned us. Individual restaurant owners, such at Fritzel's, we all stopped what we were doing, and it was all out of greed. Merchants in all fields just stopped trying down there. Of course, I'm the greatest Chicago chauvinist that ever was. I think Chicago is the greatest city in the world. But I think the Loop will come back strong. I'd make it work. With middle-class and upper-class housing down there, I think the Loop will begin to come back.

"My feeling is that independent restaurants, Don Roth, Bill Contos, Arnie Morton, around twenty of us, are better than public-owned corporations. We eat here at our own restaurants.

"New York has a couple of very great restaurants. I think the single greatest restaurant I've been in is '21.' But still I would say that Chicago holds it own with New York and San Francisco."

"The purpose of a restaurant is to send away happy customers. I like to say I'm 5 feet 4 inches tall, but in my restaurant I'm 6 feet 3. I walk outside, I'm 5 feet 4 again."

Trying to distinguish between customers and friends is difficult when you operate an establishment with a combination of your heart and your head. "Close to 1,000 . . . " customers or friends? "In life I am blessed with five very warm, dear, close friends whom I trust to call even more than friends. Then you go through life and meet 1,000 acquaintances. . . . My five people, when one of us is cut, the other bleeds. The other 1,000, when they're cut, you hurt for them. Friendship and loyalty is very important to me."

A long session with Sage brings the man and his methods into sharper focus. You are left with the feeling that he knows where he's at, he's happy being who and what he is, and the future may depend on no more than the next promotional brainstorm, though the streak of humanism in the man is clearly visible.

226

On James T. Farrell: Not Resting in Peace

When James Farrell died on August 22, 1979, at the age of seventy-five, many people, writers, critics, and readers were surprised that the author of the *Studs Lonigan* trilogy (written almost fifty years before) was still alive. Farrell's peculiar fate was to have written an American classic in his late twenties, early thirties, and then plunge into oblivion.

He went on to write over fifty books, including *Sam Holman,* said to be his last novel, finished only five weeks before his death, and the first to be published posthumously. His files are bulging with unpublished manuscripts.

"They say I'm washed up," he once said. "Editors and publishers tell me I should have quit writing years and years ago. They think I should have conveniently died at thirty. But I won't die. I'll keep on writing."

Either the critics ignored him after *Studs,* or the times changed (naturalism became passé), or Farrell became so locked into the singular passion of exploring what he knew best—working class Irish of Chicago's South Side, and 1930's America, which haunted him—that no other subject, no refinement of his own craft, interested him. He was that obsessed. His mission was clear-cut: to become America's Balzac, to get down every aspect of life at that time in telling detail. "I don't follow any form when I write. I just make my points. My idea of writing is simplicity over simplification," he said.

Sam Holman is Farrell's story of leftist philosophies and politics among New York intellectual circles in the 1930s. Farrell, with his own socialist leanings, knew that scene well, and in some ways has written a *roman á clef* depicting the lives and motivations of certain characters who would later make the headlines concerning the history of the Communist Party in America.

He does this in the plainest prose, a simple (often plodding) piling of detail upon detail, incident upon incident, leading his main character, Holman, through a rather mundane life of changing beliefs, insufficient drama, until the life and the story end. It could be a newspaper account; it is that straight. Yet he captures a time perfectly, and a man within that time so preciously, that you will never forget Sam Holman or that period of American life.

This book may disappoint those still expecting Farrell to deliver another

227

Studs Lonigan. It is not that. And I question the right to expect Farrell, or any other writer who has delivered to us once in classic proportions, to deliver again. And again. And to bury him if he doesn't.

The country changing, his audience diminishing, critics ignoring him, his eyesight fading, a bout with the bottle, his personal life in shambles, Farrell moved from Chicago to New York, from hotels to smaller apartments, his income dwindling, but still writing nine, ten, twelve hours a day. Continually publishing books—his one long, long story of American society, the 1930s— and continually ignored.

"They looked at my stuff and said it wasn't Farrell," he once said. "Every goddam thing I do is not Farrell. Who the hell is Farrell anyway? If I ever find the sonofabitch I'll have him killed."

Sam Holman is Farrell. It's another piece of an enormous and significant body of work by a Chicago writer, an American writer, with the stamina to believe in himself and his art.

Farrell died with less than $10,000 in his estate.

He left a fortune in literature.

Flake-Out at the Skin-Flicks

It was one of those October/April mornings in Chicago: rainy, windy, gray, cold, where the only warmth in the air seemed to hang in the tempting colored lights of theater marquees. Under such circumstances, a movie house is the only place of refuge.

Where Eagles Dare, screamed the Chicago Theater. *The Killing of Sister George,* blinked the State & Lake. *Funny Girl,* laughed the United Artists. *Vixen,* winked the Loop. But you've already heard and read and talked about these. No surprises. *Vixen?* Nope. Too much the "in" flick at the moment. Maybe a work of art, said someone. Leave it to the critics, the film buffs, the suburban voyeurs.

On an October/April morning in Chicago, the only flicks worth seeing were the ones nobody would admit seeing. The ones the critics seldom wrote about. Take a good old skin flick, just for laughs.

The Ecstasies of Women, tittered and panted and blushed at the Capri. The kind of local color worth walking in the rain for. Warmth. Sanctuary.

Except for the marquee and the box office, the Capri doesn't even look like a theater. All of its gaudy, popcorn smelling, maroon and blue ushered, bright candy-wrapped sisters are making hay at this time of the morning with the women shoppers, the kids, the visitors on and around State Street, while here huddles the Capri, south of all the action, but willing to cradle the lost, wet male who just happens to be passing by.

Nobody buys popcorn at the Capri. Nobody munches on candy. Everyone comes in empty-handed. There isn't a shopping bag in sight. Never a woman. You take a seat in the battleship gray decor and sit in silence waiting for the few lights to go out and the show to begin.

At 9:55 a.m. fifteen men of various ages are already scattered about. Nobody looks at anybody else. No one expects to be seen in such a place. Everyone sits rows and chairs away from each other. If there were some candles and a cross up front, you'd think, for all the maddening silence, that this was a house of worship. Maybe it is. Lights out.

My God! In living color? What's become of the old stag-like black and

229

white? The grainy film? The single twitchy crooked magnified hair that always does a dance across the silver screen? The more than occasional blackout? The visible splices? The gravel throat dialogue?

It's all new now: everyword a bell tone, every scene in focus. My god, mammary glands moving in living color at this hour of the morning!

And there are real people up there, Hugh Hefner cutouts. Harry, his name is, out for his final bachelor night with the boys. Tomorrow the wedding bells ring. But tonight it's the four of them drinking and living it up in this Go Go place. And the girls, right behind and above them, are go-going all the while these guys are saying something original about the good old days . . . "Tomorrow ends it all." Harry? Harry's dreaming of those days while above him those mammary glands keep time. And about every ten minutes he has a technicolored flashback to those days of seduction.

And we're right there with him! All fifteen of us in the Capri on this cold wet morning. Only our number has multiplied. Maybe thirty by now. (Can't say we don't know enough to come in from the rain.) And more and more business-looking men making the scene. But everybody still keeping his distance.

Harry flashes back now to a Los Angeles bar, going up to this chick and hitting her with that classic opening, "Pardon me, Miss, is this seat taken?"

"No," she says with a smile. "Are you on vacation," they both seem to say. What does Harry do? "I prepare ladies for the four seasons," he says. "I sell lingerie." "Kind of an interesting job," he says or she says. You can't really tell with these two because they both keep muffing their lines. Harry, in particular, is a rather energetic young actor who not only muffs his lines but breaks up and laughs in the camera.

But you forgive Harry for this and even his dead chick. Good acting, after all, is a rather natural thing. And these people are so natural they sound as if they were reading their lines and practicing very hard to act naturally. Give any guy in the street a script, tell him to read it like an actor in the movies, and there you have Harry. The chick is even beyond this. But what the hell, what do we (now fifty strong) here in the Capri care about art? Action, baby, action!

First a toast from Harry the lingerie salesman: "Bottoms up, and may they all be covered or else I'll have a bare existence."

Nobody laughs in the Capri.

Continue with Harry's onslaught? "Have you ever modeled lingerie?"

"I haven't had many private demonstrations," she says.

Where's he from? Where's this guy Harry from? How do they always find these willing chicks waiting in the bars in L.A.?

"I'm from Intercourse, P.A.," says Harry.

Nobody laughs in the Capri. Nobody ever laughs in the Capri.

"It's right beside Paradise," he continues as they both chuckle, "and not far from Hell."

Silence.

But where's the action? Seventy-five cold, wet men did not abandon the Chicago streets this morning for laughs! Get on with it, Harry. Get on.

And so he does. First in the car. Gold convertible, top down in the L.A. sunlight. They embrace. Harry's travelling salesman's hands begin their long day's journey into night. Close up (perfect focus) on a detailed French kiss. Sound (all the way up) on some pretty heavy breathing. But that's all for now. Next stop: Harry's little yacht called, naturally, "High Life."

Since when did leading men in skin flicks own yachts? Even in flashbacks?

They're on the boat. "Bartending is my second specialty," says Harry. We all know what the chick says. "That's a little something you'll have to discover," he retorts.

"You're going to crush my dress," she says.

"Then why don't you change? All my samples are hanging in the other room." Harry does some more practicing on his second specialty, while the camera moves in just behind the bar and focuses perfectly on this great sign, the only real laugh on the boat: THIS MAY NOT BE THE MAYFLOWER BUT MANY CAME ACROSS ON IT.

Nobody in the Capri saw the sign.

But everybody saw Harry and the chick finally make it on his yacht. Everybody heard the amplified sounds of passion. And everybody felt her moving final line, fluff and all: "I'm just wicked," she said, "but I love it."

The crowd in the Capri has grown to over a hundred men, each still enjoying *The Ecstasies of Women* in his separate seat, his own row. Each warm and glad to be safe inside. Not one seeing any humor in the production.

Some flashbacks later (or is it the real scene? but does it matter? no) and Harry's talking to this topless dancer named Frenzy. "What's your first name?" he asks the mammary glands. "Summer," she says. "I have two sisters, Fall and Winter. And a brother named Strange."

Still no laughs in the Capri.

What does Summer Frenzy's father do? (Full's his name, by the way. And the mother, Half-a.) "He's a honey-dipper," she says.

And where, oh, where, is Summer Frenzy from? Are you ready, all of you guys out there in the Capri? Ready?

"I'm from Climax, Arizona," she says.

Laugh, damn it! Look at Harry breaking up.

"This is one of the worst experiences of my life," he says. And we believe him. All of us do. All 150 of us in the Capri.

The plot thickens with more present-perfect, past-future flashbacks of seduction. The women get younger and lovelier, the color more technicolored. One chick on the beach asks Harry, "What do you think I want to do? And where we do it doesn't matter." (Of course it's on the "High Life," Harry's only scene in this production.)

"How do you dig men's clothing?" he asks.

232

"In the closet, sweetie," she replies.

The dialogue reaches trite-classic proportions as Harry vows, "Your skin is as soft as a baby's behind." And, "You are gorgeous." And her sweet-simple reply: "Some men are so easily pleased."

Yes, they are, but they'll never let on. All two hundred of us sitting there in the Capri, waiting out the wet morning hours of a cold city, sitting back in separate silence wondering who Harry will get next.

Everyone enjoys the ecstasy, but no one appreciates the agony of it all. Maybe when you consider the serious straits of the skin flick today, there is nothing to laugh about. *The Ecstasies of Women* is, after all, just an up-dated attempt to keep the crude and passing art of the classic skin flick safe and separate from the new nudity (obscenity denied) now playing for the whole family at you local neighborhood theater.

What's a man to do on cold Chicago mornings when skin flicks become safe for democracy?

Laugh?

Hell yes. Finally. See them all at the Clark's Classic Skin Flick Festival maybe five years from now.

"Bottoms up, and may they all be. . . . "

Dixie: On the Outskirts of Town

You can find a little Dixie in Chicago in some pretty respectable places. That's the whole damned problem. Take a good woman, give her a comfortable surrounding, and you end up with a bitch of a bad imitation. We all know what happened to that great little restaurant next to the alley in that bad-news part of the city—you can't afford to go there anymore.

Take Dixie. The respectable people get a hold of it, give it a boater hat, striped shirt, grandfather's mustache, arm garters, put red, white, and blue lights on it, and invite all their friends from the John Birch Society to come and see what they've found: yes, folks, just a little bit of Americana. Quaint the way things used to be. Pleasant. "Is that you, William, keeping soft time with the right heel of your new $50 Florsheim shoes?"

What's a good man to do? Search the outskirts of town, of course. As Mike Royko once put it, "I never eat inside the El tracks." Ditto Dixieland—or anything else you want the roots of. Watch out for Chicago Jazz on main streets in bright lights.

Once upon a time in Dixie, in a joint outside the city limits, hot jazz by Franz Jackson, the Salty Dogs, and others lit up the night-time sky. They called it The Red Arrow. It was on the far west side, in Stickney on Pershing Road, a no man's land of sorts bordering the sanitation district. A good place for jazz. The Red Arrow itself—a roadhouse, one of those frame buildings in the middle of nowhere that always attract a crowd just because the location was Limbo, U. S. A. A safe place, where nobody would see you. And, with this added touch of excitement, the perfect place to drink beer to oblivion. The perfect place for Dixie to march the saints right out of you. The perfect place to be.

The Red Arrow died over three years ago. Stickney is all built up. An anonymous apartment building and a vacant lot mark the spot where people once abandoned their cars and lost themselves for hours in booze and jazz.

If the Red Arrow in Stickney was far out, Rene's in Westmont is way out—and still alive. Way out west in the perfect shoddy atmosphere for Dixie.

There's an address painted on the rural mailbox outside the joint: 202 W. Naperville Road. Try and find it.

235

If you're driving west on 47th street in LaGrange, then cross the Burlington tracks to Chicago Avenue in Hinsdale, which remains Chicago Ave. as you continue due west through Clarendon Hills, then through someplace three blocks long called Blackhawk Heights . . . and you're still not there. Suddenly the sign Westmont looms up, and though you're still on Chicago Ave. until you cross Cass Ave., you now discover that Chicago has turned into Maple. Confused? That's nothing. Keep going a few more blocks and Maple magically becomes Naperville Road. At the corner of Naperville and Washington, the northwest corner, SURPRISE! there's Rene's.

It's been waiting there for you for years. I've seen it only once in daylight, and I'd rather not describe it. At night it looks sleazy as any roadhouse. And there's a little marquee beneath the pulsing pink neon sign, "Rene's" that announces in wobbly red letters:

Sun.   D   XI

I   E.

Sunday, 8 p.m.: Dixieland at Rene's in Westmont. But that's only half the story. Abandon your car in the gravel and chuckholes. Come on in. Already "Tiger Rag" is running wild, right through the walls to greet you.

Inside on your left is a small platform where four great guys calling themselves "The Chicago Footwarmers" (although their name is not on the marquee, on the bandstand, or anywhere else for that matter) make Dixie—or Hot Jazz, as Kim Cusack, leader and clarinet man, calls it. So just who are these "Chicago Footwarmers"? There's Mike Walbridge on sousaphone, Eddie Lynch on banjo, Glen Koch on drums, and Kim on clarinet. And they play hot jazz at Rene's every Sunday night—been playing there, in fact, for the past seven years.

Rene's on the inside is something else. The walls are decorated in appropriate ivy-print corrugated paper. Throw in a dark landscape painting, and two more of those Woolworth classics of tiny children with big sad eyes. There's a U-shaped bar with standard electric beer signs and mounted fish caught somewhere on sale. Overhead, tiny Italian Christmas lights keep Christ in Christmas all year round. And behind the bar, Rene himself, heavy, almost neckless, keeping tab of who's drinking what and why the hell aren't they drinking more! It's Sunday night, for crissake, and these guys aren't playing Dixie for my health.

The rest of Rene's is a story problem of how many tables and chairs one man can squeeze into a small room with a bar, a bandstand, and two washrooms. And how many people can stand and drink all night for the sake of Dixie?

Plenty. Plenty, for this group.

Mustachioed Mike Walbridge, co-leader, is a young tall man playing a hell of a big instrument, the sousaphone. "I attack it like a trumpet," he says. A lab technician by trade, he is considered the purist in the group. Eyes closed, face up-tight (man!), he concentrates on precise sounds! Why Dixie for him? "My dad was a jazz musician. He had this great record collection. That started it. It's

236

such a loose freewheeling style of music." The state of Dixieland? "We're the only group in the area that plays authentic jazz."

Glen Koch, "the 80-year-old hippie of the drums," as Kim calls him, has a long history in music that includes everything from society dance bands to playing for six months in a ship's band on an around-the-world cruise. An insurance broker now, he gave up music entirely for twenty years. "I never played Dixie till I met these guys." And so every Sunday night he's there at Rene's: "Sunday night is not a job to me. Might as well call it a jam session."

Eddie Lynch on banjo makes you feel good just watching. He's big and heavy and smokes a pipe. He sits down, plops that banjo on his belly, and plucks away like it was nothing at all. A cab driver ("I'm a musician by profession, but a man's got to eat.") he claims he gave up four bands just to play Dixie. "It has the beat. It has the feeling. It portrays any feeling you want. This is the way music was meant to be. This is what I intend it to be for my life."

And then there's Kim, the Clark Kent of the group, a man who passes as a quiet, nice-guy English teacher by day, only to shed that disguise at night for a clarinet, red suspenders, a bottle of Miller's and hot jazz. If only his students could hear what he does with a clarinet, hear him explain why he digs Dixie, "Because it's music that's got a lot of guts." If only they could see him on stage, enjoy his wit and wisecracks, as he M.C.s the music and the madness. "That can't be Mr. Cusack," they would say. Of course it can't. We all know that Mr. Cusack is a member in good standing of the N.E.A., guardian of grammar, keeper of the word, "professional" all the way. (Who says a man can't lead two lives?)

And play he does. They all do. Listen. Listen to the opening set of "Struttin with Some Barbecue," "Chicago," "Tiger Rag," "Just a Closer Walk with Thee," and "Evolution Mama." Kim Cusack moving the carinet around like it was stuck in his mouth. Kim stomping out the time, bringing the rest of the group in with a wave of his head or hand. Kim singing. Singing! Mr. Cusack? Teacher of lost causes? "Oh, evolution mama, don't you make a monkey out of me. . . ."

Rene's was a happening before someone discovered the term and proclaimed it an art. Given any Sunday night, these four guys, their music and the people, things inevitably happen.

Sometime before the second set, the door will burst open and in will walk a musician called Jack-the-Bear. Why bother with more description? Jack-the-Bear! How do I know what his last name is, where he came from, what he does? Bearded Jack-the-Bear is here. He gets a big hand from the regulars, cheers himself, takes out his white trombone, and plants his rear end on the jukebox, a little to the left of Big Eddie.

Now for some fun. Like Kim deliberately going into numbers that require no trombone whatsoever . . . and Jack-the-Bear getting his licks in anywhere— usually just a long note—wherever he can . . . much to the delight of the audience who give him a big hand for his every stabbing vooooooommmmm.

Things continue to happen. Eddie Lynch singing, sounding so very much like Louie Armstrong. Or just playing softly and calling, "Quiet," so Mike Walbridge can be heard. And then, after Kim, the music getting hotter, Glen stirring it all up with sticks, and Eddie yelling out, "All right, let's go!"

Or some nights Lew Green walks in with his cornet, introduced as "the world's foulmouthedest cornet player," and Lew stands tall in the midst of them and works beautifully with Kim in music and witty patter.

And, of course, the people. You can't forget them. Jazz buffs like Bob Miller (who died just recently) and his wife who never missed a Sunday out at Rene's. Bill and Lol Walker. Chuck and Bernice, who dance their hearts out to this music. And Kim will say, "This is what I like about Rene's. Guys like Chuck who keep everything going. All these same faces. They've gotten to be friends of mine. A 'kiss-the-weekend-goodbye' crowd."

A good-time crowd. A cross-section crowd. Young and old. Everyone from the Oak Brook set to a guy sitting at the bar in his ENCO uniform. A couple of middle-aged women maybe looking for action, and some tired old men sitting at the bar glassy-eyed, glad to get away for the night from all the real action at home.

I have been in Rene's when a big blonde, from god-knows-where, with a mink stole and black dress began doing a dance straight out of *La Dolce Vita*. And another time, any number of times, when a man or woman walks up to the band and belts out a tune just for the hell of it . . . only to receive Kim's classic comment, "That was contestant number 69, folks," Madame X, a secret suburban housewife, was there just the other night singing, "A Good Man Nowadays Is Hard To Find," just like another red hot mama from years back.

I have been there when a little old man, refugee from some Bohemian neighborhood, I'm sure, went around from table to table selling horseradish. I only wonder what he thinks of Dixieland.

I remember the times (almost every Sunday night) when Nancy, Kim's wife, dressed to the teeth in black slacks, regulation gray sweatshirt, and army fatigue shirt, yelled out, "Play 'Poor Butterfly'!" (which Kim never does). He answered her request with a gesture. Which she returned. If Kim is the M.C. on the bandstand, Nancy is the M.C. in the crowd. A great team—show biz and otherwise.

There was once a night when writer J.R. Nash, looking very much like James Cagney, thought he was Bix Beiderbecke but couldn't find his horn (or was it his lip?).

And another night when a former Rene's regular, now a west coast artist, Lew Allen, returned to Rene's dressed like Wild Bill Cody. "This is the only thing I miss in Frisco. There's no Dixie. No Rene's."

Somewhere between 11 and 12 p.m. Kim swings into a "Chicago Theater ending," as he calls it. "I Want a Little Girl" is the tune, and after you've heard it the first time at Rene's you won't forget it. You know the band is saying

239

goodnight, and no matter what Rene does, no matter how many songs are punched on the jukebox, the mood is gone and the crowd is leaving. "I Want A Little Girl" gets softer and softer as Kim introduces the men: "Let's give a hand to the world's biggest banjo player . . . and that 80-year-old hippie on the drums. . . . We're the "Chicago Footwarmers". . . . Don't go away folks, Rene's still got some beer to hustle. . . . Time to go back now to that real world. . . . See you next Sunday." And with those words and a deafening flourish, it's the end. And Dixie dies in Westmont, on the outskirts of town.

Jerome Holtzman:
Chicago's Dean of Baseball

"In this city [Chicago] sports fans do not do the Wave. They do not wave hankies. They do not paint themselves in team colors or wear goofy costumes. They watch the game."—Dirk Johnson, *New York Times*

Which accurately describes the work of Chicago sportswriter Jerome Holtzman, as well: to watch the game.

On December 6, 1989, Holtzman was named winner of the prestigious J.G. Tylor Spink Award for 1990 by the Baseball Writers Association of America. Which puts him in the Hall of Fame in Cooperstown. Not bad for a kid who grew up in Jake Avery's 24th Ward (the West Side Jewish Ghetto) and was twice in the Marks Nathan Jewish Orphan Home on 15th and Albany.

He's a throwback to the days of old newspapermen, a dying breed. Ring Lardner comes to mind, or Ben Hecht, Damon Runyon, Jimmy Cannon. The way it used to be. Copy! Dealine! Scoop! Where the hell's the story?

It's in his eyes, his hands, the way he carries himself. He's been around. You don't study sportswriting in college, bub. Give him an old Underwood on which to peck and pound facts into lines of hard, clear words. Pure, simple prose. A guy with a great grasp of the story and an understanding of the past from which to put today's game in perspective.

"Among the beauties of baseball," he wrote in his column for the *Chicago Tribune*, "is that despite the designated hitter and artificial turf, evils both, essentially the game hasn't changed. The bases are still 90 feet apart, as in the days of Father Chadwick. The mound is 60 feet, 6 inches from the plate, unchanged since 1893. To hit .300 it is necessary to get three hits in every 10 at-bats, same as it was in 1903 when Cleveland's Nap Lajoie won the American League batting championship with a .355 average."

How's that for good old fashioned, hard-nosed baseball writing, sports fans? (How's that for Advanced Sportswriting 300, future sportswriting students?)

Sometimes you go out and find the story; sometimes the story comes to you. At the moment I'm looking Jerome Holtzman right in the face in Door County, Wisconsin—not his usual stomping grounds. There's not a press box, a baseball diamond, a scorecard anywhere in sight.

I've read his work for years, never expecting we'd ever cross paths, given my distance from Chicago these days.

Yet here he is on my homefield, Door County, where he and his wife Marilyn retreat in fall, after the World Series, after another baseball season.

Holtzman paces the quiet of my coop late on an October morning, plunk in the middle of nowhere, nothing but trees and fields of silence outside the windows. A Chicagoan, a sportswriter, definitely out of place, he unwraps a big Honduran cigar, acts a little befuddled. No cheering in the press box, indeed. [*No Cheering in the Press Box*, by Jerome Holtzman, a solid and fascinating collection of interviews with some of the greatest American sportswriters; Holt, Rinehard and Winston, 1973.]

Here he sits (for a moment), the bulk of him: plaid shirt, suspenders, barrel-chest, curly graying hair, bushy eyebrows, puffing smoke, looking me straight in the face with a classic Chicago mug of his own that says, "So what's the deal?" Getting his two cents in first: "So tell me about small town life."

I shrug and suggest what he already knows: it's no Wrigley Field.

Let's talk sports writing. Let's talk baseball. . . .

"I started on June 25, 1943, in Chicago at the *Daily Times* as a copyboy in the sports department. And I was seventeen two weeks later.

I stayed at the *Times* from June of '43 till September of '44. From September '44, just after my eighteenth birthday, I went into the Marine Corps for two years. I came back in September of 1946. I went back to the *Times* and I was a copyboy. As a copyboy I was doing the baseball averages. We had a scorecard on the back of the paper every day. I was twenty years old."

His knowledge of sportswriting and love for print journalism go back to high school, where he was sports editor of the *Crane Tech Chronicle*.

"Crane Tech High School was unique in this respect. Because it was a technical high school, we had all shops—fifteen different shops, electric shop, wood shop, machine shop, forging, welding. We also had a print shop that had kids learning how to work linotype machines. And they had a little press room there. And as a result, because of these kids learning the production end of the print shop area, Crane Tech had a daily paper! Every day but Monday. We were told, and I'm sure it's correct, that we were the only high school in the country that had a daily paper. Now Lane Tech was twice the size of Crane Tech. Lane Tech had 10,000 boys, Crane Tech had 5,000. But Lane Tech's paper was mimeographed. Ours was printed. In my last two or three years in high school, I was a sports writer for the paper, and as a senior I won the Inch Award. We had a banquet at the Graemere Hotel on the West Side of Chicago. I'll never forget it. I broke the record as a senior. I wrote more inches of copy than anybody who

242

had ever written before on the paper. And I was the sports editor. So that really qualified me as a copyboy when I went to work at the *Times*. I knew what bold face was. I knew what an eight-point slug was. I knew certain minor things.

"In those days [after the War in '46] a copyboy was really a pretty good job. I did a lot of work. I did the clerk's work, I did the averages, I did the morning lines. The *Daily Times'* biggest edition was the turf edition. We sold a lot of papers at the race track and around town. It was the big turf edition in Chicago. The *Times* was known as a racing paper. They might not like to hear that, but that's pretty much what it was.

"The turf edition came out about eleven o'clock in the morning, as people were going to the track. We'd come in there about seven or seven-thirty in the morning and change the morning lines and new jockeys. The point is, I was doing a lot of stuff. I was setting down the race results. I also picked the horses as a copyboy. I was Ann Joy for a couple of years because the guy who did it, didn't want to do it any more, so he shoved it on to me. I picked the horses, I handicapped the horses . . . all as a copyboy. No one knew it. I didn't know a lot about racing at the time, but I learned how to read the racing form, and I was a fair picker. I did this even before I went into the service. In 1944, I think if you followed my selections, you would have made about $40.

"So when I came back in 1946, I got my old job back again, doing the same thing over again for the first couple of weeks. Finally I said to the assistant sports editor, a guy who just died, 'Ted, I'm going to have to leave. I'm doing the same thing I did before.' It was a Friday afternoon. This guy's name was Ted Damata, a wonderful guy. He said to me, 'You can't quit. You gotta come here Monday and see the sports editor and tell him.' The sports editor was a guy named Gene Kessler. I came in Monday morning and Gene Kessler said to me, 'Well, from now on you're going to start covering high school sports.'

"And so, when I was twenty years old I started writing for the paper on a daily basis and became what is called a prep writer. I did it for eleven years. In the spring of 1957, I went on baseball. The Chicago *Sun* and the *Times* merged about '47, '48. I met my wife that way because there was a printers' strike in 1948, and Marilyn was a typist. In those days they typed the paper. And that's how we met. We got married in '49. She was a beauty from Lake View High School—just north of Wrigley Field.

"I moved to the *Tribune* in August of '81. And when I moved, I had thirty-eight years at the *Times* and *Sun-Times*, including my two years in the service. They gave me credit for that. I'm sixty-three years old."

Holtzman relights his cigar, sits down, gets up, glances out the window, and begins pacing again. He needs a whole ballpark to move around in. "So tell me about small town life," he says.

"Tell me about sportswriting, then and now," I reply.

"Well, I think it's more competitive now. There are only two papers. When I covered, there were four. The quality of the stories is just as good or better. I'm not really positive, but I think the quality is better. When you have four papers, if somebody had a scoop, three guys were scooped. One guy had it and three didn't. Where there's two guys traveling together, only one guy is scooped. And so therefore it's a more competitive situation.

"And there's more pressure I think on the baseball writer today. But there are other compensating factors. Today the baseball writer gets two days off a week when he's home. Today the baseball writer is encouraged to take a two-week vacation in season. Now two days a week off when you're home may not seem like very much, but the baseball job, I think, is the toughest job on the paper. I know that may sound self-serving, but the fact is people think it's a constant joyride. It isn't. It might be a constant joyride for the first three or four years, because you're a fan and you enjoy it. But after you've covered baseball for four or five years, you're no longer a fan in the regular sense. You're going to work. My office is the press box. I had a desk at the *Sun-Times*. I have a desk at the *Tribune*. I never use it! In fact, the people at the office know that. They give the two baseball writers one desk. Because neither of us is ever there.

"You are no longer a fan, you're an objective reporter. You are going there to observe and report on what happened that day. I was talking to somebody recently, and it was a typical conversation. The guy said to me, 'Gee, you must be terribly disappointed if the Cubs are going to lose.' I said, 'If I was going to be crushed every time the Cubs lost the pennant or finished in the second division, there'd be nothing left of me!'

"You're emotionally involved. And when you're emotionally involved, you write good stuff. But you're not a fan. You don't die because the team dies. If the team dies, you've got to live and write the story on how they died. You can't die with the team. You've got to have enough left over to be able to go on to your typewriter and write how and why they died."

"Chicago a good sports town?" I ask.

"Oh, it's a great sports town. The only sports town I'd compare to Chicago is Boston. Boston I think is a great sports town because there are just a lot of people interested in sports. Wrigley Field and Fenway Park . . . well, one of my daughters went to the University of Massachusetts [in Amherst], and I said to her, 'Be sure to go to Boston and to Fenway Park. Go to the ballpark because it's a cultural experience. It's like going to the Museum of Fine Arts in Boston. It's part of the city!' And I feel that way about Wrigley Field, and to a lesser extent about Comisky Park.

"What makes a good sports city? It's the people, it's the ballpark, it's the history of the teams, it's the traditions. Chicago's got a great sports tradition, the Chicago Bears, the White Sox, the Cubs, the Blackhawks. And now they have a professional basketball team that's a going entity. They never had one before. You know, basketball had been a bust in Chicago until recent years. Chicago was a basketball wasteland for twenty years."

The image of Chicago . . . so many images, good and bad through the years. How does a tream contribute to the overall image of a city?

"Unfortunately, some people seem to think—these are immature people—that the image of a city depends on the success of its professional sports teams. I can assure people that I was in Oakland in the middle of the 70's when Oakland won three consecutive World Series. And having won the second and third World Series did not make Oakland any more attractive a city than it had been before. People shouldn't regard the success of their sports teams as a reflection on the city at all. Chicago's a great city! And it's just as great if the Bears win the Super Bowl or if they lose the Super Bowl. All this talk about Chicago being a team of losers. I think it's very upsetting, this image that, well, the Cubs always lose. Well, that's not true. There are a lot of teams that always lose. Sure, the Cubs haven't won a pennant since 1945, which is the longest stretch. But the fact is that the Cubs have had some pretty exciting teams. They've been competitive for the last fifteen, twenty years. They almost won in '69. Also, if they had won the pennant in '69, which was the year of the great flop, it's my professional belief that they had such a good team in '69 that they would have won two or three more pennants after that. That winning one pennant begets another."

"Any particular team which might be considered *the* Chicago team?"

"I always thought the Cubs, the sleeping giant in Chicago. The Cubs because of the location of the ballpark. I once read many years ago that a quarter of a million people live within walking distance of Wrigley Field, and I assume that's still true. Of course, since the *Tribune* bought the Cubs, the Cubs have become America's team because of their exposure on WGN. However, they were on WGN before the *Tribune* bought them. WGN has grown into a super station, but it was a super station before the Cubs were purchased by the *Tribune*.

"It's been my experience in Chicago that the Cubs, when both Chicago teams were finishing in the second division—and god, the Cubs finished in the second division for almost twenty years in a row—that the Cubs had an advantage going into any season by about a quarter of a million in attendance over the White Sox because of the location of their ballpark. It was—I'm not sure if it still is now—a more desirable neighborhood. It was easier to get to. They played nothing but day games, which I think played a very significant part in increasing their fan base. When both teams were finishing poorly every year, the Cubs didn't have to have a good team to draw a million people. The Sox did.

"Also, the playing of the game was very important. I don't even think old man Wrigley ever understood why. Maybe he did. Mothers used to send their kids to Wrigley Field with a lunch. They'd put the kids on the El or the streetcar, and the kids could go to the ballpark and be home by dinner time! In those days there was never any threat of violence anywhere, certainly not the way it is now. So as a result, with these little kids going to Wrigley Field then, the Cubs had the youngest fan base. These young people developed into fans, and then they'd bring their kids there. The Cubs have had this benefit of a renewal situation in regard to fans, and the Sox, by playing at night, didn't have that advantage. It was more of an adult crowd."

"How do you see the father/son aspect of baseball?" I ask.

"That's part of the renewal I was talking about. Baseball is the national game. It's an offshoot of an English game. The Hall of Fame people insist that baseball was founded in Cooperstown in 1839 or whatever. It wasn't at all. Abner Doubleday did not invent baseball. There's a whole Doubleday myth. Baseball is an offshoot of an English boy's game called rounders. It's a pastoral game . . . it's played on a green field, a large green field. And it's been played for so many years that there's a mythic quality about it. There's a whole mythology of baseball heroes. There's a whole pantheon of baseball heroes.

"The father and son thing . . . we were talking about the green field. I think that Americans have this pastoral yearning. Americans have become citified, and yet there's this gnawing suspicion that things were nicer and better when we were a rural country. A green field is rural, and there's some kind of instinctive pull that we have, which I can't really describe. There's an element of that attraction in baseball. It's a country and a town game. I think this romance of a rural and small-town America still beats within everybody. Also, if you go to a baseball game, you sit next to your neighbor and talk . . . between pitches, between innings. It isn't like watching a football game where there's a play every thirty seconds. Or basketball, which is constant action. Baseball . . . fathers bring their sons. And their sons bring their sons."

What is it about the game itself? What does a man like Holtzman see, who has watched thousands of games in his lifetime? How would he explain the game to someone who knew nothing about it?

"Well, first of all, for me every game is different," he says. "The problem with being a sportswriter, especially a veteran sportswriter, is the tendency to think 'Well, I've seen this before.' But you very seldom see the same game twice, especially in baseball. Baseball's such an unpredictable game, and there are so many players, and there are so many possibilities. I remember times when I was bored, and I realized I was bored because I was not watching closely enough. If you watch closely enough, you see things that you haven't seen before.

"In spring training, for example, or sometimes during the season, I don't sit in the press box. I sit behind the plate. And it's a much better game down there. The players aren't so far away. You can see the skip of the ball, and you can see when the ball is hit. You get a better judgment on the speed of the ball, and the degree of difficulty—when you're sitting upstairs, fifty feet further out, you don't see the degree of difficulty as you do when you're on the field. It looks much easier when you're up there watching because you're not close. When you get down close, you realize it's a difficult game. People say, 'Baseball, it's just a kid's game.' But when the professionals play it, it's not a kid's game.

It's a whole different game. The worst professional player is enormously better than any amateur player. This really isn't true in the other sports.

"I'd explain to anybody that you've got to understand the rules. You've got to understand that the whole purpose of the game is to score runs. That's the essence of the game. I don't care what happens during the game, the purpose is the manufacturing of runs: you don't win without runs. Sometimes you can score without a hit. The essence of the game is to advance the runner. If the runner's on first, you've got to advance him to second. And from second to third. And from third, home. That's really what it gets down to. I'm surprised that in the statistics more emphasis isn't put on the people who score the runs. This is where speed comes in. Some people get on base and manage to score more runs than others. To me, that's an underrated aspect of the game. To understand the game, you've got to understand that the whole purpose is to score runs."

Hollywood seems to have rediscovered baseball lately: *The Natural, Bull Durham, Field of Dreams, Eight Men Out* . . . what does an old sportswriter think about baseball movies?

"They're too sentimental. I'm sentimental, but I don't like being sentimental. I think that the movies give a false picture of baseball on the major league level. When the earthquake hit in San Francisco this year, it hit on Tuesday night, twenty minutes before the game was supposed to have been played, twenty minutes before the first pitch. The teams took the next day off. And then

247

Thursday, they started working out again.

"Some people were killed during the earthquake, although not as many as everybody thought. Reporters went to the workout on Thursday, and the conversation between reporters and players was mostly to the effect, 'Well, do you want to play? How do you feel about playing during this great natural disaster? Maybe you shouldn't play. It seems sacreligious to play a baseball game and resume the World Series under these circumstances.' Then Dave Parker with the Oakland A's, a veteran player, said to some reporters, 'Well, you guys are working. Why shouldn't we be working too?'

"And I thought he was right. That's his job. He's a professional baseball player, and he wants to do his job. Nobody was complaining that the reporters were there working. Why didn't they take a day off? I feel that way about it, that these guys are professionals. Hollywood takes things and makes them all bigger than life. Everything is glossied up. The baseball movies that I've seen have very little relation to the lives that I have seen in the major leagues."

What of the lives he's seen? Holtzman, as deep in the woods and as far from professional baseball as he is on this day, nevertheless has a hitting streak in my book: everything I throw at him, he wallops out of the park. I begin mixing them up—everything I've got—and wait for the Holtzman thwack.

SOX PARK: "An old baseball palace. It was called the baseball palace of the world when it was built in 1910. It's a very fair park for pitchers and hitters, and it's prettier now than it ever has been."

HARRY CARAY: "A guy who cultivates the fans. He's made himself the superfan, and as a result the fans identify with him. He's worked that side of the street. A comparison—when we used to get off the charter planes coming into O'Hare—and Bob Elson was the announcer, a very popular announcer in Chicago, there were people meeting the plane at the airport, and they saw the White Sox coming, and they would run, all the players would give autographs and so forth . . . as soon as Bob Elson saw this, he would run the other way. He wanted to get away from the fans. He was a very sophisticated and aristocratic kind of guy. When this happens to Harry Caray, he just walks into their midst. That's the difference."

BILL VEECK: "A delightful guy in many ways. He had an impish sense of humor. The greatest stunt in baseball that I know of was sending the midget to the plate. Bill Veeck understood that baseball was entertainment more so than any of the other owners in his time. He wanted people to have a good time going to the ballpark. The exploding scoreboard, which he put in in 1960, has since been copied. He was a pioneer in a lot of ways. He was also a very hard-headed guy."

ERNIE BANKS: "He's one of the nicest persons I've ever met. I've known Ernie Banks for about thirty-five years, and I've never known him to say a disparaging word about anybody. Never."

ZIMMER: "Zimmer's a kind of hard-headed guy, very sensitive to criticism.

He's really a meat-and-potatoes guy. He's a good manager. He knows the business. He has a fairly good understanding about people."

CASEY STENGEL: "Casey Stengel was wonderful. He had that quality . . . he was just nice to people and people were nice to him. Casey Stengel was a very shrewd guy, and he understood everything he was saying. He was a very astute baseball man—nine pennants in ten years. He was a fun sort of guy, not a grim guy. He didn't go around with the world on his shoulder. And he was very nice to reporters. He treated reporters like human beings. He understood they had a job to do. A lot of people don't understand that; they regard reporters as necessary evils."

DIMAGGIO: "DiMaggio . . . it's funny. I know DiMaggio now as a very quiet, introverted sort of guy who protects his privacy. And from what I've seen, a very loyal guy who expects people to be loyal to him. The moment they're not loyal, he drops them. He's really a kind of basic American hero."

YOGI: "You got all these stories and sayings of Yogi Berra, half of which he didn't even say. Yogi Berra is one of those supposedly unlettered guys that has a doctor's degree in baseball. He's earned his Ph. D. in baseball, and he's also a very smart guy. He's living proof that you don't learn everything in the classroom."

LARUSSA: "A very serious guy. I knew LaRussa as a player: he played with both the Cubs and the Sox briefly. I've never known anybody who takes as much time and gives as much thought to making out a simple lineup as Tony LaRussa. He agonizes over his lineup—at least he used to when he was with the Sox. He's a very nice guy. I think he thinks too much. He's a very deep thinker. The strange thing about LaRussa is that everybody says that because he has a law degree, this makes him a smarter manager. Having a law degree does absolutely nothing. It's of no help. I think if he had been a lawyer, he would not have been a distinguished lawyer. But he's obviously a distinguished manager."

EARTHQUAKE SERIES: "The fact that Oakland swept them badly in four games will not be remembered as much as the fact that it was the Earthquake Series."

MICKEY MANTLE: "Mantle is the only player I can think of who was an inspiration to his teammates. They really held him in awe. Willie Mays was held in awe also, but not quite the same way. Willie Mays was always whining and complaining—that's what always came back to me. Mickey Mantle was kind of a quiet hero, and the players all realized this. He also played with a terrible injury. I think that Americans like the silent hero. They like the John Waynes, the Gary Coopers. Mickey Mantle to a certain extent was that kind of an 'aw shucks' farm guy, a small town guy from Oklahoma."

BEST TEAM THE CUBS EVER FIELDED: "The '69 team was probably the best team yet, the best team with the worst manager—Durocher. Durocher was an older man at that time. Durocher wasn't the same manager in Chicago that he had been in Brooklyn or with the Giants. By the time we saw Durocher in Chicago, he was a safety-first manager, which he hadn't been previously."

WRIGLEY FIELD: "It isn't so much the Cubs that are the attraction, it's Wrigley Field. Because the players change. There's always a new generation of players, but the ballpark is the same. The ballpark remains."

You realize that with Holtzman (as with Studs and Royko, two other Chicago institutions, national treasures in their own right) the work and the man become one with time, become art. Nowhere is the man more alive, more at home, than in doing, being what he is: Holtzman. Even at this moment, even in Door County, even without a game to report, he is Holtzman. He carries the players, the fans, the history, the whole ballpark with him.

Holtzman's wife Marilyn is perhaps enjoying this brief vacation in Door County; not her husband. No matter how he pretends to be having a good time, this is just a seventh-inning stretch. His interest in my small-town life is mere small talk. For all the green fields here come spring, this place would never measure up to his own field of dreams.

During the course of our talk, we drive to another village on the peninsula for lunch. In the midst of the meal, he says again, "So tell me about small town life." I reply, "Point to anyone in the dining room, and I'll tell you their story." He smiles.

On our way back, I take the backroads to give him another taste of life in the country . . . small farms, old orchards, a lot of peace and quiet. Up ahead, I spot something that might appeal to his curiosity about life here. "I'll show you something you've never seen in Chicago," I tell Holtzman, and begin slowing the car. "See that mound in the land there? See the door right into the earth?"

Holtzman, puffing a cigar, turns his head slightly, gives a momentary glance out the side window. "Yeah?"

"That's a root cellar," I tell him, "where old-timers used to store potatoes and other vegetables. Perfect temperature."

Holtzman tips the cigar out of his mouth and says, "That's interesting. . . . What else you got?"

To understand and appreciate a Jerome Holtzman, to understand and appreciate a sportswriter (Chicago and Chicagoans), you've got to understand "What else you got?"

"How do you define a Chicagoan?" I ask him.

"I'm happy where I am," he replies.

"We've all heard the story about every newspaperman being a frustrated novelist. Might a sportswriter like himself be a frustrated ballplayer?"

"I'm not a frustrated baseball player," says Holtzman. "I was a very good athlete when I was a kid. I played baseball and basketball. But I always wanted to be a baseball writer, a sportswriter. I've been a sportswriter since I was fifteen. When I went around the press box my first year of covering the major leagues, my biggest thrill wasn't meeting Mickey Mantle or Willie Mays or Ted Williams. Sure, I enjoyed meeting them, I can't say I wasn't thrilled to meet them. But I was much more starry-eyed when I met Dan Daniel of the New York *World Telegram*, when I met Gordon Cobbledick of the *Cleveland Plain Dealer*, John Lardner, who was working then for *Newsweek*, Red Smith, Jimmy Cannon . . . they were my heroes! These were the guys!

"Baseball is 50% nostalgic. Baseball has this advantage over any other sport because it has this enormous reservoir, this literature, things written about baseball, this great history. It's almost a mythical history. It borders on mythology. It's American mythology.

"It gets bigger all the time. Just in the few years that I've been working — forty years—it has grown enormously in all aspects. It is now a large industry where they make a lot of money on it. They've commercialized all aspects of the game. Corporate America has latched onto sports as a good image-builder. All of these big corporations pay millions of dollars to be officially affiliated with baseball, basketball, football."

Though snow dusts the fields of Door County today, though another desolate winter is about to set in, my feeling is that Holtzman sees none of this. He's halfway to Arizona already, looking to green fields, opening day.

"The season begins for me in spring training. I see thirty ballgames in spring training—that's more than 90% of the people see all season. Opening day . . . there's excitement in the air, but I always have the feeling that opening day is for amateurs, because the people you see on opening day, including the media people, you never see again for the rest of the season. I'm a 162-game man. So for me the season really begins the second day. Nobody's there.

"People say to me, 'Isn't it boring covering a losing team?' I've probably seen more losing games, having covered both the White Sox and the Cubs, than most sportswriters. I've seen only one pennant in thirty-five years, since I started in 1957. That was the White Sox in '59. I've never seen either team since in a World Series. And people say, well, I've been deprived. I've *never* felt deprived! Because my job . . . I'm always more concerned with the story I write than whether the team wins or loses. My job is to report, not to win or lose.

"Sure, it's more exciting to win, but the fact is I don't go home and say to my wife, 'The Cubs lost today.' I'm more inclined to say to her, 'Gee, I wrote a lousy story' or 'I wrote a good story.' That's what's always been more important to me.

"If Ryne Sandburg goes 3 for 4, that's great. But I want to go at least 1 for 3. I want to be a .300 hitter. And if I'm not a .300 hitter, I'm not going to be writing very long.

"I said before that a baseball writer has the toughest job on the paper. I'll tell you something about the long season—it wears you down. It wears the players down and it wears the reporters down. In the first eighteen years or so when I covered the game, the only time we ever had a day off was at the All Star break. You had two and a half days off in the middle of the season. As a result, you're working every day. Even when the team is off, in the rain, you gotta

251

write a story. There's no off-days for the reporter, no open dates. So you learn how to pace yourself. You have to pace yourself because you can't write a good story every day. And it's a tough assignment on the paper because you're under deadline pressure. When you're covering night games, you've got forty-five minutes to write a new story. We're writing the equivalent of about two thousand words every day for the paper, because of the early stuff, the late stuff, the middle stuff. We're writing the equivalent of three stories a day. People don't understand it.

"Baseball writers are under a lot of pressure, but it gets so that the more you do it—there's no pressure at all. Because that's the way it's done. I remember once somebody asked Red Smith, 'How long does it take you to write a column?' You know what he said? 'How much time do I have?'"

Aiko: Poetry in Paper

The outside reveals nothing. All the meaning lies within.

An oriental screen in the window suggests a Japanese tearoom. There is a single clay vase with a soft spray of pink flowers. One clay bowl. Two hanging lamps.

Aiko's Art Materials Imports (714 N. Wabash) appears on the only door, which you push and hear it open into silence.

I am reminded of a haiku by Sodo:

> My hut in spring!
> True, there is nothing in it—
> there is everything!

Only this is Chicago, electric horizons, mechanical shifts in tone, a building of concrete, brick and glass . . . a stony density of things. And not spring, but the white edge of winter moving in. . . .

> The voice of Snow
> That flight of egrets, if they gave no cry,
> Would be a streak of snow across the sky.
> —Sokan

Inside Aiko's, an emptiness of morning sunlight spreading through the white screen. You hear the heat. It wraps itself around you like summer.

Artist's supplies everywhere. But you must look, or you will be absorbed by the brevity of the room, the exact emptiness of everything in its place. Carving tools for woodblock prints, inks, watercolors, brushes, grinding blocks and ink sticks. Books on Japanese arts and crafts, origami to haiku and Zen greeting cards and stationery, modern Japanese prints. And paper, mostly paper, handmade Japanese paper . . . a whole wall of it . . . the colors, the textures, the prints, overwhelming to the inner eye. Aiko's . . . a Japanese paper garden . . . a certain suddenness of color . . . a burst of wildflowers at your feet . . . everything and nothing . . .

> Here on the mountain pass,
> somehow they draw one's heart so—
> violets in the grass.
> —Basho

253

I hear the sound, "Good morning," rising from the heat. I turn to see a gamboge butterfly, Ruth Nishimura, in a brilliant smock, hovering near a small open office. "Mrs. Nakane [Aiko] will be here shortly."

I continue my silent journey through a store no bigger than a living room, moving before a rack of greeting cards, listening occasionally to the customers as they pass in and out the door.

"I want to do some batik . . . can you tell me what kind of paper I should use?"

"For batik, you have to have pretty strong but absorbent paper," advises Ruth Nishimura as she reaches for a roll of paper, gently spreading it out like the finest linen tablecloth.

Hot process, cold process; soft, hard; absorbent, nonabsorbent . . . intimations of Zen in the very essence of paper.

Greeting cards . . . I'm held by them more than momentarily. Prints by Azechi . . . "White Animal," "Mountaineer," beautiful grained paper. And inside, no message at all . . . only a blank invitation to write what you say, tell who you are. Batik cards, Hiroshige prints, twelve in a set, $3.60, floating pictures on paper . . . birds, sunsets, children, fishermen, plum blossoms . . . "Girl with Canary" . . . "Morning Moons."

Letter sets in Japanese paper, $2.75 to $3.50. The package itself a gift of heavily grained handmade paper, orange, red, green . . . even a page of explanation from the people who make Inaba paper. It reads like a poem . . .

Gathering the materials from the fields and mountains.

Steaming the materials in the furnace and the first barking which is done to take off the useless bark.

Beating up the materials.

Mixing the beaten materials in water containing mucous liquid taken from natural plants and dipping up the proper quantity of mixture onto a bamboo-lined frame, by shaking which properly, a form of wet paper is made.

Drying each sheet of half dried paper individually on a polished board.

A ringing telephone shatters the stillness. Ruth Nishimura takes an order. Only a few feet away, I can barely hear her voice. My eyes are held by three boxes of pebbles . . . black, white and whatever color a plain pebble appears to be . . . $1.50 a box . . . so beautiful, so smooth.

"Would you like me to hang your coat up?" asks Ruth Nishimura. She has been with Aiko's for almost ten years and explains what some of her being there is all about.

As for time and seasons, "Saturday is the busiest day. Many come from out of town. August and September we have colleges ordering supplies for art departments. Then from October to Christmas is our peak, many people buying paper to make their own Christmas cards. The only time we are not too busy is around June and July. About 60 per cent of our business is mail order."

I assume there is another store like this, perhaps somewhere in Chicago.

And if not here, certainly the East Coast or the West Coast. "No, we are the only store like this in the whole country," explains Ruth Nishimura. "Orders come to us from California, Maine, Canada, Hawaii, Alaska. We've even had an inquiry from Thailand. Mainly it's our selection of handmade paper which we import from Japan. We have at least three hundred different varieties of paper."

And how does one make a living in paper: What kind of business is this, sometimes selling a single sheet of paper to a person? "People usually buy about $3 worth. The least expensive? A penny a sheet, I suppose, but it's a small piece of paper. And it can be as expensive as $5.75 a sheet for this gold leaf. Tie-dye, batik, are $1.75 a sheet. The majority are 24-by-36 inches. It all depends on the frames the framers use."

And of what use is handmade Japanese paper? (Of what use, a blade of grass, a butterfly, a cherry blossom?) "Gift wrapping, silk screen, decoupage, woodblock prints, shelf lining, collage, wall covering, even covering windows—you know, when you want light, but people can't see through."

I love the very names of these papers, some of them, 14-by-20 for woodblock printing: Nishinouchi (38 cents), Gekkeikan (22 cents), Wakasa (20 cents). The names of these papers, what do they mean?

"Some are the locales where the paper is made, the villages. But you know how the Japanese are. They like to put poetic names to things."

She attends to the wishes of another customer, unrolling rolls of colored paper in such a festive air and with such delicacy of fingers, patiently answering each question, nodding approval, suggesting. Moments later, my hands lost in the pure form of earthly pottery, the hollowness of baked clay, I hear her quiet voice behind me.

"Would you like some coffee?"

I sit at a small desk in the open office, completely content in the peace to be found in a paper store. The only sound now is the clinking of my cup and saucer.

The phone shatters the stillness once again. She answers. The subject is paper, the question is red. (A message of pure Zen, to be sure.)

"We have a red red," says Ruth, sliding the color into the silences of a telephone conversation. "Something called somegami red. It's a deep red. Yes, we have another, but not as brilliant as a somegami red. It's a very pure red, medium thickness, dyed only on one side . . . the other side is white.

A woman wearing a crazy black hat with a faded red rose appears at the paper counter and questions Ruth about strengths of paper and the whole batiking process. She seems a light-headed type, bordering between zany artist and frivolity. With her black hat, coat, pants, dangling faded rose and magnificent green sweater, she's perfect for a paper store—purity and the Zen mystique of no mindedness.

I drift into Japanese Prints for a fresh breath . . . a display of work by Yoshitoshi Mori. I mention his work to Ruth Nishimura, in passing, who responds to me, almost in a whisper, "According to Mrs. Nakane [Aiko], Mori is very weak physically, but his prints are very strong."

After Mori, I discover the other modern print masters . . . Hashimoto, Uchima, Sato, Fukita, Watanabe. The color and form and feeling are infectious. Poetry, again, in the simple naming of a picture . . . "Small Bird" by Nakao, "Inner Garden" by Hashimoto, "The Flower of Distant Memory" by Amano, "Object: Arrangement of Waterfall" by Yoshida, "Breath (Earth)" by Takahashi, "Poem 72-45" by Haku Maki.

"Good morning," still another soft voice hovers in the midst of the poetry of such prints.

I first catch the smile, then the face of a beautiful, gray-haired Japanese-American woman, Mrs. Nakane—Aiko, herself. She has a touch of all seasons about her, but in her gray and red smock, her spiritual energy, her laughter and clear pools of quiet, I think of winter, I think of spring. Like her saleswoman, Ruth Nishimura, she exudes the mystery of being there and not being there. She does not question, impose, implore, she is just there, somewhere nearby, when you need her.

I ask about Japanese prints, the West's fascination with such art. What does an American see in such work?

"Color combinations," says Aiko, "and subject matter. And then the subtleness of it all seems to be pleasing to the American people."

She continues with a discussion of the artist's red seal on all the Japanese prints, and explains how the seal is part of the total design.

"You see, another difference between the Japanese and the Chinese is right here. In China, when the print is passed down from person to person, each man adds his own seal to the work to show previous ownership. So sometimes you see a print covered with red seals—the design, lost. It's too bad for the original artist.

"Materialism, that is the basic difference between the Japanese and the Chinese. The Japanese would like to be a little more subtle in these things."

She delves deeper into a discussion of these two cultures, with great understanding and love for both, it appears.

"Japan is all inhibition—the Chinese, no inhibition. It is not that open, Japan. They have always been islanders, you see. They keep to themselves. Zen is part of all this."

Aiko talks about papermaking, the village of the Kurotani, which she has visited. She tells how the villagers raise the plants, make the paper—the whole cycle from beginning to end to beginning again. And how this too is passing, the villagers abandoning the old ways for the technology and comforts of the city.

"The western influence," she says. "First radio, then TV, now colored TV. Industry is going full speed—new, faster, more and more of the same progress. Making handmade paper like this won't be enough for them. And technology

256

will be of no help. Racing water. Pure, no chemicals to bleach. That is why this paper will last for thousands of years."

Aiko's taste in books reflects the very nature of Aiko herself, the whole Japanese mystique—subtlety, grace, silence, beauty. "How to Wrap Five Eggs—Japanese Design," "Tamba Pottery," "The Hokusai Sketchbooks."

Hokusai has always fascinated me, and I ask Aiko what more she can tell me about the man.

"He was an artist. Everything that he ever saw, dreamed or heard became picture, became drawing. I don't think he ever considered it art. He just wanted to draw, make art."

Hokusai, best known for his forty-six woodblock prints, each reflecting a different view of Mount Fuji, had this unique insight into his own artistic nature:

From the time that I was six years old I had the mania of drawing the form of objects. As I came to be fifty I had published an infinity of designs; but all that I have produced before the age of seventy is not worth being counted. It is at the age of seventy-three that I have somewhat begun to understand the structure of true nature, of animals and grasses, and trees and birds, and fishes and insects; consequently at eighty years of age I shall have made still more progress; at ninety I hope to have penetrated into the mystery of things; at one hundred years of age I should have reached decidedly a marvelous degree, and when I shall be one hundred and ten, all that I do, every point and every line, shall be instinct with life and I ask all those who shall live as long as I do to see if I have not kept my word.

The books alone, probably less than seventy-five in all, can hold you still like a humming bird in Aiko's for most of a morning, all of a day. "The Ideals of the East," by Okakura; "The Book of Tea," by Okakura. Japanese cookbooks, books on flower arrangement. A shelf, and then some, of haiku. "A Net of Fireflies," a beautiful title, an anthology of 320 Japanese haiku with 33 haiku paintings in full color, including an essay on haiku and haiga:

Each true haiku is a swift record in words of one moment of Satori, of the sudden flash of Enlightenment which grants us a transcendent Insight into the Suchness of things. For one second, the Eye of Metaphysical Realization opens, and we are transformed into Buddhas. The next it closes, and we re forced to resume our separate and mortal selves again, imprisoned in the illusion of ordinary life.

I pick up another beautifully boxed book—titled *Poems to Eat*, by Takuboka. I taste one . . .

even whistled
in my sleep—
in fact, at 15
whistles
were my poems

257

I swallow another . . .

>   always come
>   to this gloomy bar
>   the late sunset
>   reddening, shines
>   right in my drink

These books by Reps, I ask Aiko—"Zen Flesh Zen Bones," "Unwrinkled
Plays, Square Sun Square Moon, Zen Telegrams" . . . Reps, an American with a
Swiss name, who seems to wander the Eastern Landscape in mystery putting
down drawings and words, Zen messages all . . .

>   Drinking a bowl of
>   green tea
>   I stopped
>   the war

Is he real? Does he know!

"I guess he does know," says Aiko. "But Zen is something you cannot real-
ly explain with words. You cannot really teach others by writing or talking
about it. If someone says, 'I understand it,' he really doesn't understand it. You
have to say you don't understand it, you don't know how to explain it. Then
maybe you do."

"Even the Zen believer may not know what he's doing, why he's doing. But
you see it in results. Good and bad come out in all the cultural things we have
now.

"I didn't realize it, but it's in everything in Japan. Even the Christian way of
thinking is judged and affected by Zen."

The story of her store?

"There is nothing else like it. People tell me to grow, but I know my limi-
tations. It all started by accident. I went back to Japan almost thirty years ago,
and my goodness all the beautiful little shops, such beautiful tools and brushes
and paper and inks. So I just picked them all up, here and there, and brought
them back as a gift for a good friend of mine, an artist.

"He showed all this to other people, and they thought I could write and order
them a set of this, of that. I said no, I couldn't do that since I picked them up
one at a time from many different shops throughout the country.

"So Zeke, my friend the artist, said, 'Why don't you open a shop, and I will
help you?' I was so naive. I thought I could open half a day and do whatever I
liked. But there is always more and more.

"It has been eighteen years now."

She finds it difficult to put such a way of life into so many years. She
knows that Zen itself is best understood unexplained. But I am studying her ink
grinding blocks, brushes, ink sticks, and she seems to pick up my silent interest
in sumi (a quick drawing in ink, a fast brush stroke) and she tends to discover

my questions before I ever give them voice.

"Sumi is a black ink made from the soot of carbon collected from vegetables and pine trees, roots and branches. A much finer grain. The soot is mixed with animal glues, water, cooked down to mass and kneaded. Sumi black is permanent like no other black.

"Sumi technique, sumi art, was developed from Zen again. It is something that you put down on paper, the feeling that you had at the moment. This pure Zen painting is the kind of art for you, yourself, and not any other people. If it satisfies you, it serves its purpose—that is the purpose.

"Black is better than color because the viewer can imagine any color he wants to. If you use red, it is red. Blue is blue. But black is not color, and so it is all color. Zen."

She holds a black ink grinding stone (suzuri) in her hand and an ink stick, explaining the motions of the sumi artist.

"If your water is pure from the stream, then your ink will be pure. If your thoughts are pure while you are preparing the ink, grinding the ink on the stone, then your art will be pure. It's all very different from your American philosophy of why waste time . . . use bottled ink.

"Even the paper, absorbent, non-absorbent. The Western world want to bend nature to its design, making paper non-absorbent. But the Japanese try to use the natural form of paper, working with it to get the best, the most the paper will absorb.

"In sumi, you can never hide in a wet stroke. You make a mistake, it shows. You cannot hide your thought. And it's only for your own enjoyment, for your inner self. That's the purpose, the end."

And the name Aiko, what does it mean?

"Love child," she flashes a true line above her eyes with such a sumi stroke, scattering cherry blossoms with her smile.

Paul Romaine:
A Writer's Bookseller in Chicago

He was a dapper, white-haired man with a neatly trimmed mustache, a pipe permanently fixed between his teeth, and a somewhat studied facial expression, about to break into a knowing grin. He handled his books with reverence, turning pages with the care a monk might display, examining an illuminated manuscript.

Romaine may not have been everyone's kind of bookman, but he suited me perfectly: a young man from Cicero, in love with Chicago, unhappy with himself and the world, mostly in school or between jobs, mostly wanting to become a writer but too ignorant to begin, too insecure to reveal his desire to anyone, mostly riding the El back and forth to the Loop unexplainably, wandering Chicago's streets, searching for the city's literary past and present, hanging around the main public library on Randolph and Michigan, reading the Chicago papers at Pixley & Ehler's across from the library each morning and often at night. Seeking sanctuary on rainy, grey Chicago days in a bookstore owned by a man like Paul Romaine who seemed to be almost waiting for your arrival to talk books and writers and *belles-lettres*. This was the mid-1950s and into the '60s. This was my own "moveable feast," the closest I would ever get to Paris in Chicago—for the time being.

There were other bookstores to my liking as well in those times: both the Central Bookstore and Economy Bookstore had much to offer a young writer on the lookout for bargain used books on Clark Street. There was also the Post Office News at 37 West Monroe Street for newspapers and magazines from all over the world. But on LaSalle Street, just north of Randolph, was Romaine Imported Books, as independent a bookstore owner as to be found anywhere. Downtown Chicago was blessed with real bookstores then.

261

There was a time when bookstores sold books (new and used), not toys, stuffed animals, games, greeting cards and bestsellers to exist. A time when a bookstore was named for the man who owned it, a man knowledgeable about every book in his store, a man who greeted his customers by name and catered to their needs, a man conspicuous on the premises.

So many bookstores today seem indistinguishable from each other, pandering to bestsellers and nonbooks, run by computers and sales clerks with blank expressions who think Danielle Steele is literature, and Dostoevsky (unpronounceable) the latest California guru who writes self-help books on cosmic personal growth through banging one's head on the wall till the stars appear.

Not that true bookstores no longer exist in the Chicago area. One must seek them out. (Which is one characteristic of a first-rate independent bookstore: its inconspicuousness. It doesn't leap out in front of you on busy streets or in shopping malls, as most of the chains, suffering from the sodden similarity of franchise fever.)

There is Roger Carlson's superb little bookstore in Evanston, Bookman's Alley; Stuart Brent's (perhaps the dean of Chicago's independent booksellers) on Michigan Avenue; Richard Bray's Guild Books on N. Lincoln—a lively and important center for readings by Chicago writers and visiting authors as well; Kenan Heise's Chicago Historical Bookworks in Evanston; Barbara's Bookstores;

and the granddaddy of the all, Kroch's and Brentano's on Wabash (an exception to the rule of "big bookstores") which, truth to tell, sells a lot more than books these days, yet nevertheless maintains a top-notch staff of book people, and has always supported Chicago books and Chicago writers.

There are, no doubt, other small, independent, excellent bookstores scattered about other parts of the city as well. But there is no Paul Romaine's, to my knowledge.

Just as there is no longer an Ira Adler in the book department of Marshall Field's, who knew first editions, rare and valuable books, who purchased entire private libraries and sold individual items to his book-loving customers, who first introduced me to Kenneth Patchen's *The Journal of Albion Moonlight*, William Carlos Williams' *Kora In Hell*, and Frank Harris' *My Life and Times*.

But for me back then (and for many years to come) there was Paul Romaine, standing in his rather dimly lit bookstore on LaSalle just north of Randolph, his radio always tuned to classical music on WFMT (an habitual listener to Studs Terkel), puffing away on his pipe, either engaged in literary conversation with a customer, or quietly reading a book he had taken down from a shelf.

As I remember the scene now, there was seldom anyone in the store but Paul Romaine when I usually frequented it: late morning or early afternoon. Which was perfect for me. I had the bookman all to myself. I could ask the most ignorant questions about writers and books and not be embarrassed that others might hear. And (like only a classic bookman with a shop of his own filled with volumes he loved and knew, memories and ideas he was eager to share) Romaine had time, time, time on his hands to explain, to tell stories, to show books. Even to read passages from them.

I associate the mood of those days, the mood of the streets, the mood of the bookshop on LaSalle, with a peculiar Chicago mood, something Nelson Algren caught in words as his own Chicago image: "An October sort of city. . . ."

Whatever excitement and despair I may have experienced in those young days in the city, there was this mood of Octoberness about it. Grey on grey. A shadowy light angled across old buildings and storefront windows a la Hopper (Romaine's bookshop would have made a perfect Hopper study). To be in the scene but outside of it. A solitude suggestive of a haunted past. Promises of more loss, loneliness, dreams deferred. ("Have you ever read the poems of Langston Hughes?" Romaine would ask. "Gwendolyn Brooks? *Native Son* by Richard Wright?")

Late that same grey October afternoon, climbing the steel structure to the El (the truest raw hunk of native, "industrial" art, rivaling even the city's own Picasso), standing on the windy El platform, city of the big iron shoulders, boarding the Douglas Park home to Cicero, looping Chi-Town, my back to the diminishing downtown, the river, the skyscraper lights. Up in the air with Kerouac's desolate angels, the ups and downs of broken back stairs, electric blue flashes on brittle brick walls, visions of half a man and half a woman seated at a silent kitchen table in a second story window of torn white curtains, brightening the dark. Neon night coming on. Alleys of no forgiveness. Love on a one-way street for the black-haired harlot from Hammond, Indiana, abandoned again to her own devices, who never remembers your name. Me, clutching Algren in the window's reflection: *Chicago: City On The Make* goes through me like a song.

I remember the top shelf, near the storefront, where Romaine kept Algren's books. I remember his telling me the story behind Algren's original Chicago story, written for *Holiday* magazine (whose editors were not pleased with his words for the article). Not quite "Chicago, Chicago, that wonderful town" in Algren's eyes:

"The nameless, useless nobodies who sleep behind the taverns, who sleep beneath the El. Who sleep in burnt-out busses . . . the useless, helpless nobodies nobody knows: that go as the snow goes, where the wind blows, there and there and there, down any old cat-and-ashcan alley at all."

There were at least a half dozen copies of the slim, dark green-jacketed volume of Algren's book on the shelf (Doubleday, hb, 1951, $1.50) all of them remaindered, pencil-marked in Romaine's own cryptic code (usually inside the back cover) "1st ed." or "o.p." and the price. Romaine had reduced it to a dollar. I bought one copy and, in time, purchased all the rest for friends. Two copies of the first edition remain in my possession, plus a copy of every new edition that appeared since the first in 1951.

Which is yet another indebtedness to Paul Romaine: introducing me to the art of book collecting, without my ever giving it much thought at the time.

Some authors today look back upon writing programs in famous universities, workshops under the tutelage of major poets and novelists, as significant experiences that helped shape them into the kind of writers they became. I had the city of Chicago, and Paul Romaine.

Not that he was ever conscious of his role. He was, after all, just a bookseller. And I, just another customer. But there was time and room and books enough for the relationship to develop far beyond that, into the world of specific ideas, particular works and writers, literary movements here and abroad, literary history, rare books, magazines, and even art.

He couldn't mention Algren without talking about Sandburg, Farrell, Whitman, Baudelair, Simone de Beauvoir. And you couldn't talk Farrell without getting into Dreiser, Frank Norris, Upton Sinclair, Anderson, Lewis, Jack Conroy, Hemingway, Bellow, back to Ring Lardner, Ben Hecht, George Ade, Eugene Field, Finley Peter Dunne, into the heartbeat of Chicago's Renaissance, Edgar Lee Masters, Sandburg, Floyd Dell, Margaret Anderson's *Little Review*, Harriet Monroe's *Poetry*, Hecht and Maxwell Bodenheim's *Chicago Literary Times* (to be resurrected after a fashion by the legendary Jay Robert Nash in 1961 as the *Literary Times*) . . . Chicago, "the literary capital of the United States," said H.L. Mencken, way back then.

Who?

Mencken, said Paul Romaine. Never read Mencken?

Which is how a good part of my literary education went. "To know this city, you should know Herman Kogan and Lloyd Wendt's *Chicago: A Pictorial History*," he suggested.

"Suggestion" is the important word. And total immersion of a writer's consciousness into a particular literary past: knowing who and what came before so you would have some knowledge of what might be expected of *you*.

I was as green as they came. Not to mention as white, ethnic, and blind to social injustice in my own neighborhood, Cicero. My experiences of the Negro in my early childhood amounted to "Amos and Andy" on the radio and the black man who carried our coal from the street each fall.

No one in high school or college ever told me of the work of Richard Wright whom Romaine described as his "friend," the Chicago writer Richard Wright. Romaine handed me *Black Boy* and *Native Son*, then guided me on to Willard Motley, the poetry of Gwendolyn Brooks, and Langston Hughes (who wrote for the *Chicago Defender* at one time), not to mention Ralph Ellison's *Invisible Man*, which I felt was the greatest American novel I had ever read, up to that time.

But there was "Negro" art as well (before the word "black" became part of our language). "Did you ever see the work of Beauford DeLaney?" asked Romaine, opening a magnificent book called *American Negro Art*.

From Negro art to the world of art, Romaine seemed to have it all as his fingertips, in books, magazines, file cabinets, portfolios. "This is the work of Kathe Kollwitz" — a signed lithograph of a desperate image of mother and child. "This is the Mexican muralist, artist, Siqueiros" (a self-portrait, signed litho, limited edition I could not afford then, $75).

The connections then (even now) kept coming, continued to merge, separate, veer off in other directions. You can't read about a Mexican muralist, Sequeiros (wish to own his self-portrait, stuck in a file drawer in Romaine's shop) without running into the revolutionary painter Diego Rivera and his sense of history, both Mexican and American. Or the passion for the poor which Orozco seemed to paint with brushes dipped in fire. And then turn to the quiet, color drenched images (Mayan to modern) of Rufino Tamayo, who seemed almost European by comparison.

I can't imagine any of this happening in today's bookstores, including our discussions of Henry Miller, his *Tropic of Cancer* (which was still banned in this country at that time), his life in Paris, his watercolors (which he traded at the time for any donation to his existence, even clothes), his experience in Chicago (see *The Air Conditioned Nightmare*), his return to the U.S. and life in Big Sur. "Write him," urged Romaine. And I did, on a number of occasions. And he always replied.

And though Romaine may have had Miller's notorious Tropic books hidden somewhere in the store, he never made an offer to sell any of the works to me and seemed content instead to merely bring Miller's work to my attention, especially his Rabelaisean way of life.

And where could I find the "unbanned" Henry Miller in Chicago except in Paul Romaine's bookstore? Who else would have publications like *The International Henry Miller Letter* ($1.00) out of the Netherlands? Or a limited edition, #50, of Miller's second book, *Aller Retour New York*, privately printed, 1935, for $7.50? Or the classic essay on his own watercolors and the true spirit of the artist, *To Paint Is To Love Again*?

When I traveled to Mexico for the first time much of what I had learned in Paul Romaine's bookstore stayed with me. I searched the bookstores of Mexico City looking for copies of Henry Miller's banned books: *Tropic Of Cancer* and *Tropic of Capricorn* (Obelisk Press/France) and found them. Two small, hard-backed copies, one red, the other green, printed in English on very thin paper.

I also saw Diego Rivera's murals for the first time at the Palacio Nacional.

And in one of the rooms of Chapultepec Palace, high on a scaffold, stood a grey-haired artist, David Alfaro Siqueiros, just released from prison again for revolutionary activities, painting a new mural, still wielding his brush with a life-long commitment to art for social protest's sake.

Like Rivera (though tougher in spirit and deed) Siqueiros could identify with the Rivera penned in manifestoes of the painters' syndicate to advance the cause of fellow working men and the spirit of the Mexican Revolution:

"We are on the side of those who seek the overthrow of an old and inhuman system within which you, the worker of the soil, produce riches for the overseer and politician while you starve. Within which you, worker in the city, move the wheels of industry, weave the cloth and create with your hands the modern comforts enjoyed by parasites and prostitutes, while your own body is numb with cold. Within which you, Indian soldier, heroically abandon your land and give your life in the eternal hope of liberating your race from the degradation and misery of centuries . . . ."

All of this may seem like a long way from a downtown Chicago bookstore during the '50s and '60s; a long way from Algren, Conroy, Farrell, Langston Hughes, Richard Wright, old copies of *New Masses*; talk of Dalton Trumbo's anti-war novel *Johnny Got His Gun*, Arthur Miller, McCarthyism, the stories of Harvey Swados; and the question of what constitutes an obscene book. D.H. Lawrence's *Lady Chatterley's Lover*, Henry Miller's *Tropic of Cancer*, and the re-issue of the eighteenth century novel *Fanny Hill*—which Romaine sold and was prosecuted for in an obscenity trial in Chicago in the '60s, sentenced to two year's probation, and fined $1,000. (The judgement was later overturned by the Illinois Supreme Court).

All of this began to come together; the books, the magazines, the authors, the art, the particular passions of one man, Paul Romaine, purveyor of ideas that seemed to some, at the time, against the American grain.

And Paul Romaine, whose sympathies certainly reflected concern for workers, the politically oppressed in all countries, the American Negro, the Jew, the free press, freedom of expression in the arts, was indeed suspect of socialist/ communistic sympathies, though his cause seemed to me (then and now) the greater cause of human rights and dignity.

Certainly the man who put Thoreau's essay on Civil Disobedience in my hands and explained to me Thoreau's influence on Gandhi could not be that "UnAmerican."

Granted there was a touch of the clandestine about him, even an air of intellectual arrogance at times that seemed to suggest he did not easily suffer the greater world of fools—political fools in particular. He was not against the law, but opposed to the unjust law. I suspect that "under the counter," somewhere in the store, were works of literature banned in America, though I never saw them.

What he did produce for my benefit was a small copy of Mark Twain's "obscene" classic "1601": "With such a tongue as thyne, lad, thou'lt spread the ivory thyghs of many a willing maide in thy good time, an' thy _____ be as handy as thy speech," said Ye Queene. And a pirated edition (ten pages) of *The Collected Poems* of Ernest Hemingway:

The Ernest Liberal's Lament

I know monks masturbate at night
That pet cats screw
That some girls bite
And yet
What can I do
To set things right?

I bought a copy of these books for fifty cents apiece. So much for corruption in Chicago via obscene printed matter sold by Paul Romaine.

As for the "Communist influence," he had another ploy entirely: imported books. These were mostly hardbacks (and some paper) beautifully printed in English, frequently illustrated with drawings, etchings, and photographs, all published by the Foreign Language Publishing House, Moscow. All $1.00 to $2.50 per book.

His "subversive" influence, as such, was to place Russian literature in my hands: the short stories of Chekhov, a set of Maxim Gorky (including *My Apprenticeship*), *The Garnet Bracelet And Other Stories* by Alexander Kuprin, *Shadowed Paths* by Ivan Bunin, *Evenings Near The Village of Dikanka* by Nikolai Gogol, *White Nights* and *Poor Folks* by Dostoyevsky, *Old Odessa* and *Red Cavalry* by Issac Babel, and other collections of essay, poems, and stories by Turgenev, Sholokov, Zoshchenko, Paustovsky, Ananyan, and Mayakovsky. There was even an intriguing collection of *Modern American Short Stories*, which included Dreiser, Anderson, Faulkner, Hemingway, Steinbeck, Saroyan,

Dorothy Parker, and Meridel LeSueur.

A book of essays about the writing life, *The Golden Rose*, by Konstantin Paustovsky, became one of those priceless/precious works ($1.50) a young writer returns to again and again for orientation, for passage through the dark times of confusion, defeat, and self-doubt. Paustovsky, detailing personal experiences in his own sojourn through art, would prove to be an incomparable guide, a true believer in the beauty and strength of words, the transformation of all men through tales.

And how could a young writer not remember Babel's story "The Beginning," wherein he described his own life as a young writer, wandering through Petersburg from one publishing house to another, his short stories in hand, finally calling on Gorky, then chief editor of a monthly magazine, *The Chronicle*, who told him to leave his work and return in a few days. "Gorky invited me into his office and what he said to me there determined the course of my life," explains Babel.

"There are small nails," Gorky said, "and there are nails as large as my fingers here," and he brought his long, delicately shaped finger close to my eyes. "The life path of a writer, my dear scribe, is studded with nails, mostly of the larger variety; you'll have to walk on them barefoot. You'll lose plenty of blood, and as the years go by, you'll bleed more profusely. If you are a weak person, they'll buy you and sell you and shake you and put you to sleep, and you will wilt while pretending you are a tree in bloom. But if you are an honest man, an honest writer, and a sincere revolutionary, you will think it a great honor to keep walking the path, and it is for that uncomfortable journey that I wish you the best of luck, friend, and give you my blessings . . . ."

I gleaned from Russian literature a sense of continuity between generations of writers: a sense of place, a sense of history, a sense of common human values, and the writer's responsibilities to make these things known through his art.

Romaine and the types of books he chose to sell in his shop (Colin Wilson's *The Outsider*, Camus' *The Rebel*, Ralph Ellison's *The Invisible Man*, the small pamphlets and books appearing almost every other week from Kerouac and Ginsberg's Beat Generation) were valuable to a young writer who knew in his bones that a good part of the life and art of anyone serious about the written word was the very act of rebellion: social, moral, and political.

But aside from the political and social issues of the day, it was mostly the older literary link to Chicago's past that I cultivated through Romaine and his bookstore. The link to Paris of the '20s (where Romaine lived from 1925 through 1927, a friend to many of the leading literary expatriates). The link to Hemingway and Sherwood Anderson.

I remember Romaine going through a file cabinet one day, opening a manila folder, and showing me letters addressed to him from Hemingway.

I remember him telling me about a publication of his, *Salmagundi* (even then a collector's item), featuring some of Faulkner's early sketches plus a poem by Hemingway. Romaine contended it was the only publication where two such future literary greats appeared in the same issue, neither writer having ever met the other. (He had at least one copy on hand to show me, as I recall).

But Hemingway in Chicago—this was heady stuff.

Years later I would learn (mainly through my memories of Paul Romaine's conversations and Carlos Baker's two books, *Ernest Hemingway: A Life Story* and *Ernest Hemingway: Selected Letters, 1917-1961*) more of the details of the Chicago/Hemingway/Romaine connection.

269

Ben Hecht

I would be surprised to learn that Hemingway was upset at Romaine's attempt to enlist him in the Leftist cause:

"As for your hoping the Leftward Swing etc. has a very definite significance for me that is so much horseshit. I do not follow the fashions in politics, letters, religion etc. If the boys swing to the left in literature you may make a small bet the next swing will be to the right and some of the same yellow bastards will swing both ways. There is no left and right in writing. There is only good and bad writing . . . I'm no goddamned patriot nor will I swing to left or right."

He was also suspicious of limited edition publishers (Romaine's *Salmagundi*) and Romaine's intentions in writing him in the first place. "Publishers of limited editions make a practice of selling the personal letters of writers," he responded in August of 1932.

In the same letter, Hemingway dismissed the concern of others (Romaine included) regarding the subject matter and direction of his work: "I wrote, in six weeks, one book about a few drunks and to show the superiority of the earlier Hebrew writers over the later quoted Ecclesiastes versus G. Stein. This was some seven years ago. Since then I have not been occupied with this so-called (but not by me) lost generation."

The Hemingway myth looms large in the minds of many American writers, and his Chicago roots had always intrigued me. Romaine once mentioned that Hemingway and Sherwood Anderson were in Chicago during the same period of time.

There was another myth, that certain romantic element of the writer's life that Anderson provided in the way of direction and inspiration for all struggling writers in the Midwest—Andersonian grotesques in their own right, yearning to break through the isolation of small town-mindedness (neighborhood, suburb, village), to break out of the bounds of questionable moral codes, bad marriages, routine jobs, intent to seek a freedom of self-expression through art only the great cities of the world seemed to provide, Chicago, New York, Paris.

Anderson had escaped.

I would return to the neighborhood from Chicago on the Douglas Park El, sit in an all-night coffeeshop on 22nd Street, or at the desk of a small writing office I had created in a basement storage shelter of an apartment I was living in, read Sherwood Anderson's short sotry, "Milk Bottles," and see myself in his tale:

"I lived during that summer, in a large room on the top floor of an old house on the North Side of Chicago. It was August and the night was hot. Until after midnight I sat—the sweat trickling down my back—under a lamp, laboring to feel my way into the lives of the fanciful people who were trying also to live in the tale on which I was at work. . . ."

I would be immediately caught up in the life of a writer, in Chicago, craving the mood, totally absorbed in the fiction.

271

Sometime during the 1960s, Romaine moved his street-level bookstore operation from North LaSalle to an upper story at 212 North Clark, a block away, across from the Greyhound Bus Depot (where Helmut Jahn's new building, the State of Illinois Center, now stands).

I did not see Romaine as much in the late '60s as previously. For one thing, I was finally beginning to cross that bridge from wanting-to-become-a-writer to actually writing.

Also, there was a little sadness to his new location, almost an atmosphere of defeat about the old man, the past, the times and ideas he stood for. I seemed to be moving ahead, anxious to both seek and address the greater world at large, though I could never let go of the man or the bookstore completely.

I would ocassionally visit him at his new place, riding an old cage-type elevator with a black metal gate that scissored open and shut. All the floors seemed deserted, all the offices quiet.

His "store" had been reduced to the space of about one small room overlooking the rooftop of the Greyhound Bus Depot, the El above Lake Street, old office buildings with watertowers and black iron fire escapes, and a hint of the blue waters of Lake Michigan far beyond. In a late afternoon sun, it was all quite beautiful through the one window, the perfect backdrop. Old Chicago. Old Romaine.

The man himself seemed the same as when I first walked into his bookshop on LaSalle Street in the mid-1950s. He had the same interest in literature and politics and looked upon the whole world somewhat bemusedly, the pipe still firmly clenched between his teeth, every white hair on his head in place, his mustache perfectly trimmed.

He was still pulling offbeat books from the stacks, odd curiosities to share with curious book lovers. A small book of poems, *Paroles*, by Jacques Prevert; a signed copy of Henry Miller's essay on justice *Maurizus Forever*; Camus' essay on capital punishment, *Reflections on the Guillotine*. Something by Knut Hamsun (once a Chicago streetcar conductor). Books by Anais Nin, Celine, Pio Baroja, Brecht, Colette, Andre Gide. Copies of *The New Masses* from the 1930s.

The last time I saw Romaine was in this store, sometime in the '70s. I had left Chicago to write from the relative isolation of a rural landscape, but I missed Chicago, and I missed Paul Romaine's bookstore.

The two stores begin to merge at this point in my life, though the earlier one on LaSalle appears more vivid in my memory. For there, in that bookstore with Romaine, time was most alive for this writer.

There, one rainy afternoon in fall, after I dropped out of the graduate program in English at the University of Chicago (wanting to *be* the writer, not the scholar who studies the writer) Paul Romaine introduced me to one of his customers, Walter Ryberg, day city editor, from the City News Bureau of Chicago, 188 West Randolph, just around the corner. (The CNB is the oldest news service in operation and is considered by some to be *the* school of American journalism).

We talked. He considered my interest in writing. He explained the function of City News in Chicago, sensed I was looking for work, and invited me up to the newsroom for an interview with "Gersh"—Issac Gershman, managing editor and general manager of City News. Two days later I was hired as a cub reporter, $35 a week. My eyes were opened to city life and parts of Chicago I never imagined.

From an ink monkey, battling ditto machines and the notorious tube system in the back of the newsroom, to checking morgue reports, to the teletype and tangled lines of the switchboard, to tagging along with a more seasoned cub reporter on one of the many beats covering the city, to being a "gofor" on the night shift (coffee and donuts at Pixley & Ehler's across the street, under the El on Wells), to gradually assuming a beat of my own a few times a week, to learning to gather and report news, to working days, afternoons, midnight to eight, to eventually being assigned my own beat, which in time led back to the newsroom and learning the art of the rewrite man, to that final hurdle of "the desk."

It was an incredible system of tutelage in the best school of journalism anywhere. It took at least a year, often longer, till one "graduated" to the outside world of Chicago dailies. But whatever the time spent there, and whether one ever made it to "the desk" or beyond, there was a pride and history to the place not soon forgotten. For some, it meant more than any college degree.

As much as I enjoyed it, there were conflicts almost immediately on the homefront, back in the neighborhood: I was prepared to teach, but wasn't doing it; I had dropped out of a Master's program and all its guarantees for success in education; I seemed to have no plan, no future, nothing but a desire to write, which I was unable to share with anyone, and which offered no security whatsoever. Then suddenly, almost unexplainably, I found myself working for $35 a week as a cub reporter, thinking perhaps newspaper writing was the life for me.

The hours were crazy, the work both boring (on the inside) and exciting. Best of all to be on the streets of Chicago at all hours . . . on foot, on buses, standing on El platforms, in good and bad neighborhoods. To sit in courtrooms and police stations and try to begin to understand justice and the lives of Chicago cops: an introduction to the city's dispossessed, headed for the lockup.

I began to understand how writers (especially newspaper writers) develop a tough coat of cynicism and a language of satire to survive. The human comedy is mostly tragedy.

I stopped in to see Romaine only occasionally during my City News days. There was never enough time now to browse. The hours were wrong. Reporting assignments changed by the hour. There were no days of the week, only days and nights. There was less and less time for books. Life had replaced literature; I did all my reading on the El, coming and going, day and night, Chicago to Cicero and back.

Few, I'm sure would recall my time at City News, with the possible exception of Royko, who had served his apprenticeship in grand style (already a legend before his time) and was then poised at the night desk, reading, willing and able to be snatched up for the Big Time.

We played pinochle around his desk at night, in those quiet, small hours of morning when Chicago supposedly slept. His love for the city combined with a personal history and sense of politics, people, and place that brought a wry smile in the telling. A neighborhood kid with a good punch, he learned when and how to throw it—with the proper, street-smarts impact. It was obvious, even then, he would serve Chicago and its readers well.

I never made it to re-write man or the desk. My first stint at City News was short (less than half a year) and in the shadows at best. I made it from the back-room to the street, covering fires, various police beats—the Central police station on South State, most frequently. I was never assigned a specific beat, my next step.

Once again, restlessness, uncertainty, doubts that a newspaperman's life was the real life for me. I lacked the aggressiveness. I disliked being on the "inside." I preferred the streets. I grew tired of facts, found journalism, the news story, too restrictive. I needed to see and understand my own life through the lives of others on more intimate terms, to tell stories real enough to be imagined.

Gwendolyn Brooks and Jack Conroy

I left quietly. I wanted to travel, I explained. I returned to a private Chicago I had mapped out for myself: coffee shops, department stores, restaurants, bars, bookshops, downtown streets, Grant Park, the lakefront, the library, the Art Institute, the Field Museum, railroad stations, the river, Old Town, the El. My hangouts.

Occasionally I hired out for the day, the week, as a substitute teacher in my old neighborhood, at my old high school, J. Sterling Morton in Cicero.

Occasionally I wrote short stories at the kitchen table early in the morning, waiting, dreading that phone call before 8 a.m. and the cheery voice seeking to place me in yet another classroom as sub-teacher/victim for the day. If no call came by 8:30, I was out the door, down the street, on my way to catch the El to the Loop. First stop: Paul Romaine's

"I think I'm going to Europe," I announced one day. Romaine understood even if no one else did. Paris, of course—*de rigueur* for any young man intent on a writer's life.

I set sail for a first taste of the continent, my own moveable feast, (a journey which would ultimately include all of Great Britain, Scandinavia, Western Europe, Yugoslavia, and Greece by bus, train, and boat).

Somewhere in the middle of the Atlantic on the S.S. Rhyndam, the third day out . . . a sunny day, a calm sea, a mood of great expectation, I recall stopping to read the world news headlines from a yellow sheet of teletype paper posted near the ship's library: July 2, 1962: Hemingway Kills Himself in Ketchum, Idaho.

Later the same year I return to the U.S. from Portugal only to find myself, within days, walking the same Chicago streets, visiting my same Chicago haunts, again without work or direction. Again in Paul Romaine's where, on my very first visit, I once again run into Walter Ryberg from the City News.

"Come back," he says. "You can have your own beat. $65 a week."

I can't decide.

I'm convinced of only one thing since my return from Europe: I'm going to write—whether anybody else cares or knows. My head is filled with stories and images of the old world, though I am still uncertain what to do with it all, how to begin. (I have but one published short story in an obscure little mag to my name).

I have almost decided to return to City News, spend half a day there talking to people, when a call comes through offering me a teaching position at twice the money—with summer free to write.

I take it. And spend the next seven years teaching (and writing).

Throughout the teaching years, I try to write mornings, evenings, weekends, and summers. Chicago remains as close to me as ever—for escape, for entertainment, for inspiration, for material. Every day ever spent in Paul Romaine's pays off handsomely: in the classroom, in my writing. (I create and teach "units" on Negro literature, Chicago writing, Russian literature . . . thanks to Romaine).

Nelson Algren and Mike Royko

While Europe still occupies much of my daydreaming (I want to return, to live and write there a while) I discover the potential of my own ethnic neighborhood and the city of Chicago as subject matter (I study Issac Singer, Farrell, Algren, Harry Mark Petrakis) and begin publishing narrative articles (first person journalism) for Chicago newspapers and magazines—in addition to fiction, some of it set in the same ethnic domain.

Somewhere around the late '60s, early '70s, Paul Romaine becomes my agent.

I have a first book of short stories ready (originally titled *The Restaurant Stories*), and a novel-in-progress about teaching, about Europe, about Mexico.

Romaine is unable to place either manuscript, and for the life of me I can't remember what ever happened to our author/agent relationship, where the manuscripts were sent, or if they were ever returned to me. I begin to separate myself from the city, content that Romaine cares enough about my work to want to help.

My one regret: I am unable to get editorial approval anywhere in Chicago to do a story on Paul Romaine, though my pieces on other Chicagoans are readily accepted and frequently published in the city's major newspapers and magazines. (Romaine is still too hot to handle, I surmise. Either his politics or his obscenity case over *Fanny Hill*)

By the mid '70s I have drifted away from Romaine and the bookshop completely.

The first collection of short stories is revised considerably and published as *The Hour of the Sunshine Now* by Story Press in 1978. The novel on teaching is completed, rewritten, rejected, returned to the files, only to be resurrected and published as *Adventures In An American's Literature* (Ellis Press) in 1982. Both books win critical praise as small press publications, plus some awards. Both reflect insight, learning, refinement garnered in a Chicago bookshop owned by Paul Romaine (though I am uncertain he knows whatever became of me).

Around 1984 my publisher tells me about an old white-haired man he met at a bookfair on the North Side of Chicago. "He used to know you. He spoke highly of your work," my publisher says. I describe Romaine to him as I remembered him. The description fits. I am reminded again of the story he deserved.

One morning in this rural landscape far from Chicago, I open the newspaper at the local coffeeshop and discover Paul Romaine's obituary written by Kenan Heise in the *Chicago Tribune*: Paul Romaine, Dealer in books, Pal of Authors, February 27, 1986.

All this comes back to me.

I owe Paul Romaine a story.

He was a dapper, white-haired man with a neatly trimmed mustache . . . I finally begin.

Bringing the Good News to Skid Row

"Go out quickly into the streets and lanes of the city and bring in hither the poor, and the maimed, and the halt, and the blind."–Luke 14:21

I guess I'll begin with that. A man must begin with words that speak to him. And if that man in is tune with his God, he listens to such words till the words become a voice, and a man hears and acts—and understands his mission in life.

The Rev. Robert N. Coleman, of the First United Pentecostal Mission, 1000 W. Madison St., seems to be that kind of man. I say "seems" because I am always a doubter among men who profess God too openly. Coleman would call me a sinner. But he is a believer, a Christian, a good man. And I am not all of those. But there are differences in men.

Before visiting his mission on skid row, I spent a fascinating morning with Coleman in the basement of his church, 1350 W. Erie, watching movies he had taken of the men and the mission on skid row. It was good of him to give such an introduction to the poor, the maimed, the halt, and the blind.

But there were moments when I wondered whether it was right—Coleman in suit, shirt, and tie, out there in the street, smiling in the camera while shaking a drunk awake in a doorway; the Reverend walking down the long line of men outside the mission, sizing it up in a way, patting the men on the back, smiling, and always looking into the camera. The men sometimes monkeyshining, but mostly waiting patiently and not giving a damn. (So who am I to question whether or not they belong in the movies?)

The last reel was special: "Mr. Blei, I like to show this one fellow here to as many people as I can. Now this'll turn your stomach. You just won't believe some of this until you see it in pictures." As he ran the reel, Coleman continued the commentary: "See that fellow coming in now? Now you just watch him. [The man is led into the mission by Coleman and seated.] Now you watch Brother Behnke there." Brother Behnke, Coleman's first skid row convert and now superintendent of the mission, begins to roll down the stocking of the seated derelict, while the camera comes in for a close-up of a leg that looks like raw salami. "See that corruption coming out that fellow's leg? Them are maggots." And they were. And because it was a movie, they moved—and were very vivid.

But I do not write to make light of this man, any man, and his mission. Coleman is a good man. God knows how many lives he has saved on the row. God knows he is necessary there and doing far more for men than I and many others. But there are differences in men.

Coleman has religion, although he won't call it religion. He's very skeptical about the intellectual approach to God. He's very skeptical of other faiths, their doctrines, their interpretations of the Bible, their mumbo jumbo. "Religion isn't the answer, salvation is! Religion has failed. Religion is a mental concept of what people think about God. Salvation is an experience with God!"

He will tell you this again and again, why his mission, one of several on skid row, has such a great following: "Why, all the others is just chuck full of religion and not an ounce of salvation.

"I'm not a fanatic, Mr. Blei, but I believe the Lord has laid it upon my heart to help these men. And I don't mean rehabilitate. I don't like that word. Rehabilitate is only temporary. There's got to be a lasting change in a man or he'll go back to his old habits."

I can't deny that. Nor can I deny that Coleman practices what he preaches. "The best sermon I can preach is my life." He fully understands that to win the confidence of these men, he must be above reproach. He does not smoke, drink, swear, admit to any worldly temptations whatsoever. His converts must act accordingly. "I have never been to a drive-in movie. I have not read a comic book in thirty years." One can only wonder how far a man can cut himself off from the world, how he is to recognize the new names for sin in our time?

It is necessary to understand a man's conversion to know who the man is today. Coleman was a "sinner" at one time. He did drink and indulge in the common sins of most men. He spent a year on the bum, riding box cars from New York to California. Then, on his way west, he once stopped at a little church in Marion, Indiana, where his brother-in-law was pastor. Nothing much happened that first time. "I acknowledged the fact that there was a God. I knew he existed." So the Rev. Coleman went on to California and arrived at the time of the Depression. He found some work picking dates, but after a few months he went back the way he came, back to the little church in Marion, Indiana, where his brother-in-law was pastor. "That's where I found people who lived right every day. These people lived their religion. People who believed that salvation is an experience, not just a belief. In order to get along, in order for anyone to live a Godly life, they've got to get rid of sin in the first place. The secret of these men on skid row is they're gonna have to get rid of sin in their very breast."

And so came Coleman's conversion: "I went up to the altar of that little church and said, 'God, if there's anything in religion, I want the whole thing.'

And I repented, and I went to my brother-in-law and told him I wanted to be baptized in Jesus' name. It was cold then, but they cut a big hole in the ice in the river and I was baptized. Then my brother-in-law said, 'Now you can have the Holy Ghost, and when you get the Holy Ghost, you get power.' So I went up to the altar that night and asked for the Holy Ghost. And at 9 o'clock, God filled me with the spirit, and I was just babbling away in different tongues. . . .

"And so I called home that night and said, 'Mom, I'm saved. God filled me with the Holy Ghost.' When I got back home to New York, I baptized my own Mom and Dad in the name of Jesus."

Coleman came to Chicago almost twelve years ago from Warsaw, Indiana, where he was pastor of a small church. "I felt a burden on my heart for Chicago." He took over a church at Roosevelt and Ogden, then later the present one on West Erie. But it was Rev. Reed who took him for a ride one day down skid row. "I saw the street lined with these fellows, and Brother Reed said to me, 'This is the street of forgotten men.' And God laid on my heart that someday I would have a mission on Chicago's skid row to work with these men who were forgotten.

"Our first approach toward the program was street meetings. I had to win the confidence of these men. We told these men that we were there not to make fools out of them, and we would appreciate it if they did not make fools out of us. I knew we were going to have victory because of the street meetings. Our mission materialized after eight years passed by."

The first mission on Halsted Street lasted a little over three months before it was razed for a new Holiday Inn. But Halsted Street was where Ed Behnke wandered in. Ed Behnke bummed the country from coast to coast on freight trains and can call off every skid row in America the way the roll of states is called in political conventions. Ed Behnke drank a quart of whiskey a day, and ironically lived right above the Halsted Street mission, and one day walked downstairs "and gave his heart to God." He is superintendent now of the new mission at 1009 W. Madison, and has been with Coleman and God and the men for three years.

When we come to these men, the mission, and Rev. Coleman, it becomes much easier to see the works of Rev. Coleman, and much harder to understand the words of men: "Skid row is "hell"—for Coleman, the men, and me. A man need not believe in a heaven to recognize this. And if the words "eternal damnation" mean anything, they must mean "the men of the row who cannot get off."

Each afternoon around 4:15 (except Friday and 3 p.m. on Sunday) these men, 175 to 200 of them, begin to line up in front of the First United Pentecostal Mission at 1009 W. Madison.

Inside, Ed Behnke and a staff of six or seven other men, all former alcoholics, all converts, all living testimony to the work and words of Rev. Coleman, prepare for the evening service.

These men live in the mission. They receive no pay. They help collect food, mend and distribute clothing, clean the mission, work on the food-line, partake in the religious service, and go out into the street and help the sick and injured. Ed Behnke remains on call twenty-four hours a day.

These are good men and they are fascinating. They all have stories; they all have lived lives most men would fear to dream, lives on and over the edge, lives, almost all of them, beginning with broken homes. There is some schooling, but never very much, and young manhood that begins or ends with work or women or wandering, but almost certainly leads to nightmare journeys of alcohol from one private or public hell to another.

Coleman will tell you about some of them. He will tell you how one of the men came to the mission while going through D.T.s. How the man saw little green men running around his body, kicking him. How Coleman took that man to the altar of the church on West Erie, and the man was shaking all over. Coleman addressed the congregation, saying, "How many of you believe that the Lord can save this man?" And they all did. "And all at once the man stopped shaking. He was just as quiet and still as could be. I baptized him in Jesus's name. And God filled him with the Holy Ghost and the sign of speaking in other tongues."

This man is now a part of Coleman's mission, like Ed Behnke, originally from Cleveland, Ohio, who went on the bum at eighteen and didn't stop until three years ago at the age of thirty-nine when he walked into that Halsted Street mission.

"I always had the urge to travel," Ed Behnke will tell you. "I got off at the Greyhound bus depot, and I didn't know where I was. I never been to Chicago before. I was looking for a place to work and a place to stay. So I just kept walking until I found a place that was hiring men. Then I needed a cheap place to sleep. And I found that near where they were hiring. And I didn't know it, but all along, all the while I was on Madison street. I was on the row."

There is this young Spanish-American, Joe—"Bandido," Ed calls him—who has been a convert for a month or so. His father's death set him off, brought him down hard: twenty-four years old and not a single link with the past. "I was lost. I have nobody left." Now he has the fellowship of these men, and he believes he's found himself through Christ.

There is elderly Marshall Moore, who was impressed by the long line in front of the mission and came in one day and was saved.

And Brother Richardson who spent nineteen years in the penitentiary for armed robbery.

They live, most of them, in a back area of the mission which has been sectioned into various sized rooms, one little larger than a closet. They sleep on cots, live with makeshift furniture and wear clothes donated by the church on Erie and others as well. It is "make-do" all the way. Yet the men are clean, healthy looking and neatly dressed.

O yes, there is Brother Ernie. Ernie, especially, I cannot forget. Coleman

282

refers to him as the Hippie because of his appearance when they met. "Why, he [Ernie] came in here with this big beard and mustache, and you should have seen the sight!"

Ernie, now clean-shaven, has been in and out of Chicago since 1955. He's been a convert since July. We sit in the downstairs kitchen just a little before 5 p.m. when the front door is opened and the mass of men file into the mission.

At 39, Ernie is far past the hippie age bracket. What he had in common with that movement were intellect and a dissatisfaction with society. A "drifitng philosopher," Rev. Coleman calls him, a man who bummed around the country and part of the world most of his life. "When I drank, I never played around. I drank. I drank the best and I drank the worst."

I want answers from Ernie. How does a freethinker end up on skid row? What has he read? How much formal education? What's wrong with society?

Ernie stares into space. You have the feeling he could destroy you with the words stored up somewhere behind those eyes.

"Radicalism," he says. "I had no use for anybody, anything. I couldn't see myself with a house and kids, going to work every morning with a lunch bucket. For what? I wanted to be self-sufficient. I wanted to be Friedrich Nietzsche if I could have been. He went mad, didn't he? Maybe I would have."

So he was a reader, I thought. God, what a waste! A mind [and this is true of all the men I met] with such potential. Why? Why? Why? What other philosophers has he read?

"None. Anything a philosopher doesn't need, it's another philosopher. I can find more philosophy in a 35-cent novel."

He admits, like most of the men, that he came to the mission expecting to take a "nosedive" [first declare yourself for Christ, then be fed] but he found something else. He found in Coleman a man he could trust. And that is very hard to find on the row—especially among Christians. And he found that what he might have been searching for all along was God. "I been to these places before. I came for the material, that was all. Something to eat. They all try to sell you Christ. Well, I tried to detect a phoniness about this mission, but there was none. He didn't get to me the first time. I kept coming back. I listened. I saw what was happening to the men."

Coleman interrupts at this point and describes how Brother Ernie finally came to the mission with his knapsack, emptied the cigarettes on the floor, and repented. But he hasn't got the Holy Ghost yet. Coleman says that not all men get the Holy Ghost right away. It's different with different people. So Ernie's still searching.

"You can't find anything greater than what we have here," says Ernie, and leaves the table to go upstairs and help Ed Behnke seat the men who have waited, some of them almost an hour now, for their first meal of the day. We all go upstairs . . . but first we pray for help.

283

Brother Wayne Worthen enters, assistant pastor of the church, to lend a hand. Rev. Coleman signals Ed Behnke and a phonograph begins playing some Jesus music. Then the procession from the street of forgotten men begins.

They come in blinking under the mission's stark, fluorescent light. They are young, they are middle-aged, they are ancient. They are dying, all of them. They are black, Spanish-American, Indian, Southern white, Northern white. They are clean shaven, unshaven, crippled, crooked, and straight. They are dressed in every conceivable get-up, from military overcoats to tee shirts and sweaters. They will wear anything, especially now that it's cold. They fill almost the entire room—two hundred chairs. And they wait. They mumble to themselves. They argue. But most of them quietly wait within themselves, for they are hungry. And they have time, these men, time, time, time, time.

Looking into their faces, you see their craving for liquor. You see how it works. You realize that some of them carry knives to protect themselves from each other, but mainly from the constant threat of young jackrollers. These faces could easily include a Richard Speck—and who would know the difference?

What shocks you after the first minute is not what they are and how they must live, but how much they resemble any man you have ever met. Look hard enough, and you see the guy next door, the men in offices on Michigan Ave., an uncle, a cousin, a TV personality, a sports figure. Find the right man and look exceptionally hard, and you can almost see yourself.

When they are all in, Coleman asks everyone to stand while he and some of his men pray out loud, each man shouting his separate prayer, speaking, in a way, in different tongues. Coleman stands on a green platform with a banister and pulpit. He begins directly—almost man to man. "How many you men had the flu?" Hands are raised. Too many hands. Everybody's got the flu. Even Rev. Coleman. Then the first pitch: "Some people tell me Heaven's like Chicago!" And for those who are tuned into him, there are a few chuckles, a few shouts, some laughter. [Of course these men know what Heaven's like.] "SOME PEOPLE TELL ME HEAVEN'S LIKE SKID ROW!" More response. He's off, and many of them are listening. Who else has talked to them today?

But they're hungry. And now it's time for some music. Brother Worthen plays an electric guitar. Another man plays a violin. Ed Behnke sings. So does Coleman. They all join in singing, "THERE'S ONE WAY, ONE WAY TO GOD." More sermon. More song. "LAST NIGHT I DREAMED AN ANGEL CAME." A black man closes his eyes and sways gently with the song. "Say 'Amen'," says Coleman. "Amen," reply the men. Coleman is really warming them up now. More and more response from the men. Some with him, some against. Coleman is open to all their words and will skillfully weave them into the text of his sermon, for Coleman's is that old-fashioned religion which you don't see much of nowadays. He needs no pulpit, certainly no set speech. In fact he's already up on the banister creating the sermon out of everything he hears, sees, feels. "THAT'S ALL YOU MEN ARE, IS DIAMONDS IN THE

ROUGH! THAT'S ALL! THAT'S ALL! AM I RIGHT MEN? AM I RIGHT? HOW MANY OF YOU MEN THINK REV. COLEMAN'S RIGHT?" "Yes, Rev. Coleman. Yes, yes." "NOW ALL YOU MEN THERE SAY, 'AMEN.' " "Amen. Amen." One man is giving the Reverend a little trouble. Ed Behnke keeps an eye on him. But the Reverend turns it over to all the men. "How many of you think we should throw that man out?" It's unanimous. The men are with Coleman. Ed Behnke moves to ease the man outside. "I ain't doin' nothin'," he shouts. "I ain't doin' nothin'." "HOW MANY OF YOU MEN THINK HE OUGHT TO STAY BUT KEEP HIS MOUTH SHUT?" Coleman turns the other cheek. Less than a unanimous reaction. "Throw the monkey out," somebody yells from the back. But the Reverend holds on, and the man quietly sits out the rest of the service.

Time for some music. "SOMETHING GOT A HOLD OF ME THAT NIGHT." Somebody thinks it's a funny title and laughs. But everybody listens till the song is over, till Ed Behnke and some of the others testify once again how they found the Holy Ghost, till there is one more song and one more prayer, till Coleman tells them all to say, "Praise be the Lord." When they do, he tells them, "You know, that's the most sensible thing you said all day!" And it is time then to eat.

They begin to file down the stairs to the basement. I don't know how the crippled get down. I don't want to know. I know, though, that "basement" is the wrong word. "Cellar" would be more like it. There is dinginess and dampness to a cellar, this long, narrow, poorly-lit sepulchre under West Madison.

There are no tables as such, no chairs, no chance for the men to put their plates down. There are only two long stand-up chest-high tables of a sort, and the men lean up against them and fill their stomachs fast.

The men first line up along the west wall and move quickly toward the back kitchen where some of Coleman's men distribute food from large cardboard barrels.

Food. Finally. And the barrels are full. Food a couple of days old. Food left over from vending machines. Take your choice. "Take five apiece, fellas." Take your choice of cold sandwiches: tuna salad, hamburger, salami, ham, bologna, egg salad, hot dogs. All individually wrapped and smashed in cellophane packages. And take two or three sweet rolls, wrapped and smashed. And take a plastic, Day-Glo tumbler of hot coffee. Hot.

It may not be the proper diet, but it's something. Enough for Coleman to be thankful to the A.R.A. Vending company for donating leftover sandwiches every Monday, Tuesday, Thursday, and Saturday. "Can you imagine, they used to burn this good food before I found out. And these men are starving." And Campbell Soup helps out twice a year with four hundred cases of soup.

There seems to be no end to this pitiful procession of men grabbing sandwiches and sweet rolls, stuffing them in their shirt pockets and shopping bags;

taking a hot cup of coffee then moving off to the stand-up and back out into the street for another night.

Coleman talks to many of the men as they go through the line. He's looking, of course, always looking for another convert. Still another life to save from skid row. He asks some of the men to step out of the line and sit down at the small kitchen table and talk to me. I've had enough of these men, but he keeps sending them, keeps talking. "You've got the flu, don't you?" he shouts to a man, one eye bandaged, sweat pouring from his face. "You got the flu, man. We got to get you to a doctor." And the man suddenly beams and nods his head yes, like a child. It was probably the first time in months anyone talked to him like a human being.

"Duke, come over here. I want you to meet someone." He brings Duke to the table, a heavy man with a thin gray mustache who even talks like a duke, English accent and all.

"I almost died," he says. "It's my heart. I been in County for days. They just released me and gave me these pills." I listen to Duke's story and discover another incredible life. Duke is the man we've all read about, the classic story of skid row: a man with three degrees (one in law) who had a fortune and blew it, a master in all the manly arts of self-defense, who smiles and says to you under his breath, "I could kill you." And you know damned well, although he's just out of the hospital and fifty-seven years old, he could.

Yet he's a gentle man, a former espionage agent who jumped behind German lines in a black parachute. Duke has stories and stories and stories. And who's to deny them?

What does he want now? "I got to make another mission tonight down the street where I can get a flop. Then tomorrow I need some fresh clothes. Rev. Coleman will give me some clean clothes. If I can find a nice place to stay, the Welfare says they'll help me out. Then maybe I can get off the street. What would you do? What would you do? I can't go back to sea. I was a captain once. I'm too old. I could do a lot of things if I could get off this street. But I can't fill out an application. I can't account for all the time. I wish I could believe in God the way Rev. Coleman does, and all these fine men. I know all of them. It would be nice to live here and help out. But it's too hard. I can't give up smoking. I've smoked all my life. And I can't work here for no pay. Yes, it's nice here. One of the best missions on the street. I'll tell you what else I like here. The music. I listen to the music. Oh, I'd like to hear some Beethoven instead, or Brahms or Mozart. You don't hear them on the street. But the music here is nice."

There were others besides Duke at the table, but for me the stories were over. The man on my right slumped over and asked me to feel his forehead. I heard Coleman say that "the man's got to get to the hospital or else he'll die."

I guess that would be an end of sorts. But there are so many endings here because there are so many stories about the men, the mission, and Coleman. I don't know where to begin.

Coleman, I am sure, needs help. I am sure he thinks I can give it to him [Brother Blei, he finally called me), but I doubt it—not the kind of help that's really necessary.

Coleman has plans. He needs larger quarters. He wants to buy a building down the block for $35,000. He has raised a good amount of the down payment already. He thinks that with more room he can do more good for more men. He can get some of them back to their families, as he has already done. He can save more men through repentance, baptism, and the gift of the Holy Ghost.

He realizes, too, the importance of getting men off the row entirely, off to a farm someplace. After he's done this, he wants to start a mission in New York's Bowery. And still another mission in Little France, New Orleans. But that's the future.

I hope he gets whatever the men need. But I'm still not convinced his religion is the final solution for these men. I hate to think one helps the mission by taking movies and pictures of lost men. Why are the chairs upstairs in the mission and not downstairs? Why not feed the men first and give thanks later?

I asked Coleman how long a man could keep coming to the mission for food and not be converted, and still not be turned away. "Our purpose is to get new men in," he said. "Nobody deserves to hear the truth twice if they heard it once."

I hope he didn't mean it the way it sounded.

What of the other men his staff, Ed Behnke, in particular, and Ernie, the hippie? I kept asking these men about the life ahead of them. They were well now. They were healthy. They had a firm hold of themselves. What about education? Work? Marriage?

Everything now seemed to depend on the will of the Lord. They were committed now to the mission.

Although that may be a noble life, indeed, is it living? Is it enough? For a second Ed Behnke said something about travelling to the Amazon someday and studying tropical diseases. That's what I was looking for. But it was only a second, and then we were back with the Holy Ghost.

I don't know. I hate to see men imprison themselves one way or another.

As I said in the beginning, Coleman is a good man. And I no doubt am a sinner. But there are differences in men.

287

"My son. Five days old. Good-lookin' kid, ain't he?"

Bill Mauldin, Up Front

The best nights I've spent in the field have been in barns. And the best night I ever spent in a barn was when I woke up and found a cow standing over me. She had a calf but I shouldered the little creature aside and milked the mother in my best New Mexico style. —from *Up Front*, by Bill Mauldin

He's beginning to look more and more like his famous World War II characters, Willie and Joe, now at age 55, with a scraggly beard, a few wrinkles, a bit of a mournful look about his face at times. But a quick down-home grin, a burst of laughter, a shout, an undying enthusiasm for life in the global village puts Bill Mauldin back in the center of things, quietly holed up as he may seem, far away from it all, in Santa Fe, New Mexico.

To a soldier in a hole, nothing is bigger or more vital to him than the war which is going on in the immediate vicinity of his hole. If nothing is happening to him, and he's able to relax that day, then it is a good war, no matter what is going on elsewhere. —Up Front.

I stand inside his spacious home in Santa Fe—sun, mountains, space, serenity, a swimming pool . . . as tranquil a setting as one could imagine for "layin' back," as they say. Only this Southwest is headquarters for Mauldin; the mission is the continuing examination of Carter, energy, ecology, George Meany, the '70s. "If it's big, hit it," is his maxim; whatever grabs hold of his mind and fingers to make us smile and think.

He has opened the door, he is answering the phone; a Siamese cat scurries into the living room, a dog is barking up a frenzy at the stranger, Mauldin is hanging up the phone, talking to the dog . . . "You got him scared to death" . . . making excuses to me for the dog: "You don't want to discourage 'em too much when they're learnin'," and opening a new bottle of Johnny Walker in good old Chicago style, in laid-back Santa Fe hospitality.

The barking diminishing, the glasses tinkling, the room awash in a Santa Fe afternoon sun, Mauldin begins to explain why he has moved his base of operations here. "We had an apartment back in Chicago. It was all sort of a gradual thing during the past year or two. I went to Yale (to teach) two semesters, '74 and '75 . . . I hate the weather in Chicago, the winter. I bought this house seven years ago. My wife was from here . . . she died in 1971. I'm a native New Mexican."

Chris, whom he married in 1972, enters the room: long blonde hair, pretty, natural . . . a native Chicagoan at heart. "I was born in the city," she says. "We lived for six years in the Swedish section of Chicago. Later we moved to Wilmette. But I'm really delighted to be here." Mauldin commutes to Chicago, and the *Sun-Times* on occasion, using his own plane; he pilots, Chris navigates.

The key to the cartoonist's emancipation from the *Sun-Times* office, however, is a little miracle of technology in his New Mexican headquarters known as an AP Laserphoto machine which transmits Mauldin's cartoons each day (five a week) from Santa Fe to Chicago.

Hours on the job, though, are difficult for him to calculate. Like any artist, Mauldin's imagination is churning all the time, feeding on daily newscasts, books, newsmagazines, periodicals of all sorts. The man dreams cartoons, no doubt, though his real ritual for putting it all together seems to begin each morning in the bathtub . . . extremely hot water, he explains (according to World Year Books), "to let my brains boil."

"Sometimes it takes a while, but it never fails. Although I have never been able to figure out, let alone explain, the mental processes involved in converting current events into cartoons, I think it is a sort of filter system, like an automatic coffee maker, combined with what psychoanalysts might call free association.

"One morning, I might sit in the steam thinking about Congress, which would lead me to the Senate, which might point to the White House—several senators have become presidents lately—thereby bringing to mind the secretary of state, then the Defense Department, raising the specter of nuclear warfare, which causes fallout, creating air pollution, which takes me back again to congressional debate. Somewhere along the line, one of these subjects will mate with a news topic, giving birth to an idea—an interesting feat for an automatic coffee maker."

A large oval mirror projects above his desk from the windows beside him. Not as sophisticated a tool as the Laserphoto machine perhaps, but a necessity indeed for a cartoonist who strives to get it right. Mauldin often poses himself in the mirror to get accurate gestures in his drawings.

"Say," he says, "that call before was about some furniture I ordered for the porch. It's down at the railway station. You mind riding along with me to go pick it up? Chris!" he shouts. "Chris, you know where my good-ol'-boy hat is?" He is running around, looking for his hat. "Ah, the hell with it." He steps out the back door with a sign on it: GOOD FRIENDS, PLEASE KNOCK BEFORE ENTERING AND CALL BEFORE KNOCKING. Stepping back in, he pops out again moments later with a beat-up Western style hat on his head.

Then into a Chevrolet pickup with a gun rack. Mauldin turns the ignition key, gritting his teeth. "If this runs without blowin' up," he says, talking to the

290

machine which will not turn over. "I think I better have a look," jumping out, opening the hood, watching gas leaking from the carburetor rather steadily, slamming the hood down.

I've got a friend's pickup, I suggest. "Great. I'll drive and you ride."

Mauldin is at the wheel, explaining his relationship with the *Sun-Times,* the freedom he enjoys: "I think that one thing that works in my favor is that their share of syndication pretty much pays my salary. (His work appears in 250 newspapers.) So, I'm sort of paying my own way. Besides, I've been in this business so long that I don't have to be in the office. I do as much reading here or more. I've always considered Chicago a basically friendly place, but I'm getting old enough now that I like to be back in my hills. I know I'm gettin' away with murder in a sense, but I believe in working. I think my work is better off here . . . and so is my employer.

"I've always resisted being on the editorial page of the *Sun-Times.* Some days I don't even know what our policy is—and if I did, I'd probably oppose it. The only time I ever worked closely with the editor of a page was when I was on the St. Louis *Post-Dispatch.* But even then I never attended editorial meetings."

Winding down the streets through the beautiful scene which is Santa Fe—something to do with the New Mexican light, something to do with the people who just roll with the day—Mauldin reflects upon his love affair with the area. "It's a lot like Mexico. I've been living here on and off for over thirty years. I was born in a place called Mountain Park, no longer on the map. The logging trail stopped there then. The nearest place to it would be something called High Rolls."

Santa Fe is booming these days, property at a premium, damned near everyone wanting to be a part of it, everyone accepted, no questions asked. It is home, or hide-out, even to John Ehrlichman, who holed himself here for a while to write and contemplate, and who only recently left to begin serving his sentence.

"Everyone wants to be the last son of a bitch to get here," Mauldin says and laughs.

He backs the pickup to the platform of the Santa Fe freight station and begins checking around to locate his furniture. Mauldin is telling a Chicano working at the desk: "Yeah, 'Mauldin,' Bill Mauldin . . . M-A-U-L-D-I-N." Only part of the order, it seems, has arrived. We throw one large box on the back of the pickup and head for home.

"Lifestyle? I don't think I have one, really," he says. "One of the great charms of Chris is that she takes things like I do. She gets up about six to work on her book; I do, too, to work on a drawing. We go to about noon, and then we go off on an adventure. A lot of the time wasted commuting, we put to good use.

"Although this is not hot and desert-like country (Santa Fe is at 7,000 feet elevation), even so, everything productive you want to do, you do it in the morning so the afternoon is yours to siesta or do anything else you want to do. Before the energy crunch, if the mood was upon us, we'd fly out to the Arizona place and spend the afternoon there beer drinking, whatever. But our style has been crimped a little bit."

As for fame, the two-time Pulitzer Prize winner, recipient of numerous honorary doctorate degrees and associate fellow of Yale University seems to handle it pretty well in Santa Fe, judging from the fellow at the train station, who never heard of him. "As you saw," Mauldin laughs, "I'm really a local celebrity. That's what's great about this town: Nobody gives a crap. When Ehrlichman came here, I bet he was hoping he wouldn't be noticed; but I'll bet by the time he left, he wished he were."

Keeping up with the news from his vantage point, keeping in touch . . . "We watch all of the network news. Genevieve (his secretary at the *Sun-Times*) often sends me news summaries of the day on the telecopier. I keep a pretty extensive picture file of people. Trips down to the morgue [the newspaper library] are handled on the telecopier. Any photos needed are sent via the telecopier. The two key expenses are: I pay Genevieve's salary, and I also lease the Laserphoto from AP. But I think it's worth it.

"You miss hanging out at Riccardo's, though . . . I miss Riccardo's. I miss sitting around and drinking with people like John Fischetti. I miss Royko. Oh, we reconvene it when we go there," Mauldin says with a wicked grin.

We pull up to the house again, unload the box of furniture, carrying it to the porch where he and Chris begin setting it up. "Good stuff, huh?" he says obviously pleased with the merchandise. "I think we'll sit out here. Let me go in and refresh our drinks."

It's a late afternoon sun just off the Mauldin porch in Santa Fe, the glowing New Mexican hills in the distance . . . the whiskey flowing real fine, the new furniture about as comfortable as any man can set his body in, and Mauldin drawing more and more on old Chicago feelings.

"When I first went to Chicago, I liked Daley," he says. "I accepted him. It's a tough town, they want a tough guy running it. And like Paddy Bauler said—hey, you know Paddy Bauler lived here, by the way? 'Chicago ain't ready for reform.' I thought Daley would end up being a nice, colorful, sort of James Curley type, but more uncouth. But then the terrible things of the '60s . . . and the '68 convention just ended it for me. He just became another Mussolini. People approved of him because he made the trains run on time, but that ain't enough. I think he got more hard-headed as he got older."

There was no Mauldin cartoon when Daley died, I remind him. I was waiting for one; so were many others. "I don't believe in picking on dead people," says Mauldin, "and to do anything else sounds hypocritical." National politics is Mauldin's battleground. Only, with Carter, there hasn't been much battling.

292

"I have a problem with the national scene in that so far I approve of Carter. I will not carp at him just to prove that I have sharp teeth. I approve of his election. So far I approve of what he's done. I'm being almost totally non-critical, which is supposed to be deadly for a cartoonist. I would welcome any opportunity to savage him, but I'm not going to fake it. But it's a dangerous thing not to be critical of your current President."

Where's Mauldin going? Is Santa Fe the end of the line? "I enjoy my work. I want to stay at it. I probably have ten or fifteen good years left before I just start hanging in there.

"I'm fifty-five now. I've never known anyone who passes seventy in this line and continued to do good work. I don't want to die in a harness. I don't want to ever do bad work. I've got at least four books in me, like a log jam. I love to write, I think writing helps drawing. I do a lot of photography too, land-scape stuff. I'm fascinated with light. This is the greatest place in the world for light. I like to go up in the mountains and just do scenery . . . I just love it. People don't sit around here and lotus-eat.

"We better go in," says Mauldin. "It's our last shot at the news for the weekend." He wheels a portable color TV in front of the sofa, then plunks himself down to watch John Chancellor; a cat curls up on his lap. "We watch NBC and then ABC. I watch the Today Show at six. NBC is sort of the Rock of Gibralter. I can't stand Brinkley, though . . . he's always cracking up over the most horrible story."

Carter's news conference is the lead story. "I like the way he handles himself," reflect Mauldin, never taking his eyes from the tube. "I like the way he handles George Meany. Some of this may be a naturally conservative nature as I grow older, but I see labor guys like Meany and Fitzsimmons dragging us into something like they got in England . . . and we're going to be screwed. The Russian dissident situation . . . I think Carter has handled that well."

Carter is talking on the tube—gracious, serious, eyes-a-twinkle, tie slightly askew. Mauldin, in a loud guffaw (scaring the cat off his lap): "I think he's a smoothie, oh, what a smoothie, a lot of Kennedy style, and a lot more substance. I'll really be grateful if he gives me an excuse to hate him . . . I really will."

Aside from the network news programs, Mauldin keeps tabs through major (and minor) news periodicals as well. "I think *Time* and *Newsweek* have both gone to hell. The only news magazine I've trusted for years is *Business Week*— no editorial policy at all."

Mauldin moves back and forth in time, sparked by a question on my part or by something in the news: "The late '60s . . . I think the kids saved the country. And in doing so, they messed up their own lives. I think there should be absolute, total amnesty. . . .

"As a general thing, you could say this about them: a lot of kids were smoking pot and thinking deeply in '74. By the fall of '75, a lot of them were drink-

293

ing like fish and beginning to act like kids in the Eisenhower '50s. Back to panty raids. I prefer the dope smokers . . . I think like a cartoonist, hyperbole is my stock in trade. The spirit of the '60s faded fast, the spirit of the '70s came on. I really think the '70s are going to be a replay of the depressed Eisenhower '50s."

The Santa Fe sun creeps down even more, mellowing the room, Mauldin and even the evening news. He turns to ABC, Carter, again . . . the man, the image beginning to haunt Mauldin, it seems. The President playing to Mauldin? Mauldin playing to the President? He sketches Carter's smiling face in his head, but cannot dig out the line, the work to bring him down. He watches the President as if it were a sporting event, moving his arms, his legs, his body . . . listening, even talking to him, telling Carter on the screen: "Right, right!" Hooting a hurrah for the way he's handling the Russians. Then, turning to me with a grin, "You know why I like this son of a bitch? Look at his tie . . . sloppy. His suits fit him the way mine fit me." Mauldin laughs, but still listens . . . the old platoon sergeant looking for an opening, waiting for the salvation of some kind of Carter miscalculation to call for the direct thrust of the Pulitzer pen, the perfect line or word drawing insight and laughter enough to smooth a cartoonist's troubled conscience.

"I just can't hit the guy if he doesn't give me a target." Mauldin is talking to himself . . . "if it's big, hit it," repeating his own directions to Jimmy's face, trying to shake off the Carter charisma, keeping a steady bead on him, not letting him out of his sight,

Ben Gingiss: Tuxedo Junction

In the beginning there was Gingiss.

Back in the days when you were starting your formal love life with the high-school prom, there was Gingiss, somewhere around the corner, to tux you up fine with your first touch of class.

Or if you were cementing a relationship, there was Gingiss again, just around the corner, to help you tie the knot, outfit your wedding party, and throw in monogrammed drinking glasses for the bride and groom.

I'm on my way now to meet that man Gingiss, and he's right around the corner, high atop the John Hancock wedding cake where the chairman of the board of Gingiss International, Inc. resides.

My shoes could use a shining. My clothes remain forever unpressed. I am dressed informally, to say the least. Will Big Ben give me a dressing down?

The time was (proms past) when I was the first on my block to rent a plaid dinner jacket from Gingiss with a dashing black cummerbund and dance all night to the music of Ralph Marterie.

And the time was, years later, when Gingiss dressed me in an eggshell-white dinner jacket as a member of the wedding (my own)—and threw in that free gift of glasses. (Which was probably why I went to Gingiss in the first place, brought up in the neighborhood tradition of always dealing with a merchant who offers something for free.)

It was a good feeling, that "tux" feeling. Clothes, by God, did make a man! I felt I belonged, destined to live a formal life at dinner parties, charity balls, opening nights at the opera. No matter when, not matter where, if Tuxedo Times were upon me, Gingiss was there.

Because Gingiss was everywhere.

Silent fifties, revolutionary sixties, mysterious Carter seventies—the right to dress, or undress, remains one of those certain inalienable rights. Though I have not worn a tux in some time (and would feel right strange wearing one in the land of Oshkosh B'Gosh), memories linger, questions persist: How go the days and nights of formal wear in these times? Where is Tuxedo Junction anyway? And who is Benjamin J. Gingiss, our father of formal wear?

Evidence of his presence litters the American landscape. Even in fiction.

Pick up a current novel of international intrigue, *The Twenty-Third Web* by
Richard Himmel. Look at page 218:

"What I really called for was to see if you can do me a favor."

Moynihan exploded. "Favor? What makes you think I'd do you a favor?"

"Because you're sweet and lovable, as well as being even-tempered and soft-
spoken."

"As long as you understand my real nature, Frankie, I'll make a sincere at
tempt. What the hell do you want?"

"Do you know anybody at Gingiss, the tuxedo rental place?

"A tuxedo? What the hell do you want a tuxedo for? Come to think of it
you're going to need a tuxedo. After I kill you tomorrow they can lay you
out in it."

"Do you know anybody there?"

"Sure, I know Ben Gingiss. Why?"

"I need a tux for tomorrow night. I know damn well that if I go in tomor-
row, and get a shnook salesman, he won't even talk to me. They need at
least 24 hours for delivery. I though maybe you could exert some clout."

"Do you want a pink one or a blue one?"

"Tell Gingiss I'll be in his downtown store first thing in the morning."

Inside a private office across from his apartment, I meet Gingiss himself, an amiable man, a veritable Gentle Ben, age sixty-seven. This man founded his business in 1936 with five hundred borrowed bucks and tuxedoed it to a sales volume of $18 million a year. He is untuxed himself, at the moment, but dressed in impeccable taste.

The walls are filled with photographs, awards, memorabilia galore, reflecting his indisputable power and his place in Chicago history (the late great Mayor Richard J. Daley in top hat) and in the history of the world. And all this from dressing people up in style—frequently, no doubt, making them look and feel better than they really were.

I am introduced to Ben's son, Joel Gingiss, thirty-five, upon whom the mantle of the presidency (chief operating officer) of Gingiss International, Inc. has fallen. "Jody became president three or four years ago," explains Ben. "He resisted becoming president, but he was a natural for the job. When he finally was elected, I just got out of the office, he got in, I went on a trip, and no one even remembers me."

"My father had gotten a little removed from all the day-to-day operations," explains Joel. "All his kids were grown. I was off flying airplanes. My mother and dad love to travel. My understanding of the business came from growing up with it. My dad would come home from the office and cite all the miseries of it. I started at the botton and became president. One reason I went to the Naval Academy [a 1964 graduate of Annapolis . . . one of the most decorated pilots in the Vietnam war . . . twenty-five awards, including the Distinguished Flying Cross . . . 206 combat missions, assigned to the carrier Kitty Hawk] was to get away from all of it. By the time I came in, the company was just getting into the franchise business. It was a challenge, and that's what put me over."

While Joel talks, Ben remains in the background, looking immeasurably proud of his son. When I ask Ben about his present role as chairman of the board, Joel replies, "This is the board, for all practical purposes. We're still a family company, going now from a small operation to a medium one. We now have 151 stores across the country, thirty states, nineteen in Chicago. Nineteen are company owned. The franchise program is only nine years old."

The phone rings. Somebody needs two special tuxedos . . . a big cocktail scene. . . .

"It's like this all the time," says Ben. "People who need something special."

Joel, it soon becomes evident, is into the hard numbers, statistics, percentages, projections, franchise operations . . . the pure technology of the tux, while Ben, though certainly profit-oriented, has the personal history of people and friends to excite him, the lore and love of it all.

"The woman is the crucial decision-maker," says Ben out of the clear blue. "The average guy, when he gets married, doesn't care. Our message is aimed at the woman. I think we were the first men's-wear dealer to go into bridal magazines. We are generally looking for an audience eighteen to thirty years old. Today we sell more new formal clothes than anybody else in the world. We've been selling formal wear for about thirty years.

"All our stores together do $18 million in business, ten percent of that new formal wear. Our market is 75-percent weddings, 15-percent proms, and the rest what we call 'the other business'—conventions, society parties, openings of the opera, show biz. We've sold every governor of Illinois his formal clothes for the past twenty-five years. Carter, for his son's wedding in Atlanta. In fact, Chip wore one of our garments at the inauguration."

To go back to the beginning, the father of formal wear pauses a moment, to regain his sense of history. "It was during the Depression," he starts. "Late 1936. My sister was marrying a fellow 6' 3". The best man was 6' 5". We were looking for formal wear and there was nothing. My younger brother and I felt there should be a market for good clothes. So we bought the finest clothes we could buy on credit, and we were an almost instant success.

"I remember in the first few months getting a call for seventeen cutaways. We didn't have them. And Michael Howlitt's sister was getting married. Since we couldn't fit them, we went to the house, measured them, and then went out and bought them. We started out with $500 thay my mother borrowed on my father's insurance policy. Before we got the walls put up, the carpet down, it was gone. A tux was costing us $25; we rented it for $5.

"We had different sizes. . . . We bought clothes to suit the customer. We were just busy as hell and in financial trouble all the time. Just when we paid our last obligation, Pearl Harbor broke, December 7, 1941, and then it became illegal to make formal clothes. We kept the shop closed, but we had an answering service."

That one wedding with the order for seventeen cutaways eventually accounted for 876 new customers, which was one of the ways that Gingiss began to grow. In almost every wedding party there was usually someone planning a wedding in the near future. And Gingiss inevitably got him.

"When the war was over, we threw everything out and started from scratch," continues Ben. "The first store was where the Greyhound Bus depot is now. We were on the second floor, above a saloon. Often you stumbled over the drunks. Gingiss Brothers it was called then. When we went into Evanston, we went on the second floor, too. There's a reason for that. In the early days, men weren't too keen on renting formal wear. Gentlemen didn't rent formal wear, they owned it. The rental business didn't have much of a reputation. But as our reputation became firmly established, we moved to the ground floor. Of course, the rent was cheaper upstairs, too."

Formal wear, as Ben Gingiss sees it, can be divided into five categories: full dress, cut away, stroller, black tux, and white dinner jacket. And as for building his own rental business, Ben kept on his toes when it came to styles.

"We invited the bridal consultants and men's-clothing-store people to see our things. We kept the fashion people informed of new trends. I was constantly trying to find out what men liked to wear, what they looked good in. We would suggest these things to manufacturers. Another thing we watched was what the custom tailors made for the rich. I would be watching what people were wearing in Palm Beach, the resort areas, what people wore on cruises. Old money set the tone for formal wear."

Aside from personal observation, Gingiss, always a student of history, became, in fact, an authority on the history of clothing throughout civilization, building one of the best personal libraries around, serving even as a consultant to Amy Vanderbuilt.

"My father," Ben adds, "used to make a lot of the chorus wardrobes for the old Balaban and Katz theatres. When times were hard, my mother would make wedding gowns and veils for brides. I guess that was always cooking in my mind."

After three and a half years of college, he worked in a number of businesses—"all of it saleswork," he says. "I just hated everything I was doing. I was twenty-five years old when I got into this. No one had the idea of renting clothes as an elegant first-class establishment back in 1936. It all had the aura of a second-hand clothing store business then, like a costume business. There were at least fifty people in the business when we got started, but by the time the war broke out, we were number one. The minute something went out of fashion, we would sell it to orchestras, glee clubs, waiters, magicians . . . get rid of it fast. About two years ago, we gave ten thousand outfits to Goodwill Industries. Having what's right is important."

Though Gingiss himself does not necessarily call the shots when it comes to men's formal fashion wear, he has been known to shoot down a particular item (like the Nehru jacket) when he feels it is wrong—and ugly besides.

"That was the most fun thing I did," he confesses. "Many stores were coming out with Nehru jackets. Lord Snowdon started it. Then it was copied by Teddy Kennedy. It was worn with a turtleneck shirt and no tie. Manufacturers of formal wear thought they had to try it. I did some research on it and found out it was started in prison—Prime Minister Nehru of India adopted this garment when he was in prison. It just did not seem appropriate for formal wear.

"After it had been going for about six months, I called a press conference and explained that not only should it have never happened, but that it would die a quick death. And anyone who bought one from us could bring it back and I would replace it with a brand-new garment. Sure enough, it died just like I said it would. You could not mix informal clothes with formal clothes. It was a sloppy looking garment. I just couldn't live with it."

Hundreds of newspapers carried the Gingiss story with the headline: "The Nehru Is Dead." And it was. Ben Gingiss killed it single-handedly.

It's one of the more fascinating aspects of history, just what men wear and why. "In the early days of our country," explains Ben, "life revolved around the church. As people became more leisure-conscious, a lot more activity began to revolve around country clubs and schools. I think formal wear took up on that. I would have to say that all through history there have been specific types of garments for specific occasions. The Indians had their war bonnets. You always had people dressing in a certain way, sort of to please the gods.

"One might say that a man's dress often mirrors the history of the time he lives in. His clothes are intended to relfect his status, tastes, and sometimes his profession. With formal wear, men are wearing something elegant and completely different than what they wear at any other time, to dignify and celebrate a specific and memorable occasion. We are fortunate to be in a business that is part of this tradition."

Ben, in fact, will go so far as to expound on a system of ethics, morality, all related to what men wear.

"Formal weddings have less likelihood of ending up in divorce court," he says. His son Joel describes an informal joint study that Ben made with Judge Julius Miner, who consulted his own records. They found that those who had eloped, those who had gone to a justice of the peace, had a higher incidence of divorce than those who had formal weddings with the whole family involved.

"Taking the whole wedding as a serious matter," says Ben, "the aura about it was: What you can get into easy, you can get out of easy."

As for today's tendency of the young to go with whatever moves them, Ben shrugs his shoulders. "Let's say there's a line between practicality and common sense. During the Vietnam war, the kids were rebelling. Anything their fathers wore, they were against. If we had kept the traditional tuxes, we would have been out of business.

"There was a slow down in the late sixties and early seventies. We found instances where they didn't even have proms. In terms of kids, I think we lost them for a while—when they were getting married out in the cornfields and parks. In some ways, we are a barometer of people's attitudes. Our business almost anticipates the outlook of people. I think the Vietnam situation was a reflection of that."

"But today," counters Joel, "I think we take care of the prom kids better than anyone else in the world. We really try to take care of them. The wedding business has been in a decline the past several years. Lately it has started to increase, but slowly. One of the factors involved is that the average age of people getting married has increased."

"Also," adds Ben, "we're getting the kids who have been living together for two or three years and after that want a big wedding."

The word "tuxedo" first came into the language of formal wear in 1886 at a country club in Tuxedo Park, New York, when Pierre Lorillard substituted a shorter coat for evening dress for the formal swallow-tail coat. If, according to Ben Gingiss, the years after World War Two were marked by a great resurgence in formal wear, with the new double-breasted tuxedo in full bloom, the fifties were marked by the introduction of lightweight fabrics and synthetics, the single-breasted and the shawl-collared tuxedo, called the Tony Martin and manufactured by After Six. Cheers, too, for the cummerbund, which held the gut of a guy like a huge sash, finished the top of the pants, and added a bit more class.

Fashions in the history of formal wear, indeed. What did we wear in the terrible sixties, a decade that some of us would rather forget? Formal wear still fought for a piece of that action with the introduction of pastel colors in tuxdom. (Color, and why not, when the street fashions of the hippies blossomed in a sea of blue denim?) Formal wear may have lost the flower children, but tuxes would get a little livelier as time went on.

The revolution of the seventies in men's formal wear came about when a manufacturer called Lord West brought out a tux they dubbed the Prince Edward. "It came in brocades and velvets and colors," says Ben. "A three-quarter-length jacket, double-breasted, six buttons, satin lapels, worn with a ruffled shirt, ruffled or lace cuffs. It caught on like wildfire. During and after Vietnam, only the kind of colors and styles that came on the scene would have attracted young people and gotten them out of Levis and T-shirts."

We break for lunch and I follow Ben Gingiss and son down elevators, through a maze of hallways, byways, back streets, and on to the Carlton Club. Heads nod and bow, hands extend, greetings are exchanged with every other step. I have the feeling that, at one time or another, Gingiss had personally outfitted every Chicagoan, for everyone seems to know Ben Gingiss. I have a fleeting image, as we make our way through the multitudes, that a chorus of tuxedoed angels hover in our wake. As Joel confides to me at one point in our journey, "He's sort of our resident miracle worker."

Ben Gingiss can tell tales and more tales, and someday he'll have to gather them in a book. It's difficult to mention a celebrity that doesn't elicit a Ben Gingiss story.

"I'll never forget when James Roosevelt was in town," Ben says over lunch. "He needed a tux in a hurry. Within half an hour Roosevelt was dressed and on the dias. Afterward he left a note: 'This tux fits me better than my own.'

"Bob Hope was giving a speech here one time. 'Fellows,' he said, 'this is not going to be a long speech. The man from Gingiss is waiting to pick up his tux.' "

Magic in the name Gingiss? They once took a poll to determine the public's familiarity with the name, and the recognition factor was surprisingly high.

Joel puts in, "It became a catchword primarily through my father's efforts in going out, promoting the business, meeting people, making them feel special."

"Well, the big thing," says Ben, "is that when an important time in life came about, the big occasion, I was there.

"Take Dirksen for example, giving an exclusive interview on all the TV networks while he was buying a tux from me. And, you recall, we did the whole Kennedy inauguration. We shipped 2,000 suits down to Washington, six trailers loaded with clothes. There was a lot of controversy then over whether Kennedy would wear a top hat. I said he would. And he did.

"Every cutaway Daley ever wore was ours. Daley had his tuxedos made here. We imported the grey top hat from England for his daughter's wedding. He was a fashion plate, Daley. When the kids [Daley's sons] all went to the proms, the mayor would personally come in with them to see that they were fitted right."

Still, one wonders, especially in these free-and-easy times: Do clothes really make a man? Do we pander to, even foster a pseudo upper-class image with the whole tuxedo mystique?

"I don't think it was contradictory at all that Kennedy was at home playing touch football, and yet he wore a white tie and tails with the Queen of England," says Joel.

"What people are doing is emulating other people they look up to," Ben explains. "It's Hollywood! He's going to look at his picture for years afterward, and he's going to look like a duke to his family, always.

"The real bedrock of our business is middle-class America. They don't have huge country-club parties just because they are bored. Take Ford City—as blue-collar as you can get—and that's one of our biggest stores! People have always had a need to make special things—weddings, proms, celebrations—special!"

Later I leave Ben Gingiss high atop the Hancock and proceed with Joel through the white-collar, blue-collar streets to the source: The Gingiss warehouse, which supplies all the Gingiss stores in the Chicago area with more tuxes than anyone can imagine.

Along the way, a few more particulars. As to cost: "The average rental now is about $35, which included everything but shoes—five dollars extra. We have a suit as low as $29 and one as high as $42." (Actual value: $275.)

Style is an expensive factor. To add a new style to the line costs Gingiss about $140. There were five styles at the beginning of the tuxedo business. "Now we must have 27, 28 styles. Now there is style obsolescence as well as wear. We developed a policy of replacing it before it looked sad. Generally we feel we can get three seasons out of a tux. Back in the old days, it would be cleaned and pressed and altered thirty-two times. Today we get away from a lot of that alteration by buying three pairs of pants and one coat."

Joel Gingiss estimates the nation's formal-wear sales and rentals at $300 million annually, with some two million weddings each year. May is the biggest month, with most of the prom business concentrated in the last two weeks of that month and on into June weddings. But August has taken over as the biggest month for weddings, with September coming up fast.

The warehouse, from the outside, is an unimposing building at 555 West 14th Place. There is a store in the place where sales are held on old tuxedos. Roman Pisockyj, plant manager and recently promoted assistant vice-president, says in his inner office that by the end of prom week "We will have put out a total of 4,200 to 4,300 coats. Normally the event is on Friday or Saturday. They pick up on Thursday, and we expect the people to bring the tuxes back on Sunday."

Moving inside the warehouse, I spy another small room inhabited by an unheralded but valuable link in the Gingiss tuxedo line: Mannou Younan, a Lebanese, who is the master tailor on the premises. With needle in hand and thread in mouth, he manages to nod and smile. "He primarily works on damaged merchandise," explains Joel. "He is almost entirely remaking parts of these coats."

But the view beyond Mannou, the very soul of the warehouse, is almost too much for my eyes to absorb. I rub them, blink them, try to get some kind of bearing on this veritable horde of tuxedos. Rows of them! Rainbows of them! Tuxedos actually moving along a line by themselves, very mysteriously, like specters looking for a body to inhabit. There goes a yellow one . . . here comes that blue one again, assigned, it would seem, to some kind of limbo, remaining forever aloft, never to touch down again. . . .

This is it: Tuxedo Junction!

There is a cleaning and pressing room here. "Trousers are checked to make sure nothing is in them," explains Joel. The king of the cleaners is a smiling black man, C.C. Coleman (a Baptist minister), thirty years a Gingiss man and the ace spot remover of them all.

"C.C. can get out any spot that's ever been put in," smiles Joel confidently. "In fact, the American Dry Cleaning Institute calls him when it has a problem. He's our supervisor of dry cleaning."

What does C.C. stand for, C.C.? I ask the spot man.

"Caesar Cornelius," he smiles.

"I never knew that," says Joel. "He's always just been C.C."

The rebirth of a tuxedo follows an unalterable process at the Gingiss warehouse. From cleaning it moves on to a first inspection, where two people check the buttons, the lining, finally moving it down the line (a fully automated line that goes down, around, up, and down) where the tux mysteriously heads like a huge homing pigeon for its particular rack (style), roosting there momentarily till the pickers come by with orders to grace someone's body once again.

"Line fifteen takes them to a final check," explains Joel, "making certain that the proper order has been filled, that the suit is in good shape. Then it is bagged and sent down the line to be delivered to whatever store it is going to."

Like that light-blue tuxedo still going around and around the line, the tales of Ben Gingiss are endless and stay with you long after his own story has been told.

Like Abe Gibron: "Try fitting 350 pounds of Abe Gibron into a tuxedo."

Or Burr Tillstrom: "I even made tuxedos for Kukla and Ollie."

Or best of all: "I once got a call from a gentleman farmer in Michigan who wanted to buy a tuxedo, but it had to be one that had been worn by some special celebrity. So I sent him a tuxedo once worn by Sarge Shriver and charged him $200 for it. But the money didn't matter. He'd pay anything. He just wanted the tux to dress a scarecrow."

Nelson Algren (1909-1981):
Buried Alive in Chicago

"Well, we're all born equal and anyone in Chicago can now become an expatriate without leaving town."
—Algren

Some thoughts on a hometown writer who died not too long ago but was actually put to rest twice: first in Chicago and finally on the East Coast. Second City, Windy City. Lady of the Lake who likes playing hard to get. Chicago always had a knack for blowing away its toughest lovers, its most creative souls. "There are a number of answers to the old query about why writers so often take a one-way flight from Midway or O'Hare and never come back," he once said.

Algren was probably better understood and accepted in other parts of the world than the Chicago he captured in heightened prose, loved, honored, and, like no writer since Sandburg, came close to carrying forever on his big shoulders.

For it isn't so much a city as a vast way station where three and a half million bipeds swarm with a single cry, 'One side or a leg off, I'm gettin' mine!' It's every man for himself in this hired air. . . . Yet once you've come to be a part of this particular patch, you'll never love another. Like loving a woman with a broken nose, you may find lovelier lovelies. But never a lovely so real.

Algren was an extension of Sandburg, and the city's legitimate poetic heir. His *Chicago: City on the Make* remains the truest map of Chicago's heart ever penned. That book and Sandburg's *Chicago Poems*. Two American classics.

Algren was a joker, a comedian, a satirist, a fall guy. He laughed at himself and said many memorable things, including everybody's favorite piece of advice, "Never play cards with any man named Doc. Never eat at any place called Mom's. And never, ever, no matter what else you do in your whole life, never sleep with anyone whose troubles are worse than your own."

With Whitman he agreed: "There shall be no difference between them and the rest." He loved to mock the righteous, the pompous, the self-serving. Chi-

305

cago newspapers (editors and columnists in particular) were among his favorite targets. They, in turn, took pot shots at him. They were none too pleased with his love poem to the hometown, *Chicago: City on the Make*. The Chicago *Daily News* called for "revocation of the author's poetic license," while the *Tribune* held its nose: "A more partial, distorted, unenviable slant was never taken by a man pretending to cover the Chicago story—a book unlikely to please anyone but masochists—definitely a highly-scented object." Algren retorted, "a busy little object who didn't smell too sweet himself typed busily away at *The Tribune*: the job of assistant travel editor was open."

Division Street had more soul than Lake Shore Drive (the Gold Coast, the Near North, Kenilworth, and City Hall). The average junkie, card shark, pool hall hustler and prostitute harbored more human decency in his book than most downtown merchants, politicians and publishers, including the late great Colonel McCormick of the Chicago *Tribune*.

Therefore its poets pull the town one way while its tycoons' wives pull it another, its gunmen making it the world's crime capital while its educators beat the bushes for saints. Any old saints. And everytime a Robert Hutchins or a Robert Morss Lovett pulls it half an inch out of the mud, a Hearst or an Insull or a McCormick shoves it down again by sheer weight of wealth and venality.

But you takes your swipes at the powers-that-be in Chicago (or at the New York Literary Establishment) and eventually you pays. As New York refused to accept his kind of town, his kind of writing, Chicago refused to acknowledge its writer with the golden hands as one of the boldest sluggers to throw a knockout punch in any literary slugfest, anywhere in the world. Even Papa, when asked who was the greatest American writer, answered, "Faulkner." And when asked for other names, simply said, "Algren." Even Papa recognized the power of the streetfighter from Chicago climbing into the literary ring: "This is a man writing and you should not read it if you cannot take a punch. Mr. Algren can hit with both hands and move around and he will kill you if you are not awfully careful," said Hemingway.

"Great qualities of insight into people, a heart of pity, a gift of cadence and song," countered Sandburg, "and often when you're near heartbreak, he throws in comic relief."

Chicago's gusty winds of indifference blew cold in Algren's face. He wasn't writing the "big" books—not after *Never Come Morning, The Neon Wilderness, The Man with the Golden Arm, Chicago: City on the Make, A Walk on the Wild Side*. It was almost as if the wind had stolen his breath, taken his art, his heart away. After *A Walk on the Wild Side* (1956), the city, the country, the world would wait almost twenty-five years for the next novel, *The Devil's Stocking* (published posthumously). "A woman once told me that I was a devil's stocking—knitted backwards," claimed Algren.

306

Indifference, neglect, contempt . . . "nobody knows my name." Chicago was full of it. The Lady of the Lake offered him hard lessons in the art of unrequited love. "You can belong to New Orleans," Algren admitted. "You can belong to Boston or San Fransisco. You might conceivably—however clandestinely—belong to Philadelphia. But you can't belong to Chicago any more than you can belong to the flying saucer called Los Angeles. For it isn't so much a city as it is a drafty hustler's junction in which to hustle awhile and move on out of the draft." Eventually he moved on and out of the draft.

In 1975 he too took a one-way junket out of the City That Didn't Care Enough and headed toward the East Coast (to work on the book that would become his last novel, *The Devil's Stocking*) and eventually die somewhat a stranger from Chicago, buried in a strange land—Sag Harbor, New York. THE END IS NOTHING THE ROAD IS ALL reads his gravestone. Chicago still owes him. We'll leave it to the ghost of Algren to pick up the marker someday.

I recall only a few years ago, thumbing through the card file of the main Chicago Public Library and discovering most of his works unlisted, including *Chicago: City on the Make*. True, Algren was never very kind to those forces within the city which refused to recognize the humanity he happened to find amongst Chicago's losers: thugs, addicts, gamblers, murderers, prostitutes, con artists, all those living on the edge with no voice of their own. The gospel, as he interpreted it, still belonged to Whitman:

I feel I am of them
I belong to those convicts and prostitutes myself
And henceforth I will not deny them
For how can I deny myself?

That was his real strength, his faith. It was for them he wrote. For them he gave voice, and in so doing, found his own, rendering it into a language both real and lyrical that became literature far beyond the boundaries of Chicago: "The nameless, useless nobodies who sleep behind the taverns, who sleep beneath the El. Who sleep in burnt-out buses with the windows freshly curtained; in winterized chicken coops or patched-up truck bodies. The useless, helpless nobodies nobody knows; that go as the snow goes, where the wind blows, there and there and there, down any old cat-and-ashcan alley at all."

Aspiring writers everywhere had their Hemingway for a model of prose, a model of macho. But no manchild dreaming himself a writer in any Chicago neighborhood could remain untouched by the power of the Man with the Golden Arm. Algren was King of the Hill. And his shadow loomed large down every Chicago street, gangway, alley, and under the El tracks. (It looms even larger today in his absence.)

I have friends who spoke of him fondly as "Nelson." I know writers who claim they knew Algren very well. I never met the man at all. I hungered for

307

news about him from Herman Kogan, Paul Romaine, John Fink, Jay Robert Nash, and any publication that merely mentioned his name. I hoped to bump into him one day on some Chicago street or in Paul Romaine's bookstore.

Once, when a meeting might have happened (something arranged by a writer friend), connections were missed, dates bungled, and shortly thereafter I was the dreamy young writer on a one-way ride to Europe, and he was the Old Master boarding a ship for the Far East. Our paths never crossed. (I'm not sure I had the confidence to face him, anyway, for I'd heard he was very rough in the presence of admirers.)

In the end, all I really had were his books, his words. When I found myself in the high school classroom, I passed them on to others. (I was always teaching Chicago to kids in the grassy western suburbs whose parents were hell-bent protecting them from the experience. And Chicago to me was Sandburg, Farrell, Richard Wright, Gewndolyn Brooks, Petrakis, Sydney J. Harris, Royko, Studs Terkel on WMFT, and Algren, of course.)

"This is Nelson Algren," I'd say. "This is Chicago." And I'd begin reading him aloud, surprised to hear my own voice turn close to song:

An October sort of city even in spring. With someonebody's washing always whipping, in smoky October colors off the third-floor rear by that same wind that drives the yellowing comic strips down all the gutters that lead away from home. A hoarse-voiced extry-hawking newsie of the city.

By its padlocked poolrooms and its nightshade neon, by it carbon Chirsts punching transfers all night long; by its nuns studying gin-fizz ads in the Englewood Local, you shall know Chicago.

By nights when the salamanders of the El bend all one way and the cold rain runs with the red-lit rain. By the way the city's million wires are burdened only by lightest snow; and the old year yet lighter upon them. When chairs are stacked and glasses are turned and arc-lamps all are dimmed. By days when the wind bangs alley gates ajar and the sun goes by on the wind. By nights when the moon is an only child above the measured thunder of the cars, you may know Chicago's heart at last.

It was Algren on a roll. You could hardly stop his words from singing. And when I seriously began to write, the sound of his prose echoed and echoed and echoed in my head.

And when I cut the ties to a fulltime job (salary, pension, insurance, security) and began to live the writer's life of insecurity, it was often the knowledge of Algren just eking out a quiet, Chicago neighborhood existence that spurred me on.

Hollywood (Otto Preminger) had taken him to the cleaners on movie rights to *The Man with the Golden Arm.* A "big" book, it had taken years to write, and it would take Algren years and years to write another as good, with no guarantee of success. And the literary hustlers were raking in fortunes manufacturing bestsellers, and where was the greatest American writer next to Faulkner? Holed up in his Wicker Park flatt, playing a little poker, doing a little journalism, existing on book reviews and the kindness of friends, his writing growing more and more unfashionable, unable to command big bucks from big New York houses. Algren moving into the field of also-rans and has-beens.

"No, I won't do another big book," he told H.E.F. Donohue in a fascinating book called *Conversations With Nelson Algren.* "There's no chance of thinking about a big book. . . . You've got to cut everything else out. You're never free . . . unless you're able to do stuff that's been done before, like the battle of Chickamauga. If you're able to go to a library and reconstruct fifteenth-century London or something—that's one way to do a book. But I don't have any way of doing a reconstruction thing. The only way I can write is to try to make something that hasn't been done before, and in order to do that you can't just take notes. You have to be there. You write about your own reactions to the scene. And you have to get all the details that nobody knows about. You have to be specific."

Here was Algren keeping the faith in a literary world running more and more amuck.

Some years later in New York he told Jimmy Breslin, "People say to me, 'When are you going to give us the big one?' I say, 'When you start reading the little ones.' "

I've also come to respect the fact that Algren had little use for academics, who never understood just who the hell he was and where he was coming from. His works just didn't fit the old patterns. They thought (still think) you write novels about literature, while Algren made literature out of life.

I like the fact that in a moment of weakness he accepted an invitation to teach at the Iowa University Writing Workshop (see "Hand in Hand Through the Greenery" in *The Last Carousel*) where mostly he played poker, acted the wise guy, and was eventually fired. Take the money and run—an old Chicago street game Algren knew well. And when you get a chance, bite back: "Its Creative Writers' Workshop is a good place to go to become a tourist. For it provides sanctuary from those very pressures in which creativity is forged. If you want to create something of your own, stay away."

Sometimes I wonder how Algren might have survived the country, how a Division Street aficionado would have dealt with an acre of birch. There is so little of nature in all his writing.

I recall he once left Chicago for the Indiana Dunes to face, no doubt, Ma Nature herself, not to mention the ghost of Mr. Thoreau who haunts the heart of evey American writer. "So, what's this all about?" I can see the puzzled look on Nelson Algren's face. The closest he ever came to extolling the virtues of country was probably the Hawthorne racetrack. Algren high-tailed it back to Chicago from the Dunes before anyone really knew he had left.

I was in Chicago when I heard of Algren's death. I recall scouring the major bookstores downtown in search of his work, for one book in particular, *The Last Carousel*, which I had loaned to someone and was never returned. But not a single title of Algren's could be found on any bookshelf.

I asked the man at the information desk of one of those computerized bookstore chains if they had Algren's *The Last Carousel*.

"Who?" he asked. I repeated the full name, adding, "The Chicago writer."

"How do you spell it?" he asked. I spelled it.

He glanced over his shoulder to call the name out to a woman who was checking the inventory on another machine.

"Algren?" she questioned, mispronouncing his name, then laughing out loud.

Nelson would appreciate that, I thought. The irony. The humor of the situation. The laughter. Though he, no doubt, would have the last laugh:

" 'Laughing even as an ignorant fighter laughs, who has never lost a battle,' the white-haired poet wrote before his hair turned white.

"But the quality of our laughter has altered since that appraisal, to be replaced by something sounding more like a juke-box running down in a deserted bar. Chicago's laughter has grown metallic, the city no longer laughs easily and well, out of spiritual good health. We seem to have no way of judging either the laughter of the living or the fixed smirk of the dead."

Sing a Song for Van Buren Street

State Street remains, historically, that Great Street, Michigan's a Magnificent Mile, and even Wack, Wack, Wacker Drive has a song going for it. But who sings of old Van Buren Street, groveling there like a lost hymn under the El tracks, holding the line of the Loop's south end?

If you start west down Van Buren from Michigan, you're nowhere . . . you've only just begun. Burrough's is on one corner, the prized Adler & Sullivan Auditorium Building on the other. Signs lead you to believe this is the Central Chicago Bike Trail, and also ILL US 34 and ILL US 66, but there's no refrain or even kicks on this part of old Route 66.

A touch of elegance, then, for a beginning of this block: the Chicago Club entrance with its esoteric Night Bell button: Joseph P. McMahon, Florists. But then at 61 E. Van Buren: STORE FOR LEASE 708 Sq. Feet. Vacancy . . . a sign of the times?

On the northeast corner of Van Buren and Wabash, a new red building looms ghostly, smugly, and seemingly so out of place: CNA Plaza. Lights on in the lobby but deserted. Another artificial architectural wonder of our Chicago times where perspectives of old buildings bordering old streets are methodically replaced by monuments that somehow shut out all the life despite the infinite invitation of glass.

CNA, let me in! Open this red-metal cage! The pulse of Van Buren beats beside you. (Maybe the view from the top is different, but that's so out of reach.)

Ducking momentarily into Old St. Mary's across the street . . . another shot at ultra modern for old Van Buren, the facade looking like a tiled shower in suburbia. The interior sports an altar like sculpture, a flashy-restaurant style. Lord, pass the thousand island dressing, please. But who's to deny comfort and solace wherever and however you find it, especially along Van Buren St.? One woman, seated, holds her hands and her head in prayer, while one man stands in the aisle wondering, wondering.

Outside . . . I'm hit! Scccrrrrrrreeeeeeeeeccch! The El crying above in its bend down Wabash . . . and Van Buren, suddenly, lovingly, coming alive. Clack, clack, clack . . . screeech . . . screeee . . . stretching the sound out till it tingles along the spine, while pigeons splash in the air.

Roll, you motha, roll! I shout to the iron-trellised heavens. Who can hear me now, huh? Who says Old St. Mary's has the corner on faith, hope, and charity . . . not to mention peace and joy? Give me a screeching El above my head any damned day! Thank God for such a wonder. My first flight was the Douglas Park El, going up to the top at Pulaski, hovering above Van Buren some twenty minutes later. El, you were my 747. May you hang up there forever!

Under the tracks now, across the street to Pixley & Ehlers. P & E's are special places for downtown people; they will never win any awards for great food, or ever be listed in all our Chicago guides for trendy dining adventures. Yet P & E will be there when you need it. When it's a bad day, when your head is hanging somewhere down around your ankles, when you're lost in the metaphysics of the Loop, when you're down to your last two bits, when you prefer everyone in the world to just leave you alone. . . then Pixley's has a place for you.

This one on Van Buren today advertises MIDGET HAMBURGERS 18 cents. I think a Midget Hamburger for breakfast is just a real fine suggestion for Van Buren St. in the morning.

Inside, I recognize the decor immediately: instant depression. Same old orange chairs, wobbly tables, and gravy colored food for the down and out downtowners . . . 2 eggs, potatoes, tomato juice, roll & butter, 99 cents . . . oven baked beans, roll & butter, 77 cents.

"I'll take five midget hamburgers and a cup of coffee."

"We don't sell no midget hamburgers no more."

I should have known that was just an old sign of the way things were down Van Buren St. I'll just have a cup of coffee. And please, don't change the sign.

Stepping off again, crossing the alley behind Goldblatt's, I pause to praise pigeons, alleys, and lamp posts all alive and well and living along Van Buren. Here's to downtown alleys baroqued in black fire escapes, pigeons reflectively roosting over love and death in every crevice, and intricate old lamp posts lost in the insignificance of their incandescent days.

State and Van Buren, a crossroads of sorts in old Chicago. One of the busiest El stops in CTA lore. Sears on one corner, Goldblatt's on the other, shoppers hurridly rattling up and down those heavy stairs. And, years ago, Minsky's Burlesque just a few doors down State. I went to hear the comics. And study the mechanics of pasties with propellers.

And approximately at this point, heading west, Van Buren's history comes home to roost. Minsky's is gone, but there's an Adult Book Store on the southwest corner, and for the next few blocks a heavy air of desperation hangs about the street, relieved here and there by a couple of stores with some history, good restaurants, and a few landmarks.

Ah, dirty old Van Buren with pigeons in your hair, newspapers drifting down the block, broken booze bottles in the gutter glinting in the sun, lost men bumping around, intersected as you are by sinister, sisterly South State, you have seen better days, and may live to sing a survival song of sorts.

You're on the drawing boards, no doubt, of our urban renewal visionaries: Banish the bums! Build the new city college! Poison the pigeons! Dismantle the

El! Let the sun shine in! Rendering is the architectural lingo . . . surrendering is the usual result.

And when they finally pull you apart screeching from under the elevated tracks, drive out the pigeons and the honkytonk people, administer face lifts to those buildings of some promise, pave the streets smooth and, by God, even plant trees! Van Buren your song will be stilled, and your name only a legend.

But for the moment, Van Buren lives in a haze of boozy breath and the flash of iron wheels. A bum burrows in the waste basket looking for crumbs and yesterday's news, while a man with tavern pallor descends into Ye Old Corner Cellar Restaurant to heighten his day.

In keeping with the Van Buren Street elan, there's a Wig Store, a Jiffy Tie Store, and an Earring Store, 95 cents. Not to mention the first of those classic Heartbreak Hotels at 12 W. Van Buren called, simply: HOTEL . . . Low Rates. Hot and Cold Water in Every Room. One of those last stop places for Chicago wayfarers at the end of their lines.

Next door, the Rialto Tap with a sign in the window: WE SERVE ALCOHOLICS.

And another with a mirror inviting the streetwalker to SEE THE FOOL. The Rialto and Van Buren don't especially appeal to any subtlety in men's hearts.

A couple of jewelry stores, pawnbrokers and then the Plymouth Hotel . . . FOR MEN ONLY Permanent-Transient. All the dark windows seem scaled in grime and nailed shut forever. One, opened a crooked crack, admits a ray of sun for a dying plant. Green is not Van Buren's color.

Working the south side of the street now (across from the Rialto Tap) I stand before Stebbin's Hardware with windows chock full of neat displays: mailboxes, scissors, locks, brooms, lamps, all kinds of tools . . . a store any Chicago neighborhood would be proud of. Yet here it sits, almost lost in the Van Buren Loop.

Manager Stebbin Younger says that though he's been in the business only 20 years, the hardware store has operated on Van Buren since the early 1900s.

Who patronizes such a hidden hardware store? "Everybody. Insurance men, office people, suburban shoppers, builders. We have lots of everything. They know they can find a greater selection of pure hardware items here than most stores."

And how's old Van Buren Street these days? "Oh, it's pretty much the same. It's always been the honky tonk area of South State, always kind of underneath the elevated . . . probably not the most desirable location, but we've been able to conduct a decent hardware business over many years. We'd like to stay, but the Chicago City Junior College plans to take these whole two blocks from State to Plymouth, Jackson to Congress. We'll just have to wait and see."

A few doors down is Bailey's Military Uniforms, whose ads I've seen in the newspapers for years. I can still remember looking down upon this store from the El when, a small World War II child, I envied every uniform in the window.

Once inside, it's obvious that Bailey's has seen better days. With the U.S. pretty much out of the war business at the moment, and heroics at a low level, there's not great rush for military glamour. Dust settles heavily in Bailey's. The sales people are all at parade rest. Faded stripes and ribbons . . . unpressed and out of date uniforms . . . it's a military museum of sorts . . . a Battle Hymn of the Republic sung backwards.

I try the old chain of command, but nobody will talk, not even a name, rank, or serial. Finally, someone squeezes out a few answers. To him, I'm just holding up the war.

"52 years in operation . . . Bailey's? Originally the name came from Barnum. So when we took over, we took out some of the letters from the sign to read 'Bailey's'. Always a combination store. At one time we did three times the business we do now. So now they buy work clothes, fatigue pants, surplus, anything military. . . .

"Camping is the biggest now. We got camping . . . and western riding apparel, English riding apparel . . . boots and shoes. Van Buren hasn't changed much. The people are afraid. The college? Huh, you tell me? We're not even thinking of that yet."

There's the Dill Pickle Delicatessen & Sandwich shop on the corner of Plymouth Court and Van Buren, serving hot corned beef on Rosen's rye. And the Fisher Building across the street, it's grand old entrance and design contrasted, Chicago-architecturally, with a couple of cool, modern upstarts just under the El tracks down the street: the Amalgamated Trust & Saving Bank (Michigan Ave. sophisticate beyond redemption) and the new Federal Penitentiary, rising above the whole crusty Van Buren scene like a Claes Oldenberg sculpture in honor of the computer card.

The whole south side of the street at this point, between Dearborn and Clark, gets unbearably classy and glassy now, opening up with grass and trees and sky alongside the elevated tracks. Even the pigeons seem to have abandoned the scene in confusion.

To recapture the old reality, I tune in again to the vibrations of the El and glance across the street, where the Esquire Hotel languishes in splendid squalor above the Beacon Discount Center.

And here comes the world's oldest flower lady, right down the middle of the street, underneath the patterned sunlight filtering through the tracks. She wears a long printed gown. Her gray hair is flecked with a bygone red. She carries a purse and a shopping bag. She's pushing seventy or maybe she's immortal. She's shopping for hope this sunny morning down Van Buren Street.

I brave the entrance to the Esquire Hotel, with the smell of old smoke and stale beer. DOORS MUST BE CLEAR AT ALL TIMES. Upstairs, a large lobby of old wooden tables and busted chairs . . . a blaring TV . . . men sitting

314

around everywhere untangling lost dreams, determinedly not seeing anything. Gold Eagle Liquor waits, for now, forever, at the corner of Van Buren and Clark.

Looking up and west from the corner of LaSalle, another remembrance of Chicago things past . . . the old, ochre colored El station with the tiny bare light bulbs hanging down . . . Van Buren rococo.

And just across the street, the granddaddy Van Buren Street institution of them all (characteristically misnomered) the LaSalle Street Station . . . allll aboarrrrrrrrd! If you have a thing about train depots, here's an old dying dinosaur.

A study in sadness, a mighty station now a mere shell. Trains and people pass through like shadows. The Rock Island Line may have been a mighty fine line, but today the emptiness of the tracks and the stillness of the depot leaves a manchild lingering at Gate 7, wishing the new world still had old-world symphonies of steam engines, bells, and whistles that wooed one through the night.

Now there's the Blue Island Suburban Line coming through, they say. And the Joliet Main Line. Train passengers have been replaced by commuters. Three people sit down on the long wooden benches. There's not a Red Cap in sight, all the trains are numb, and the shoeshine man sits alone in his own chair.

How's business? "A few in the morning . . . a few at lunch."

Outside, across the street, almost next door, the Ft. Dearborn Hotel sits solemnly, once inextricably linked to the life of LaSalle Street Station, once, at a time along with Van Buren, when railroads and Chicago were one. With the depot only a memory, the Ft. Dearborn Hotel holds on like an aged harlot to her baubles, bangles and beads. Mahogany walls of burnished lustre, brass stool ashtrays on the floor, paintings, crystal chandeliers imported from Italy.

I talk to Thelma Defort, a resident of some twenty years, who is pinch hitting for the manager today. "The hotel has been here some sixty years and had five hundred rooms. People nowadays look for places where they can park their cars. They want to be close to everything. So we're mostly permanent guests now . . . we're two-thirds permanent. We have two ladies who have been here since '39 and one since '38."

"Van Buren these days . . . it's dirty, so dirty. They're trying like hell to make it survive though. But after five the place is deserted. Not like when the trains used to run. Still, this is a very nice hotel. We try to keep the riff-raff out. Sometimes we miss but not often. Everybody who stays here with us is pretty famous. I'd like to see it [Van Buren] come alive again. But I'll never see it in my time . . . never."

For me, this part of the street is the end of the line for Van Buren. Up ahead the El loops northward, it's character diminished. What comes after isn't half so captivating. Criss-crossing my way back now, I weave here and there around corners in the hopes of some final discoveries.

Around the corner from the Esquire Hotel, just a few feet down Federal Street, which lingers there like an alley, drunks and sleepers and wide-awake people holding up the walls, hangs a sign: FEDERAL INN. Dust, darkness, and an ominous entranceway. I lean in and give it a whirl.

Surprise indeed! These are not the people I left behind on Federal Street or the Esquire lobby. By God, a vision of a Michigan Avenue class hideaway with smart people dressed to the teeth. Can this be? Off Van Buren Street?

Squeezing into a spot at the bar, blinking to ease off a back alley blindness, I order a quick gin and tonic, perusing the place in celebration of my find. Perfect, absolutely perfect for an assignation. I coax a menu from a beautiful waitress, and my mouth waters over all the possibilities . . . Lobster, Fresh Ocean Perch, Colorado Brook Trout Almondine . . . all reasonably priced.

Bartender, what's the deep dark secret to this place? I find the owner, Frank Bianchi (in partnership with Gerald Slaterilli) who lays on a little history, in between seating customers and handling reservations.

"One way or another this restaurant has been in existence for the past sixty years. It's gone under various names . . . Happy's Cape Cod for twenty years. The Federal Inn since 1966. We deal with a multitude of people . . . insurance brokers, commodity brokers from the Board of Trade, Continental Bank People, lawyers and FBI men. We're close to all of them." (Wouldn't you know the FBI cased this place before me!)

We kick Van Buren Street around a little more. "The location," Bianchi confesses, "because of its very confinement, is known mostly through word of mouth . . . strictly a five-day, out of the way operation."

Shhhhh, I feel like thanking him as I turn up my collar and leave through another entrance . . . which immediately destroys all the mystery for me: suddenly I find myself in a brightly lit foyer. For the Federal Inn, in all honesty, is on the first floor of the famous Monadnock Building, another architectural wonder, the highest brick-walled building in Chicago, designed by Burnham and Root in 1891 and bordering both Van Buren and Jackson. For me, though, a lover of all mystique, the Federal Inn shall always remain a kind of nefarious and wonderful spot to be entered from Federal Street, and preferably after a long walk down Van Buren.

I hit a place called Quincy #9 on Plymouth Court for a quick beer and a good steak sandwich. The atmosphere is "timeless neighborhood tavern. Homey . . . "We've got the oldest liquor license in Chicago," says the bartender. "We don't cater here to no Van Buren types."

Just across from Quincy #9 on Plymouth Court is a place called Binyons. Caught in the middle between Jackson and Van Buren, with the John Law school next door and the Standard Club across the street, Binyons don't 'specially cater to no Van Buren honkytonk people, neither.

A green-striped awning entrance, three beautifully furnished floors for dining, and 128 years of Chicago history somehow deadens the memories of that dirty old street down the way. With a Chef's Special luncheon today of a Baked Stuffed Pork Chop going for $3.25 plus a full meal (lunch and dinner) packed with suggestions such as Turtle Soup, Smoked Thueringer, Chilled Alaskan

Crab Legs and home made Apple Strudel in brandy sauce, who cares if anyone's feeding the Van Buren Street pigeons?

Hal Binyon himself explains, "Since 1925 we've expanded from one floor to three floors. It's a family operation. I'm the second generation, and I have two sons. The cusine? German at one time, but now we're pretty much Americanized.

"Board of Trade customers, Federal Building people . . . the whole financial district. We cater to some of the merchants from Van Buren too. They talk about revitalizing it [the street], and with the new city college we have been advised that they are going to try to relocate us."

From the heights of Binyons, I descend once more down Van Buren Street for a final fling under the El tracks, sauntering a street that rolls under foot for many a honkytonk man, remembering and suddenly laughing out loud at the epithet Frank Bianchi of the Federal Inn hurled at the street:

"Van Buren? I've always called it Pigeon Shit Alley, but with the changes coming about, I see nothing but an upgrading of the area."

The El rumbles, a drunk whistles "Tea For Two," LaSalle Street Station sends one slow train down the tracks. Pigeon Shit Alley stands on its final leg while I step to the Van Buren Street shuffle, downbeating it all the way home with a lone pigeon pecking out time behind me, covering my tracks.

317

Dance With Me Petros!

The parking lot is full across from the Dianna's Restaurant "Opaa" on Halsted. The bouzouki music pours out into the dark Chicago night, warming the heart, teasing the senses of any stranger on the street. The Greeks, of course, have a word for it: *Filoxenia*—love for the stranger. And for me, for many non-Greeks and Greeks alike, the Dianna is home.

Inside the saganaki (flaming cheese) is on fire at every table, the avgolemono (egg lemon soup) begs to be slurped, and platters of roast lamb tantalize any mouth especially conditioned with bottles of retsina or roditis.

The chanting begins . . . Petros, a 6-foot-2 reincarnation of Alexis Zorba, Chicago-style, is kissing all the women at the door, laughing with all the men, table hopping, gesturing to his waiters in great classical Grecian sweeps, waving a large Macanudo cigar proudly between his fingers and lips, listening for the crescendo of the chanting, laughingly, lovingly cheering them on: "PETROS! PETROS! PETROS!" His invitation to dance.

"Welcome home, cousin," he smiles, and pours the red wine, "I'll be with you. First, I got to dance."

The Greek experience. You can travel the world a stranger and receive nothing but the cold shoulder, but then you move into Greece where you are hit simultaneously with a landscape that brings you down to your knees, and then a people who pick you up again with a bear hug, invite you into their lives and share their joy. You wonder why the hell you ever bothered to travel anywhere else in the world. Petros is like that.

I remember first seeing him as a waiter in the old Diana Grocery, in the '60s, just down the street a few blocks. His brother Pete seemed to run most of the show. Petros had just recently come over as an ex-schoolteacher to learn the Greek restaurant business.

The old Diana Grocery was a classic village tavern: nothing fancy. Real. Groceries in front, a small restaurant in back . . . the smell of olives and feta cheese, lamb, bread, wine, would knock you out at the door, carry you aloft on a pure Mediterranean high. There was always laughter, always music. And on

319

Friday and Saturday night, always a long line waiting for tables in the back.

But then Pete, or the brother Ted, or the new waiter Petros, would come out of nowhere, hand an empty glass to everyone waiting in line, break open a bottle of Metaxa, and we would drink to Greece, or to Pete, or to just waiting for an empty table. "God bless America and all the Greeks!" was the usual toast of the Kogiones bothers. No one, no restaurant in Chicago, ever treated its customers (the stranger) with such hospitality.

As a young waiter in the old Diana Petros was quiet, somewhat serious. He didn't use the English language much. Pete the sheriff, in his cowboy hat, and Ted, with his great mustache and hugs for the women, dominated the scene.

Gradually Petros began to loosen, began kidding the women, kissing them. And then the time came when Petros began to dance with the other waiters, with the guests, and finally alone, balancing a glass of wine on his head. We all loved him and cheered him on.

In the spacious mod-Greek elegance of his new Dianna's "Opaa," we relive some of this past. I try my damndest to get behind the good Greek's act (if it is one) which he has raised to an art. If you harbor the slightest bit of Chicago cynicism in your heart ("Never eat at a place called Mom's"), then Petros is the big Greek con artist. Yet if there is the smallest bit of affection in your soul for all that is human and alive, then Petros is the surest sign of real life you'll find anywhere in the city. And getting whacked out with him over good wine and food at the Dianna has to be about the best and only way to survive on these sometimes mean city streets.

"I came back from Nestani," he tells me, "around Tripoli . . . 1961. I was a schoolteacher. I got my diploma from the Pedagogical Academy of Tripolis, prepared to teach elementary. But I only taught for a month and a half. Listen, cousin," he laughs, "I was very revolutionary. Why? Because I always thought the kids were as good as the teacher!"

He gets up again, to kiss another woman, greet another guest . . . all "cousins," as he refers to anyone who steps into the Dianna. Petros is a man who cannot sit still. For Petros, to live is to move. And Petros seems everywhere at once, though always returning to take up the thread of conversation, or to explode with his two favorite expressions: "Opaa!" a kind of Greek trademark he popularized at the old Diana, and "fantastic!" which he uses more and more these days with a Greek flavor, emphasizing the syllables till the word sounds something like "van-tas-tic!"

His understanding of Greek food goes back to his own home, and his experience in the army, where he was in charge of the Officer's Club, and where, according to Petros, "I was exposed to the very best. We had civilian cooks, and we prepared food for the lowest class officer to the highest. Two chefs, up to colonels. And from there on we had special cooks for the generals. Prince Constantine ate there . . . and commanders of NATO!"

320

We talk of the old Diana's, and his explanation of what went on back there in 1961. "The main emphasis at that time was the grocery. They [his brothers] had opened a restaurant three years before that—no chef, no waiter, they just served a bite to eat.

"I told them we should bring in a chef . . . my brothers would prepare a casserole of lamb a day. I was the waiter, the busboy, the dishwasher. We did not serve more than fifteen meals a day. At the same time, I was going to school—Industrial Engineering College. Later, I transferred to the Central YMCA where I study psychology, business administration . . . English. I knew very little English."

Old Greek Town was changing at this time, though. Circle Campus would be coming in. As Petros describes it, "The Greeks were leaving, most of them going to Central and Harrison and Lawrence Avenue. From 532 Halstead, we moved to 310." And it was there, at the old Diana, where the Kogiones brothers developed their style, and where Petros, in a sense, was born, and remained for ten years.

Speaking of the first restaurant he explains, "I brought in all the students from the Industrial College one time. Look, I told them, why not come here for dinner at very low prices? I told them I'd buy their dinner, if they wanted to. But they paid anyway. And for the first time, the place was filled up—seven tables!

"Then I went to the YMCA and one night I brought all the teachers over, on me. But the next day, they sent me a check for $110!"

Throughout the conversation Petros is interrupted again and again by his guests, his "cousins" . . . women, especially, who seem to hover about him, appear out of nowhere. Petros, sending out this "van-tas-tic!" Greek energy whereby he can look in the eyes of a woman ten tables away, and within minutes she has her arms around him.

"What happened?" he says to another. "Don't I deserve a kiss tonight? . . . Ah, I love you, I love you!"

Returning to his success story (a woman trailing her hand across his shoulder) he explains, "That's when I decided if the place was going to make it, we had to work with the Americans. So we stayed there till 1963, Before we left, the seven tables were packed. Then we moved to 310 [the Diana Grocery] and we doubled the space. We got more waiters, more chefs, more everything. That was the one big thing which became an institution! All the brothers (Peter, Ted, George, Demos) were working there, and I was in charge of the dining room. We were there ten years, and then I opened the Dianna's Opaa." (All the brothers were involved, but rather in the background, with only Petros in full command.)

"Opaa!" he yells, for the hell of it, and all the restaurant (seating some three hundred people) returns the call. "Van-tas-tic!" he laughs, claps, waves his hands, and puffs away on another cigar.

Opaa, I say. Translate it.

"Hurray!" he says . . . "Ole! Higher up . . . either in spirit or you can be up

321

physically. Whenever I was in a taverna, and we had a little extra drink, we went 'Opaa!' I used to do a little dance, the *hassapiko* . . . no mistakes to be made as long as you are rhythmical. Then I put a wine glass on my head, and gradually I created the stability. Then I put a bottle on my head, and everybody went 'Opaa!'"

Petros the performer, then. But Petros the restaurateur also. "About a year and a half after I came, I heard so much that the customer is always right. How could I be right when I knew nothing about their customs, their food? So at Dianna's I said: 'I come first! You come second . . . for your own good!'

"I know that my criterion is best, is much higher than anybody else in the business. I am the most educated in Greece, from Greece for the Greek restaurant men. I was more educated at the academy than anybody else. Furthermore, I was experienced to what the best was served to the highest ambassadors, to even the king!"

His personal Grecian formula: "You must like people! And you must like what you're doing . . . if I might say, love. Second, you must believe in it. You must buy the very best meat, U.S. Choice. We don't serve anything here that I don't like! It has to be good for me first, or I don't serve it. Concern! You must treat everybody as a VIP."

Petros is warming up now. It's the wine, it's the women, it's the sight of his Dianna filling up with the late night crowd, everyone enjoying his share of "The Greek experience" which Petros and I are still trying to define.

"I think my secret is women," he says. "I treat all women as ladies. And they are all beautiful as far as I'm concerned. I was kissed in appreciation by my first customer. We have no customers, by the way. They are all guests, friends . . . yes, cousins!"

We return to the way Petros, and others, have in a sense "marketed" an entire people, a way of life. How receptive Chicagoans have been toward this. The givingness of the Greek people. And now Petros, so often buying drinks, bottles of wine, entire meals for his "cousins" for no reason at all.

"I think we represent Greece at its best. First of all by not taking advantage of the ethnic food that it presents. You get a good name for something Greek when you present quality. Dianna's happens to be better than anybody else because of my beliefs. Second, to be seated in a pleasant atmosphere. Third, occasionally I do buy them a bottle of wine or a drink. Fourth, the guest deserves the best attention. That's why our motto is WELCOME HOME! It means that everybody is like a guest at my home. And that is because of my father who had an open house in the village. Always, strangers came by and my father invited them in. You must not think of dollars. Do your job right, and the money will be there. I want everybody to be happier than when they came in."

Petros is invited to another table for a drink. Wherever he moves around the restaurant, hands reach out for his, women stand to be kissed! His presence is incredible—a modern Greek myth of his own making. There isn't a politician,

322

preacher or pope who wouldn't like some of that adulation. McDonald's has its golden arches; the colonel has his Kentucky fried hustle; but Petros has his heritage, his "Opaa!" his own self.

Showtime now . , . Petros, standing tall in the middle of the room, makes a few announcements: "We serve the best!" applause, whistles, opaas. He asks for silence, and when he doesn't quite get it at one table, he gently reprimands them: "I come first . . . or else get out of here!" Applause . . . foot stamping. "I was born to teach, not to be taught!" More laughter, including his own. "I would like at this time to say—if you are something, and you don't like it, change it! And if you don't like it the second time around—that's too bad!" More applause, whistles . . . Petros turning around in circles, laughing, yelling out: "VAN-TAS-TIC!"

"It is the custom," Petros continues, "to celebrate happy events such as birthdays, anniversaries, divorces . . ." which brings laughter and applause. "And also tonight we have a couple who have managed to live together for forty-one years! Mr. and Mrs. Morris. Let's give them a hand. OK! You are all beautiful. We have celebrated everything tonight. Applaud yourselves, everybody! Opaa!!"

While Petros is closing down his act for the moment, I turn to a table behind me and ask one of the women, Gloria, for her off-the-record impressions of the man. "He's a friend to me," she says. "Very different. Oh, I think all European men are different. And Petros . . . with Petros he just makes you feel special, feel sexy."

To the point where most women are dying to go to bed with him? "Listen, don't say that . . . that's how I lost one of my boyfriends! I don't care how he is with other women, as long as he's a friend. He makes each one feel special."

Or, as the other woman, Pam, says with a smile, "He's got a beautiful way of bullshitting." She came tonight because "I wanted something different. Petros has a way of making people feel comfortable. When he talks to you, it's as a person. The fact that he makes me feel like a person, that's why I came. You go to any other restaurant, and you just go there to eat."

Petros returns, notices the woman named Pam hasn't finished her steak. "Listen," he says. "I'll give you a steak to take home—uncooked."

"No, no," she replies. But Petros has already ordered one of the waiters to wrap up a steak for the lady to take home. "Yes, yes," he laughs. "Take it with you. Anything the lady wants, huh cousin?"

The perfect woman? I ask him. "Receptive to a compliment, and pleasant to be with you. A woman should never stop being a lady . . . to give all they got!" he laughs, claps his hands, shouts, "Van-tas-tic!"

All of which sounds like Zorba, I remind him. "Zorba? He's related to me! To portray the true Greek . . . I am the one, because I live it!"

"This is the most beautiful thing I've felt for a long time," says Pam to Pe-

323

tros, concerning the whole evening at the Dianna.

A young man, from a long table of enthusiasts, grabs Petros around the shoulder and asks, "Are you going to dance tonight? You don't mind if we get a little wild?" Petros waves him off, assures him he will dance in a little while.

He leads me into the back, then, into the cooler, the kitchen, and finally his private office, pointing out the particulars of his life along the way, dramatically holding a head of lettuce in his hands, tomatoes, onions, a hunk of beef . . . shouting, extolling the wonders that go into his cooking. "Got to be the very best! Tomatoes, look. I swear to you no one will buy these tomatoes but me! The best! No matter how much it costs, it is irrelevant. Look, ochra, zucchini, egg plant . . . I buy directly with my own truck. I use Romano for fried cheese.

"Lamb," he slaps one, "got to be small, 32 pounds. They're spring lambs, more expensive than 65 pounders. Steak . . . U.S. Choice, has to be, has to be. Baby octopus, look at this, cousin. Gyros, you keep it always fresh. We make our own, 15-per cent lamb, 85-per cent beef. Look at this shishkebab . . . to be marinated overnight. Fish, beautiful fish. Not frozen . . . fresh!"

The Petros madness continues in the kitchen, as he begins hollering in Greek to the cooks, pulling out pans of pasticcio, uncovering pots of avgolemono, pans of vegetables, chunks of beef. "We cook everything!" he yells. "Come," he leads me to his private office.

Inside, in the corner, a huge portrait of a Greek soldier dominates the room like an icon. "My father," he says, "Big Nick. Came to this country in 1907 and helped build the railroads in the West. In 1912 he left town and helped to fight the Bulgarians. Better to be No. 1 in the village than the last one in a big town. What I am today, I am because of him, liking people, loving them.

"My father was the strong member of the family. My mother's still living there, and I'm going every year to see her. A big celebration. She wants to see us."

There are mementoes, too, of former Vice President Agnew. Petros shrugs his shoulder. "We can't help but think well of him because he's the only Greek-American who made the high office."

It's a more reflective, more sober Petros I see now behind the desk, in the quiet of his own office. He still chomps on a rich man's cigar. He's still the affable Greek. But here, surrounded by the relics of his past, the reminders of his origins, Petros exudes a certain humility. There is even an icon near him of St. Nicholas.

"It seems to me that when the going's rough, inevitably we turn to God. Not by going to church every Sunday . . . But I think there is a God, and we feel the effect . . . whether we like it or not.

"There is no country like the United States with the most freedom and opportunities known to human life. The people are by me the most hospitable in the world. In France, they would kill me overnight. Americans have a tendency to support the ones who try to make it.

"Most of my life is Dianna's. That's another reason why I haven't been married." And then he opens a file cabinet full of fan mail, letters, thank you notes, which he spills out all over the desk. "A close relationship with everyone," he explains.

"Dear Petros," they all begin, "We loved being with you. The new place is fabulous. Love, Your favorite blond." "Dear Petros, Thank you for trusting people and having one of the best restaurants in Chicago. Our check for $24 is enclosed for the case of wine. We drink to your health. Opaa!" "Petros, Love is your theme, but when your body tires, there's no one to take your place. How's about taking 'loving, tender care'—of you, Petros?" and . . . "Petros!!! Try to remember. I met you in Beirut, at the Phoenecia Hotel Pool, around September of last year. I'm the tall blond dancer who loves to eat tabulli salad. Have you remembered who I am yet? Oh, I just love being a mystery. Do you ever get to New York? Let me know if you do. I'd love it. . . ."

"When you receive this, you don't feel tired. You may be physically exhausted, but you go on because you are what the people made you to be. Age? Petros is the age for all women," he smiles.

He shows off a pair of cuff-links from Agnew, with the vice presidential seal. "We had egg lemon soup, Greek salad, lamb, wine. It was the most exciting evening of my life."

And he also pulls out a letter dated Oct. 31, 1974: "Dear Mr. Kogiones: During all the confusion since my trip to Chicago, I wanted to be sure that you knew how much I appreciated the bottle of wine that you so kindly gave me. This was just so thoughtful of you and I truly appreciate your kind gesture of friendship. I am very thankful that I have had a speedy recovery from my operation and feel better each day. I so enjoyed my visit to Chicago and hope to resume an active, full schedule soon. The President joins with me in sending our warmest regards. Sincerely, Betty Ford."

After that, what next for Petros? A cookbook, maybe? Petros now has one of his own: *Petros' Famous Recipes (An Adventure in Greek Cookery).*

It's a delightful book, pure Petros, a little rough around the edges, but filled with excellent recipes, a little history, philosophy, too many introductions, and colored photos of Petros and Famous People . . . Petros dancing, Petros dining, Petros personified. It reads, at times, like a night out at Dianna's Opaa. It even includes his famous recipe for saganaki:

Flaming Cheese (Saganaki)
1 piece of cheese cut in a triangle
(Kasseri or Kefalotire)
1/2 lemon
1 egg
1 whiskey glass of Metaxa or another brandy
Flour cheese, dip it into beaten egg, and then fry it in an oiled or buttered frying

325

pan, turning it over two times. Have a hot pan ready and put the cheese in it. Then pour the Metaxa on the cheese, light it with a match and say "opaa." Extinguish the flames by squeezing the lemon over the pan. (Serves One).

And for a finale? Well, Petros dancing, of course. His "cousins" are restless in the dining room without him on the scene. The chanting has begun: PETROS! PETROS! PETROS!"

As he steps in, the room resounds in "Opaas!" Men, women, even children, feeling the Greek's love of life. "PETROS! PETROS! PETROS!"

He moves into the crowd like royalty, shaking hands, kissing women.

Strangers sidle up to me and say, "He's a hell of a guy, isn't he? He's nuts. He's really great. We came here just to see him, just to feel good." And, "He's Chicago's greatest host," says another. "He makes every woman feel special. Everybody's Greek tonight."

Yes, maybe everybody feels Greek tonight. That's the fantasy Petros helps to create, as the bouzouki music is toned down at his command, and everyone listens to him speak:

"First of all, I'd like to apologize for not being at the door to kiss all the women when they came in!" . . . PETROS! PETROS! PETROS! . . . "You are VAN-TAS-TIC!" PETROS . . . PETROS . . . PETROS . . . "I have to apologize for the upper level because the wine is getting to their brain!" . . . PETROS! PETROS! PETROS!

There is no way they are going to let him say another word. The music from *Zorba* begins; Petros smiles and prepares to give them what they want. The sound of the bouzouki is turned louder. The audience claps at a maddening rhythm, the bright lights are turned off, red and blue lights wash the center stage. Cigar in mouth, Petros turns . . . removes his jacket . . . throws out his arms . . . closes his eyes . . . turns to the music, bends to the floor, kicks . . . listens to all that is Greek inside of him, turning, turning, taking it all with him, taking us all home.

Sam Karnick: Window Washer

Where are you, Sam Karnick? What heights have you scaled today? What depths will you plumb tonight? What's the way of a window washer anyway?

I've got a lot of questions for you, Sam, and I can't find you. I don't know if you're lost for good, or if you'll ever make the papers again except for the possibility of another fall. Maybe the last fall.

"I've fallen seven or eight times," he was quoted as saying a few months ago when he hung for twenty minutes from a broken scaffold thirteen stories above E. Huron Street. "It's nothing."

But it must have been something. Sam made the papers this time. His and his partner Brian Joseph's lives were in danger over at the Westbury Hotel. Firemen and newspaper people and spectators were everywhere, all sharing the drama. "Hey, there's a man falling down!"

There is always an audience for a man in a public predicament. What do we make of that? Why does the possibility of death command the public's attention so? I see him hanging there, calling to the crowds below. Why do we thrive on witnessing disaster?

How many people could you count pulling for you, Sam? How many people down there in the darkness of their hearts secretly imagined a bloody fall . . . buckets and water, all articles of the trade, and most of all, finally, you, Sam Karnick, thirty years of window washing experience taking the final count of gravity? Head first or feet first? Half gainer or somersault? Eyes open or shut?

I have this feeling about Sam, though I've never met him. Intuition tells me he is a stranger to a scream in his free falls. Intuition tells me he might even ham it up a bit, break into a swan dive and song.

"I once hung sixteen stories up, and once I fell off a six-foot ladder and broke my leg."

All I know about Sam is what I read in the newspapers, what I discovered from others over the phone, and what I imagined visiting the settings where he most recently touched down. Sometimes this is enough.

"It's a fast buck. And if you go, you go."

A simplistic philosophy, perhaps. Easily stated . . . easily done. Few of us

327

have fallen that far to prove it. Every man has heard these words, uttered them himself a few times: "If you go, you go." But not every man has had the occasion to measure the depth of his immature heroics at the moment of truth . . . or even a few minutes thereafter.

Sam Karnick said, "If you go, you go," thirty minutes after he was rescued from a broken scaffold. Most of us would not be so sure of those words, so soon.

Most men would thank God and the fire department and find it difficult to hold back the fear and the feelings. Most of us would vow to follow the straight and narrow road, empty our buckets, become believers. Most of us would listen to our harried wives and worry about our families. Most of us are good at finding some alternatives.

But Sam Karnick, 56, a window washer for thirty years, is accustomed to living alone and on the edge of things. His partner, Brian Joseph, 27, claims his mind was blank during the whole hanging-from-the-edge scene. And Brian Joseph will no doubt find some alternative to window washing—unless he was apprenticed to Sam Karnick's soul as well. Brian Joseph, in fact, has already left town. "I think he went to Oklahoma or somewhere," said his last employer.

But Sam Karnick, shortly after his fall, had a cup of coffee, a shot of vodka, and said he was ready to go back to work. Most of us would first empty the vodka bottle and then start thinking about a new line of work.

What kind of man's work is window washing, anyway? Men sometimes wash the windows of their car. Women wash all the windows of their house from the inside, then send the old man around on the outside with a six-foot stepladder, a clean rag, and a bottle of Windex. That's the extent of the average man's acquaintance with window panes. That and the fact that a perfectly clean window is an illusion. One always leaves a smear somewhere.

Height is confined to the top step of the ladder, just high enough to still feel a safe extension of both feet on the ground while reaching for the top of the first story window. If the second story is your habitat, then it's either an extension ladder poking at those dizzying heights or sitting outside on the window sill making grand, fast sweeps for clarity while the good woman holds onto your feet and life from inside. "Harry, be careful!"

We do have this thing about clean windows. We readily judge individuals, nationalities, businesses by whether their windows are clean or dirty. The ethics of window washing: "You know her . . . the one with the dirty windows."

It's a question, then, of height, bordering on philosophy, that separates the neighborhood Windex washer man from a Sam Karnick. Karnick's life, you see, doesn't really have any meaning at all until he finds himself far above the average second-story window. Height increases the quality of his living.

So, I have these questions for you, Sam:

What's it like way up there?

When, if ever, does the dizziness begin? From the 49th floor, shall we say, does a window washer look up or down or just straight ahead? Is there a corresponding feel of power with every inch of the wench upward, or a diminution of the human spirit when you consider the way all men must plod below, and how you're never really above them for good, and sooner or later you must come down?

What's it like up there in the sun, pieces and patches of sky, and the inconsistency of clouds? How about the rain? Your greatest threat, I recall, is wind. Wind can put an end to your ambitious heights on some days. Wind can ground you for a long stretch.

Too much wind and no pay. . . . I can see you mulling over your drink those long windy days, nervously fingering the glass, your fate up to the elements, feeling, I would imagine, something akin to what pilots must feel when entire airports are shut down because of bad weather, and there is no getting off the ground, no matter how strong the urge to fly.

And what do you see, Sam Karnick, through the looking glass? Beyond, above, below? What stories and poems do windows reveal? What pictures do they show?

How do you look, Sam, in reflection? Any older? Wiser? How many more windows to wash for a man 56 years old? How high can you still climb in the years you have left? Or do you hit the ground at 65 and just stay there, banished from above, two feet on the sidewalk, reaching the easily attainable heights of street windows with a long-handled squeegee?

How does it feel to wash a window so clean it can sing? And is that the extent of your pride?

Somehow, I think it isn't. Somehow, I think you may be one of those impossible men always climbing for a fall. Somehow I think you're disappointed in the days that go almost too well—days in which you go up, do your job perfectly, then come down again safely. Days like that a man like you may wish to throw his buckets down an alley, head for a bar, and get gloriously drunk just to put the whole world in proper perspective. "Hell, I didn't even come close to any serious falling today!"

Somehow, I think you reveled in that latest scare. "We were all set to secure," you said. "The next thing I know I'm punching buttons [on the winch] and nothing stops. First he [his partner] starts coming down. Then the buckets are coming down. Then I know I'm up that creek without a paddle until the firemen showed.

"First they tried to unscrew the bolts [to the window]. Then I said, 'Bust it, I'll pay for it.' Someone else, a fireman, shouted, 'Bust the son of a bitch,' and I said, 'That's my man.' "

That's my man: only you would recognize the truth of that characterization. You and those of us here on the ground working out a life almost totally devoid of any drama. Those of us who live in safety belts every day of our lives because we've found our alternative to danger.

We need an occasional Sam Karnick teetering on the edge just to remind us what it was like once, perhaps as far back as childhood, when we knew we were alive.

I have still more questions for Sam, but I'm glad he's not around to answer them. I like to think he wouldn't have time to entertain such foolishness.

I've been looking for Sam. I checked with the ABC Window Washing Company on Fullerton. But it seems he didn't make a big hit with them, judging by their attitude as to his whereabouts.

"No, he doesn't work here anymore. No, he only worked for me for about three weeks. No, I don't know where he is. His partner? He's not here anymore either."

Sam could be on Skid Row for all they know or care.

"It's a fast buck," Sam said. So I ask the former employer just how much a Sam Karnick is worth.

"$214 a week is the standard scale," I'm told. "But I don't know how much Karnick was making."

And what manner of man was he? Do you remember him?

"I just saw him when he came in to pick up his check. That was all."

That's my man.

Checking the Westbury Hotel, 150 E. Huron, where Sam took his publicized plunge, I find little else about him worth recording. The Doorman? He doesn't remember the incident. He's new on the job. The maintenance man washing the revolving window door?

"Yeah, I remember the guy fallin'. Right here in front. No, I didn't talk to him. Never met him. The housekeeper might know. She was up there then. You try the housekeeper. She's down that way."

The housekeeper remembers Sam Karnick hanging from the scaffold. She was working then. She saw him. She never talked to him, though. He's never been back to wash windows since.

Would you remember him if you saw him?

"Oh yes," she says. "I'd know him if I saw him in the street. I'd know his face."

That's my man.

Over at the Regency Hotel, 19 E. Ohio, Sam's last residential address, I come a little closer before acknowledging a dead end. The Regency Hotel seems one of those halfway hotels to nowhere: not quite the end of the line, but on the route, one of those classic city dead-end habitations, regardless of how many floors there are. A man could die of loneliness in any one of the rooms. All the windows need a good washing.

The desk lady fills the chair as if she's been dumped there and will never move. Every question is an intrusion; every person is a stranger in her territory. There are no "guests" in her book.

Does Sam Karnick live here?

"He's gone."

Do you know where he went?

"No."

Any forwarding address?

"No."

How long did he live here?

"About three months . . . listen, I'm busy."

Do you remember him?

"You bet I remember him." She says something about a busted-up room.

Outside, I meet a man in an undershirt with tatoos on his white arms, sitting on a box. He thinks he remembers Sam Karnick.

"He told some stories," says the tatooed man. Nothing more, nothing less.

But neither the desk lady nor the tatooed man has ever scaled the heights of a building. Neither one was very versed in falling. Sam knew greater heights. And maybe he only busted rooms without windows.

And though he may be lost or out of place at the moment, somehow I see Sam undoubtedly up there somewhere, still making a fast buck, riding for another fall.

The Petrakis Story, 1980

I could tell you that Harry Mark Petrakis is fifty-six years old; looks tanned, healthy, dapper in a striped summer sport coat, blue shirt and blue tie; and seems content with his lot in life as a storyteller—novels, collections of short stories, the autobiographical *Stelmark: The Petrakis Reader*, always a new novel about to appear, and more works in the making.

I could tell you he is smiling his classic Good Greek smile, infectious as ever, as much a part of him as his laughter, his gestures, his resonant voice, his ability to tell so dramatically a story about damned near anything. I could point to this bowl of avgolemono (egg-lemon soup) before me and say, "Harry, tell me a story about this soup." He could . . . he does: "I had a bowl of avgolemono for lunch, but it was not as good as this. Too watery. This is good and thick. To make good avgolemono. . . ."

I could tell you that we are sitting in the downstairs darkness of The Taberna, 303 East Ohio, in the Time-Life Building—not exactly Petrakis' neighborhood terrain. But we are here instead of the Greek enclaves of Halsted Street or Lawrence Avenue because he is too well known there; it would be noisy and people might be a bother, and here it is quiet and cool, and Petrakis can pass relatively unnoticed, though a few people do come up to him, and one woman (on our way out) takes his hand and says, "I've had a secret passion for you for years." For the the first time in the entire evening, Petrakis is without words.

I could tell you how I read his first published story, "Pericles on 31st Street," in *The Atlantic* in 1957, sitting in a rooming house, wanting to become a writer, but going to college instead to become a teacher because in my neighborhood a man had to be something, and being a writer meant nothing. I loved what Petrakis did with Pericles, and for the first time I forgot the expatriates, forgot Sartre and Camus, and began to think of my own neighborhood. When I began to write, I would begin there.

I could tell you about his first book of short stories, *Pericles on 31st Street*, about their sense of place: ethnic Chicago. Their sense of character: classic comic/tragic individuals in a neighborhood homeland. Their themes: love, loss, courage, dignity, joy, freedom, death—as old as the golden age, as new as any of the stories inside The Taberna this evening.

It takes a Petrakis to create a Simonakis (from "Pericles"): "We gave the world learning and courage. We taught men how to live and how to die. . . . Laugh, barbarians. . . . Laugh and forget your debt to Greece. Forget the golden age and the men like lions. . . ."

In a time of so much dark fiction, Petrakis' stories glowed with warm laughter and love. Only a handful of short story writers in America make a reader feel good anymore. Petrakis is one. Saroyan, another. Yet neither man today publishes many new stories. "It's the market." "It's the audience." It's one of the things I want to talk to Petrakis about.

I could tell you that at fifty-six, Petrakis still feels like a young man, that "Pericles" was only yesterday, that another life decision will soon be made, that Petrakis still has a lot to say and looks forward to the age of sixty when, he informs me, the great Greek writer Kazantzakis did much of his important work. "*Zorba,* for one, was written when Kazantzakis was in his sixties."

Hope, confidence, determination are the essence of Petrakis' stories—and the spirit of the man himself.

I could tell you how I intended to present Petrakis in tape-recorded answers to questions prepared in advance: Petrakis' words and wisdom in the structured clarity of the Question and Answer format. But tape recorders diminish all writers, and prepared questions allow no room for imagination, for failure and mistakes, for the reader to imagine what Harry Mark Petrakis is all about. Images speak the more memorable truths.

Picture Petrakis writing for ten years, from age twenty-two to thirty-two, before selling his first story to *The Atlantic.*

Picture four of his stories rejected by *Playboy*, and the same four stories accepted and published by *The Atlantic.*

Picture Petrakis, a young writer, carrying in his wallet a standard rejection from *Harper's* with a hand-penned note: "We're interested. Send more."

Picture Petrakis, some twenty years later . . . five novels to his name, two collections of short stories . . . sending off a new story to *Harper's.* . . . and receiving a standard, printed rejection slip. "I have come full-circle," he smiles. "I will let you imagine how that must feel."

"I must have put stories down on paper in my teens," says Petrakis, "dreadful stories full of violence, prostitution, pimps, sexual abberations . . . all of the things that obsessed me and I didn't know anything about. None of the sexual aberrants were Greek," he laughs; "just sort of neutral.

"I think that two years of illness as a boy (early stages of tuberculosis), between the ages of eleven and thirteen, really brought me in contact with stories, with books. My parents began to bring, by accident, books home. My father would bring five or six books from a notions store. Scott, Scaramouch . . . I can't remember them all. I think probably it was a tremendously stimulating period for me. I was frightened . . . there was talk of the possibility of a sanitarium—which I viewed as a dying room I wouldn't return from.

"When I finally got up and went back to school, it was as if two years of illness had disrupted my ability to cope with the real world. There is something about illness and the imagination . . . Thomas Mann, of course, *The Magic Mountain.* I worked at different jobs, worked in the evenings in a liquor store. Then, about the age of seventeen, I funneled all my energies into gambling.

"When I started gambling, there was no writing, very little reading. I became an obsessive gambler. I couldn't leave it alone. Then, when I got married to Diana, I pledged I would stop gambling. But I couldn't. She almost left me two or three times that first year. I kicked it slowly, very slowly."

He recalls a scene, a turning point in his life etched somewhere upon the soul of a man leading a wasted life, but determined to redeem himself (find himself, explain himself). He tells how he owned and managed a luchroom at the time, a losing business. There were gas and electric bills to pay. He was behind on rent for the apartment, behind on the mortgage on the lunchroom. His wife, Diana, was pregnant with their first child. He recalls a visit to his father, a Greek Orthodox priest, to borrow $150 to pay off his depts . . . and then, on the way home, losing it all in the bookie parlor on 63rd Street.

"I remember returning to the lunchroom, the door locked, and Diana, pregnant, standing inside. Looking back on all this now I would say that today I am a writer because I was ill two years as a boy and because of those years of excessive gambling. When I kicked gambling, I had to fill the void. Yes . . . if I didn't have tuberculosis, and I wasn't a gambler, I wouldn't have been a fucking writer. So much for hand-chosen destiny!"

So much for the down-to-earth stuff of life, of story-telling. But how to discover the difference between the real and the imagined? How to find and know that power?

"I took a course at Columbia Colleg—I was twenty-one or twenty-two—to become a radio broadcaster. People said I had a good voice. One of the assignments was to do a story on the theme of Christmas, so I did a little two-page story about a waiter who comes home on Christmas Eve with a tree and some presents for his alcoholic wife. He finds her in a neighborhood bar drinking with a couple of gigolos. He takes her home. Hits her. Washes her. Puts her to bed. Stays with her till she has fallen asleep. Then takes the small Christmas tree from the porch, decorates it, puts the presents under it . . . figuring in the morning things will be all right.

"I read that story in class and at the end there was dead silence. The teacher asked for criticism. The general reaction was that this was a true story written out of the agony of personal experience. One guy said he would stake anything that it was all true, that I had an alcoholic wife.

"That story had an important impact on me: I had created people on those two pages so brimming with life that the class refused to see them as fictional!

That's when I started to write stories again. I started with stories because the novel was more than I could handle at the time. Some people start with stories, some with novels. The people who start with stories never make big, billowy novels."

You do not talk "technique" to Petrakis. He is unwilling to entertain such a concept in explaining his art of storytelling. All the technique in the world will not create a Simonakis, a Matsoukas, a Father Manos, a Kanthos. Writing programs teach technique, turning out writers of consummate skill but little feeling, never a Steinbeck, or a James Jones, a Farrell, or a Petrakis with his knowledge of the way men live and die outside the university, plunging into personal discovery, retrieving a recognizable and valued sense of humanity, elevating it at times to myth.

"Technique? Nothing I've ever worried about as such. I don't suppose I've thought about it as my technique. I think of telling stories. My stories have always been told in terms of character, emotions, revelations.

"I began simply by writing—the emotional outpouring of story. The early stories must reflect this. I tried to write like Wolfe wrote. The only difference was Wolfe was a genius and I wasn't.

"Overwriting was my pattern . . . drunk with words. Then slowly coming to a realization that passion wasn't enough. My inability to discipline myself to school, to storywriting, cost me extra time to learn to tell a story, to write one.

"The short story comes as close perhaps for me as I will get in working with forms of poetry. I think the short story is magical in what it can accomplish."

There is a tendency among some literary critics to separate "ethnic" writers from our flashier urbane or academic ones. A tendency to label artists for easy identity, then leave them there as if the world (New York) were done with them, and they have nothing left to say.

"My early stories were pages of characters who had no life. I'm not sure when I turned and went back to writing about the Greeks. It seemed very natural that I would write about them. I knew them. We have to begin with that which is ours. That which we know . . . love, loneliness, sorrow . . . there is no ethnic label you can pin on those. I write of Greeks because I know Greeks! But I don't count myself an ethnic or parochial writer.

"Chicago has obviously been good for me. It's provided me people, a sense of place, which I have used in my stories. But I think any place . . . if you're a writer, you should be able to work any place."

I could tell you that I am distressed by the plight Petrakis shares with many short story writers in America. His second and last collection of new stories, *The Waves of Night*, was published in 1969. (*A Petrakis Reader,* a compilation of his first two books of stories and one new story, was published by Doubleday in 1978.)

Obviously new stories by Petrakis and other seasoned American writers are just not being written today, not being published. They are simply lost Ameri-

336

can stories. For twenty years or more this country has lost (and continues to lose) a whole body of literature by craftsmen who labored and learned the art of storytelling only to abandon it.

"You move into the novel for economic reasons," says Petrakis. "I think it's ... suddenly you can get advances for novels, and you can't on a book of short stories. Novels get reviewed and make money for you, and you can therefore live and write another novel. . . . The poet can't make the move to the novel like the short story writer can. But the poet is conditioned to accept this.

"I don't miss it [short story writing] like I did in the early years. *A Dream of Kings* [his bestselling novel which became a movie] had a definite structure for me. In *A Dream of Kings* I first came to grips with the form and requirements of the novel. Now I'm intrigued by it.

"I would like to be able to get a contract from a publisher to do twelve stories in the next year," Petrakis says. Yet he sees that possibility as remote.

"I've done about five short stories in the last five years. I've probably been averaging about one a year. No, I don't write more than one or two a year now—economics again. I have book contracts on which I'm two and one half years behind now. To turn to the short story would be just adding to this obligation of time, without being assured that the time will be compensated for. That sounds very mercenary, but that's the reality of the situation. Man can dream visions of art, but when he becomes a master carpenter, he wants his hourly rate."

As for the state of the short story in America today, "I think people for years now have been getting their stories on television. And to think of plodding through a story now, as exciting as it might be, is a world apart from a Baretta, a Kojak. Those who read the short story today have to be true lovers of the short story, like lovers of poetry."

Still there are the Updikes, the Cheevers, the Singers . . . that small and precious body of story writers in America who do continue. "But you're talking of men who have national, international reputations, and they have a market for their stories. Their motivations are hard to know. *The Stories of John Cheever* could become a bestseller."

I could tell you that the hour has grown late at The Taberna, that the food, the drink, has gone to our heads. But that is not entirely the reality of the situation. I could tell you that the demeanor of Petrakis has changed slightly since we began talking. That in place of the exuberance in which he began there is now quietness, reflection.

I think of what he said Kazantzakis accomplished after the age of sixty and wonder aloud of the possibility of Petrakis pulling up stakes someday, making changes, going home to Greece, perhaps, for the inevitable discovery of life and story that awaits him there.

"Twenty years ago I had to make a decision, and I may be close to one now. I've gotten comfortable. I've got some security now, and I don't want to give it up. I can do it . . . I can make that break . . . but I'm scared."

Hidden in my briefcase throughout our conversation were Petrakis' first two collections of short stories—*Pericles on 31st Street* and *The Waves of Night*. While he was telling me about where he finds himself today, I carefully removed both books from my briefcase and placed them before him on the table, *Pericles* on top . . . and then sudden silence.

I asked what came to mind upon seeing these two books again. His faced softened from surprise to sadness to love to revery.   "Pericles. . . . I think of the wonderful excitement when these stories were first put out in book form . . . and the picture of myself on the back with so much more hair . . . the face, relatively unravaged. You know, this fucking book goes for $45, $50 today?

"*Waves of Night* . . . I think that title story is the main reason this book was published. Yet I was never able to sell that story. I think it went to twelve, fifteen magazines, and I was never able to sell it. It never came out till book form. . . ."

Petrakis gently touching the books, flipping through the pages of stories he crafted so well, so long ago . . . scanning the lines, feeling the binding, then closing the books before him, sliding them gently aside, though his eyes cannot leave the cover of Pericles.

"You asked what comes to mind when I look at these books now? A good question. Ghosts," he sighs. "Ghosts. Haunting in a way . . . haunting."

Studs: The Art of Talk

"I find some delight in my job as a radio broadcaster. I'm able to set my own pace, my own standards, and determine for myself the substance of each program. Some days are more sunny than others, some less astonishing than I hoped for; my occasional slovenliness infuriates me . . . but it is, for better or worse, in my hands. I'd like to believe I'm the old-time cobbler, making the whole shoe."
  —Studs Terkel, *Working*

I hear the voice first. *That* voice, joking with one of the maintenance people in the building. Then we meet at the elevator and shake hands. It's been a couple of years. We are going up to his office and the studios of WFMT where he will be doing his daily program, the same program Chicago has loved since 1952. To love the program is to love the man.

I am not his guest today, though I feel fortunate to be in the presence of a master interviewer, to relate to his questions, to observe him work. I'm here today to watch him in action, the man who was Mr. Talk Radio in Chicago before the concept was even born and bastardized to the banalities of the media today.

I vaguely recall seeing/hearing Studs for the first time in the early days of television, around 1950, '51 or '52. There was Dave Garroway, there were Kukla, Fran and Ollie, and there was Studs' Place, where people sat around in an old saloon and talked and sang. It was as real as the neighborhood where one lived, improvisation at its best. Pure Chicago style. I didn't know what improvisation was at the time—that would come later, thanks to Studs and his love for jazz which he spread over the air.

My most memorable image of that early television program was Studs answering the phone, saying, "Studs' Place," in that inimitable voice. First there was the voice. The then laugh . . . that "Heh, heh, heh," in a rat-a-tat-tat fashion. The rest of the image (visual and oral) would fill in later.

I'm not sure if my parents ever watched the program. The one person who really tuned me in to "radio culture Chicago," vis-a-vis Studs Terkel, was the old Chicago bookseller, Paul Romaine. You could not visit his shop any day without encountering the voices and music of WFMT. It was the only station he listened to. And if you happened to be in there mid-morning, you heard the voice of Studs talking to someone. Romaine would tell you who the guest was, and you would either softly talk books over the voice of Studs, or you would quietly drift through the store while Romaine puffed on his pipe and the voice of Studs floated in the air discussing music, art, literature, history, life in general . . . whatever interested him. He was infectious. Whatever interested him, almost immediately interested you.

Studs has that knack: to put you on his wavelength, something great teachers do, great artists.

I follow Studs from the elevator to the main office of WFMT. He walks with a certain briskness, sometimes beside you, sometimes ahead of you, always talking. You have feel his mind is on everything at once—past, present, future—and he can't possibly absorb one more appointment, one more visitor, one more phone call, one more question, one more idea . . . but he does. There is a call waiting for him. His guest has arrived. There will be somebody else in to see him later. He shakes it all off. Just-another-day-in-the-life-of-Studs, a Chicago legend pushing eighty, with miles and miles to go before he sleeps. He introduces me to the receptionist then says, "Come on, let's go. My guest is here."

I follow him down a long hallway. Photographs of well-known WFMT personalities, such as Marty Robinson, hang along one side. It's a veritable maze of modern, white office space. We go through what must be the incredible WFMT record library and into the rather spacious and sterile studio itself (unlike Studs' office which seems cramped and a mass of organized confusion).

The first time I saw Studs in person had to be about the mid-1960s. I had become somewhat of a regular listener, not to mention a subscriber to the old WFMT Guide—that long, narrow, rectangular publication that gave you a rundown on the station's programming for the month. It was especially valuable in providing classical music listeners/lovers with all the details of a specific album (artist, record company, etc.) played on a specific hour and date of the month, in the event that listeners (such as myself, who had only recently begun to appreciate the classics) wanted to buy the record.

I spent many an hour, many a dollar downtown at the Discount Record Shop

on Lake Street (under the El tracks) building a large record collection—classical, jazz, opera, spoken arts—thanks to the station and the Guide. (How else to account for these now collectors' items of Maria Callas and other magnificent Angel recordings? Not to mention albums of authors reading from their works [the Spoken Arts series] that include Dylan Thomas, Brendan Behan, Henry Miller, Carl Sandburg, Robert Frost, H.L. Mencken, Langston Hughes, Ferlinghetti and all the Beats [the San Francisco revolution of poetry and jazz] James Baldwin, Ernest Hemingway, etc.)

That was another unique thing about WFMT, the Guide, Studs, the Midnight Special, the announcers, all the programming: it became a kind of homebase for anyone in Chicago interested in the arts, in love with the vitality and spirit of the city. It was the station that you talked about, that talked to you. You got the interviews, ideas, social controversy, human drama, laughter, jazz and culture from Studs; the classical music and concerts from other announcers; and the offbeat, Nicholas and May humor, Big Bill Broonzy Blues, folksongs, the laidback, slightly wine-drunk-and-full-Saturday-night-feeling every week on the Midnight Special. And this was the purest Chicago radio coming to you, and you knew you were back home in Chicago, among friends, tuned to 98.7 on the FM dial.

WFMT was our Carson, our Letterman, our Saturday Night Live and our Prairie Home Companion all rolled into one.

The WFMT Guide served as a sort of newsletter: what the faithful could expect to hear over the air day and night, each month. There were ads and articles as well. For as small a magazine as it was, it provided insight and access to a Chicago we felt was ours: a first class kind of place to be, never a second city to us. Not by a long shot.

It was in the Guide that I probably first saw a photograph of Studs and first read an article about him. It was somewhere around that time when Dylan Thomas was in full bloom . . . when he was being talked about by Studs, when WFMT was playing his recording (especially, "A Child's Christmas in Wales"), when I went to the Goodman Theater for the first time to see a performance of Thomas' radio play, "Under Milkwood." In the lobby of the Goodman stood Studs Terkel.

That's what I remember: the voice, the man, suddenly coming together. Surprise. Awe. Here was *the* voice of Chicago's conscience. Chicago's spirit. I had nothing to say to him, yet angled to be closer, within earshot, just to hear him in ordinary conversation. There was no ordinary conversation with Studs. He could have been talking on the radio.

He was surrounded by friends. He was telling them something. He was entertaining them. I don't remember how he was dressed, how he looked, or what he was talking about. But I had seen and heard him. And now I had something to tell others: Studs Terkel. I saw him once at the Goodman Theater.

I'm fairly certain he wasn't dressed the way I see him today entering his studio, wearing his legendary Studs Terkel garb: blue sportcoat, gray pants, red socks, gray hush puppies, red-and-white checkered shirt, and red knit tie.

He dresses in a style my father (a white-collar worker all his life) called "race track clothes," a style I grew more comfortable with as I grew older. A take-me-as-I-am style.

A Chicago style, I'd say.

How impossible to imagine Chicago someday without him—a Chicago without Lake Shore Drive, State Street, the Trib Tower, the Magnificent Mile.

He is the hometown boy made good: Louis "Studs" Terkel, actually born in New York City, nicknamed after the character in Chicago writer James Farrell's classic neighborhood novel, *Studs Lonigan*, though there is no fiction to Studs. Only character in abundance.

Radio man, television man, graduate of the University of Chicago Law School in 1934, actor, author (winner of the Pulitzer Prize in 1985 for *The Good War: An Oral History of World War II*), narrator for a PBS documentary on the Spanish Civil War, *The Good Fight*, movie actor in "Eight Men Out" in which he played the reporter, Hugh Fullerton, who helped break the 1919 Black Sox scandal in Chicago.

Chicago. There it is again. Chicago/Studs . . . impossible to separate the two, though the man has covered with world with his tape recorder in search of yet another story, another voice to join his, to share with listeners. He keeps bringing it all back home to Chicago.

The same world, in fact, comes to Chicago. Comes to seek out Studs, to stop by the station and talk awhile. Just like today's guest, sitting there in the studio waiting for him, a famous jazz musician, his face recognizable all over the free world, and the not-so-free-world as well. . . . including Russia, recently visited. And which he now brings to Studs, to share with him and his listening audience — the recording of the live concert, "Moscow Night," and his own memories of that and the jazz world at large.

Dave Brubeck rises (all six foot plus of him) and the two men warmly grasp each other's hand and arm. They are old friends. Studs' life is rich with talented and fascinating old friends. It is no wonder he loves so much, and is loved so much, by so many in return.

Immediately his enthusiasm for Brubeck, for jazz, for Russia, for the world, for today's program, for life itself takes fire. And we are off! We are entering Studs' territory, putting a program together of voices, music, commentary, spirit.

Brubeck is accompanied by his producer, Russell Gloyd, and for a moment the studio seems overflowing with conversation, laughter, and introductions. Studs begins going over a possible program approach with Gloyd and the engineer while Susan Names, the public relations director of WFMT, steps in to take some photographs.

I just happen to have some old albums on hand for him to sign: "Jazz Goes To College," "Brubeck Plays Brubeck," "Jazz Goes To Junior College," "The

Riddle," and "Jazz, Red Hot and Cool."

"Oh, my goodness," he smiles, flipping through album cover memories of another time . . . a younger Brubeck with black wavy hair, the black rimmed glasses.

"I remember a piece about Chicago you once played at the Blue Note," I tell him. "You were working with the sounds of the city, everything from fire sirens to church bells. I loved that piece. I was so in love with Chicago myself at that time, jazz in the city, and here you went and put it all into a musical composition."

His evocation of the city came out of nowhere and stayed with me like Sandburg's poem. But I never found it on a recording, never heard him play it again. Another time at the Blue Note I caught him between sets in the packed room and asked if he would play the Chicago number I had heard him do before. He said he would try. I waited around with friends at the Blue Note all night, but he never got to it. I was bitterly disappointed.

"I'm sorry," he says. "But you know, I did record that. It's called, 'Sounds of the Loop.' I'll sign them all," he says, taking the albums.

"That's one of my favorites," I tell him, referring to the album "Jazz: Red Hot and Cool" which he holds in his hand.

"You know who that is?" asks Brubeck, pointing to the sexy lady in red, cigarette in hand, leaning against the keyboard like an old torch singer, shoulder thrust forward, eyes only for the piano man. "That's Suzy Parker, the model. That is not a dress. And she came in with a slip and a brassiere, and walked up to the piano, and then they draped this over her. And Paul [Paul Desmond, alto sax] knew who she was. And I didn't. And Paul was all ahhhggghhhoooo. We just didn't know it was going to be her. She is beautiful. And can you see that that's not a dress?"

In the background Studs says, "What should we open with?"

"What about opening with 'Take Five' from Russia?" says Brubeck.

"Hey, that's a great idea! 'Take Five'," exclaims Studs.

"Especially on this station with the Shostokovitch theme," says Russell Gloyd.

"That's great. This is a classical music station, you know," says Studs.

"I can talk about this," says Brubeck.

"It'll be wonderful!" says Studs. " 'Take Five.' That's a great opener. Now what do you think for two?"

"I'll tell you what. We'll still talk about Russia and we'll do number four here on the CD, 'Unsquare Dance'."

"What's that called?" asks Studs.

" 'Unsquare Dance'," says Gloyd. "It got the Russian audience applauding."

"Okay. Then we'll talk in between. We have an hour you know . . . about fifty-five minutes," says Studs.

"Do you have a copy of the book *The Great War* ?" asks Gloyd.

"Oh, sure," says Studs.

"Do you know that Dave's in it?"

"Yeah, who? who? . . . " Studs seems flustered.

"304," says Brubeck. "Page 304."

"My God, he knows the page!" yells Studs. "Yeah, that's right! It was my friends Ray Wax who booked you. You know what his real name was?" (And Studs reveals the name.)

"Damn, that's why I didn't recognize him!" shouts Brubeck. "I read it and I said, I don't remember this guy!"

In the book, Studs interviews a WWII vet named "Ray Wax" (a real operator, as Studs describes him) who angled himself into a position to produce shows to entertain the troops. Wax explains, in *Working,*

Someone came to me and said he wants to organize a band. I said, "Who've you got?" He said, "I play sax and I think we got a piano player." I talked to this piano player: "What's your name?" "Dave Brubeck." I said, "Who do you play like? Stan Kenton?" He said yeah. I said okay. I pulled his form 20. Brubeck was a rifleman, an infantryman. When I pulled his form, he couldn't move forward. It's like he disappeared. That's what I did with eighteen people in the band: I held their form 20s. They stayed alive and I had a band.

"Okay," somebody shouts. "No more talking." Studs is back to trying to put together today's program, trying to give the interview and the hour some shape. "Okay, four. What is number four? 'St. Louie Blues'. . . . So that'll do it. With the talk. It's about nine minutes. And 'God's Love' [from another album] is what? About five minutes? . . . that sounds good.

"Ray Wax!" Studs shouts again, picking up another loose thread from the stories and conversations flying around his head. He begins to impersonate Wax: "That guy, Brubeck! Goddam! I saved his life!" Studs, the actor, has everyone laughing.

"In a way he did," says Brubeck. "But I saved his, and he doesn't talk about that."

Studs continues lining up the day's program in his own head, scratching down a few notes which he stuffs into his pockets — and inevitably loses track of.

"So, we're set. We'll keep it very free and easy. I like working this way."

The program is about to begin. Everyone appears relaxed, especially Studs. Brubeck and his producer sit together, and Studs faces them across a large round table. The microphones have been tested and set. Studs has one sheet of paper in front of him and a pen in hand.

Who knows what else goes through his head at this point? Where the program will begin? How it will develop? Where it will end? All Studs knows for

certain are the four Brubeck pieces he will play, and the time of each piece. Not much, perhaps, to build an hour's program on. Then again, this is Studs doing what Studs does best: shaping human voices into one-of-a-kind interviews that run the gamut of the heart's emotions, the mind's hunger. An artist of the air at work.

"Well, we're on our way," says Studs excitedly. "That's 'On Our Way to Canaan Land!' I always think of Mahalia Jackson saying that: "I'm on my way to Canaan land!" he laughs. Both Brubeck and Gloyd join in, then grow still. A sudden quiet descends on the studio, and Studs begins his show for the day:

"What a delight, the delight of having a virtuoso as a guest, Dave Brubeck," Studs opens, "who, as you know, is considered an artist in the world of jazz . . . some say, a legendary figure, and indeed he does play his own kind of music. With him is his colleague, Russell Gloyd, and they've been travelling to various parts of the world, especially, recently to the Soviet Union. And of that we'll hear some musical examples, some of their reactions to it. And this is by way of saying Dave and his group will be performing Sunday night at a place, at an auditorium that has good accoustics, the Fourth Presbyterian Church . . . I'm thinking, Dave . . . it was thirty some years agow when we first met."

"Yeah," says Brubeck. "Thirty-seven years ago. At the old Blue Note. With Frank Holzfeind. The first Blue Note, before they moved a few blocks away."

"It was on Clark Street," says Studs. "Upstairs . . . no, upstairs was the second one, on Randolph."

"And I had driven in from California to play there," says Brubeck, "and about five people showed up, and I said to Frank, 'I want to go home to San Francisco.' This was my first tour. And he said, 'Why?' And I said, 'There's nobody here to see us. And I can't stand playing here.' He said, 'Look. You let me run the club. And you play the music. But do me one favor, promise that you'll never work for anybody else in Chicago.' I said, 'Okay.' The next time we came, you couldn't get into the club! Lines of people, clear around the block! And he had a hunch we were going to hit, and he was right on. And I *never* worked for anybody else."

"I should point out this last fact is very important," says Studs. We're talking about jazz artists, and what a remarkable man was Frank Holzfeind, who *knew* something about you, who *knew* you had that special ingredient . . . and had faith in the artist."

"We really honor our long term commitments and we believe in them," says Russell Gloyd. "You know, it's amazing, over the years that is what has come back to us. The people who have put the faith in Dave when no one else would."

"Recently," says Studs, changing the direction of the interview, "you and Russell and the group were in the Soviet Union . . . in what is quite a remarkable time of almost a revolution within the revolution. I want to come back to you and the early days, but what . . . first reaction, the Soviet Union, the music, the one you choose to open with, and have long been associated with."

"Yeah, I chose to open with 'Take Five' because most of your listeners do associate me with that," says Brubeck. "But I've been playing that piece since 1958, and I would say at almost every concert because the public always wants to hear it. And we had played five nights in a row in Moscow, and the fifth night we were televising for Moscow, and we were recording, hopefully. And we got to 'Take Five' for some reason . . . became the theme of the Shostakovich Fifth which is what I start playing in 'Take Five.' That is the *key* . . . when I was a kid that made me want to write for orchestra. And that theme *changed* my life. And here I was back in Russia playing that theme in a jazz 5/4 time."

"It's especially moving," explains Gloyd, "because the Shostakovich Fifth Symphony represents Shostakovich's personal statement. He was the boy wonder of the Soviet Union. And Stalin loved him . . . and he then went out of favor. And the Fifth Symphony was Shostakovich's statement saying, 'I am an honest person.' And here is a statement of the artist through the symphony. Most everyone in the audience would have recognized that and understands where it is coming from. So it truly was a synthesis taking place there, in that performance."

"So, let's hear 'Take Five' . . . this is Brubeck with a touch of Shostako-vich," says Studs, leading into the music.

"With a live Russian audience," adds Brubeck.

The studio momentarily grows still as "Take Five" goes over the Chicago airwaves, and Studs and guests pull back from the microphones, and the conversation continues, unaired, contained within the studio. For private enjoyment only.

The skill of a Studs Terkel interview is part quick shifting (knowing when to change gears), part instinct. "Improvisational," if you will, not unlike a good jazz musician. It is not unlike the artistry of his guest, Dave Brubeck, who has said, "Improvisation, to me, is the core of jazz. Because I believe this, my style of piano is one shaped primarily by the material, or ideas which I am attempting to express—not by a system or a search for an identifying 'sound.' My concept has been that style is a *means* of expressing an idea, and when developing an idea, a style *evolves*."

In the course of the hour, Studs develops his own idea, creates another classic interview (a duo, sometimes a trio of voices) in his Studs Terkel style, weaving in his insights plus various Brubeckian themes: Dave's early years at the Blue Note in Chicago . . . Brubeck's extraordinary reception in Russia . . .the incredible popularity he has enjoyed there for years (via unauthorized and unorthodox tapings of his music from Voice of America broadcasts . . . including a KGB guy, a Gorbachev bodyguard/Brubeck collector and one of his greatest fans) . . . Brubeck's interest in sacred music, the composer Darius Milhaud, at Mills College in Oakland, California:

"Milhaud was the first composer," (enters Brubeck as a counter-rhythm to Studs' developing melody) "I think, to use the jazz idiom in a piece called 'The Creation of the World' . . . I think before Gershwin or anybody else. Bernstein still says it's the best piece ever written for jazz symphony. So he was a perfect master for us to go to—Bill Smith, the clarinetist, Paul Desmond—and there were five of us out of my first group that were composition students under Milhaud. It was a fantastic experience because we were so used to being told, 'Don't play jazz.' And Milhaud said, 'I want all of you in this class to raise your hands if you're jazz musicians. And I want you to know, if you're going to express America, you better use the jazz idiom because the greatest American composers such as Gershwin and Duke Ellington have used the idiom.' And he went on to say Copeland, Bernstein, Charles Ives. And he said, 'If you live in this country and you don't have a jazz idiom in your compositions, you'll never express this country.' And I couldn't believe what I had heard."

Brubeck, Studs, bringing it all back home again.

(Studs telling me once that the art of interviewing is "Listening. Especially for pauses. Why did he pause? Was it something deep? Something hurtful? Then to come back to that later. You want to create a conversation like over a cup of coffee.")

349

Studs, catching a new note in their conversation and playing it for all it's worth . . . or Studs introducing a particular refain of his own for the guest to play with, expand into a marvelous, free-wheeling composition.

As you listen to them both, it's impossible not to be held captive by the excitement in their voices, the flight of their converstaion, the moment of their being totally alive in the give-and-take of impressions, ideas, major and minor themes.

Studs then cuts to another Brubeck piece to air for his Chicago listeners from "Moscow Night" (the traditional "St. Louis Blues"—Russian style) and an air of stillness descends upon the WFMT studio than can only be described as reverential.

The eyes of both men close. Brubeck slowly builds one hell of an intro to the old jazz classic . . . the Russian people love it, recognize it, applaud it.

Brubeck, eyes closed, listens to himself in Moscow . . . and in the darkness behind his eyes . . . unconsciously begins playing his fingers over a keyboard which is the table where he sits in Chicago.

Studs, arms folded, eyes closed, head swaying, smiles and begins beating time with his Hush Puppied feet.

Here are two consumate artists at work, at play, at peace, with some sense, perhaps, that time may be running out. Each is so finely tuned that the living and the work come easy now. Almost everything that occupies their attention turns to art. For those fortunate enough to reach such harmony, there are no mistakes.

In *Talking to Myself*, Studs tells of an incident in 1956 when he and Nelson Algren went to hear Billie Holiday sing in a jazz-joint on the South Side of Chicago.

Billie's voice is mostly gone. She still wears the gardenia in her hair. The place is almost empty. Her back-up musicians are old and tired, yet music is there. She sings "Willow Weep for Me" and everyone in the joint understands the beauty, feels the sadness. Some shed a few tears—Studs and Algren included.

"Something was still there," says Studs, "that something that distinguishes an artist from a performer: the revealing of self. Here I be. Not for long, but here I be. In sensing her mortality, we sensed our own."

The World's Greatest Czech Bakeries
(Memories of Old Bohemian Bakeries)

Bakery is home. It's family, the remembrance of old times, good times, a kitchen afloat in the aroma of fresh bread. Goodness bordering on love.

5:45 a.m. I rise once again in my father's house to find my parents where I will always remember them in the early hours of the morning—at the breakfast table. I pour a cup of hot coffee and wait . . . for the sounds of my father getting up from the table, moving into the pantry, returning with his hands full of fresh bakery. For the sounds of crisp white paper unwrapped, bags torn open, string snapped with the flick of fingers.

First, the sweet smell. Then the golden sight, the colors of peach, cherry, pineapple, blueberry, poppy seed. "Take some houska," my mother says. "You'll feel better." "You know," says my father, "I had number eighty-four at Vesecky's last Saturday, and they were first calling thirty-two! Jesus, I don't know how people can wait that long." But he does. And I often go weeks, months, waiting to taste the bakery of Bohemia once again.

The French have their tarts, the Greeks their baklava, the English their scones. The Bohemians? They have it all: Babi's rye (sometimes called Grandmother's rye), traditionally a round, sour rye, with floured bottom and beautiful dark crust; babovka, a cake with a rippled top filled with either poppy seeds or almonds; buchticky, fruit-filled squares with turned-up corners; houska, a rich coffee-cake twist with raisins and nuts; kolac, open-faced coffee cakes of various fruits topped with streusel; kolacky, a smaller cookie-sized variation of kolac; moravsky, a pull-apart with a cheese bottom and apricot top. Variety and heaviness of fruit fillings characterize Czech wonders. Poppy seed is king. Rye bread is basic. Houska is close to the heart of every true Bohemian.

Exiled for years in Wisconsin, far from the greatest bakery shops in the world, I count myself to sleep with the names of neighborhood bakers along Cermak Road—Fingerhut, Minarik, Sobran, Vales, Stetina, Vesecky. I dream of kolacky jumping over the counters. I wake to a vision of houska fresh from the oven, ready to be consumed in a fit of ecstasy.

The sensory deprivation can be eased only in the bakeries of my youth, by miles of houska. I leave Wisconsin, set forth through the old neighborhood on a three-day feast.

6:30 a.m. A brisk bakery morning. Renewed by a breakfast of houska and coffee cake, I begin my assault: Charles Fingerhut Bakeries, 5537 West Cermak Road, Cicero, the easternmost bakery, makers of the famous Babi's rye, a registered trade name.

Though the front window reveals only birthday and party cakes, inside is a treasury of Czech baking: clusters of Babi's rye, counters of coffee cakes that bring tears to a hungry man's eyes, racks of poppy seed buns, salty horns, sweet rolls, not to mention twenty-seven varieties of cookies and dozens of brandy, salem fudge, and toffee tortes. The front door continually opens and closes as customers gather the soft jewels in shopping bags.

A young man in a pinstriped suit is Herb Fingerhut Jr., production and marketing manager and the cake decorator—that's how big Bohemian baking has become. On the way to his office, he explains those Donald Duck cakes in the window: "Those are our signature line. I create them and sign them. If people order something special, whatever, I'll put anything they want on it. I just got done make a six-foot standing Road Runner cake. The whole body was cake, and the neck, royal icing. Real tail feathers."

Herb has been a family baker for three years. He started at twelve as a cleanup boy, went to college for two years, then followed his father's and grandfather's footsteps to the Dunwoody Institute in Minnesota, "the best basic baking school in the country. I had the same teacher as my dad. And I'm the eighth generation of Fingerhut bakers. I've been making cakes since I was five. My grandmother always pushed me: 'Oh, it's beautiful, beautiful!' "

More than sixty years in the same location, Fingerhut (with outlying bakeries in Berwyn, Brookfield, and Westchester) is the area's biggest Bohemian bakery business, with nearly a hundred employees. It still concentrates on Czech specialties but also has bowed to the times; its party cakes cross all ethnic barriers. Everything is baked at the central store in Cicero, and the figures are staggering: "We do about 1,500 pounds of Babi's rye a day. Three-pounders, four-pounders; we actually go up to a hundred-pound Babi's rye that fits on one whole shelf. We put a ribbon on it, some flowers. We call it a Bohemian birthday cake. We do about 1,000 pounds of white bread, 1,000 Bohemian ryes. Coffee cakes and Danish, more than 800 pounds of dough. Probably 500 dozen kolacky and about 900 to 1,200 decorated birthday cakes a week. These figures will triple around the holidays. Altogether, well over 200 bakery items."

Herb introduces me to "my Italian baker, Benny Botta. He makes the buttercreams, fudge. And this is Jim Bartunek, the decorator. He's the artistic guy. He can make you anything. When I want to learn something, I watch him."

Benny is busy with four hundred pounds of chocolate-chiffon mix, his right arm into it up to the elbow, swirling it around along with the mixer. He smiles, a cake man in perfect harmony with his ingredients.

"I'm going to have about three or four wedding cakes," says Herb, who is about to be married in a few days. "Benny is going to make a cannoli—heart shaped, all white, four tiers. Jim will make a groom's cake, fudge . . . dark, for the groom. Two layers. And I'll make my own cake, eight and a half feet high. There will be a twenty-four-inch layer at the bottom and an eight-inch layer on top. There will be three separate heart-shaped cakes surrounding it to represent peace, love, and happiness. One will go to her mother, one to mine, and one for us, which we'll freeze and eat a year later. The cake will be all white, white on white. Everything white."

That afternoon, I find myself at the Manor Bakery, 5906 West 35th Street, Cicero, far off the beaten Cermak track, along the southern perimeter of Bohemia in an area known as Boulevard Manor. Chester Matiasek Sr. and Chester Jr. have been manning the ovens here for nearly thirty years. The array of Czech goodies on display in front and polka music coming from the back leave no doubt: a Bohemian baking family has made an outpost here.

Why the Boulevard Manor area? "This was the up-and-coming place in the fifties," says Chester Jr.; "Cermak Road was filled with bakeries. This was a mixed neighborhood, with young people establishing themselves, their first house. That meant kids, birthday parties, weddings. And I think now we're coming into a second generation of this."

Chester Sr. bursts in, shakes my hand like a long-lost relative, hollers, pokes, laughs as we all sit down in a small kitchen where we have been joined by Mrs. Matiasek and a daughter. Father and son talk bakery. The conversation sounds like all the family gatherings I've ever attended, in all the polka-filled Bohemian kitchens of my life.

A coffeepot appears. The old man reaches for a tray of freshly baked almond-crescent cookies and puts a heaping platter of goodies before us. "Good? Good?" he shouts. They melt in my mouth. I smile. He laughs. If there's a moral force in a Bohemian's world, it's bakery.

"You're not going to find it anymore," the old man says. "Your concentration of Bohemian people living in Cicero and Berwyn, that's going. All the women were famous bakers in the old country. When I was a kid we always had four or five loaves of bread at home. Bread, bread, bread. Christ, that's all we ate! Bread smeared with goose lard. That was how you grew up. Just rye bread and goose lard!"

Bakeries like Manor's typify Bohemian baking-family traditions. The elder Matiaseks live above the bakery; the son and his family, next door. Chester Jr., proud of his little daughter in Czech school, suddenly sets up a projector on the table and begins showing home movies, first of the bakery, then of his daughter performing in a Czech play. I'm held prisoner by father and son houska-makers who have gone into film. I comfort myself with more almond crescents and coffee while the bakers, Senior and Junior, narrate the film: "We make 7,000 rolls an hour," says Junior. "Very few bakeries have this kind of automation," says

Senior. "Look—an automatic lift," the bakers' duet continues. "It can pick up a 250-pound kettle of dough. All the scaling (weighing) is done in nine minutes. Then there's a rounder machine. Never seen one of those, I bet. It rounds out three dozen rolls every three seconds, And see that, a Swedish oven! You won't see that on Cermak Road. You can bake right on the racks. We brought it in nine years ago. A drive-in steamer and a drive-in oven!"

The polka music continues; the movies is still running. Coffee cups are filled in the dark, more talk, more laughter, more bakery. Another reel is slapped in. Can true love be found in a bakery? Yes, according to Junior: "I met my wife here. She was working in the store. She started as a salesgirl at sixteen."

Finally, we move into the back room to inspect the real thing: mixers, lifters, rounders, the works.

"See this? A new automated doughnut fryer . . . 150 dozen an hour . . . anything, long johns, sugar twists, bismarks. On St. Joseph's Day we make St. Josephs—French doughnut buns filled with custard and topped with assorted fruits. Italians love 'em. It's insane. It's unreal, those days. Like the Poles the day before Ash Wednesday, before Lent. All Polish bakers are gone from Hawthorne, so the people come here for their ponczki. It's like a filled bismark, with raspberry or cherry or blueberry. It's all day. It's crazy, it's crazy," the old man says.

I have to get out of here before Matiasek's Manor does me in. As I'm about to make my exit, Junior appears with his father's saxophone. The old man laughs. "I play with the Jolly Baker's Band, weddings, anniversaries," he says. "I have three saxophones. I had them all gold-plated." I try to make a move before he begins playing all three of them, but Junior is too quick for me: he's back with a birthday cake in each hand: "This is the Raggedy Ann cake I make. This is the teddy bear. . . ." One foot out the door, and Chester Sr. is shouting goodbyes: "Well, you can say you've seen the best. Never a thing stale left over. The Best!"

That evening, I return to Fingerhut's to meet the Baron of Babi's rye himself, Herb Sr. Still a young man, he has relinquished some of his Babi's bread power to his son, who sits quietly near his father in the office upstairs.

Heavyset, sure of himself, Herb Sr. says, "There were sixty-two Czech bakeries in this area in the 1940s, one baker per block and two on several of them. There was only one Lithuanian baker and one Italian. The big changes came in the forties and fifties. The supermarkets took over the little guys, and now we're seeing the turnaround.

"People want natural food products, no preservatives. People want quality. My folks taught me something very important: make the product as good as you can, figure the cost, and make a profit. The Bohemian is frugal, but he's willing to spend a little more if he's going to have it the next day. I can't make a white bread by mechanical means, or a coffee cake that tastes like straw.

354

"Houska, I love to eat. A piece of houska in the morning! There's a million things you can do with it: Toast it, make French toast with it, put some cream cheese on it, some fresh strawberry jam . . . a little butter first. And with rye bread you make topinky. Toast it, rub it with fresh garlic, and then butter."

As for any "brotherhood" of bakers in Cicero and Berwyn, Herb just laughs. "No one wants to talk to the other guy. Professional jealousy. Even now, when we want to find out when the other guy's going on vacation so we'll know how much more to bake, we have to call and pretend we're ordering: 'Oh, you're going to be closed for the next two weeks? OK.' Hang up and start baking."

The secret to any successful bakery is being in tune (or in touch) with the dough. At Fingerhut's, that man is Karlovsky.

"Frank is a super baker," says Herb Sr., "the best baker anywhere, bar none. He's a cake man as well as a bread man, but he's been a bread man all his life. Whatever his problems, I live with them because he's the best. Frank calls me a sonofabitch, I call him an artist. Because when he makes a houska, it looks perfect and it is. He knows how to make adjustments, even for the weather, and he does it all without thinking. Uniformity. Consistency. Two months from now, six months from now . . . it'll be the same."

Herb Jr. walks me out. Suddenly he grabs a knife and hacks off a piece of sauerkraut rye for me. Savoring a mouthful, I watch him attack a porky rye, baked with bits of bacon in it. "Try this." I nod a full mouth of approval and mutter a porky-kraut rye goodbye.

I dream of dough that night, pursued by a hundred-pound loaf of Babi's rye leaping to the music of a polka band.

9:00 a.m. the next morning, I boogie back to Bohemia's Bakery Row. Vales Bakery, 6034 West Cermak Road, Cicero, is now under the bakership of Ken Galik, son-in-law by bakery blood to the old Vales family, thirty-five years in the same location. Galik, once a Sears salesman, has been with Vales for ten years. "My in-laws retired, and here I am. Jim Vales, the original owner, was a baker all his life."

We're at the rotating oven, which is turning over and over with pineapple-cherry cake, coffee cakes, ribbon cake, eight-inch yellow layer cake. There's no timer. "Just by touch," says Galik. "You feel it, you know it's ready. I start at ten every night, six days a week, seventy-two hours a week. I sleep from noon till around four. You get used to it.

"Houska, that's our biggest thing. If you went to any bakery they'd tell you it's probably the best around here. We take more time. We start making them around 11:30 at night, and they don't get done till 9:30 the next morning. Ours are big. We let them set longer, then proof more.

"We also make a lot of small stuff—six-inch pies, half-pound breads. Besides the new trade, we get a lot of old people who can't eat much. So we make little

355

cakes, all kinds of little stuff. A lot of the old-timers still speak Czech . . . we even have some Chinese and Japanese people who ask for houska.

"Coffee cakes are big—apricot, prune, cherry, poppy seed, cheese. There are all kinds of names. But people just come in and say, 'What is that? ' and buy it that way."

Jack Budzyn, of Polish ancestry, unloads a tray of steaming-hot pineapple-upside-down cakes, the cherries and pineapples glowing like gems. "Whatever bakery shop does something special, the Bohemians go for that," Galik explains.

"We probably sell as much houska as loaves of bread, way over three hundred a week. And at Christmas, you do that in a day. At Easter, we make the lambs [cakes]. My wife decorates all of them. She's been doing that with her father since she was a little girl."

The morning bakery eaters drift in and out, picking up a houska, a coffee cake. "The window display, that's a big thing," says Galik. It sure is: mini-pizzas of cheese, pineapple, blueberry, apricot, 43 cents each. French doughnuts filled with custard, hot dogs in a bun, large kolacs, apple and poppyseed strudel. I think of how great it would be to come in one day and say, in my best Bohemian, "Wrap up that whole window, please."

As I leave, two old men come up to the counter and buy twenty-nine loaves of rye bread. A Bohemian-rye orgy! I eye them suspiciously, then beat a path down Cermak Road.

By afternoon, my legs feel like dough. At 5919 West Cermak Road, Cicero stands a green-tiled bakery once called Hruska's. Now the sign in the window says SOBRAN'S home bakery. Ever since 1952, Charles Svec, a Sobran son-in-law and a baker for seventeen years, has been in charge.

It's an old store. It looks the way old bakeries used to look—sliding glass doors, a ceiling fan, a warm wooden bench over the radiator, and people who come in, take a deep breath, and exclaim, "Oh, it smells so good in here!"

Specialty of the house? "Rye bread," says Charlie Svec, who seems a bit tight-lipped and wary. "Hearth-baked rye bread in an old-time brick oven built in 1925, originally wood fired, now oil. Our rye bread is made from scratch. We've been making a cocktail rye, too, for Old Prague [the famous Czech restaurant across the street] for more than twenty-five years."

To Svec, everything else he makes in the Czech tradition is the usual. "The usual coffee cakes, Danish type. Bohemian houska. Everybody makes it the same. They may say they put all butter in it, but I don't believe it."

"I love baking. I was once a buyer for J. C. Penny, but I like starting with raw materials and ending up with a finished product. I put in about eighty hours a week, two a.m. till noon, sometimes till three, four in the afternoon. Just one other baker helps me out, Charles Bacigalupe. You got better control over your product this way. Never anything stale. . . . We're able to make our filings and icings ourselves because we're that small.

356

"I've been baking since I was eighteen. The problem now is that a bakery today is almost impossible to sell as a bakery. The hours are terrible. The work is hard. But I'm not going anywhere."

Neither am I. The next morning I'm back on the street, determined to leave no houska horizon unexplored.

Stetina's, 6516 West Cermak Road, Berwyn. What can I say? Classic Czech bakers. You look at all those rococo rolls and coffee cakes in the windows, all the perfection of bread and houska, and you know that the golden age of Czech bakery isn't dead yet.

The Stetinas are third-generation bakers, going back to the 1930s on 26th Street (and before that to the old neighborhood on California). Their shop has been here since 1946. Mike Slezak, thirty-five (his mother is a Stetina), took it over from his father in 1968. "I grew up right upstairs," he says. "I've worked for my dad since I was eighteen."

Slezak is aggressive, a baker who gives everything his best. "We make all our rye bread from scratch. It comes out of the ovens three times a day: 5:30 a.m., 8:30, and 11. Our people know this. They get it fresh. They run home, put some butter on it."

He catches me lingering over something he calls Black Forest cake.

"It goes for $5.50. Three layers of cake, two chocolate, one yellow. Cherry filling, cherry liqueur, whipped-cream-filled, and topped with whipped cream, cherries, and shaved chocolate. Next to it, that's a Texas cheesecake for $3.25 with wild blueberries, Philadelphia cream cheese, and butter streusel on top. I got the recipe from Neiman-Marcus in Dallas. It's not a cheap cake to make." Neiman-Marcus comes to Bohemia?

"I try to change every week, give the public a little variety. You experiment. Go out and see something else and try to duplicate it, make it a little better. I love to cook and bake at home, try it out on my kids. No machinery at home; it's all done by hand. The only difference is the quantity."

Yet with bakery booming in these environs, Slezak seems more pessimistic than some of his colleagues: "I think bakeries are going to die out just like the little butcher shops. It's not profitable to make bread, for instance. It's a service to your customers. Same thing with sweet rolls. A lot of people are more weight and cost-conscious these days. The diet of people has changed. Bakeries will have to become specialty shops to keep going.

"I'd say our average sale is three dollars, twice a week. Some customers buy the same thing every day, and others come in and spend $25. I think what keeps a bakery going all these years is that in no other store can you put ten dollars on the counter and walk out with an armful of food. At a butcher shop, you carry it out in one hand."

What makes Bohemian baking the best? "First, there's appearance. People wind up buying it because they can't resist the look of it. Second is taste. The

357

taste has to be so good that the housewives will want to make it themselves. They call me up, want to know how to make it. But they *still* can't make it. I always say: you give them the recipe, but you can't give them your hands. You can give the recipe to four people, and it'll come out four different ways."

While Slezak checks the oven, I gaze at four Czech bakers, including one who speaks seven languages. The tables of tempting coffee cakes would demolish any weight-reducing class in Chicago: an artist's palette of fillings, the deepest, warmest colors imaginable, from the richest apricot to the brightest cherry red.

Joe Hamouz, thirty-two years a baker, is filling the ovens. And Jerry Jerica, a round, white-haired, bouncy baker, seems to be rolling his whole self into bread dough, smiling with every breath.

I watch as he rolls it, forms it, bounces it in his hands. Red-faced and smiling, he forms two good-sized balls of rye dough, aware of its soft sensuality. He suddenly breaks into laughter as he brings the two round handfuls of dough to his chest, raising his eyebrows in Old World memories.

Ah, yes, you old bread man, you remember her well.

On to Minarik's, 5832 West Cermak Road, Cicero, and images of all the neighborhood bakeries I've known: bakeries in spring, bakeries and birthday cakes, bakeries in the dead of winter, a snowy day, and now the window of Minarik's—warm with poppy-seed babovka, assorted buchticky, grape coffee cakes, plum, pineapple cheese, and swirls of cheese and apricot—brings more comfort than the Florida sun.

Inside is the folksy Czech touch: paintings of the old country, Czech cookbooks for sale, a crystal chandelier shining over the rye bread, a sign on the wall (in Czech, roughly translated: Give Us This Day Our Daily Bread. Good, old-time Bohemian breadbasket religion.)

Mrs. Minarik is a Czech bakery queen of sorts. Says her baker-husband Frank, "If you listen my wife, you no be able to put in all she says." A true Mother Czech, she sits me down in the back and serves coffee and fresh butter horns, instinctively knowing that it takes bakery to get things going.

Minarik's is Old World style and taste at its best. The goodness, the skill, she attributes to her husband: "A baker forty-six years, all life. His recipes are from all his trade, all his life. We specialize in apple strudel, houska, kolacky, and delicious bread, Bohemian style—Minarik's rye bread. Coffee cakes, open face, all kinds fruit, even plum and grape. We have always fresh fruit—strawberries, plum, grape, peach. Houska we make with raisins and almonds on top . . . lots of butter. We are old-fashioned. We believe in nothing but butter, honey. Fresh everything.

"Why so much bakery, Czech people? Just European way. People like to eat bakery. Like your *maminka* [mother], why she must have buchticky? Why? European people maybe never have enough meat. Never. They finish off meal then with bakery stuff. They fill up on bakery. On the farms there, they have the milk, the butter, the eggs.

"Well, now, five years, I want to sell. I am old lady now. Husband is old man. I am married thirty-four years, thirty-four years baking, working, working . . . nothing else to do. What do you think? Honey, I need rest. But I *love* it! This is our life.

"I like apple strudel, I like bread, I like it all, all bakery. That's why I am fat! My doctor say to me, 'No sugar.' I say, 'Doc, are you crazy? I got a bakery shop, how can I cut out the sugar?' So I cut out--maybe two months. Then I go back to the bakery, honey."

The nimbus of another night in the old neighborhood. A nightmare of all the Czech bakeries mysteriously disappearing, replaced by supermarket packaged pastries. I wake up to kolacky withdrawal. 1:00 a.m., 2:00 a.m. What are the bakers up to?

3:00 a.m., Vesecky's, 6634 West Cermak Road, Berwyn, the last stop of my Bohemian bakery binge. The wedding cakes glow like ghosts in the nighttime windows. A phantom baker in white is already filling the window with kolacky for the traditional Saturday-morning onslaught of customers who will converge on all the bakeries of Bohemia in hours, stashing it away for the weekend. No bakery till Monday is a Bohemian fear worse than death.

Entering the back door, I am visually, sensually overcome by the madness, the light, the aroma of a bakery in full swing: nine men dressed in white, all whirling in a world of flour, dough, whipped cream, and fruit fillings. Hands, hands, hands, an intricacy of hands, working wonders through the night, trying to keep the clock from reaching six, when the store must open and the bakers magically disappear.

Jim Vesecky, Sr., seventy-one, welcomes me with open, floured baker's arms. His son, Jim Jr., slaps his hands clean to offer a hearty handshake. (I have been here before. In the sixties this was my neighborhood bakery.) "How you been?" they ask. "How about some coffee, some kolacky?"

At the oven, Joe Samec is pulling out coffee cakes like there's no tomorrow. (Nearly fifty different kinds. Who knows what they're all called? You make them, buy them, eat them because they look like the answer.)

Quarts of lager beer appear and disappear in their doughy bread, their own special way of making it through a Vesecky night.

Samec is orchestrating the ovens containing twenty buttercream streusels. Bob Miksa mans the houska detail along with young Mike Opat ("My dad owned a bakery on 26th and Ridgeland"). Old Jim Vesecky brushes the houska with an egg wash to make them shine. Young Frank Holas lends his skill as well. Grandsons Randy, twenty-four, and Dave, twenty, help out, learning the ropes.

I devour an apricot kolacky as the houska detail swings to the white dough. A chorus of seven bakers conquers globs of dough on two large tables: salty

359

horns, hot-dog buns, butter crust.

Jim. Jr., wrist deep in cheese and prune, says of his baking sons, "I didn't en-
courage it, but the business still has a good future, and nobody wants to be a
lawyer or anything. There are probably too many college-educated kids who
can't do anything, anyway. Nobody wants to go in the trades."

Old Jim Vesecky takes a swig of beer and begins loading trays of fresh bakery
for the front of the store, where racks of bread--bucket rye, small rounds, large
rounds, large white, cocktail rye, poppy seed, potato rye--already await the day.
At four a.m. on Saturday, Helen Tyler and Mrs. Vesecky will begin the feverish
task of preparing for customers.

Changes in the bakery business? "The number of retail bakeries has been de-
creasing since the 1940s," says Jim Jr., "but by last year, the number had stabi-
lized. It's people looking for specialty items and natural foods. You just can't
go into general baking any more. Either you have to cater to an ethnic group,
like we do, or make specialty items. People always say, 'Why don't you move
out to the suburbs? We need a good bakery.' But I think the shopping habits
are different there. Most of our customers are men these days. They come in to
pick up an order, and then I suppose they see other things or the salesgirls talk
them into something else."

Mrs. Vesecky enters the room. Old Jim, who seems to be everywhere, now
has his two grandsons rolling--hands, arms, bodies in a dance of dough. Jim. Jr.
appears. And for this one brief moment at the workbench, three generations of
Vesecky bakers demonstrate the Bohemian baking tradition. Fifty years and still
counting.

The Vesecky grandsons, along with Frank Holas, get ready to head out for the
opening of pheasant season. Jim Jr., in the back of the shop, begins to fill box-
es with rye bread and coffee cakes. "For the boys," he says with a smile, "to
bribe the farmers to let them hunt on the land. They've found that bakery helps
them get in."

Cake decorator George Hruska, a thirty-year man, is burrowing through a stack
of cake orders, preparing to build himself a whipped-cream cake for sunrise. Joe
is taking out houska, six at a time; old man Vesecky helps Mike with the salty
horns. "A bakery ain't got these, it ain't a bakery," Mike says.

George is mumbling again. Jim Jr. wipes his hands. "George is getting a
little grumpy. Today he's got all these cakes to do alone. I'll have to give him
a hand." George is taking it all out on some tiny rolls, whupping them with an
overdose of whipped cream.

"I don't dream of bakery anymore," smiles Old Jim. "I used to, years ago. I
dreamed of kolacky once. We used to pile them up high like this. And I
dreamed they were so high that they started coming down on me." The old man
leans back, pushing with both hands, trying to hold back an avalanche of ko-
lacky.

Night and day blend into one for the baker. Bakers appear and disappear, leaving behind golden buns, racks of houska, and showcases full of their handiwork.

All alone, George whips his way to sunrise, talking to himself, dolefully peeling bananas, slicing them off with vengeance to top a cake. Then hitting hard with a whoosh of whipped cream. Smoothing it out along the edges and around the top. Then back to a fancy whipped-cream border, head bent in total concentration, bringing his work to perfection. He mumbles a lasting tribute to himself: "Made by the all-around baking man."

It's like a dream. To make sure I'm awake, I taste a cheese, a pineapple, and a poppy-seed kolacky.

"There are more coffee cakes here than anyone can name," says Jim Jr.

"Take some more bakery," says the old man, smiling.

"It all has to be out by six," says Mrs. Vesecky.

"Jesus Christ, I'm flying like lightening," says Helen.

Joe, the oven man, drifts out the back door with his arms full of bakery.

On the street, an old man presses his face to the darkened front window, covers his forehead with both hands, and waits for the lights to go on in all the bakeries of Bohemia. Waits for the sight, the smell, and the sure sign of home.

Back to the Neighborhood: The Houby Parade

If you are any kind of lover at all, you never let go of your first love of the streets: the old neighborhood. You never tire of romancing and remembering her.

To have come of age in any neighborhood, especially a Chicago one, you are a marked person the rest of your life. It will not let go of you, you can never let go of it.

Nostalgia is the heart of the homebody suffering from "time passes." Whether it's an honest human emotion or insincere, who can be certain? But it's better than a bad memory. And no matter where in the world you are, and time indeed is passing, if you came from an ethnic Chicago neighborhood, you will find friends.

In the winter of 1988, I found myself in Managua, Nicaragua. The second night there I met an elderly widow, Mrs. Adolph Svec—who once lived in Cicero. I remembered her husband, a distinguished educator in the community and my Boy's Club instructor in Cicero in the 1940s. (He taught us to turn old bowling pins on a lathe into lamps.) Small world. Big memories. We talked "neighborhood" on into the night—thousands of miles from Cicero, in a poor but proud neighborhood of Nicaraguans, struggling with their own sense of place and past.

Suffice to say that my neighborhood of Cicero and Berwyn is alive and changing, deteriorating in some areas, gaining new strength in others. Struggling, to say the least. The last movie house (the Olympic Theater) recently closed. It was one of my favorite Saturday matinee haunts. My Grandma and Grandpa Papp once lived in the Olympic building. My Grandpa ran the boiler room—and gave me free passes to the movies.

The house where I grew up remains. My father still lives there, although most of the old neighbors are gone. A Spanish family moved into the house next door. My father says they are good people. And the hot Mexican food they offer him is very different from Bohemian cusine.

Sometimes I walk the old neighborhood, sometimes I drive. But I prefer (much as my father) to walk up the streets, down the alleys, always in touch with the familiar landmarks of backyard gardens, corner bungalows, neighbors in windows or sitting on steps waving as I pass by. There is this immediacy of place, human contact, acceptance, which we lose sight of in today's world of suburbs and shopping malls, an immediacy which the neighborhood ethnic equates with life in the village.

Each time I return, I return to my youth: walking the alleys, the block, the streets. Smelling the freshly cut grass. Remembering piles of leaves along the curbs burning and smoking in autumn evenings. Mothers on front steps calling their children in before dark—"when the streetlights go on."

I was back in the neighborhood again just recently—though even "just recently" becomes more and more vague in the lore of neighborhood, when time present/time past seem always to merge, and my being there a year ago, a week ago or in two weeks to come, seems all one and the same.

But I was back there for the annual Houby (Mushroom) Parade in October not long ago, perhaps not a great event or honor for some. But a local celebration of considerable magnitude for a once neighborhood kid who lived for years in relative neighborhood obscurity. This was a benchmark of sorts—you *can* go home to the neighborhood again. What's more, you can even be in a parade.

With the publication of *Neighborhood* (Ellis Press, 1987), I began to achieve a bit of notoriety in Cicero and Berwyn, thanks to stories and photographs which appeared in the *Cicero/Berwyn Life*. I was a guest on local radio and Metrovision Cable TV, hosted by Len Petrulis. I did some autograph sessions at Pancner's and met a lot of old friends.

M. Pancner's became my neighborhood headquarters, thanks to Jean Pancner Lundberg, the daughter of the late Miles Pancner. She, above all, helped center "the local author" in his old neighborhood again, refresh his sense of the old language, Czech history, customs, neighborhood lore; saw to it that people who wanted the book, or were looking to make contact, knew where and how to find me. (She continues to provide this lifeline, for which I am grateful—a true neighborhood sweetheart.)

My "local author" fame continued. I spoke to a large gathering of the Friends of the Library in Berwyn. I returned to my old high school, J. Sterling Morton, to talk with students photographing the old neighborhood, thanks to their teacher Margaret Trybus. (A lesson for me as well, since through their eyes, their images, I saw how much the old Czech culture was changing to Spanish, Italian, and other ethnic groups. Changes, as well, in the school itself. Yet there was something in the attitude of the students, the clean and solid appearance of the school itself that filled me with pride.)

I was invited to be the guest speaker at a number of marvelous reunions of former Morton High School students: in Long Beach, California (Morton Group of Southern California, organized by superman Ernie Alessio [Class of '39] and associates) and another in Tampa/St. Pete, organized by two wonderful old neighbors, Lydia and Ed Libery, whom I had not seen in more than twenty years. Ed was my old scoutmaster.

Though I've never attended any class reunions of my own (for all kinds of personal reasons) these two events were two of the best "remember-the-old-neighborhood" experiences I will ever know . . . Meeting high school sweethearts/graduates, Fred & Dorothy (Church) Weick, of the class of 1918 . . . meeting so many people with vibrant, loving memories of our past. People who remain "neighborhood" to the core, no matter the time or distance . . . ("Did you bring any Babi's rye," they would ask. "Any Bakery from Vesecky's? How about some praszky, jaternice, tripe soup?") Ah, the stomach of a neighborhood. How it remembers.

In May of 1989 I was invited to deliver the commencement address at my alma mater, Morton [Junior] College in Cicero. Once again I returned to the neighborhood. Once again I felt pride as I donned the traditional robes of a scholar and academic (though I am neither) and attempted to tell them who we all were from this same nieghborhood, what we came from, where we should be headed . . . always remembering to glance back a little over our shoulders.

The graduating class, young, middle-aged, old, was defintely "neighborhood"—a cross-section of Americana, including one black woman who crossed the stage to accept her degree, making history of her own in Cicero.

To change, to celebrate, to not forget where we came from. To be happy in our work. To take whatever risks necessary to achieve whatever it is within ourselves that needs to be heard and shared.

Our neighborhood college (M.J.C.) was looked upon with humor at times: the "Bohemian Harvard" some called it. Or, "Czech Tech." But we could smile at this ourselves, knowing full well our parents were saving a bundle giving us the first two years of college in our own neighborhood at cheap tuition, living at home. Most of us completed bachelor degrees and beyond at other universities. Most of us succeeded, and did the old neighborhood proud.

Czech humor is alive and well on the streets, in the homes and shops of Cicero. Prague and its great literary tradition was never that far removed. To take a common mushroom (the houby) and make light of it and a culture (the Bohemian mushroom hunter) by turning it into a parade, a profitable, annual celebration that gives a whole community some sense of identity is no mean task.

Yet, at the Nineteenth Annual International Houby Parade (which I was a small part of) sponsored by the Cermak Road Business Association, even soon-to-be-President George Bush came along for the ride and spoke to some five thousand people in front of one of Cicero's landmark restaurants, Klas, on Cermak Road. (Some 70,000 people were on hand along the parade route.)

What Bush said was, "We celebrate family, we celebrate faith, and we celebrate freedom. None of us will ever forget there is not freedom in Eastern Europe, and I have pledged as president I will never forget that." So much for neighborhood ethnic politics, on the national level. (Though I wondered if all the Hispanics present felt he had anything to promise them.)

This was the second president I had seen in my old Bohemia along Cermak Road. In the 1950s I stood in the street by Western Electric amidst thousands of factory workers (my mother included) who cheered Ike.

Politicians have always fround their way to this neighborhood.

A few signs along the route hounded George Bush's first neighborhood Houby Parade: "WHERE WAS GEORGE?" Including one held by an old Bohunk in a window above Cermak Road that was far and above politics: "I AM 98 YEARS OLD." (A scene right our of a Czech film or story. How could even a future President of the Eastern Establishment *not* smile at these poor, Eastern European working folk? Just so long as he didn't patronize them—as politicians are wont to do.)

On the small marquee attached to the grand old sign that announces Klas Restaurant (where the next president of the United States was addressing the ethnic minority) evidence too, of both the friendliness of Czechs and perhaps a touch of their kind of ironic humor Czechoslovakia has given the world in books and film—literary masterpieces such as Jaroslav Hasek's, *The Good Soldier Schweik.*

WELCOME GEORGE BUSH TO KLAS, said the marquee in bold, black letters. While just above it, a more permanent part of the sign, a Czech proverb that has greeted every neighborhood shopper, walker, drinker, eater, down through the years: ENJOY YOURSELF IT MAY BE LATER THAN YOU THINK.

Somewhere in some neighborhood pub in Prague (or Cicero) the ghost of Soldier Schweik wipes the foam from his lips, puffs his pipe, and smiles on Houby Kings, politicians pandering to ethnic (slavic) souls, the absurdity of power, the comedy of man.

"I once knew a Czech author personally, a chap named Ladislav Hajek . . . He was a cheerful gentleman, he was, and a good sort, too. He once went to a pub and read a lot of his stories there. They were very sad stories and they made everybody laugh, and then he started crying and stood us drinks all around—"
—Soldier Schweik

M. Pancner's:
A Czech Shop on Main Street/Cermak Road

It's been a neighborhood landmark since I was a child: M. Pancner's Cards & Gifts (Cicero Book Store) 6038 W. Cermak, in Cicero, Illinois.

Cermak Road (named after Chicago's Czech mayor, Anton Cermak) was the life of the neighborhood. It remains so today, but nothing like it was then, when it dominated the entire community, defined a culture (basically Czechoslovak and Eastern European), and the shops along our Czech "Main Street" hummed with the language of the old country, the smells from bakery stores and butcher shops.

The sidewalks were filled with bushels of fruits and vegetables. Old babi (grandmothers) with leather shopping bags filtered in and out the stores speaking their native tongue. Men walked, rode bicycles, waited on corners for streetcars, or boarded the Douglas Park El for the Loop at one neighborhood station or another—Cicero Ave., Central, 58th.

Kids moved down the street alone, in bunches, in the hands of their mothers or grandmothers, sometimes thumping and humming along the concrete pavement in a handmade wooden scooter made from fruit boxes, a 2x4, and roller skates.

It was a time when drugstores had soda fountains that served Black Cows and Green Rivers; when butchers gave small children warm frankfurters to eat while mothers ordered fresh cuts of meat from fat men in bloody aprons; when there was sawdust on the floor; when women wore babushkas and men wore fedoras; when white poster-painted glass windows advertised SALES that were really sales; when store signs at night were rainbows of neon; when "the 5 & 10" sold 5 and 10-cent things; when produce stores sold hard little green peas (ammunition) to kids on Halloween for the pure devilment and sure aim of pea shooters; when a ride to, around the Loop and back on the EL cost a kid three cents; when looking in store windows was what we did before we had TV to imagine our lives.

Young and old, we windowshopped the neighborhood, both sides of Cermak, till we were exhausted from all we thought we had added (or soon would) to our lives. All our new found fantasies. From clothing (Jack's Men's Shop); to Furniture (Kobzina's); to food (Stein's); to drugstores and all their alchemy; to bakeries, delicatessens, Art's Bicycle Shop (Schwinn), auto showrooms, featuring Buick "Roadmasters," sporting goods, kitchen appliances, hobby and hardware stores.

Storefront windows were our catalog pages, our newspaper and magazine ads, sometimes, even our geography books made real. At nights, in the magic of concentrated light, the windows held us like stage sets—which we entered through shining glass.

Pancner's window, from my earliest memory, was another world entirely, the old world: Czechoslovakia, a world I had only heard about in the conversations of grandparents, neighbors, visitors. But I had "seen," was aware of Czechoslovakia in those varied artifacts of Czech culture with which the old timers decorated their homes.

You would look in the beautiful window displays of Miles Pancner and almost always see *something* that reminded you of home, of your grandma's house, of what Czechoslovakia must be like. Perhaps it was the Hummel figurines which pulled you in . . . those old world pastoral evocations of children sitting on fences or near trees singing, swinging, feeding geese; children playing concertinas, violins, and horns . . . an old shoemaker with boots under his arms . . . a chimney sweep carrying a ladder. Images of the old world, of village life, what Grandma and Grandpa talked about, sometimes with tears in their eyes.

Or all the delicate glass that held one's eye—the red crystal vases, bowls, and goblets which Czechs showed off in their dining rooms, saved for special occasions, or kept locked forever behind glass china cabinets.

There were ethnic plates as well with images of old world castles . . . porcelain cups and saucers. Religious goods—carved crosses and saints. And above all "Easter" eggs—not like any you could ever color at home, but intricately designed, hand-painted eggs, from Europe—chicken and goose—which were small works of art one normally found in museums.

And books. From Czech/English dictionaries, to collections of old recipes, to Czechslovak history and literature. To see the written language on covers alone: *Cesko-Americky-Zpevnik* held both mystery and delight.

When I "rediscovered" my old neighborhood as a young writer in the 1960s, rediscovered the Czech culture and language, it was Pancner's I stepped into after *many* years absence, to purchase a book, *Progressive Czech*, by Bohumil E. Mikula, once a teacher of Czech at Morton High School.

Pancner's in the 1960s . . . was like Pancner's in the 1940s . . . is like Pancner's today, and on into the 1990s. No other store on the street has changed so little. It's a perfect time capsule of the way things were: from the long glass-case counters that run almost the entire length of the store from the front door to the rear storage area; to the center display cases, racks of greeting cards, book shelves . . . to the stool by the front window where old Mr. Pancner used to sit watching the world go by down Cermak Road, greeting the customers as they entered his shop.

He always wore a white shirt, tie, sweater or scarf and fedora. Always had a cane in hand. Always seemed anxious to speak Czech. There was more than a touch of the debonair, the European aristocrat about him. He exuded a sense of old world class. What he loved to talk about most in his later years were his experiences in the army in World War I, when at the age of seventeen he fought for four years against the Italians, was wounded in action, cited for bravery, and was given many gold medals. He was a born storyteller.

A native of Kyjov, Czechoslovakia, he left at the age of twenty-one and joined his brother in business in Chicago. He married Marie Alexander (of Lisov, Czechoslovakia) in Chicago in 1926. And on their third wedding anniversary, October 3, 1929, they opened this store, Pancner's Cards & Gifts, at 6038 W. Cermak Road. (A somewhat similar Pancner store, F. Pancner, in Berwyn, was founded by his brother, now deceased, and now run by two sons.)

Marie Pancner had a natural instinct for quality gift items (especially imports) whether they were toys, dolls, crystal, figurines—as opposed to the usual items found everywhere else.

371

This is even more true today, with the store in the very capable and caring hands of daughter Jean Pancner Lundberg (a successful teacher, writer, and mother) who took over the business after the death of her mother in 1980, and whose major concern was the care of her father (who lived above the store), the expansion of her collectible doll line, and keeping the Czech tradition alive a while longer on Main Street/Cermak Road.

She keeps alive as well her memories of the two loving parents who most shaped her life: "My Mom was the workaholic; Dad, the Father, the personality man, the charmer. My Mother was my inspiration, my lifeline to the past. She always had a kind word, so many words of encouragement for me . . . telling me I could accomplish whatever I strove to achieve. I learned these skills from her, plus sticking to a task until it was accomplished. These are some of the legacies I have passed on to Derek [her son]."

The store today, though it may look the same as it did sixty years ago, no doubt holds three, four, five times the amount of merchandise: miniatures—animals, birds, doll house items; collectors' ethnic plates—German, Italian, Czech, Scandinavian; porcelain statues—Bing & Grondall, Llardro, Hummel, Gerold; crystal from Germany, Czechoslavakia, Yugoslavia, Poland, Italy, Hungary, Argentina; anniversary items; bells—German, Czech, Polish; banks; nightlights; paperweights, music boxes; ash trays; religious goods—rosaries, jewelry, medals, crosses, statues, ("We sell *lots* of St. Joseph's to people trying to sell their homes," says Jean); stationery and office supplies; mugs; plush animals; wood carvings; books—classics and a few current paperbacks, foreign language dictionaries, cookbooks for various ethnic groups (Czech and Italian the most popular); wallets, pens, bookends; greeting cards—an international line hard to find anywhere else in Chicago, with words and verses in Italian, German, Polish, Czech, Spanish, for all occasions . . . and *all* languages for the holiday season, including Portugese, Chinese, Swedish, Lithuanian, French, Russian, German, Czech, Slovak, Norwegian, Hungarian, Ukranian, Polish.

As for ornate dolls, Jean (exhibiting many of the qualities of a fine porcelain doll herself, a genuine Czech doll in her own right) has a world-class collection to offer in her little shop, dolls from Alexander to Effanbee, Gibson, Bradford, Royal, Steiff, Vogue, Tanzupi.

To current charcter dolls: Liz Taylor, Rhett Butler, Marilyn Monroe, James Dean, Reagan, Alexis, Babe Ruth, approximately a hundred or more types/companies combined. (She is also the founder of a doll collector's club and publishes a newsletter which reaches more than four hundred members.)

So the small Czech shop on Main Street/Cermak Road extends far beyond its neighborhood borders. Much farther than Miles and Marie ever expected, sixty years ago, thanks to their hard work, thanks to neighborhood tradition, and thanks to their daughter, Jean. (And the help and understanding of her husband, Lloyd, and son, Derek, as well.)

"I was reading some of your work to my father," Jean told me at one of the autograph sessions for *Neighborhood* held at Pancner's (where I had come "home," full circle to the store where I once bought Modern Library editions of the classics, nurturing a secret desire to someday write). "He said your stories remind him of the Czech author, Hasek, *The Good Soldier Schweik.*"

"Tell him, *děkuji, děkuji,* from me," I smiled. "Hasek is one of my favorites."

With the death of old Mr. Pancner, the neighborhood lost not only one of its oldest shopkeepers but a certain presence as well that lent character and value to a street that both celebrated and defined the lifeblood of its people.

What a memory the man had of European and Czechoslovak history. He would begin almost anywhere—but eventually return to the war, his life in the military, which for a man in his late eighties had to have been a time of youth both celebrated and denied.

He was a man filled with stories: how he once set up a printing press in the basement of the store to print his own cards in Czech. The time a member of Cicero's legendary Al Capone mob tried to muscle into his store and put in slot machines. "But I said no. In my store come a lot of kids. And I throw the bum out."

"I hated the war," he told me the last time I would ever talk with him. "Lots of killing. I was seventeen years old. They give me gold medals, and I bury them. I not proud. No sir. Remember only . . . I was brave."

The storyteller's gone. But the shop of Miles Pancner on Main Street/ Cermak Road remains — a neighborhood legacy. *Nazdar!*

> *But there isn't enough of anything as long as we live.*
> — Jaroslav Seifert, *Dance-Song*
> (1984 Nobel Prize)

Libby & Jana: The People's Restaurant (L&J Lounge: The People's Bar)

When I first met these two Bohemian beauties they ran the People's Restaurant in the Boulevard Manor section of Cicero.

It was quite the place, and they were quite the talk of the neighborhood—at least among Bohemian men who have an eye for a pretty face, a pretty leg, a pretty Czechoslovak zena.

What I saw then went something like this:

They keep drifting in and out of the People's Restaurant in Cicero—the neighborhood hungries. Women with shopping bags. Men of all ages (especially oldtimers) coming in for their roast duck, tripe soup, fruit dumplings. Coming in for a bellyful or an eyeful. Stepping in perhaps just to see Libby and Jana, two Bohemian treats not usually found in a neighborhood ethnic restaurant.

There is a touch of Czech classic in the People's Restaurant, 5916 W. 35th St.: clean, crisp, tiny, a few native artifacts for decoration (cutouts of houby pasted to a mirror); plastic lilies of the valley in milk-glass vases on each table; and two prints of Prague.

And the sound of native tongue spoken fluently and loudly. And the aroma of native cooking (roast pork, dumplings, and sauerkraut). Add two buxom, mini-skirted sisters, waiting tables, washing dishes, and helping mama in the kitchen.

Libby Kohout (thirty-eight? . . . ageless), waitress and dishwasher, blond, mother of two, slightly serious, claims that she worked on construction for fifteen years in Czechoslovakia and left in 1968 because, "My husband didn't like Communism. This is better."

Jana Cerveny, thirty-six? ("I'm twenty-five! I'm twenty-five!" she insists),
blond, delicate, mother of two, waits on tables with a bubbly flair but once was
a singer in Czechoslovakia. "I sing, 'Kiss Me Kate,' Offenbach, was Eliza in
'My Fair Lady'."

Marie Hradecka, mother and chief cook, (all the old world recipes in her
head), surveys the whole scene from her kitchen, stirring pots of boiling soup,
shoving trays of homemade bakery goods into the oven, filling empty plates, yet
all the while keeping a trained eye on her two daughters.

The food is very fine and reasonable—$2.60 for a small portion, $2.90 for
large, and $3.00 for roast duck, the most expensive item on the menu. But that
doesn't matter.

What matters is the broken English, the local color, and the mother, Marie,
in the restaurant at 7:00 every morning, preparing her best for the people.
"Everyday, homemade soup. Everyday, everything baked fresh," explains Libby.
Marie is too busy for explanations.

What also matters (mostly for men) are the two vibrant waitresses, the likes
of which are usually reserved for downtown cocktail lounges and credit card cus-
tomers, far from this neighborhood.

And so the oldtimers, one eye on their forks, one eye on Libby and Jana,
keep dropping their silverware, checking the legs, the scenery, coming up for
fresh air, breathing a sigh for days gone by.

The old country was never like this—neither was the new. The taste for life
lingers a little longer when dished up by Libby and Jana, two Bohemian refugees
at home in the People's Restaurant. That's what matters most.

When you no longer live in the old neighborhood, and no matter how often
you may visit, you lose touch. Parts of it keep slipping away: streets, stores,
schools, restaurants, people, neighborhoods within neighborhoods.

Entire places disappear, and it might be years before you wonder "What ever
happened to 'the Greeks'—the restaurant next to the Villas Show?" "Whatever
happened to 'Army' who sold papers on Central & Cermak and, legend had it,
booked the ponies for the neighborhood horseplayers?" "Whatever happened to
that small Bohemian restaurant in the back, next to the alley on Lombard?" "Is
the Berwyn Dairy gone?" "Why have all the Bohemian tailors disappeared?"
Whatever happened to Frejlach's Ice Cream Parlor on Cermak in Berwyn (and on
26th Street in Cicero) which served the best malted milk shakes in the world?"

Is that great mural in the Berwyn Post Office of an ethnic family picnicking
(a concertina player and all) still there? Why isn't there more of that kind of art
in the community, which reflects and celebrates basic human values, neighbor-
hood traditions, instead of the crap outsiders foist upon us in the Cermak Shop-
ping Center—such as the proposed 'Spindle,' made of nine cars impaled on a
50-foot spike, and the existing trash here, 'Bill Bored?' Why isn't all of this
dismantled, put in a dump truck and returned to shopping center owner, David

Bermant of Santa Barbara, California, with strict instructions: "Here, put this shit in front of your own house. This 'art' reflects neither the spirit nor the tradition of the hard working people in this community. And they don't particularly enjoy being made fools of—especially by California dreamers and creeps."

It was somewhat in that frame of mind ("Whatever happened to . . ?") that I first learned from my Aunt Lorry, who lives near the People's Restaurant, that Libby and Jana and the mother sold the place and "they're not there anymore."

And that was it. The restaurant remained, but my Czechoslovak lovelies had disappeared into the fabric of the neighborhood. Or maybe moved on. Or returned to the old country. Who knows? The restaurant's there . . . but "it's different people."

It was the weekend of the 19th Annual Houby Day Parade, and I was back in the neighborhood.

The day after the parade George Bush had returned to Washington or somewhere, the neighborhood was recovering from its annual fifteen minutes of fame and I was soaking up the old neighborhood a while longer, staying at my father's, riding the El downtown as I did when I was a kid, visiting friends.

I was on Cermak Road. I was thirsty. I was looking for a cold beer. I was looking for a friendly neighborhood tavern, but the places I knew years ago were all gone.

I approached Marik & Sons Funeral Home (one of a number of highly respected, traditional Czech undertakers in the neighborhood) where my mother, my grandparents, other members of the family, and friends had been waked. And then I remembered. . . .

What does a funeral parlor have to do with a neighborhood tavern?

Everything — if you're Czech. If you've got any European blood in you at all. If you've ever attended a true ethnic wake anywhere in Chicago.

Show me a Czech funeral parlor in an old neighborhood, and I'll show you a tavern next door or near by. Celebration: that's what death, "being laid to rest," "waked" is all about.

With this in mind, I stepped toward the tavern next door to Marik & Sons on Cermak, never knowing the name of the place or who owned it, yet with a sense of déjà vu.

I recalled it was the "place next door" we went to when things got a little too heavy in the funeral parlor—a widow breaking into heartful sobs; too many mourners mourning too loudly; feeling a little confused yourself over the death of a friend or loved one. "Let's go next door for a beer and something to eat." And you would quietly disappear, leaving all the sympathy and sadness behind you, hoping to change the mood.

I took a seat at the bar of the "tavern next door to Marik," ordered a Gosser on tap from the barmaid who was speaking Czech to a guy at the other end of the bar, but all the while drawing a tall cold one for me, gently controlling the rich, thick head of foam . . . yes, this is the place.

I remember coming in here for a drink with a couple of my uncles at my Grandma's funeral. The bar. The red checkered tablecloths. I remember coming back later with my aunt and others for a bowl of soup and a roast pork sandwich on rye. (I remember thinking my mother hadn't died, and we were all sitting at the table here, eating, drinking, laughing, telling stories.)

It is good to be back on a late afternoon in a neighborhood tavern feeling home, though I don't know a soul in the joint.

I take a closer look at the barmaid. She's blond, and I love hearing her laugh and speak Czech with most of the men at the bar. I am reminded of the stories of one of my favorite Czech authors, Bohumil Hrabal, "Listen, Olympie, when I look at you . . . how shall I put it? Anyway, I may have found a girl or two behind the bar of The Monika or the Barbara that's in your league, but nowhere have I ever seen anyone with eyes like yours. You always seem so bedazzled."

Immediately I feel transported to yet another location. This is my Bohemian neighborhood, yes, but echoes of Europe, the old country are everywhere.

The front door is open. The blonde barmaid stares out the door and says to no one in particular: "I had a beautiful maple tree out there, then they fix the sidewalks. This new one, locust. Is small . . " and she throws a kiss to it . . . "but it grow up. Is Indian Summer, and look, the leaves still green."

She wears a short skirt, black stockings, and a T-shirt which leaves no doubt she is a strong and healthy European lady. Then she is suddenly joined by another beautiful blonde barmaid. I'm not seeing double. Yet. But I'm beginning to put things together.

They look and talk like the Gabor sisters—though more sincere. More down-to-earth. More fun.

Libby and Jana! Of course. (We are instantly reacquainted.) They sold the People's Restaurant and got into the tavern business: The L&J Lounge. "You made us rich!" they laugh.

The Czech conversation at the bar gets more animated as soon as the "stranger's" presence is explained. The language shifts from part Czech to part broken English, to a lot of gestures, smiles, and free drinks. The hometown boy has returned.

"I was 145 then, 175 now," laughs Libby.

"Hello, my darling," says Jana, looking her beautiful self in a black dress, black shoes, shimmering blonde hair. "No miniskirt, I am sorry. I didn't know you be here! Every three years I change boyfriends . . . younger and younger."

I flash on a Bohumil Hrabal story again, "Romance", about a young man falling in love with a gypsy girl: "When gypsy girls are young, everything about them is beautiful. And I am young." Two blonde Bohemian sisters behind one bar: only in the old neighborhood. What better place to drink, eat, tell stories, have a good time?

"I am still younger," says Libby.

"I am beautiful in the dark," says Jana. "I am still thirty-nine."

"She is still thirty-nine but before she was twenty-five. I am always thirty-eight," says Libby.

The talk, the music, the laughter grow louder. A sign above the bar says, "Enter If You Dare." The Czech language begins to explode up and down and behind the bar. I'm thinking I'd like to run away to Praha for the week with Libby and Jana. Hell, we'll all be thirty-nine. Now everyone begins singing. The woman from the *Nědelní Hlasatel* (*Czechoslovak Daily Herald*, the oldest Czechoslovak daily paper in the free world) sings to the man next to her. Libby asks if I'm hungry, and before I can answer, brings me a bowl of soup. Jana pours me a drink. I am retreating further and further into the old world.

"I am looking for a man now . . . only money," says Jana. "No more poor men."

"I don't want a young man," says a lady customer. "Too wild."

"Not for me," says Jana. "I like the honeymoon only. After the honeymoon, forget it."

The earmark of a true neighborhood tavern is a bartender who drinks with you. One grows weary of downtown bistros and suburban lounges where bartenders dressed in regulation bartending uniforms keep an arm's distance from the customer, say nothing but "Would you like another drink?"

Give me a Libby or Jana who will drink along with you. What's more, have the spirit and heart of a true old fashioned bartender to "occasionally" (and then some) buy a round or two.

The place is getting crowded. More people are drinking. (I can't remember if this is my first, second, third or fourth visit to Libby and Jana's. I am talking with a man named Will DeMuth about the Czech writers, Karel Capek and Franz

Kafka, and the old photographer, Josef Sudek, and the young, earthy one, Jan Saudek . . . and another guy interrupts, Ivan Bican, a refugee who speaks the King's English, knows our Constitution by heart, and recites it now at the bar, and pretty soon L & J's begins to sound like an intellectual cafe in old Prague, and I'm wondering why the hell I ever left this neighborhood for the empty fields (and taverns) of Wisconsin. More people are eating at the bar, both Hungarian goulash and bowls of tripe soup. The place smells of beer, goulash, smoke, whiskey, dumplings, perfume . . . all the things that matter in a man's life.

Jana pours two glasses of "Green Death" (she calls it) . . . one for me, one for her. I notice her gold bracelets, gold rings . . . Czech class . . . only in a neighborhood tavern.

"Maybe the legs are not what they used to be," says Jana. "Last night, the Houby Festival, was sooo busy here. I drink too many this. Never used to drink before, me and my sister . . . but now, ooops! Last night, ooops! My sister, she like vodka. Me? This stuff: Green Death. That was last night. Too much Green Death. No, maybe the legs not the same," she says, checking them out herself, then tossing back another Green Death. "Too bad!" she laughs. "Tonight? More death!"

I make my way out of the bar, out of the arms of Libby and Jana, out of the arms and into the darkness of the neighborhood . . . feeling better than I have in days, weeks, years. "Everyone has something he loves," says a character in one of Hrabal's stories. I love the neighborhood. I love Chicago. I love every connection I have with the old country, all the native blood within me—Czech, Hungarian, Croatian, German. The language still alive. The old world. And the new. I love being able to tell about it. Imagine all the possibilities. Hope, in this way, *nothing* will ever change. The neighborhood, the people, the culture, Libby and Jana, will be here forever, forever young.

I water flowers when it rains, in sultry July I pull my December sled behind me, to keep cool on hot summer days I drink up the money I put aside for the coal to keep me warm in winter, it makes me nervous to think how unnervous people are about how short life is and how little time there is for going wild and geting drunk as long as there is time, I do not treat my morning hangover like a sample possessing no commercial value, I treat it as if it possessed the absolute value of poetic trauma with a touch of discord, which should be savored like a sacred gallbladder attack . . . I am a corresponding member of the Academy of Palavery, a student in the Euphoria Department, my god is Dionysus, a sozzled, winsome lad, Good Cheer turned man, ironic Socrates is my Church Father, conversing patiently with one and all, hoping to lead them by his words or their tongues to the threshhold of ignorance, Jaroslav Hasek is the first born son and inventor of the beerhall story, he had a gift for living and writing life, for humanizing prosaic heavens, and his human qualities made the others feel uncomfortable with their pens. . . . —Bohumil Hrabal

380

Epilogue: Coming Back

This is probably my last book of nonfiction set in Chicago. Hopefully, there's another novel out there and more stories. Certainly more short stories. The backlog continues to increase. But I grow more uncertain about my own time and place, where I might be coming from.

The city and I are no longer on intimate terms. Partly, it's that old love affair I suggested in the beginning. You come back. You renew those old and simple pleasures . . . the morning newspaper and coffee . . . a walk down Michigan Avenue, a visit to the Art Institute, Kroch's and Iwan Reis on Wabash, the El rattling overhead, a visit to Field's, a bench in the park, a beer at the Goat, up north Michigan, perhaps, toward Water Tower Place, exploring new territory. Then suddenly you realize it's not yours anymore, no matter how many stories you still wish to write. It's an easy place to fall in love with all over again. It's a very difficult place to leave or forget.

I left in 1969. Chicago slowly turned into a bad love affair, a deteriorating relationship. Maybe I wanted too much. I definitely wanted to exist on my own terms as a writer. I wanted more commitment—a newspaper, a magazine, a publisher to take me under its wing. Protection. (Thank God for prayers unanswered.) Freelance writing was not enough economically or emotionally. I had stories, novels, poems, books to write. I had already quit teaching. I needed to cut the ties, move on, even though I knew full well little or no security awaited me.

I loved and hated freelancing: the excitement of moving into a story, the uncertainty it would ever see print or bring the payment I expected. I renounced it a hundred times, but kept running back for more. (A bad love affair, indeed, a masochist's dream come true: enough? No. Never.)

Freelancing Chicago can humble the apprentice. It is a difficult taskmaster, a great education (along with the City News Bureau). Every beginning writer

381

should pick up the lance—a minimum of five years. Live on the edge. Survive by wits and guts. No running to a university writing workshop to become a certified Poet or a licensed Novelist. No begging the government for a grant. No hiding in academia. No petitioning a writer's colony for admittance to the confines of the green woods where one might find peace in himself and finally begin the Great American Novel, once the climate's good and somebody has packed a lunch. That's no way to begin. That's already the end.

I remember Petrakis' words during a particularly depressing period when I had to freelance to eat, needed to write short stories to survive: "Nobody said you had to become a writer."

You want to eat and write? Take up the lance. Do the Big City. Learn it. Love it. Fight for every story, every word, every dollar. Wait for the check that never arrives—or, when it does, it is never enough. If you're married, it's almost impossible. If you're single, it's easier. Try to keep that together. Keep looking for more stories, more publications, and editors who believe in you. When your work is accepted for print, try not to compromise—your subject, your style, your self. Live by your words. Carry the spirit of the freelancer with you for the rest of your writing life.

Freelancing guarantees all the craziness and hunger you'll need to survive over the long haul—when things might appear a little easier but are actually only a little different.

My own period of craziness lasted more than ten years. It began soon after I left the city: a period of adjustment, a trial separation. I thought that even though I had left, for economical and emotional reasons, I could still keep the homefires burning. I did for a while.

It became a schizoid life at best, manic-depressive at worst. Was I here or there? I felt down in Wisconsin, up in Chicago. Back and forth. Back and forth. Only the road felt like home. City-man moved to the country, unable to let go of the bright lights, still knocking on the door late at night for another rendezvous, expecting her to be waiting for my arrival with open arms. In time, each grew unfaithful to the other. We were using each other, pure and simple. (Who, after all, is a bigger whore than the freelancer?)

True, there was something serene about being the writer-in-the-country, though I knew in my bones I was too young to die from an overdose of the bucolic. There were solitary days and nights of walking the solitary lakeshore, the fields, the dark roads spangled with stars above . . . quiet enough to make a grown man scream in the dark. I longed for sirens, newsstands, all-night coffeeshops . . . one of Sandburg's painted women under the gas lamps luring this farm boy.

I was fast becoming a 1970's back-to-the-land writer, lost in the woods with a 1950's, 1960's desire for that red-lipped Chicago lady I left back there under the El tracks one Saturday night. Next morning would find me running back in desperation (spiritual and economic), knocking on her door again, "working" her as we worked each other. Satisfaction was guaranteed—for the moment. (Next week, same trick. There was never any money in the bank.)

Gradually the 1970's commitment to human relationships made my intentions obvious: I was merely leading the lady on. I could not move back. I *lived* in Door County, Wisconsin. I had dug in and begun to make a life: house, family, dog, responsibilities. Besides, I was already involved in a new love affair with Santa Fe, New Mexico. Where the hell does a writer live anyway? Does he ever belong?

Chicago too was changing. I felt double-timed, jerked around, cut-off, abandoned. The city's newspapers and magazines were into demographics. What does the North Shore read? What about the inner city? Does anybody read? Anybody care? More visuals, less text. Less literature, more ads. My editors, markets, stories were disappearing. "Nobody cares about the things you write about anymore," I heard. This was news to me. I thought I was simply trying to deal with the old universals: people and place. Beginning, middle, end. Storytelling. You mean we really didn't care to hear about ourselves anymore? Chicago journalism was turning strange. An editor whom I admired was accused of turning the magazine into a literary showcase and lost his job. He had occasionally published Algren, Petrakis, poetry as well. Chicago seemed hell-bent on living up to its Second City reputation, taking its cues from New York and magazines there: The "Best" of this and that. What's "in," what's "out." Beautiful people . . . unreal, no heart. Chicago wasn't my kind of town anymore. (I longed for a Chicago publication to lead, not continually to follow.)

At one time back there I felt briefly that I belonged to a community of writers who hung out in Riccardo's and O'Rourke's. In the beginning, a writer sorely needs camaraderie, a sense of others like himself, in the same place . . . and a sense of what it might take or mean to become a part of a Chicago literary tradition. I imagine this camaraderie still exists, though I doubt the identification card means as much now as it did then.

In my book there are two ghosts every writer who claims Chicago as home must deal with: Sandburg and Algren. Sandburg (despite visiting writer Jan Morris' recent putdown "now that nobody reads Sandburg"; who the hell gave her the scoop?) remains vintage Chicago: language, people, "a papersack of invisible keepsakes." Algren peels away its soul and remains the conscience of every writer who follows.

The measure of any man's work is clear: Would Algren approve?

Faith plays a role too. Something about being raised Catholic in an ethnic Chicago neighborhood shadows your way. Once an altar boy, always an altar boy. *Introibo ad altare Dei.* (I will go to the altar of God.) Some great spirit out there must be implored and embodied. It has something to do with language and liturgy, the old Latin mass or one in Czech. Incense and holy water. Mystery and midnight mass. Nuns and priests. Flesh and spirit. Fish on Fridays. Blood, wine, and breads. *Bless me, Father, for I have sinned. . . .* Gold tabernacles and stained glass windows. Acts of confession, contrition, and resignation. The images and voices remain, no matter how far you may have distanced yourself in spiritual systems as alien as Zen, Hasidim, and Native American. *In Nomine Patris, et Filii, et Spiritus Sancti. Amen.* Mystical unions. Lenten fasts. Stations of the Cross. Candles, holy water, confessions, communion, penance, punishment, prayer. It rises in the darkness unfailingly. It's all there, where they first set it inside of you: St. Francis of Rome, church and school. One became a priest. Another, a writer. Who's to distinguish the work of salvation? Epiphany through sacrifice. *Sanctus, sanctus, sanctus.* Holy is the word.

I retreated further into the woods, further into my own imagination. I began to concentrate on stories, novels, books of nonfiction—some of the work set back in Chicago. Memory and desire, of course. What else? I began to look at life in the countryside as well.

"A writer's work is nothing but a long journey to recover through the detours of art the two or three great images which first gained access to his heart," said Camus. To continue the journey.

Nationally this writer is considered "regional," a Chicago kid relegated to the country. Wisconsin says he's one of theirs. Illinois contends, "He doesn't live here anymore."

In the end, it really doesn't matter. He's never home. No writer is. He suffers from a bad case of being out of place. Identity uncertain. Destination unknown.

Home is in the writing, the only place he lives.

Other Books by Norbert Blei

Nonfiction

Door Way
Door Steps
Door to Door
Neighborhood
Meditations on a Small Lake

Novels

The Second Novel (Becoming a Writer)
Adventures in an American's Literature

Short Stories

The Hour of the Sunshine Now
The Ghost of Sandburg's Phizzog

Poetry

The Watercolored Word
Paint Me a Picture/Make me a Poem